Lecture Notes in Computer Science 7170

Commenced Publication in 1973
Founding and Former Series Editors:
Gerhard Goos, Juris Hartmanis, and Jan van Leeuwen

Catherine Meadows
Carmen Fernandez-Gago (Eds.)

Security
and Trust Management

7th International Workshop, STM 2011
Copenhagen, Denmark, June 27-28, 2011
Revised Selected Papers

 Springer

Volume Editors

Catherine Meadows
Naval Research Laboratory, Code 5543
4555 Overlook Ave, S. W., Washington DC 20375, USA
E-mail: meadows@itd.nrl.navy.mil

Carmen Fernandez-Gago
University of Malaga, Department of Computer Science
Campus de Teatinos, 29071 Málaga, Spain
E-mail: mcgago@lcc.uma.es

ISSN 0302-9743   e-ISSN 1611-3349
ISBN 978-3-642-29962-9   e-ISBN 978-3-642-29963-6
DOI 10.1007/978-3-642-29963-6
Springer Heidelberg Dordrecht London New York

Library of Congress Control: 2012936295

CR Subject Classification (1998): K.6.5, K.4.4, E.3, D.4.6, C.2, J.1

LNCS Sublibrary: SL 4 – Security and Cryptology

Typesetting: Camera-ready by author, data conversion by Scientific Publishing Services, Chennai, India

Printed on acid-free paper

Springer is part of Springer Science+Business Media (www.springer.com)

Preface

This volume contains the papers presented at STM 11: 7th International Workshop on Security and Trust Management held during June 27–28, 2011, in Copenhagen, Denmark.

There were 33 submissions. Each submission was reviewed by at least 3, and on average 3.9, Program Committee members. The Committee decided to accept 12 papers, yielding an acceptance rate of approximately 35%. The program also includes 4 invited papers from the two invited speakers and the participants on the panel.

STM is a working group of ERCIM (European Research Consortium in Informatics and Mathematics), and was established in 2005 to provide a platform for researchers in security and trust management to present and discuss their work and to foster cooperation. One of the means to achieve these goals is the organization of a yearly workshop.

There is a long list of people who volunteered their time and energy to put together this workshop and who deserve acknowledgement. We would like to thank the Program Committee and the external reviewers for all their hard work in evaluating and discussing papers, often under intense time pressure. We are also grateful to the STM Organizers, Christian Damsgaard Jensen and Aljosa Pasic, whose work made this meeting possible. We would also like to thank Javier Lopez, the head of the Security and Trust Management Working Group of the European Research Consortium for Informatics and Mathematics, which sponsors STM. He went out of his way to support the workshop and our work in attracting papers and dealing with publishers.

Last but not least, our thanks go to all the authors who submitted papers, and to all the attendees, without whom this workshop would not have taken place. We hope that you find the proceedings stimulating.

January 2012

Catherine Meadows
Carmen Fernández-Gago

Organization

Program Committee

Rafael Accorsi	University of Freiburg, Germany
Isaac Agudo	University of Malaga, Spain
Alessandro Armando	DIST - University of Genova, Italy
Lujo Bauer	Carnegie Mellon University, USA
Jim Clarke	Waterford Institute of Technology, Ireland
Jason Crampton	Royal Holloway, University of London, UK
Jorge Cuellar	Siemens AG, CT IC 3, Germany
Christian Damsgaard Jensen	Technical University of Denmark
Sabrina De Capitani	Università degli Studi di Milano, Italy
Maribel Fernandez	King's College London, UK
Carmen Fernández-Gago	University of Malaga, Spain
Simone Fischer-Huebner	Karlstad University, Sweden
Simon Foley	University College Cork, Ireland
Michael Huth	Imperial College London, UK
Sushil Jajodia	George Mason University, USA
Martin Johns	SAP Research - CEC Karlsruhe, Germany
Aaron Johnson	Yale University, USA
Guenter Karjoth	IBM, Switzerland
Costas Lambrinoudakis	University of Piraeus, Greece
Ninghui Li	Purdue University, USA
Javier Lopez	University of Malaga, Spain
Volkmar Lotz	SAP AG, Germany
Fabio Martinelli	IIT-CNR, Italy
Sjouke Mauw	University of Luxembourg, Belgium
Catherine Meadows	NRL, USA
Stig F. Mjolsnes	Norwegian University of Science and Technology NTNU, Norway
Aljosa Pasic	Atos Origin, Spain
Dusko Pavlovic	Royal Holloway, Oxford, and Twente, UK / The Netherlands
Guenter Pernul	Universität Regensburg, Germany
Alex Pretschner	Karlsruhe Institute of Technology (KIT), Germany
Pierangela Samarati	Università degli Studi di Milano, Italy
Ketil Stoelen	SINTEF, Norway

Additional Reviewers

Arnaud, Mathilde
Berthold, Stefan
Bier, Christoph
Broser, Christian
Brucker, Achim D.
Carbone, Roberto
Costa, Gabriele
Darra, Eleni
Dong, Naipeng
Drogkaris, Prokopios
Dürbeck, Stefan
Erdogan, Gencer
Havaldsrud, Tormod
Kelbert, Florian
Kumari, Prachi

Lehmann, Anja
Ligaarden, Olav S.
Lowis, Lutz
Matteucci, Ilaria
Merlo, Alessio
Muller, Tim
Nantes Sobrinho, Daniele
Netter, Michael
Neven, Gregory
Ranise, Silvio
Rekleitis, Evangelos
Riesner, Moritz
Wonnemann, Claus
Zhang, Ge

Table of Contents

Uncertainty, Subjectivity, Trust and Risk: How It All Fits together

Bjørnar Solhaug[1] and Ketil Stølen[1,2]

[1] SINTEF ICT
[2] Dep. of Informatics, University of Oslo
{Bjornar.Solhaug,Ketil.Stolen}@sintef.no

Abstract. Trust management involves the identification and analysis of trust relations. However, adequately managing trust requires all the relevant aspects of trust to be addressed. Moreover, which aspects to address depend on the perspective of the trust management. In this position paper we relate the notion of trust to the notions of uncertainty, subjectivity and risk, and we explain how these aspects should be addressed and reasoned about from three different perspectives.

Keywords: Aleatory uncertainty, epistemic uncertainty, subjective, objective, trust, risk, trust management.

1 Aleatory Uncertainty vs. Epistemic Uncertainty

The future is uncertain and may be difficult to foresee. Nevertheless, we often make predictions about the future, be it about the weather for tomorrow, the outcome of a gambling, the stock prices, or the dependability of ICT systems. One way of making such predictions is to determine the uncertainty about outcomes of the future by means of statistical methods and probability theory. When we make predictions it is always with respect to some entity or part of reality. In the following we use the term *system* to refer to the object for prediction.

Uncertainty is often classified into two kinds [4]. On the one hand we may be uncertain about the future due to ignorance and lack of evidence. On the other hand uncertainty may be due to the inherent randomness of systems. The latter kind of uncertainty is commonly referred to as *aleatory uncertainty* and pertains to chance. Typical examples are the outcomes of the tossing of a coin, or the hands players of a game of poker receives. Aleatory uncertainty is the inherent randomness that cannot be removed from systems (without redesigning the systems). The former kind of uncertainty is commonly referred to as *epistemic uncertainty* and pertains to our knowledge about the system at hand. When making predictions about future behavior, the epistemic uncertainty is something we actively seek to reduce by gathering more information and evidence.

In determining future behavior, we may identify the possible outcomes of a situation and assign a probability $p \in [0, 1]$ to each outcome. In cases of perfect knowledge and where p is close to 0 or 1, the outcome is almost certain; there is no epistemic uncertainty and close to no aleatory uncertainty. However, if p gets

C. Meadows and C. Fernández-Gago (Eds.): STM 2011, LNCS 7170, pp. 1–5, 2012.

closer to 0.5, the outcome is increasingly uncertain, as for example the outcome of tossing a coin. Should knowledge be imperfect, on the other hand, we have a degree of epistemic uncertainty. This kind of uncertainty can, for example, be documented by using probability intervals $P \subseteq [0, 1]$ instead of exact values. The correct probability is then assumed to be a value $p \in P$. Using intervals instead of exact values is a form of underspecification that reflects epistemic uncertainty. While new knowledge is gathered, the underspecification can be reduced by narrowing the interval and thereby making a more precise prediction.

2   Objective vs. Subjective

The term *objective* commonly pertains to the existence of an object outside the consciousness and independent of the subject's perception of the object. Also the properties and qualities of the object are independent of the subject; objectivity and the objective are therefore typically associated with the true and the factual reality. The term *subjective*, on the other hand, pertains to the subject and how the subject perceives an object. The properties and qualities assigned to an object depend on the subject's perception, and may hence differ from one individual subject to the other; subjectivity and the subjective are therefore typically associated with the false and the possibility of wrong perceptions.

3   Trust vs. Risk

Trust is a relation between a trustor (an actor) and a trustee (an entity) and concerns the expectations of the trustor about the future behavior of the trustee. The same trustor can trust the same trustee for different purposes and in varying degrees depending on the purpose, for which reason there can be several trust relations between one pair of trustor and trustee.

The level of trust reflects the uncertainty about the future behavior of the trustee. When placing trust, the trust level is the prediction of the trustor and can be specified by a probability $p \in [0, 1]$ ranging from complete distrust to complete trust. This uncertainty can be both aleatory and epistemic. The aleatory uncertainty is associated with the inherent possibility of the trustee both to prove trustworthy and to deceive. The epistemic uncertainty reflects the degree to which the trustor has access to evidence about the trustee.

A further aspect of trust is that different actors may trust the same entity for the same purpose to different degrees, even if the histories and contexts are the same. This is because trust is about how the trustor perceives the trustee. In other words, trust is subjective. This is captured by Gambetta [2] who defines trust as the subjective probability by which the trustor expects that the trustee performs a given action on which the welfare of the trustor depends.

The notion of *trustworthiness*, on the other hand, pertains to the objective. The trustworthiness of an entity is an inherent quality of the trustee, and can be defined as the objective probability by which the trustee performs a given action on which the welfare of the trustor depends. When the subjective estimate, i.e. the trust level, is too high or too low, we say that trust is ill-founded. In the former case the trust is higher than the trustworthiness, which means that the probability of deception is higher than what the trustor believes. In the latter case the trust is lower than the trustworthiness, which means that the probability of deception is lower than what the trustor believes.

Trust is inherently related to *risk*, because in a situation of trust the welfare of the trustor is at stake, and there is always a possibility of deception [1]. At the same time trust is related to *opportunity*, because if the trustor performs as trusted to it may have a positive outcome for the trustor [6]. Risk is commonly defined as the probability of the occurrence of a harmful event [3]. The risk level is given as a function from the consequence (loss) of the event and the probability of its occurrence. We define opportunity as the probability of the occurrence of a beneficial event [5]. The opportunity level is given as a function from the consequence (gain) of the event and the probability of its occurrence.

When interacting based on trust, the trustor typically seeks to maximize opportunities while minimizing risks. Importantly, the opportunity and risk estimates of the trustor are subjective beliefs of the trustor that the trustor acts upon; the objective opportunity and risk can only be derived from the trustworthiness of the trustee.

In managing trust we need to understand both aleatory and epistemic uncertainty, and to understand both the subjective and the objective aspects of trust. Moreover, all these aspects must be taken into account when assessing the involved risks and opportunities.

4   Trust Management from Three Perspectives

What trust management is about depends on behalf of whom the trust, risk and opportunity are to be managed. We use an example of online poker to explain the differences. The poker web application connects the players online and serves as the house. Two actors involved are Alice who is an online poker player and Bob who is the network provider. As a trustor in this setting, Alice needs to assess whether the deck of cards (i.e. the web application) is fair and whether Bob is just. As the network provider, Bob's concern is the trust of his customers, e.g. that the online players trust him not to act as one of the online players while observing the other players' hands. The two trust relations we consider are hence one between Alice and Bob and one between Alice and the deck. There are also other trust relations, but for simplicity we focus on these two only. Finally, we have Claire who is the owner of the online poker house and whose main concern is to make money.

Figure 1 illustrates various concerns related to trust management. In the upper part we have the relevant aspects of the factual reality, namely trust (the subjective perception of the reality) and trustworthiness (the objective qualities of the reality). In the lower part we have the target of investigation when uncovering the factual reality. In the case of trust, the target of investigation is the trustors, whereas in the case of trustworthiness, the target of investigation is the trustees.

	Trust	**Trustworthiness**
Factual reality	Subjective probability of Bob being just and deck being fair	Objective probability of Bob being just and deck being fair
Uncovering factual reality	**Target of investigation** Alice	**Target of investigation** Bob and deck

Fig. 1. Uncovering the factual reality

4.1   Trust Management on Behalf of the Trustor

When the trust manager acts on behalf of the trustor, the task is to help establish the trustworthiness of the trustees involved. In other words, to help the trustor to reduce epistemic uncertainty and get the aleatory uncertainty right. With respect to our example, the task of the trust manager could be to help Alice to correctly assess the trustworthiness of the two trustees involved, namely Bob and the deck.

This kind of trust management might be thought of as a risk analysis with the trust relation as target of analysis and the stake of the trust relation as the asset to be protected. In order to correctly manage the involved risks, the trust must be well-founded, which is precisely the task of the trust manager to ensure.

4.2   Trust Management on Behalf of the Trustee

When the trust manager acts on behalf of the trustee, the task is to help the trustee to maintain or increase the trustee's reputation among a group of trustors; in principle, independent of whether this reputation is equal to, lower or higher than the trustee's trustworthiness. However, one may argue that an "honest" trust manager will not attempt to rise the reputation of the trustee beyond the trustees' trustworthiness.

With respect to our example, the trust manager might act on behalf of either the deck (i.e. the web application) or Bob. In the case of the former, the client (the one who pays for the trust management) might be the software manufacturer.

In trust management on behalf of the trustee, if the objective is to defend the trustees current reputation one could conduct a defensive risk analysis with the trust relation as target of analysis and the current reputation of the trustee as the asset. Note that the trustor's perception of the trustee is an important ingredient in such a risk analysis; it is the reputation of the trustee and not its trustworthiness that is to be defended. If the objective is to rise the trustees current reputation, one might employ the more offensive kind of risk analysis conducted by share traders where the level of risk tolerance is balanced against the level of opportunity.

4.3   Trust Management on Behalf of the System Owner

When the trust manager acts on behalf of the system owner, the task is to assess the impact of the trust relations within the system on the overall behavior or some quality of the system.

With respect to our example, the system in question includes Alice, Bob, the deck, the underlying software and infrastructure, and the two trust relations. The task of the trust manager might be on behalf of Claire to assess whether trust relations within the online poker games might be exploited to implement a scam that would ruin Claire by manipulating the players' trust in either Bob or the deck; to the extent that Alice and other players make trust-based decisions, the trust relations have direct impact on the business risks and opportunities for Claire.

Again, an important ingredient in this kind of trust management is risk analysis. Such a risk analysis would be rather conventional with the important exception that the description of the target of analysis would contain explicit trust relations. As in any risk analysis, a crucial ingredient is to make predictions and determine uncertainty. Because the target in this case includes trust relations, these relations have direct impact on the overall behavior of the system. In other words, the aleatory uncertainty of the future behavior of the system depends on both the subjective trust and the objective trustworthiness.

Acknowledgments. This work has been partially funded by the European Commission via the NESSoS (256980) network of excellence and by the Research Council of Norway via the DIGIT (180052/S10) project.

References

1. Castelfranci, C., Falcone, R.: Social trust: A cognitive approach. In: Trust and Deception in Virtual Societies, pp. 55–90. Kluwer Academic Publishers (2001)
2. Gambetta, D.: Can we trust trust? In: Trust: Making and Breaking Cooperative Relations, Electronic edn., ch. 13, pp. 213–237. Department of Sociology, University of Oxford (2000)
3. ISO/IEC: ISO/IEC 13335-1 Information technology – Security techniques – Management of information and communications technology security – Part 1: Concepts and models for information and communications technology security management (2004)
4. O'Hagan, T.: Dicing with the unknown. Significance 1(3), 132–133 (2004)
5. Refsdal, A., Solhaug, B., Stølen, K.: A UML-based method for the development of policies to support trust management. In: Trust Management II – Proceedings of the 2nd Joint iTrust and PST Conference on Privacy, Trust Management and Security (IFIPTM 2008). IFIP, vol. 263, pp. 33–49. Springer, Heidelberg (2008)
6. Solhaug, B., Elgesem, D., Stølen, K.: Why trust is not proportional to risk. In: Proceedings of the 2nd International Conference on Availability, Reliability and Security (ARES 2007), pp. 11–18. IEEE Computer Society (2007)

Trust Extortion on the Internet

Audun Jøsang

University of Oslo*
josang@mn.uio.no

Abstract. Dangers exist on the Internet in the sense that there are attackers who try to break into our computers or who in other ways try to trick us when we engage in online activities. In order to steer away from such dangers people tend to look for signals of security and trustworthiness when navigating the Internet and accessing remote hosts. Seen from an online service provider's perspective it therefore is an essential marketing requirement to appear trustworthy, especially when providing sensitive or professional services. Said more directly, any perception of weak security or low trustworthiness could be disastrous for an otherwise secure and honest online service provider. In this context many security vendors offer solutions for strengthening security and trustworthiness. However there is also a risk that security vendors through their marketing strategy create an illusion that an online service provider which does not implement their solutions might therefore be insecure or untrustworthy. This would represent what we call trust extortion, because service providers are forced to implement specific security solutions to appear trustworthy although there might be alternative security solutions that provide equal or better security. We describe real examples where this seems to be the case. Trust extortion as a marketing strategy does not have to be explicit, but can be done very subtly e.g. through standardisation and industry fora, which then gives it a veil of legitimacy.

1 Introduction

The Internet is a primary arena for human interaction, e.g. for delivering commercial and civic services and for participating in social communities. At the same time, the Internet can in many ways be a dangerous place because it exposes us to risks that are difficult to manage. Most people are aware of this fact, and most people would stop using a specific service if they perceive the risk of using the service to be significant. Losing people's trust could therefore cause a significant drop in business. Such a change in user behaviour does not need to be a rational reaction to real threats or security incidents, but could be the result of irrational perceptions and mass psychosis. In fact it has become a primary concern of online SPs (Service Providers) to tightly control the dissemination of information about security incidents and vulnerabilities, precisely because this sort of negative publicity undermines people's trust. Online SPs clearly see a need to be perceived as providing a secure IT infrastructure, which should normally be achieved by actually focusing on real security solutions. However there is a risk that organisations will implement measures aimed at inducing trust and security assurance,

---

* The work reported in this paper has been partially funded by UNIK.

but that in reality give little or no real added security. This possibility creates a potential market for "fake security", i.e. where the main purpose is to give the impression of security, and to a lesser extent to provide practical security. There is also a danger that security technology companies try to expand their marked by creating an artificial need for adopting security solutions that organisations do not need, e.g. through giving the market the impression that these (ineffective) security solutions are really needed. This would create a situation of *"trust extortion"* in the sense that SPs would have no other option than to adopt these security solutions in order to avoid losing business. This effect could be amplified by influencing the industry in subtle ways not to adopt competing and more effective security solutions. In practice it then becomes a business risk for online SPs not to implement such ineffective security solutions.

This paper focuses on certain aspects of the security industry that seem more aimed at giving the impression of security than of giving real security. More specifically we focus on the industry of the Browser PKI and of issuing public-key certificates to online SPs to support TLS (Transport Layer Security) and to software developers to support software signing. We show that the actual security provided by this technology in its current implementation is questionable, as demonstrated, e.g. by the continuing and endemic phishing attacks and more advanced attacks against web sites [16] that exploit TLS as an attack vector, and by high profile attacks such as the Stuxnet worm [17] attack which precisely exploited software signing as an attack vector to penetrate systems.

We also propose alternative security solutions to those of the traditional Browser PKI. Our proposed solutions would strengthen security and also be more economical because of its simple structure. Any new security architecture for the web needs a viable business model in order to be supported by the market. In our case one business model is based on cost savings by not using server certificates at all, and instead enable TLS security without server certificates, which is possible through the Anonymous Diffie-Hellman option. An additional business model could be based on shifting the certificate issuing business from dedicated CAs (Certificate Authorities) to DNS (Domain Name System) registrars and DNS service operators which would reuse existing trust structures and provide a simpler and thereby more secure PKI. We see a tendency in certain parts of the security industry to work against the deployment of such obvious security solutions, possibly because it would undermine their established business models.

2   Details of Public-Key Infrastructures

Secure key distribution is a major obstacle to practical use of cryptography. With traditional symmetric-key cryptography each pair of parties that want to set up a secure communication channel must first exchange cryptographic keys through a secure extra-protocol channel[1] and thereby establish a direct trust relationship. Secure extra-protocol channels and direct trust relationships are typically expensive to set up and operate, so finding ways to reduce their number can lead to significant cost savings. The main purpose of a PKI is to simplify key distribution by theoretically reducing the number of secure extra-protocol channels needed. Indirect trust in public keys is then cryptographically derived from a single direct trust relationship between the relying party and the

---

[1] Extra-protocol channels can also be called out-of-band channels.

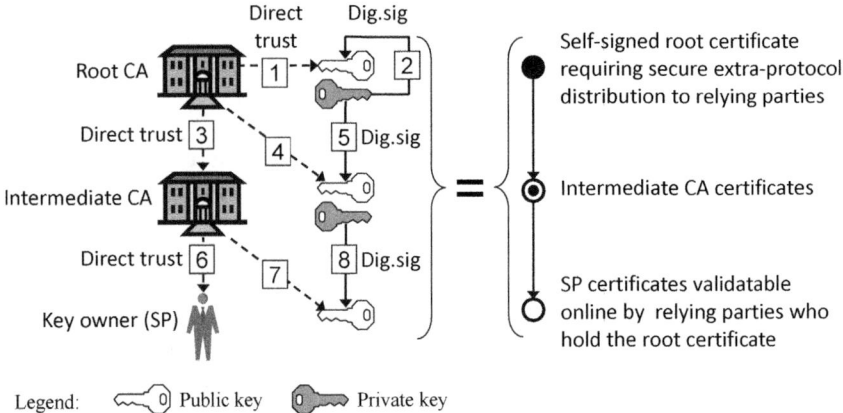

Fig. 1. Detailed trust structure for certificate generation

root CA (Certificate Authority). In that sense, a PKI allows trust to be propagated from where it initially exists to where it is subsequently needed [18]. A detailed illustration of the trust involved in a certificate chain is illustrated in Fig.1.

The left hand side shows the trust structure where the indexes indicate the order in which the trust relationships and digital signatures are formed. The right hand side shows the corresponding graphical PKI representation, where SP (Service Provider) certificates form the end point of a certificate chain. This trust structure can fail for several reason, typically resulting in false certificates being issued, as explained in Sec.3.

A public-key certificate represents an expression of trust by the CA (Certificate Authority) in the binding between a public key and a specific attribute. The most common attribute of certificates is a name, whereby the semantics carried by such certificates can be expressed as: *"The owner of the public key K rightfully carries the name N"*, or equivalently as: *"The entity named N rightfully owns the public key K"*. Such certificates are often called identity certificates because they are used for identification and authentication purposes. Any SP which can prove that it controls the private key corresponding to the public key, will have proved that it also owns the name. The proof is typically given through an exchange of cryptographic messages called a cryptographic security protocol. A certificate can also express other semantic concepts than a unique name, in which case it is called an attribute certificate. The semantics of an attribute certificate would typically be expressed as: *"The owner of the public key K rightfully has the attribute A"*. In theory, any assertable concept can be certified in an attribute certificate. Expressing access authorization is the most common usage of attribute certificates, whereby the semantic trust scope could be: *"The owner of the public key K is authorized to access resource X with operation Y"*.

It is assumed that a RA (Registration Authority) is part of both the root CA and any intermediate CA. The role of the RA is to pre-authenticate SP/entity identities based on physical world artifacts, or to define appropriate attributes in case of attribute certificates, and then to communicate this information (name and/or attributes) to the certificate issuing arm of the CA. In reality, the RA can be a separate organisation, in which case additional trust relationships between the CA and the RA are required.

Software systems are designed to store and process public-keys in the form of certificates, and are usually unable to handle naked public keys. For that reason a root public key is normally distributed and stored in the form of a certificate. In addition the root certificate is normally self-signed, meaning that the public key sits in a certificate that has been signed by the corresponding private key, as illustrated at the top of Fig.1 (index 2). Note that self-signing by itself provides no assurance whatsoever regarding the authenticity of the root public key. Despite the fact that self-signing has absolutely no security purpose, many people falsely believe that it provide assurance and a real basis for authenticity. In order to establish meaningful trust in root certificates, the root CAs themselves, and the exact procedure for installing them on a client, must be known and trusted by users and relying parties. Unfortunately, most people ignore these issues and often download and install root certificates online even without knowing.

Validation of a SP's server certificate, normally done by the relying party, consists of verifying the digital signature on the certificate and extracting the data contained within, such as attribute/name and the public key. A detailed illustration of the validation procedure and the derived trust in the SP's public key is illustrated in Fig.2. When a relying party holds an authentic copy of the root CA public key contained in a root certificate received through a secure extra-protocol channel, it will be able to derive trust in the binding between the SP public key and the SP name.

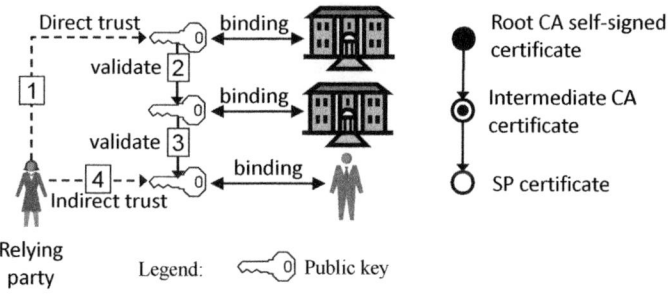

Fig. 2. Detailed trust structure for certificate validation

A leaf certificate owner in a PKI is typically a SP (Service Provider) which can be a legal entity such as an individual or an organisation, or it can be a system or process entity, or even an abstract role.

Recipients of public-key certificates, aka. *relying parties*, do not themselves need certificates in order to authenticate an entity's public key, they only need an authentic copy of the root public key. Only entities that want to claim and prove some attribute of themselves, such owning a specific domain name, need public-key certificates.

3   The Browser PKI

A hierarchic PKI can be managed by a single organisation that operates the root and multiple intermediate CAs, or by a set of separate organisations under one common root CA. The DNSSEC PKI [2] is an example of the latter model. The Browser PKI commonly used for Internet encryption has multiple roots and hierarchies, where different SP certificates can be issued under completely separate hierarchic PKIs, each with their own root. Assuming that each relying party shall be able to validate any SP certificate from any PKI, then it is required that all root CAs represent trust anchors for the relying parties. In other words, all relying parties need to receive every root CA public key through a secure extra-protocol channel, but the Browser PKI simply allows root certificates to be downloaded online, thereby making a mockery of the PKI security model. A simple illustration of the Browser PKI is provided in Fig.3.

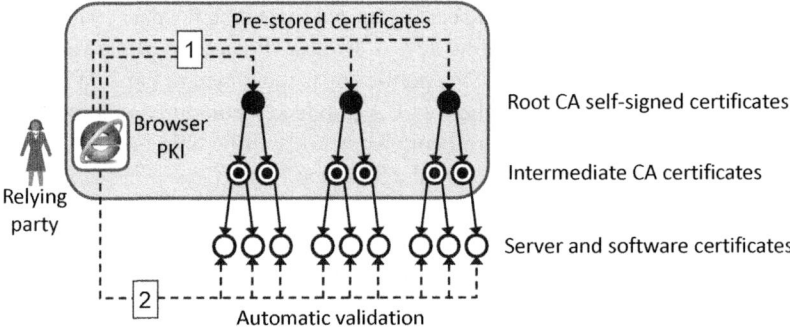

Fig. 3. The Browser PKI

The channel for distributing the root CA certificates in the Browser PKI is by hardcoding them in the Web browser distributions, as well as by importing additional certificates online. It is questionable whether the Web browser distribution represents a secure extra-protocol channel. Storing CA certificates in browsers enables automated validation of server certificates for SSL/TLS and digital signatures on software. There are typically a few dozen CA certificates in any major browser distribution. In Microsoft IE the list of root certificates can be viewed by clicking 'Tools' → 'Internet Options' → 'Content' → 'Certificates' → 'Trusted Root Certification Authorities'. Ironically many of the CA certificates have long expired, but are still being distributed with new versions of browsers. This is done e.g. in order to allow validation of legacy software, but shows that the model in fact is broken. Ignoring the validity period specified in a certificate for the sake of legacy functionality is a breach of the policy under which the certificates where issued.

The main purpose of the Browser PKI is to enable browsers to automatically validate any server certificate or software signature issued under any one of the roots. The set

---

[2] http://www.dnssec.net/

of root CA certificates in the Web Browser PKI model is dynamic, meaning that root certificates can be deleted and new root certificates can be added. This represents a vulnerability because it could be possible for attackers to replace a genuine root certificate with a false one. This attack could for example be executed by tricking the user into installing a malicious root certificate or by malware without the user's knowledge. The authenticity of a root certificate depends on the security of the extra-protocol channel through which it is received. Once a false certificate has been installed it will not be possible for a relying party to detect that it actually is false. In practice, many people install Browser PKI certificates and even root certificates based on discretionary ad hoc trust decisions, which represents a real spoofing threat for identities on the Web.

The Browser PKI structure is relatively well hidden for the average computer users who mostly ignore how it works. It is thus meaningless to speak about trust in the root CAs in this situation, because the relying party ignores what is to be trusted. The browser makes the trust decision automatically without consulting the user. Only in case the validation fails is the user confronted with a pop-up window asking her to make a decision whether or not to accept the certificate. Although most people accept certificates that fail to validate, it typically generates an uncomfortable feeling - consciously or unconsciously - especially when conducting sensitive transactions such as Internet banking. This creates a pressure on SPs to maintain current server certificates that validate automatically without annoying the user.

Having multiple separate hierarchic PKIs creates severe vulnerabilities through the fact the the whole Browser PKI is only as secure as the weakest of each separate PKI. Thus, the more root and intermediate certificates stored in the browser, the less secure the Browser PKI becomes. The whole security chain would break if only one CA issues a certificate without properly checking certificate owner's identity, meaning that an attacker would get a server or software certificate issued in somebody else's name. This happened e.g. when VeriSign, the worlds largest CA, issued software certificates in the name of Microsoft to imposters, because VeriSign failed to recognise that the persons buying the certificates were not Microsoft representatives [15]. The false certificates were never used and VeriSign survived the security breach with only a scratch to its reputation. Nevertheless, the situation was very serious because the attackers could have distributed malicious software - signed under the false certificate - that would have been automatically validated by all the browsers in the world. The whole security chain would also break if only one private key were stolen from a root or intermediate CA. This happened e.g. when attackers broke into DigiNotar CA's systems and were able to issue server certificates with false names, such as `google.com`. These certificates were used by the criminals to conduct a man-in-the-middle attack against Google services [16]. A few months later DigiNotar was declared bankrupt. The spoofing attacks that actually took place indicate the seriousness of this incident. The attackers could have generated server certificates, and probably also software certificates, with any owner name. Given that these certificates are automatically validated by the browsers it is in fact irrelevant what names they carry. A browser makes no difference between `www.mafia.com` and e.g. `www.google.com` as long as the certificate is correctly validated.

Browser PKI security is inherently weak because it depends on the security of the weakest of a relatively large number of root and intermediate certificates. It is fair to assume that the security level of each separate hierarchic PKI is only as strong as the security of the weakest member CA, because compromise of any member CA could enable attackers to issue false certificates. Let $S(\mathrm{PKI}(X_k))$ denote the security level of a hierarchic PKI named X_k, and let $S(\mathrm{CA}(x_{ki}))$ denote the security level of its member $\mathrm{CA}(x_{ki})$. Then $S(\mathrm{PKI}(X_k))$ can be expressed as:

$$S(\mathrm{PKI}(X_k)) = \min[S(\mathrm{CA}(x_{ki}))], \quad x_{ki} \in X_k \qquad (1)$$

It is also fair to assume that the security level of the whole Browser PKI is only as strong as the security of the weakest separate hierarchic PKI, because compromise of any separate hierarchic PKI could enable attackers to issue false certificates. Let $S(\text{Browser PKI})$ denote the security level of the whole Browser PKI, then $S(\text{Browser PKI})$ can be expressed as:

$$\begin{aligned} S(\text{Browser PKI}) &= \min[S(\mathrm{PKI}(X_k))], \quad X_k \in \text{Browser PKI} \\ &= \min[S(\mathrm{CA}(x_{ki}))], \quad x_{ki} \in X_k, \quad X_k \in \text{Browser PKI} \end{aligned} \qquad (2)$$

We thus see that the security of the Browser PKI is only as strong as the security of any of member CAs in any separate hierarchic PKI. With typically 50 individual CA certificates pre-stored in a browser it becomes obvious that the Browser PKI is relatively vulnerable. A CA does not even need to be attacked to represent a threat, because it is quite plausible that some CAs will be susceptible to collaborate with attackers, as indicated by the Stuxnet attack worm [17]. In this attack two separate Taiwanese companies - Realtek Semiconductor Systems and JMicron Technology Corp - that had purchased certificates for software signing produced digital signatures for the malicious Stuxnet software of the attackers, which enabled them to get the malicious software installed on the victim's systems. The companies in question have not been sanctioned, although the companies either failed to protect their private software signing keys, or they somehow collaborated in the attack by voluntarily signing the Stuxnet software.

The PKI class with the most optimal key distribution characteristics is when all SPs have certificates belonging to a single hierarchical PKI with a single root. The advantage of this structure is that the security strength is maximized and that only one root public key needs to be distributed to relying parties through a secure extra-protocol channel. In comparison, the Browser PKI model is suboptimal and introduces security vulnerabilities by having multiple separate hierarchic PKIs.

4   The Browser PKI's Failure to Stop Phishing Attacks

Current web security technology is based on the Transport Layer Security (TLS) protocol. It is normally assumed that TLS provides the security services *message confidentiality* and *server authentication*. It will become clear that the server authentication provided by TLS is only theoretical, and meaningless in practice due to poor usability.

Despite being based on strong cryptography, there are a number of security exploits that TLS can not prevent. For example, phishing attacks normally start by sending email messages that trick people to access a fake web site masquerading as a genuine web site that e.g. prompts the user to provide user Id and password. There are always people who will fall victim to such emails, and not notice that the web site is fake, not even when using TLS, because the fake web site is correctly authenticated with TLS in a technical sense. Semantically speaking however, this is not authentication because the website's real identity (domain name) is different from what the user has in mind. The problem is not due to weak cryptographic authentication mechanisms, but to poor usability of the overall authentication solution provided by TLS [11].

By analysing the security solution of TLS from a security usability perspective it can easily be seen that there are serious usability vulnerabilities that can easily be exploited by phishing attacks [12,11]. This is briefly explained below.

The standard implementation of TLS in web browsers provides various information elements to the user. Unfortunately this information is often sufficient to make an informed conclusion about the identity of the web server.

The closed padlock in the corner of a typical browser represents one form of security information elements indicating that the web session is protected with TLS. However, the fact that it does not say anything about the identity of the server is a security usability vulnerability.

Additional security information is contained in the server certificate that can be inspected e.g. by double-clicking on the padlock. The mental load of analysing the content of a server certificate is intolerable for most people, which represents a security usability vulnerability. The following analysis will make this evident.

The fraudulent phishing site: http:\\www.hawaiiusafcuhb.com targeted the Hawaii Federal Credit Union in March 2007. Assuming that security conscious victims want to inspect the server certificate for its authenticity, it is interesting to see that it actually provides very little useful information. Fig.4 shows general information about the attacker's certificate as it can be viewed through the Microsoft Explorer browser.

More detailed information can be viewed by selecting the *"Details"* and *"Certification Path"* placeholders on the certificate window. This gives the fraudulent certificate's validity period and the certification path from the root to the fraudulent certificate. However, this additional information gives no indication that the certificate is fraudulent.

The unique name of the fraudulent certificate's owner is the domain name to which the fraudulent certificate is issued, specified as www.hawaiiusafcuhb.com, which is equal to the domain name of the fake login page.

The question now arises whether this represents sufficient evidence for the user to detect that the certificate is fraudulent. In order to find out, it is necessary to compare the fraudulent certificate to the genuine certificate of the genuine Hawaii Federal Credit Union illustrated in Fig.5.

The unique name of the genuine certificate's owner is the domain name to which the genuine certificate is issued, specified as hcd.usersonlnet.com. Interestingly this domain name **does not** correspond to the domain name of the genuine Hawaii Federal Credit Union which is www.hawaiifcu.com. Intuitively this fact seems to indicate that the login page is not related to the genuine Hawaii Federal Credit Union. Based on this evidence, users who inspect the certificate could therefore falsely conclude that the genuine login page is fake.

Fig. 4. Fake certificate general info

This analysis demonstrates that the information found in the certificates is insufficient to draw a safe security conclusion, which represents a severe security usability vulnerability.

CAs in the Browser PKI industry are probably aware of this problem, and are careful to have policies that avoid any liability of practical misuse of the certificates they issue. The certificate window of Fig.5 provides a click-able button called *"issuer statement"* that opens a new window with the certificate issuance policy, which is a 2,666 word document (approximately four full standard pages in MS Word). While it might provide sufficient information to judge the legal status of the certificate, the size of this document alone clearly represents a security usability problem. In order to better understand why TLS can lead to a false positive authentication conclusion, it is useful to look at the very meaning of authentication.

According to the standard definition, peer-entity authentication is *"the corroboration that a peer entity in an association is as claimed"* [10]. In phishing attacks, an attacker claims its own identity in the formalism of TLS, and the TLS client (the browser) simply verifies the correctness of that claim. However, the claimed identity expressed in the certificate of Fig.4 does not correspond to the identity that the user assumes. Thus, the problem has to do with identity confusion, for which cryptography provides no solution.

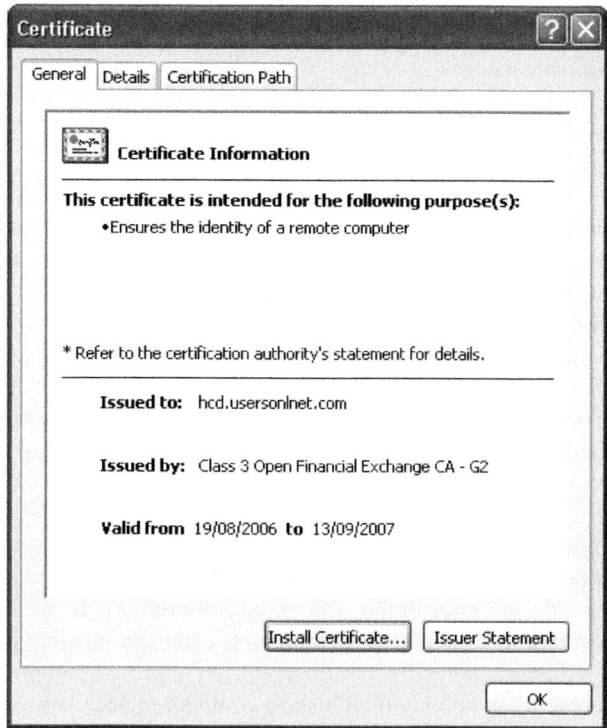

Fig. 5. Genuine certificate general info

The identity of the genuine bank assumed by the user is different from the identity of the same genuine bank assumed by the TLS client. Thus, the genuine bank itself is an entity with multiple identities. From the user's perspective, the ordinary name and logo of the bank constitute a large part of the identity. From the client browser's perspective, this identity cannot be used because normal names can be ambiguous and visual logos can not be interpreted.

Certificates, which must be unambiguous, require globally unique names in order to allow efficient automated processing. Domain names mostly satisfy this requirement and have therefore been chosen to represent the identity of the bank in server certificates. Having different identities for the same entity can obviously cause problems. A simple way of solving this problem could be by requiring that users learn to identify online SPs by their domain names. Unfortunately this will not work because online banks often use multiple domain names depending on the service being offered.

As the example of the certificate of the genuine Hawaii Federal Credit Union bank of Fig.5 shows, many companies' secure web sites have domain names with non-obvious domain names that do not correspond to the domain names of their main web sites. Another vulnerability is the fact that distinct domain names can appear very similar,

for example differing only by a single letter, or looking very similar, so that a false
domain name may pass undetected. How easy is it for example to distinguish between
the following domain names?

```
www.pepes.com/
www.pepespizza.com/
www.pepesnypizza.com/
www.pepespizzeria.com/.
```

The fundamental problem is that, although domain names are designed to be readable
by humans, they provide poor usability for identifying organisations in the real world.
Ordinary names such as "Pepes Pizza", when expressed in a local semantic context, are
suitable for dealing with organisations in the real world, but not for global online identification and authentication. The consequence of this mismatch between names used in
the online world and in the real world is that users do not know which unique domain
name to expect when accessing online services. Without knowing which domain name
to expect, authentication becomes meaningless. In other words, the users do not know
what security conclusion to draw.

To summarise, our analysis of web security has exposed serious security usability problems with TLS. These vulnerabilities continue to be exploited by criminals
to mount a large number of successful phishing attacks. Had a vulnerability analysis
like this been conducted prior to the large scale roll out of TLS, e.g for online banking applications, it would have been possible to predict and possibly prevent all these
attacks.

Current approaches to solving the phishing problem include anti-phishing toolbars
that are typically based on one or a combination of the following elements: blacklists,
whitelists, ratings, heuristics [5]. In addition, search engines typically flag web sites
that have been identified as malicious, but there will always be a delay in the detection
of malicious websites by search engines, which leaves a window of opportunity to the
attackers. None of these elements attempt to solve the fundamental problem of mapping
the unique domain name contained in the certificate to a user friendly identity that
the user can recognise. Thus they do not improve the users' ability to authenticate the
server, but is an attempt to flag malicious servers. Only the TrustBar [8] for the Mozilla
and Firefox browsers seems to provide a fundamental solution to the problem by making
authentication semantically meaningful. The TrustBar solution consists of personalising
every server certificate that the user wants to recognise by defining a personal petname
for it [7]. The petname can e.g. consist of an image or a audible tune that the user can
easily recognise. Unfortunately solutions like the TrustBar are not widely used.

5   TLS without Server Certificates

The previous section has demonstrated that the current implementation of TLS based
on server certificates does not provide practical and semantic authentication, despite
having strong cryptographic authentication from a technical point of view. Since TLS
does not offer meaningful authentication, the technical authentication mechanism becomes redundant. The principal security service provided by TLS is communication
confidentiality through encryption based on a session key. The TLS (Transport Layer

Security) security protocol [6] specifies a number of options for establishing the session key for encryption. Most options are based on server certificates, but the Anonymous Diffie-Hellman option does not require server certificates, it simply uses the basic Diffie-Hellman algorithm. That is, each side (client and server) sends its public Diffie-Hellman parameters to each other so that they both can compute a secret session key. Documentation about TLS, e.g. [4] typically describes this option as being vulnerable to man-in-the-middle attacks, in which the attacker conducts a Diffie-Hellman exchanges with both parties. However, given that TLS based on server certificates also does not provide meaningful authentication it is also vulnerable to man-in-the middle attacks, which is precisely what happens during phishing attacks as explained in Sec.4 above. TLS based on server certificates thus provides no more security than TLS based on Diffie-Hellman, both options provide confidentiality through encryption, and none of them provide any meaningful authentication.

A study of the main browsers revealed that none support the Anonymous Diffie-Hellman option despite being standardized as part of TLS [9]. We find it surprising and suspect that the Anonymous Diffie-Hellman option is not supported, because it means that TLS security can only be provided with server certificates. As a result, SPs who want to use TLS are forced to buy server certificates that they technically speaking do not need. It is interesting to ask the question why the Anonymous Diffie-Hellman option is not supported. The official answer from the browser developers would typically be that this option does not provide authentication and therefore is insecure. We have shown that options based on server certificates also do not provide any meaningful authentication, and therefore do not provide any stronger practical security than with the Anonymous Diffie-Hellman option. We therefore suspect that browser developers have been influenced by players in the Browser PKI industry not to distribute browsers with the Anonymous Diffie-Hellman option because it would threaten their business model.

In practice when navigating the Internet, authentication of web sites is not based on a server certificate, but on inspecting the web page or the domain name that points to the web page. If the user knows which domain name to expect, and recognizes the HTML content of the web page, then the web site can be considered semantically authenticated. However, when inspection of the domain name is the method for web site authentication it must be assumed that the DNS (Domain Name System) correctly translates domain names into IP addresses. The correct authentication of web sites thus depends in the integrity of the DNS. This brings the DNS into the discussion of the Browser PKI.

6   Adjacent Structures of DNS and the Browser PKI

The DNS (Domain Name System) is a distributed network of servers that invisibly translates domain names (e.g. www.uio.no) meaningful to humans into the numerical names (e.g. IPv4 address 129.240.8.200) for the purpose of uniquely locating and addressing networked devices globally.

Security threats against the DNS are many [2,14], which reduces the assurance in DNS responses such as IP address translations from domain names. The technical solution to this problem is DNSSEC (DNS Security Extension) [1] which was designed to protect Internet resolvers (clients) from forged DNS data, e.g. due to DNS cache poisoning attacks. All answers received with DNSSEC are digitally signed. Through validation of the digital signature a DNS resolver gets assurance that the information received is identical (correct and complete) to the information on the authoritative DNS server, i.e. that the information has not been corrupted. While protecting the integrity of returned IP addresses is the immediate concern for many users, DNSSEC can protect other information too, and it has been suggested to use it to protect standard public-key certificates stored as CERT records [13], thereby making it possible to use DNSSEC to distribute such certificates. However, the scheme proposed in [13] does not exploit the potential of DNSSEC for direct certification of domain names and IP addresses.

Interestingly, the leaf nodes of the DNS are the same as those of the Browser PKI, thereby making them adjacent hierarchic structures as illustrated in Fig.6 where the multi-hierarchic Browser PKI at the bottom is turned upside-down.

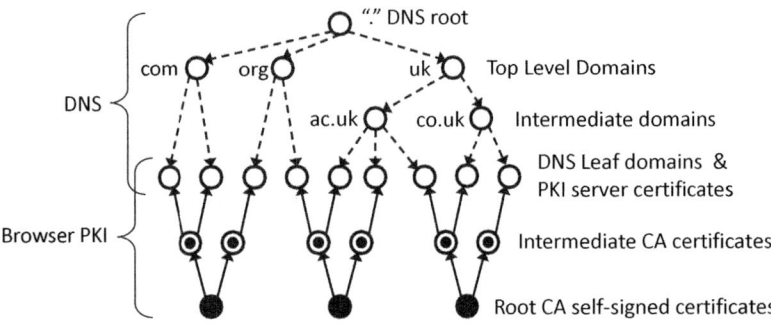

Fig. 6. Adjacent structure of DNS and the Browser PKI

When authenticating a server on the Internet, the relying party depends not only on the integrity of the Browser PKI but also on the integrity of the DNS. Should a relying party receive a corrupted reply to a DNS request e.g. in the form of a false IP address, then the relying party would be directed to the wrong server. The Browser PKI in conjunction with TLS would paradoxically validate the wrong server to be authentic. The dependency between the DNS and the Browser PKI therefore follows the principle of the weakest link, i.e. the overall security is only as strong as the weakest security strength of any of the two. Let the security strength of the current TLS implementation be expressed as $S(\text{TLS})$. By expressing the security strength of the DNS as $S(\text{DNSSEC})$ (assuming that DNSSEC is used) and the security strength of the Browser PKI as $S(\text{Browser PKI})$, then the security of the current implementation of TLS can expressed as:

$$S(\text{TLS}) = \min[S(\text{DNSSEC}), S(\text{Browser-PKI})] . \tag{3}$$

It is problematic that the correct authentication of a server depends on the weakest security of two separate systems because it reduces the overall security. The next section explains how server authentication can be simplified to depend on a single system, and thereby strengthen security, while maintaining the exact same functionality.

7   Using DNSSEC for Server Certificates

By looking at the diagram of Fig.6 it becomes obvious that the hierarchic structure of the DNS itself can be used as a PKI structure for SP certificates. In fact DNSSEC is already an overlay PKI on top of the DNS making it possible for DNS resolvers (clients) to authenticate replies to DNS requests. What we propose here is an extension of the scheme proposed in [13] where traditional X.509 certificates belonging to the Browser PKI illustrated at the bottom of Fig.6. We propose to let server certificates be signed by the DNS zone where the corresponding server is located, as illustrated in Fig.7 below.

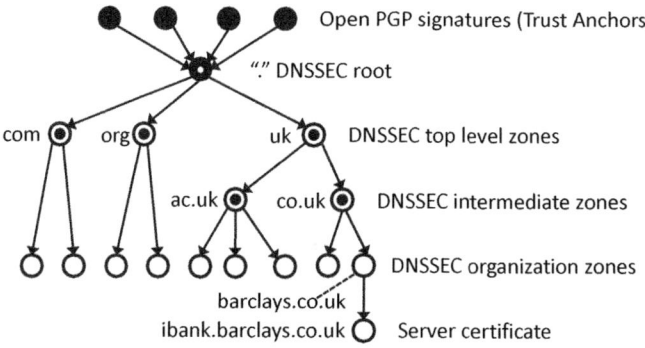

Fig. 7. DNSSEC as a platform for server certificates

In the example, Barclays bank's online banking server is called ibank.barclays.co.uk where the certificate is used for TLS connections. The public-key certificate for this server is signed by the public key of the DNS zone barclays.co.uk. The certificate can be stored as a RR (Resource Record) on the DNS server for barclays.co.uk so that it is available to all clients accessing the server.

In case of DNSSEC the trust structure is taken very seriously and multiple trust anchors represented by trusted individuals in the Internet community. Online validation of the DNS root public key is not possible, and is therefore called a DURZ (Deliberately Unvalidatable Root Zone). It does not mean that the DNS root public key can not be validated at all, instead the root public key can be manually (or semi-automatically) validated through the multiple OpenPGP signatures [3] on the root public key, as illustrated in Fig.7. So while the root public key associated with the "." DNS root can be downloaded online, its authenticity is based on some extra-protocol procedure. This can for example be that a DNS administrator obtains one or multiple OpenPGP public keys from people they trust, which in turn makes the DNS administrator able to manually validate the DNS root public key.

Integrating the PKI used for host authentication with DNSSEC results in host authentication only being dependent on the DNSSEC, so that the Eq.(3) is simplified to:

$$S(\text{TLS}) = S(\text{DNSSEC}) .\tag{4}$$

Assuming that server and software certificates can provide meaningful authentication by improving the usability of TLS e.g. with solutions such as the TrustBar [8,7] described in Sec.3, a PKI solution based on DNSSEC would be the obvious choice because it has a simple and sound trust structure. This would solve the problem of the dependancy on an separate trust structure in the form of the Browser PKI which in addition must be characterised as relatively unreliable. Not only will the robustness of the PKI be strengthened, the cost can also be reduced because of the simplified infrastructure. When DNSSEC is deployed anyway it might well be used as a platform for signing and distributing server certificates.

8 Conclusion

This paper describes vulnerabilities of the TLS based on the Browser PKI, and argues that this currently makes server and software authentication meaningless. Still, there exist business models for the Browser PKI model which in itself provides reasons for certain security solutions vendors to keep promoting this model. We argue that it is reasonable to use the Anonymous Diffie-Hellman option of TLS, because other options based on server certificates do not provide meaningful authentication and therefore must be considered equally "anonymous". The fact that most browsers do not support the standardised Anonymous Diffie-Hellman option can indicate that the browser developers are being influenced by the CAs in this regard, because the CAs see the Anonymous Diffie-Hellman option as a threat to their business of selling certificates.

The fact that the described vulnerabilities of TLS are not well understood, and the Anonymous Diffie-Hellman option is not well known or even available, online SPs feel obliged to subscribe to the Browser PKI model in order to be trusted by users, which can be described as a form of trust extortion. We argue that it is time to improve the usability of TLS, and to replace the Browser PKI model with the PKI of DNSSEC for signing and distributing server and software certificates. This solution leverages the strong trust structure of DNSSEC and thereby provides higher assurance of server authentication than is presently possible. This solution would also contribute to reduced cost because it avoids adjacent duplicate PKIs.

References

1. Arends, R., Austein, R., Larson, M., Massey, D., Rose, S.: RFC 4033 - DNS Security Introduction and Requirements. IETF (March 2005), http://www.rfc-editor.org/
2. Bellovin, S.M.: Using the domain name system for system break-ins. In: Proceedings of the Fifth Usenix Unix Security Symposium (1995)
3. Callas, J., Donnerhacke, L., Finney, H., Shaw, D., Thayer, R.: RFC 4880 - OpenPGP Message Format. IETF (November 2007), http://www.rfc-editor.org/
4. Michael Chernick, C., Edington III, C., Fanto, M.J., Rosenthal, R.: Guidelines for the Selection and Use of Transport Layer Security (TLS) Implementations – NIST Special Publication 800-52. Technical report, National Institute of Standards and Technology (2005)
5. Cranor, L., Egelman, S., Hong, J., Zhang, Y.: Phinding Phish: An Evaluation of Anti-Phishing Toolbars. Technical Report CMU-CyLab-06-018, Carnegie Mellon University CyLab (November 13, 2006)

6. Dierks, T., Allen, C.: RFC2246 - The TLS (Transport Layer Security) protocol, Version 1.0. IETF (January 1999), http://www.ietf.org/rfc/rfc2246.txt

7. Ferdous, M. S., Jøsang, A., Singh, K., Borgaonkar, R.: ecurity Usability of Petname Systems. In: Jøsang, A., Maseng, T., Knapskog, S.J. (eds.) NordSec 2009. LNCS, vol. 5838, pp. 44–59. Springer, Heidelberg (2009)

8. Herzberg, A., Gbara, A.: Protecting (even Naïve) Web Users from Spoofing and Phishing Attacks. Technical Report 2004/155, Cryptology ePrint Archive (2004)

9. Hovlandsvåg, J.S.: The support of key exchange algorithms in todays web browsers. Technical Report Assignment Paper. University of Oslo (April 27, 2011)

10. ISO. IS 7498-2. Basic Reference Model For Open Systems Interconnection - Part 2: Security Architecture. International Organisation for Standardization (1988)

11. Jøsang, A., AlFayyadh, B., Grandison, T., AlZomai, M., McNamara, J.: Security Usability Principles for Vulnerability Analysis and Risk Assessment. In: The Proceedings of the Annual Computer Security Applications Conference (ACSAC 2007), Miami Beach (December 2007)

12. Jøsang, A., Møllerud, P.M., Cheung, E.: Web Security: The Emperors New Armour. In: The Proceedings of the European Conference on Information Systems (ECIS 2001), Bled, Slovenia (June 2001)

13. Josefsson, S.: RFC 4398 - Storing Certificates in the Domain Name System (DNS). IETF (March 2006), http://www.rfc-editor.org/

14. Kaminsky, D.: Details. Dan Kaminsky's blog at dankaminsky.com (July 24, 2008), http://dankaminsky.com/2008/07/24/details/

15. Microsoft. Microsoft Security Bulletin MS01-017 Erroneous VeriSign-Issued Digital Certificates Pose Spoofing Hazard (March 22, 2001), http://www.microsoft.com/technet/security/bulletin/MS01-017.asp

16. Mills, E.: Fraudulent Google certificate points to Internet attack (August 29, 2011), http://news.cnet.com/

17. Shakarian, P.: Stuxnet: Cyberwar revolution in military affairs. Small Wars Journal (April 2011)

18. Simmons, G.J., Meadows, C.: The role of trust in information integrity protocols. Journal of Computer Security 3(1), 71–84 (1995)

Trust Areas: A Security Paradigm for the Future Internet

Carsten Rudolph

Fraunhofer Institute for Secure Information Technology – SIT
Rheinstrasse 75, Darmstadt, Germany
Carsten.Rudolph@sit.fraunhofer.de

Abstract. Security in information and communication technology currently relies on a collection of mostly un-related and un-coordinated security mechanisms. All in all, the end-user has no chance to get a good perception of the security properties satisfied for actions she is executing in the Internet. Classical approaches (e.g. perimeter security) do not work in open and heterogeneous communication environments. Federation of single security mechanisms only works for particular applications and for a small subset of security properties. Thus, new views on trust and security are required for the Future Internet. This vision paper proposes the concept of *Trust Areas* as one candidate for a security paradigm for the Future Internet and identifies some open research challenges.

1 Introduction

Security in IT systems relies on the existence of trust relations. Bi-lateral trust relations are often sufficient for secure applications. However, already in communication networks existing today such bi-lateral trust relations are not efficient and in a large scale impossible to be managed. Thus, hierarchical or federated security infrastructures have been established. Such security infrastructures are then used to define more or less static relations for VPNs, client-server applications, or network access control. So far, this approach provides a reasonable basis for the development of secure systems [1]. Nevertheless, converging networks on all layers from hardware (one device with all types of communication interfaces) to the applications (software as a service, cloud computing) creates a new networking landscape.

Current IT Infrastructures (the Internet in a wide sense) consist of various protocols, different underlying technologies to connect devices, transmit data, and different layers of distributed applications. Some of these technologies and protocols are transparent from a user's point of view. This trend towards transparent use of heterogeneous technology will continue towards seamless applications. In the long run, it will evolve to a converged infrastructure, the *Future Internet*. Thus, in the Future Internet we expect that in many cases users and also applications are indeed unaware of the underlying technology used. Therefore, the Future Internet will in fact consist of physical communication channels under the control of various network operators and a variety of overlay networks

C. Meadows and C. Fernández-Gago (Eds.): STM 2011, LNCS 7170, pp. 22–27, 2012.

such as low-level peer-to-peer infrastructures, industrial control networks, virtual private networks, service infrastructures, cloud computing infrastructures, logical backbones, or special purpose networks (e.g. for online gaming). In this Future Internet security infrastructures need to be open, flexible, cross-domain and ubiquitous. Further, user and device shall be clearly distinguished and users must have the possibility to be in full control of their data and to decide which other users or devices will get hold of this data.

Boundaries will disappear on physical and technical communication layers but also on the logical level of applications and services. Current security solutions are similar to building gated communities in the real world. Federation means that identification for one gated community is accepted by others and, in the best case, there are secure ways to get from one community to the other. However, in the Internet it is not possible to draw clear boundaries and to always make users aware of these boundaries. Similar to the physical world, security cannot be guaranteed.The approach of virtual gates and walls currently works more or less for enterprise networks, although even those are divided into distinguished network zones.The situation is even more complex in the more open Internet. Security issues go way beyond federating authentication and encrypting communication channels. Some of the relevant keywords include privacy, data collection and aggregation, user profiling, use of processing and storage power of clouds to build huge data-bases, confidentiality of personal data, accounting, money, economical processes. Many other topics could be mentioned. Additionally, the attack landscape is also changing towards more targeted attacks and advanced persistent threats that can be in place unnoticed for a long time before they become evident. Such attacks can be the vehicle of organized crime to cause high financial damage.

This position paper introduces the vision of a security paradigm for the Future Internet, the so-called multi-domain *trust areas*. These trust areas formulate the goal of suitable security infrastructures for the Future Internet. Multi-domain trust areas shall not replace existing security infrastructures, but shall complement and be combined with identity management, PKIs, security information and event management and other existing technologies. However,trust areas provide a new view on scope of trust relations and the required (and possible) flexibility of security mechanisms and also of the necessary awareness and security perceptions on the side of the end-user. The notion of trust areas can provide guidance for future research on trust and security in the Future Internet.

2   The Vision of Multi-domain Trust Areas

A fully secure Internet will remain an illusion (similar to overall security in human societies). However, in the "physical" world people have a perception of the risks they are exposed to. In a town, one can know which areas are safe and secure and which areas shall be avoided. Moreover, in physical social networks trust relations are established (often depending on behaviour, look, and "gut feeling") and identification is achieved by various non-technical means.

All these naturally human techniques cannot be easily transferred to the Internet. Nevertheless, for the Future Internet people will also build some kind of trust and security perception related to their actions in the Internet. Security and trust mechanisms need to support the establishment of such a perception in a way that it enables users to know what the risks are. Consequently, in contrast to existing information and communication technology (ICT) infrastructures, the Future Internet shall provide inherent support for trust and security in terms of so-called multi-domain *trust areas*. The next paragraphs provide a first definition of this term and the related concepts.

Trust. Historically, various different notions of trust can be found, each addressing particular aspects of ICT systems, e.g. trust in electronic commerce systems based on reputation and recommendation, or trust in public key infrastructures. While these notions support the understanding of trust establishment and degrees of trustworthiness in their respective application domains, they are insufficient for the more general notion of trust.For the notion of trust areas the term *trust* expresses the view of a particular entity or agent of the system on particular (security) properties of a system [4].

Area. For many applications, it is not necessary that trust relations are established with a huge number of entities. Trust is relevant for a particular set of entities that is actually involved in a process. In many scenarios, such a subset can be open and dynamic. The appropriate term for such an open set is the term *area*. For motivation of this choice compare with the entry in Merriam Webster:[1]

> **Entry Word**: area. **Function**: noun. **Meaning**: 1. a part or portion having no fixed boundaries 2. a region of activity, knowledge, or influence.

In the context of the Future Internet, the *area* denotes an open set of physical and logical entities, such as network components, services, but also identities or actions executed within a particular process.

Multi-domain. In current ICT networks and even more in future ones security cannot easily be build on central trusted authorities. In contrast, only subsets of network components, applications or other entities can be under a common control with respect to those properties that someone might want to trust. A set of network components and applications under a common control is now denoted with the term *Domain*. It should be noted that with respect to different properties to be trusted a single entity can belong to different domains at the same time. Processes will be *multi-domain*, i.e. they will cross different domains. Domains can intersect and that a multi-domain area not necessarily completely includes all domains it touches.

Multi-domain trust area

> A *trust area* is defined as an open cross-layer section of a heterogeneous ICT network (i.e. the Future Internet) with the following properties:

[1] `http://www.merriam-webster.com/thesaurus/area`

- Users can be aware of the actions and processes they can do without leaving the trust area.
- Security mechanisms exist that enable users to make a well-founded decision on which security properties can be trusted with respect to the actions and processes executed within the trust area.

It should be noted that trust areas are not "Secure Areas". Users need to be able to achieve a good perception of the security properties satisfied for particular actions and also of the risks involved. Also, view on security properties within the trust area can be very different for different users depending on their view and knowledge.

A trust area should cross many layers and exist orthogonal to different overlay networks. Within a trust area, users should be able to establish trust relations and users can know and can be made aware of what they can securely do and what the risks are. The concept of trust areas can be compared to a social community (or a town) where citizens know whom to trust and in which areas they can securely and safely live, shop, dine out, and in which area they should be more careful. The Future Internet shall support a trust infrastructure with inherent support for trust areas as well as trusted means to provide situational security awareness for the users.

3 Research Tasks and Challenges

Trust areas require new combinations of existing security mechanisms and possibly the development of totally new approaches in particular for supporting the users' perception of security.Clearly, a trust area will not be something monolithic. Some of the open issues to be approached are given in the following paragraphs.

Identification and expression of typical actions and processes with their trust and security needs. A careful study of cross-domain activities in the Internet with an identification of the trust and security needs of different stakeholders should give a first idea of the scope for trust areas. In addition to the obvious security properties of confidentiality, authentication, integrity and non-repudiation, some of the interesting issues to look for are accounting (e.g. world-wide cross-domain roaming services) and responsibilities (e.g. who is responsible for financial losses, breaches of national and international laws).

Identification of available security and trust mechanisms and their evolution A second parallel step needs to create a map of available security and trust mechanisms. As a trust area is not a new mechanism itself it needs to rely on a proper use of existing mechanisms and might also motivate research on totally new mechanisms. Examples of mechanisms trust areas can rely on include basically all existing and efficiently deployed security mechanisms, such as TLS/SSL for web interfaces, S/Mime for e-mail, web-service security, ticket-based authentication, token-based authentication, electronic ID cards, closed sub-networks, cryptographic protocols for WLAN, VPNs, actively monitored and controlled services, or hardware-based security. In addition to these technical solutions, trust areas can also be influenced by other non-technical things, e.g. contracts and service-level agreements or legal regulations and their enforcement. The Future Internet will continuously evolve and new attack vectors will appear along with new business models. In parallel, one can also expect new security mechanisms to be developed. Thus it will be necessary to establish advanced types of distributed security management for trust areas, including means for an adaptive evolving configuration of security measures according to the evolution of the infrastructure and overlay networks and the situational knowledge about current threats and malicious activities.

Combinations of security mechanisms / trust area security processes. Trust areas need to cross different domains and also different physical and/or overlay networks. Thus, it will be necessary to combine different security mechanisms in order to achieve assurance for particular actions or a process within the trust area. These combinations itself, but also the visualisation towards the user and the usability of the combined solutions represent one of the more difficult challenges for the realization of trust areas. Some approaches exist on the level of security patterns and also for automated reasoning on security properties and logical security building blocks. However, in general the combination and integration of security mechanisms needs more fundamental work.

Integration into Future Internet applications and platforms. Once the vision of trust areas is developed into a more concrete set of mechanisms, one next step is the integration into applications in order to make users aware of trust relations and enable the users to make well-informed decisions on their actions in the Future Internet with respect to security properties. Network components or network parts might need to provide security information for trust areas (the reliable, secure Internet backbone). Second, network components (routers, switches, but also servers) can have their own more technical view of trust areas and policies can influence the behaviour of these components relative to the current parameters of the trust areas they are in.

Usability and awareness: expressing trust and security / visualisation. In the physical world, trust is often a result of relatively clear parameters combined with a "gut feeling". This human perception needs to be replaced with some user interaction with clear semantics. The trust status with regard to a user's current actions needs to be visualised in an intuitive but not over-simplified way. The "SSL lock" in the browser window is not sufficient. One should expect users to be able to cope with visualisations as complex as international traffic signs.

Further, a proper classification and description of security properties with clear semantics is necessary. Such a classification could be based on existing frameworks for security modelling [2,3,5,6]. However, the property description needs to express all relevant parameters (e.g. the local view of the user, underlying security assumptions and underlying trust assumptions).s.

4   Conclusions

This vision paper introduces the notion of trust areas as a proposal for a new vision of security and trust in the Future Internet. This notion can be a vehicle for a more targeted discussion on trust and security issues and can also guide future research in this area. One essential component of trust Areas is the information of the user about the security properties related to the actions she wants to execute in the Internet. Obviously, this information can be quite complex. Therefore, one main task in addition to the technical realisation of security mechanisms is the visualisation of security properties shown in the context of processes and actions executed in the past or to be executed in the future.

References

1. Anderson, R.J.: Security Engineering: A Guide to Building Dependable Distributed Systems. Wiley Publishing (2008)
2. Focardi, R., Gorrieri, R.: Classification of Security Properties (Part I: Information Flow). LNCS, vol. 2171. Springer, Heidelberg (2001)
3. Focardi, R., Gorrieri, R., Martinelli, F.: Classification of Security Properties (Part II: Network Security). LNCS, vol. 2946. Springer, Heidelberg (2004)
4. Fuchs, A., Gürgens, S., Rudolph, C.: A Formal Notion of Trust – Enabling Reasoning about Security Properties. In: Nishigaki, M., Jøsang, A., Murayama, Y., Marsh, S. (eds.) IFIPTM 2010. IFIP AICT, vol. 321, pp. 200–215. Springer, Heidelberg (2010)
5. Gürgens, S., Ochsenschläger, P., Rudolph, C.: On a formal framework for security properties. International Computer Standards & Interface Journal (CSI), Special issue on formal methods, techniques and tools for secure and reliable applications 27(5), 457–466 (2005)
6. Mantel, H.: Possibilistic definitions of security – an assembly kit. In: Proceedings of the IEEE Computer Security Foundations Workshop, pp. 185–199 (2000)

Non-standards for Trust: Foreground Trust and Second Thoughts for Mobile Security

Stephen Marsh[1], Sylvie Noël[1], Tim Storer[2], Yao Wang[1], Pam Briggs[3],
Lewis Robart[1], John Stewart[1], Babak Esfandiari[4], Khalil El-Khatib[5],
Mehmet Vefa Bicakci[4], Manh Cuong Dao[4], Michael Cohen[5],
and Daniel Da Silva[5]

[1] Communications Research Centre, Canada
first.last@crc.gc.ca
[2] Glasgow University, Department of Computer Science
timothy.storer@glasgow.ac.uk
[3] Northumbria University, School of Psychology
p.briggs@northumbria.ac.uk
[4] Carleton University, Department of Systems and Computer Engineering
babak@sce.carleton.ca
[5] UOIT, Faculty of Business and Information Technology
khalil.el-khatib@uoit.ca

Abstract. In this paper, we introduce and discuss Foreground Trust. Foreground Trust, itself based on recent work in the area of Trust Enablement, is a paradigm for allowing devices in a human-device ecosystem the means to reason with and about trust in themselves, other devices, and humans, whilst allowing humans to make trusting decisions using their own internal models (whatever they may be) based on cues from the environment — *including the device(s) in use at the time*. We discuss the paradigm, and present an actualization of it in the form of Device Comfort, a model of device reasoning based on environmental cues, and the use of the device status to help users make informed trusting and security decisions for themselves. In particular we focus on the interface between user and device to help the user make trust-based decisions and use second thoughts as a means to educate and raise user awareness about their security in online and mobile behaviours.

1 Introduction

Mobile technologies, more than any other medium before them, are putting into the hands of all of us tremendous computing power, communications facilities unparalleled in history, and the ability to enhance decisions and associated actions both in terms of speed and magnitude. It is possible to take pictures and let the world see them in seconds, to post information about behaviour, location, thoughts, hopes and dreams, likes and dislikes, all, quite often with scant to no regard as to the outcomes of these actions. Not rarely enough, the outcomes can be devastating. People can be bullied, have their identity stolen, be spied upon,

C. Meadows and C. Fernández-Gago (Eds.): STM 2011, LNCS 7170, pp. 28–39, 2012.

inadvertently release more than they expected or realized, lose or compromise jobs now or in the future, and live to regret, at leisure, their 'mistakes.' Consider also that privacy is of utmost primary concern in any ubiquitous, mobile, or reputation-based environment [17,1].

As an aside, whilst this is not the place for such, there should be, and we encourage, debate and a great deal of research about whether or not indeed these are mistakes, and what the scope of the information should be. This is an avenue for initiatives such as enabling information to make up its own mind about its level of sensitivity (the idea behind so called Smart Data - see e.g. [26,21,33,23]). For the purpose of this paper, however, we will continue to refer to these unintended consequences as 'mistakes.'

These mistakes are not new. Undoubtedly for as long as people have existed in societies, there have been unintended information leaks, both personal and institutional. The advent of smart mobile technology has however multiplied the effects of what might previously have been a minor slip in the pub at lunchtime to a worldwide phenomenon by five minutes after lunch. The problem is that users are left with little comprehension about the extent to which their actions can become multiplied by the technology available to them. We can of course all assume that we are far too smart to be caught out by revealing unwarranted personal information, but mistakes do indeed happen, and given the lack of adequate privacy protection for what is posted in the various social networking sites extant today, it's little wonder. Couple this with instant access to information whenever and wherever we happen to be, whatever we happen to be doing, and it's also little wonder that even the most savvy individuals might fall victim to a phishing attack arriving, serendipitously for the bad guys, at exactly the moment these individuals are distracted (and it doesn't take much).

There are a few problems here, linked by the tenuous thread of smart mobile devices, but that thread, we believe, is enough to allow us to address it in one specific way. We can see a particularly promising pattern, that *the device itself may be key to helping address its own problems*. Indeed, we conjecture that if the device were capable of reasoning in a more nuanced and informed manner about what it was doing, and who was requesting the action, where it was, and other contextual niceties, many of these problems may be mitigated. That's not to say traditional security methodologies don't work, or won't work, merely that if we can leverage some of the sense-act powers of the device, we should try to make them work for us as much as the capabilities of the device sometimes work to our detriment, or encourage us to do so.

In any circumstance, we believe that the defence against dumbly smart devices is informed people. The question then becomes: how to inform, and make aware, the people using these devices as to the consequences of their imminent action? The user-base range is large, and goes from tweens to seniors, with all point in-between, but we are working on an approach we believe can address individual users regardless of their demographic, through adapting the notion of computational trust.[1] We take the concept a step away from traditional models of computational trust, as we will discuss below, and bring it into the foreground to allow users to see how the device itself is situated in its environment, and to make the user aware of this status and situation from the device's point of view. We conjecture, and aim to prove through simulations and experiments, that a trust-enabled relationship between device and user can help raise awareness and give second thoughts about actions for users in potentially compromised situations.

This paper introduces the concept of Foreground Trust, explores some of the areas in which it may be of use, and briefly discusses our work in the area of Device Comfort[24,25], as well as thoughts and work in the area of 'Annoying Technologies' and comfort-based user interfaces, an actualization of the Foreground Trust concept on mobile devices.

2   Trust

Trust, as a judgment with unparalleled utility, is indeed used by almost every one of these people, every day, to help make choices. Some of these choices are, or may seem, frivolous, such as from whom to buy items online, or which newspaper to believe on particular stories. Some are more complex, including the choice of jobs, friends, and deeper relationships. Trust features in these decisions because we, as humans, are mostly rather good at using it, regardless of its pitfalls, which include the fact that we can get it seriously wrong, be conned, underestimate risk, and so on. And, while there are many definitions of trust, there are likely, we conjecture, at least as many trust models (and ways of reasoning with and about trust) as there are people using it. This is not to say that we all do it differently, but that our views, estimations, and intuitions all must at some point play a part in its use within us. It is, of course, possible to find patterns and similarities, and the general behaviour of trust is well studied and understood. Both technologically and socially, we have a wide range of research available (see for example [8,2,19,12,4]). However, it remains an individual notion based on internal mechanisms and histories such that, even in exactly the same circumstances, with the same inputs, two *people* will not be guaranteed to come up with the same trusting decisions.

Computational Trust, trust from the perspective of technology – which in this instance means devices capable of communicating with each other in some way – this individuality of trust is both a strength and a weakness. It is a weakness, because seeking out a standard way of behaving and reasoning using trust is not possible, despite, and perhaps reflected by, the many models that now exist and will continue to be postulated (see [27,14] for instance). It is possible to define standard behaviours for aspects of trust, however – in a recent discussion it was

---

[1] Given the large number of articles and books on the subject, and indeed the context of this paper, we will not define the terms 'trust' or 'computational trust' here. The interested reader is referred to [18,13,20,6] amongst many others in different fields of research.

suggested[2] that transitivity was a good place to think about standardization, for instance. The fact remains that the internal reasoning models and histories that lead to trusting decisions are not standard, have their own strengths and weaknesses in different contexts, and do not reflect their human counterparts. The famously difficult problem of sharing trust values (which, inevitably, technological trust models must use) only adds to this weakness – what exactly, to a human, does a trust value of, say, 0.5 mean? To put it another way, if the trust value increases magically to 0.55, what does 10% increase mean? Can I trust the other person with 10% more of my money? Is there a 10% lesser chance the other person will betray my trust and run off with the money? Will they pay back 10% more before doing so?

Despite, or perhaps because of, these causes of weakness, Computational Trust possesses huge strengths also. Most importantly, simply as a virtue of the different internal workings of trust in humans, the internal workings of computational trust in technologies does not in fact have to adhere to a standard at all. Any and all models are possible and viable until shown to be otherwise (by which we might mean via experimentation, simulation, and/or observation of behaviour contrary to a rational human understanding of the concept). Any trust model is fine, so long as it behaves 'as if' trust reasoning is occurring.

Between technological devices, the problem of sharing trust values can be addressed because the internal workings of trust models within systems can be more closely understood (and perhaps agreed upon). Between technologies and humans, the requirements to share are likewise ameliorated because in all instances we would expect the technology to share information *in context*. Quite often we hear phrases such as 'I trust him' without justification, where further questioning can reveal context for the speaker (in fact, 'I trust him' might mean 'I trust him to vacuum the floor while I'm out of the room, and not, by extension, to bunk off or rifle through my belongings whilst I'm out, but I wouldn't trust him on his own in the house, vacuum or no vacuum.' It might also mean something completely different.) This sharing of context for humans is difficult, time consuming, and often unnecessary because much of the context is obvious or implied. We do not have this luxury with technologies, and so an explicit context sharing is often necessary, although as we will discuss later, not at the outset of a trust-based decision process.

3   Foreground Trust

In [10], Dwyer discusses Trust Enablement. Trust Enablement, described in [6], espouses the paradigm that people do not in fact need to be told who to trust, but would use available information to make up their mind for themselves. As Dwyer notes, 'the agenda of trust-enablement is to allow users to define what trust means to them in a certain situation, and to allow a user to conduct a trust relationship that is in their best interests and on their own terms' [10, Page 26]. The point here is that, since trust is a subjective judgment, it should be left to

---

[2] Many thanks to Robert Laddaga for this insight.

the subject to make it. That is not to say that the subject cannot be helped, for example in gaining context or the views of others (including electronic others) in their trusting decisions, but that the decision, trust or distrust, and levels thereof, is personal.

We can take this further and say that in fact, the trust decision is not only subjective but unique. As has been noted elsewhere [27] there are many definitions of trust, each with strengths and weaknesses. Indeed, there exist many different trust models and uses of trust within the field of Trust Management, again each of these models is unique and applicable in different contexts. The point here is that, far from being disparate, these models and definitions address different aspects of trust that are important in the contexts in which they are applied. They can co-exist within different tools, in the same space, producing their own trust values and decisions, just as humans do. Further, since they all rely on information from the environment in some way, including the reputation values of others in societies, they require to be given not what or who to trust, but what information is necessary to calculate their own particular outcome of trust.

With Foreground Trust, the concept of Trust Enablement comes full circle. Tools for enabling users to make trusting (or security related) decisions should be designed to allow the user to make those decisions absent information about the trust-based decisions of the tool itself, while the tools can exchange trust-related information amongst themselves (in smart/ambient environments) to make their own trusting decisions, which are based on potentially unique trust models. The representation to the user is not who or what to trust, but information about context that the device is able to give in order to enable the user in their own decisions. To put it another way, the device/system should not force the user to trust or not to trust, but should allow the user to make up their own mind and act accordingly. Like an efficient butler, naturally, we may allow a device to express their concerns about some decisions, but the decision is the device owner's.

Of course, the other aspect of Foreground Trust is that it is, indeed, in the foreground. The implicit acknowledgment of the value of trust in making decisions is made explicit within tools that use it both to make their own decisions and to give the information needed to allow people to make their own. From the point of view of the system of Device Comfort described in this paper, this explicit acknowledgment of trust does two things: empowers users to think more clearly about the concept for themselves, and just as importantly enables second thoughts in the actions they wish to take using their devices, and all in context. In the next section we show how we use the concept of *comfort* as a means of expressing this contextual trust-based status. Section 5 discusses our ongoing work in expressing this comfort measure in practice.

4   Device Comfort

We use the concept of *comfort* in order to insulate trust from the process in its initial stages, whilst allowing users to examine the concept more closely at will.

Thus we can expect devices to express their discomfort in context (for instance, 'I'm uncomfortable sharing your address with this requestor because this is your first meeting with them.' or 'are you sure you want John to do the vacuuming – you have to leave in 5 minutes for an important meeting.').

At its most basic, Device Comfort is an adaptation of trust in context for mobile devices that allows them to express to their users their security status. As we discuss in [25], comfort is a single measure derived from multiple inputs to a device. These inputs include location (and Comfort Zones [22]), usage (both current and historical), device hardware status (e.g., battery, camera), network and networking (e.g., bluetooth, wifi, NFC), other devices (for behavior akin to Zero Interaction Authentication [7,29]) as well as an ongoing bi-directional trust relationship between device and user (based on extensions of [20] and [36,35]). We also include policy management in the device to ensure a level of security that is more 'comfortably' understandable to security professionals and those who may own information on devices that belong to others. In all of these measures, and more that we anticipate in future, there naturally exists a level of uncertainty in a device – for instance, location may be spoofed, but different measures are available to counteract this [25] – this uncertainty can be expressed as well as an other measure as a component of comfort for the device.

Like a constitutional monarch, Device Comfort serves at least three purposes: Advise, Encourage, and Warn (we also add Prohibit, which is perhaps a more problematic action for the monarch these days). This paper is concerned primarily with the utility of these in the form of encouraging sober second thoughts, and in particular how this can be achieved through providing the user with feedback in sensible ways. As we will see in section 5, we are also not above being annoying. The remainder of this section briefly describes how Device Comfort is used within the device as a foundation of non-standard trust.

The comfort level (status in context, as discussed briefly above) of a device is something that matters most to the device and its user. To a lesser extent, it might also matter to the owner of the device if the device is owned by someone different from the user. It might also matter to the devices around it, to networks the device is using, and so on. The point here is that the internal mechanisms that the device uses in order to ascertain its own levels of comfort are of no concern to those around it. Indeed, in the normal scheme of things, this calculation is of no concern to the user of the device. In the normal scheme of things, all outside agencies need to know is the level of comfort a device has.

5   Thinking about the Interface

As in most technologies, the most important part of the 'comfortable' device is the interface between device and user. In our case, we are working with some requirements, likely not all of which are normally associated with good design:

- Be easily understood, yet allow more complex explanations;
- Be present at all times, in order to maintain user awareness;
- Be more present at times of discomfort, in order to encourage second thoughts;

- Be annoying when necessary;
- Be non-intrusive.

Indeed, these requirements could be seen as necessary for any security-oriented interface in continual use on mobile personal devices, and whilst we could add more, present interesting challenges as they stand. Our interface work is concerned with ensuring that they are all met without one of them compromising the others. We do appreciate the problems here. For instance, a device that is too annoying may be discarded in favor of using a friend's device for the immediate purpose of sending compromising material instead of used as a learning experience, or left alone altogether if seemingly innocuous changes of location result in spam-like messages about how uncomfortable the device is in one locale or another. However, we do not perceive these as a balancing act, but as a learning experience, and one based on the underlying trust and leveraged anthropomorphic tendencies of human users (see [30] for excellent insights into this). The challenge is both a design (through HCI) and a technological one, and we are addressing it from both of these angles.

5.1   Dogs and Icons: The Design of Comfort

Mindful of the principles espoused in [28] and [15], we must accept that an interface that is non-intrusive is a contradiction with the idea that it be annoying when necessary (as well as present at all times, particularly in times of discomfort).Thus, while the idea of being non-intrusive is a noble goal, ours is one that cannot follow that path. In order to help people make decisions that improve security, we are exploring two approaches that go beyond the 'normal' interface approach.

The process of expressing and even calculating comfort is not in itself particularly hard. Indeed, anyone who has a dog can attest to the fact that dogs are indeed rather good at expressing their levels of comfort. If a dog can do it, the argument goes, then so can we. Of course, it's also technically and socially difficult to calculate and represent comfort in the way we are approaching it. However, we can leverage the Media Equation [30] and allow and shamelessly encourage anthropomorphic tendencies in our goal of addressing the requirements above. This approach we call the 'Friendly Dog Interface.' Consider the dog: tail up equals happy, tail between legs is emphatically not. There are levels of comfort expressible between these extremes. There are also different ways of expressing this in context with the differing levels of comfort as well as, for instance, how fast comfort is changing.

The more challenging approach we are investigating is that of 'Annoying Technology.' Annoying technology breaks several golden rules in order to, we intend, encourage the user to take a step back and rethink their actions. An annoying technology interface could, for instance, emphasize second thoughts by presenting dialog boxes with larger buttons for canceling potentially compromising actions, and very small buttons for allowing them. We are experimenting with usability and accessibility issues in the Annoying Technology space, but believe that, for the most part, annoyance can be used sparingly and in conjunction with other approaches such as the Friendly Dog interface.

These approaches address, somewhat, our requirements when presenting information to the user of a comfort-reasoning device, in particular when the device has something to say to the user. However, pervasive awareness is our goal for building a relationship between user and device based on trust. In this instance, it is necessary for the device to always inform the user of its comfort level. And this without getting in the way. We are approaching this from a variety of directions. The first is via a status-bar icon, the second a startup (turn on) screen icon. In the status bar, a small icon can be consistently present and continually updated to represent the comfort level of the device. Figure 1 shows an example of some of the icons we are experimenting with. For the turn on screen, we can expand this with larger and more expressive icons.

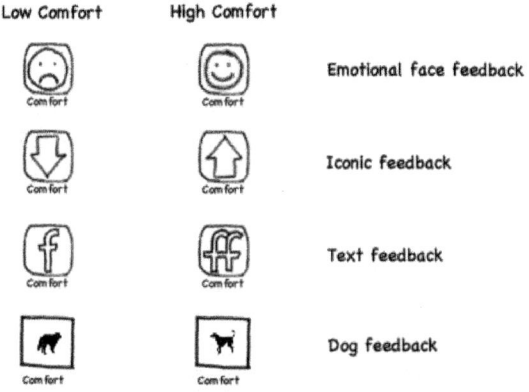

Fig. 1. A Sample of Comfort-Related Icons

Our questions then become: when do we interfere? When do we become annoying? When, indeed, do we proscribe actions? In all of these, we are pursuing research to determine not only the right way, but also the right time, to address the user in different ways to ensure that not only do they pay attention to what the device says, but that they can, for instance, learn from it how to improve their behaviour to be more secure or private, teach the device that the behaviour is acceptable in this context, achieve second thoughts, and more.

To put it succinctly, the device does not in general need to be *really* annoying, because this would indeed be counterproductive. Annoyance is potentially useful only rarely when it is used to do truly unsafe things. Most of the time we would expect the device interface to be neutral, i.e. designed to be intuitive, conform with use norms, and so forth. Also, we are examining a scale of 'annoyingness' such that small scale risks don't affect the interface usability drastically, but do let the user know that the device was uncomfortable.

Thus, a device that is generally pleasant to use and only becomes obstructive in highly risky situations has a better chance of being accepted, because if the user thinks of the device as active, then they are more likely to accept the obstructiveness if it occurs rarely.

6   Related Work

This research in part has strong links to, and lies firmly within the camp of, persuasive technology [11,15]. In [34], the regrets, because of posts, of Facebook users are examined and a set of principles are provided for how to avoid, or handle, regrets. Quite apart from addressing some of the concerns we express in the introduction, the paper expresses the need for a better design, including through sentiment analysis and 'soft paternalism' (in our terms, encouraging second thoughts). All of these techniques, as well as the ability to delay outgoing messages[3], can help provide a better sense of behavioural propriety for targeted users. Indeed all of them can be used as inputs to the device to ascertain comfort levels associated with user behaviour, and adapt trust measures accordingly. We believe the inherent relationship associated with personal device and user allows the device to more effectively encourage behaviour that will not be regretted.

Langheinrich [16] argues for allowing trust decisions to be made by humans. We are in step with this desire, but see the need, more now with the ability of instant communications, to have devices step in and help stave off regret, or to help users make not just trust decisions, but *informed* trust decisions. The Foreground Trust paradigm embodied in Device Comfort in fact directly addresses this need.

What we do not discuss at length in this paper is the power of Device Comfort in the automation of mobile device security to protect users, devices and the information that resides on them and that they share [25] – thus the device for example uses regret to ensure its actions as well as its users are 'correct' [23]). This to an extent puts the work into the arena of Ubiquitous Computing (UbiComp), which addresses, amongst others, security, ad hoc networks and contextual reasoning [31,9,5,32,3]. In this work, decisions are often made for users in the background. It is worth addressing the fact that 'for humans' may well mean that humans would like to understand more closely what is in fact happening in the background. Formal explanations based on complex trust or security models do not suffice because they are often impenetrable. We conjecture that simpler explanations, able to be expanded and further investigated, are both more accessible and more viable as a means of encouraging trust of technologies by humans. The Foreground Trust paradigm, whilst initially aimed at allowing and enabling humans to make up their own minds about situations, can serve quite as readily in enabling humans to understand better the behaviours and decisions of the technological world around them (for instance in the Internet of Things).

7   Conclusions and Ongoing Work

When it comes to personal and private information, people make mistakes. These mistakes, whilst not new, are often accelerated and inflated by social networks,

---

[3] For example in Outlook: see `http://bit.ly/saxP0m`

instant access, and 'smart' devices. We believe that the same devices can in fact be used to help people to:

– Understand their mistakes;
– Achieve sober second thoughts;
– Learn better how not to make mistakes, and improve their security.

Foreground Trust, an area of trust enablement that aims to provide human users with enough data to make informed decisions around trust, is a powerful step in the direction of these goals. The embodiment of Foreground Trust as Device Comfort is an automated approach to trust in context that uses pervasive awareness, leverages relationships between users and devices, and builds on computational trust models, to achieve the goals on smart mobile devices. The result is a non-standard model of trust because it can be different for any device and does not suffer from comparison and sharing – the device is comfortable or not, with stages in-between, the interpretation of this is in the user (and in other devices in the neighbourhood and in context).

Device Comfort is a work in progress. We are currently implementing the paradigm on Android devices (phones and tablets) and testing interfaces, reasoning models, and behaviour in several different scenarios in our respective labs.

References

1. Ahmed, M., Quercia, D., Hailes, S.: A statistical matching approach to detect privacy violation for trust-based collaborations. In: Sixth IEEE International Symposium on a World of Wireless Mobile and Multimedia Networks, WoWMoM, pp. 598–602 (2005)
2. Barber, B.: Logic and Limits of Trust. Rutgers University Press, New Jersey (1983)
3. Jean Camp, L.: Design for Trust in Ambient and Ubiquitous Computing. In: González Nieto, J., Reif, W., Wang, G., Indulska, J. (eds.) ATC 2009. LNCS, vol. 5586, pp. 1–1. Springer, Heidelberg (2009)
4. Castelfranchi, C., Falcone, R.: Trust Theory: A Socio-Cognitive and Computational Model. Wiley (2011)
5. Chen, G., Kotz, D.: A survey of context-aware mobile computing research. Technical report (2000)
6. Cofta, P.: Trust, Complexity and Control: Confidence in a Convergent World. Wiley (2007)
7. Corner, M.D., Noble, B.D.: Zero-interaction authentication. In: Proceedings of the ACM International Conference on Mobile Computing and Communications, Atlanta, GA (September 2002)
8. Deutsch, M.: Cooperation and trust: Some theoretical notes. In: Jones, M.R. (ed.) Nebraska Symposium on Motivation. Nebraska University Press (1962)
9. Dey, A.K., Abowd, G.D.: Towards a better understanding of context and context-awareness. Technical report, Georgia Institute of Technology - GVU Technical Report; GIT-GVU-99-22 (1999)
10. Dwyer, N.: Traces of Digital Trust: An Interactive Design Perspective. PhD thesis, School of Communication and thre Arts, Faculty of Arts, Education and Human Development, Victoria University (2011)

11. Fogg, B.J.: Persuasive Technology. Morgan Kaufmann (2002)
12. Gambetta, D. (ed.): Trust. Basil Blackwell, Oxford (1990)
13. Golbeck, J. (ed.): Computing with Social Trust. Springer, Heidelberg (2009)
14. Josang, A., Ismail, R., Boyd, C.: A survey of trust and reputation systems for online service provision. Decision Support Systems 43(2), 618–644 (2007)
15. Kientz, J.A., Choe, E.K., Birch, B., Maharaj, R., FOnville, A., Glasson, C., Mundt, J.: Heuristic evaluation of persuasive health technologies. In: Proceedings IHI 2010, Arlington, Virginia, pp. 555–564 (2010)
16. Langheinrich, M.: When trust does not compute - the role of trust in ubiquitous computing. In: Proceedings of Privacy Workshops of Ubicomp 2003 (2003)
17. Lederer, S., Dey, A.K., Mankoff, J.: Everyday privacy in ubiquitous computing environments. Technical report, World Bank, Policy Research Department (2002)
18. Luhmann, N.: Trust and Power. Wiley, Chichester (1979)
19. Luhmann, N.: Familiarity, confidence, trust: Problems and alternatives. In: Gambetta, D. (ed.) Trust, ch. 6, pp. 94–107. Blackwell (1990)
20. Marsh, S.: Formalising Trust as a Computational Concept. PhD thesis, Department of Computing Science, University of Stirling (1994),
    http://www.stephenmarsh.ca/Files/pubs/Trust-thesis.pdf
21. Marsh, S.: Smart documents, mobile queries: Information provision and retrieval using a multi-agent system. In: Ferguson, I. (ed.) AI in Digital Libraries - Moving from Chaos to (More) Order, Proceedings of Workshop at International Joint Conference on Artificial Intelligence, Nagoya, Japan (August 1997)
22. Marsh, S.: Comfort zones: Location dependent trust and regret management for mobile devices. In: Proceedings LocationTrust 2010: Workshop on Location as Context for Trust at IFIPTM 2010, Morioka Japan (2010)
23. Marsh, S., Briggs, P.: Examining trust, forgiveness and regret as computational concepts. In: Golbeck, J. (ed.) Computing with Social Trust. Human Computer Interaction Series, ch.2, pp. 9–44. Springer, Heidelberg (2009)
24. Marsh, S., Briggs, P.: Defining and investigating device comfort. In: Proceedings of IFIPTM 2010: Short Papers (2010)
25. Marsh, S., Briggs, P., El-Khatib, K., Esfandiari, B., Stewart, J.A.: Defining and investigating device comfort. Journal of Information Processing 19, 231–252 (2011)
26. Marsh, S., Ghorbani, A.A., Bhavsar, V.C.: The ACORN Multi-Agent System. Web Intelligence and Agent Systems 1(1), 65–86 (2003)
27. Harrison McKnight, D., Chervany, N.L.: Trust and Distrust Definitions: One Bite at a Time. In: Falcone, R., Singh, M., Tan, Y.-H. (eds.) AA-WS 2000. LNCS (LNAI), vol. 2246, pp. 27–54. Springer, Heidelberg (2001)
28. Nielsen, J., Molich, R.: Heuristic evaluation of user interfaces. In: Proceedings of the SIGCHI Conference on Human Factors in Computing Systems (CHI 1990), pp. 249–256. ACM (1990)
29. Noble, B.D., Corner, M.D.: The case for transient authentication. In: Proceedings of the 10th ACM SIGOPS European Workshop (2002)
30. Reeves, B., Nass, C.: The Media Equation: How People Treat Computers, Television, and New Media Like Real People and Places. Centre for the Study of Language and Information (2003)
31. Schilit, B.N., Adams, N., Want, R.: Context-aware computing applications. In: Proceedings of the Workshop on Mobile Computing Systems and Applications, pp. 85–90. IEEE Computer Society (1994)

32. Sillence, E., Briggs, P.: Ubiquitous computing: Trust issues for a "healthy" society. Social Science Computer Review 26(1), 6–12 (2008)
33. Tomko, G., Borrett, D.S., Kwan, H.C., Steffan, G.: Smartdata: Make the data "think" for itself. Identity in the Information Society 3(2), 343–362 (2010)
34. Wang, Y., Komanduri, S., Leon, P.G., Norcie, G., Acquisti, A., Cranor, L.F.: "I regretted the minute I pressed share": A Qualitative Study of Regrets on Facebook. In: Proceedings SOUPS 2011: Symposium on Usable Privacy and Security (2011)
35. Wang, Y.: Trust and Reputation Management in Decentralized Systems. PhD thesis, University of Saskatchewan (2010)
36. Wang, Y., Vassileva, J.: Trust and reputation model in peer-to-peer networks. In: IEEE Conference on P2P Computing, pp. 150–157 (2003)

A Proof-Carrying File System with Revocable and Use-Once Certificates

Jamie Morgenstern, Deepak Garg, and Frank Pfenning

Carnegie Mellon University
{jamiemmt,dg,fp}@cs.cmu.edu

Abstract. We present the design and implementation of a file system which allows authorizations dependent on revocable and use-once policy certificates. Authorizations require explicit proof objects, combining ideas from previous authorization logics and Girard's linear logic. Use-once certificates and revocations lists are maintained in a database that is consulted during file access. Experimental results demonstrate that the overhead of using the database is not significant in practice.

1 Introduction

In the past decade, proof-carrying authorization (PCA) [4,6,7,15] has emerged as a promising, open-ended architecture for rigorous enforcement of authorization policies. In PCA, policy rules and other policy-relevant credentials are abstractly represented as formulas of a formal logic (as opposed to a possible low-level representation in system databases or access control lists), and published in signed certificates that are distributed to authorized principals. Access to a protected resource is allowed by a reference monitor if and only if the principal requesting access produces enough certificates to authorize the access and a *formal logical proof* which explains how the certificates combine to justify the access. Through this combination of public-key cryptography and logic, PCA rigorously enforces authorization policies at a high-level of abstraction. PCA-based authorization has been deployed and tested in a variety of systems, including a web server [6], physical devices like office doors in the Grey system [7], and a file system, PCFS [15].

A significant shortcoming of prior work on PCA is the lack of a satisfactory treatment of *use-once certificates*, i.e., certificates that can be used only once for authorization. For instance, if an individual buys a movie from a pay-per-view website, the certificate authorizing her to stream the movie should be usable only once. Incorporating use-once certificates in proof-carrying authorization is challenging because it not only requires the reference monitor to track consumption of such certificates (which adds extra work, and potentially slows down the reference monitor), but also requires a change to the logic itself to track uses of each use-once certificate in a proof. As its main contribution, the present paper fills this gap — we discuss the design, implementation, and evaluation of a PCA-based file system, LPCFS, that allows authorizations to depend on use-once certificates in addition to the usual persistent certificates.

C. Meadows and C. Fernández-Gago (Eds.): STM 2011, LNCS 7170, pp. 40–55, 2012.

LPCFS extends our prior PCA-based file system, PCFS [15], which does not allow use-once certificates. First, we extend the logic BL used for representing policies in PCFS with ideas from Girard's linear logic [16] that allows precise counting of use of resources in proofs. We call the resulting logic BL^L (the superscript L stands for linear). Second, we extend proof construction and proof verification tools of PCFS to deal with linearity. Third, we extend the implementation of PCFS with a database for storing and tracking use-once certificates. All such certificates are added to the database by their creators (this is in contrast to persistent certificates that are given directly to beneficiaries), and the reference monitor marks them consumed when it successfully authorizes access based on them. An important concern in the use of the database is atomicity — all certificates present in the justification of an access must be checked and marked consumed in a single atomic step. To ensure this property, we use exclusive transactions on the database. Because marking consumption requires an update to the database, authorizations with use-once certificates incur performance overhead in the reference monitor, but we show through experimental evaluation that, given the scarcity of use-once certificates in practice, this overhead is reasonable.

A second contribution of this paper is to extend PCFS with support for *revocation* of both use-once and persistent certificates by their issuers. To this end, we include a table of revoked certificates in the database; policy creators add revoked certificates to this table, and the reference monitor checks that each certificate in a submitted request is absent from this table. Since the reference monitor does not update this table when checking the revocation of certificates, it incurs very little overhead by allowing revocation, as we confirm in our experimental evaluation. An additional design consideration is that the check for certificate revocation must be made atomically with the check for use-once certificates described above.

The rest of this paper is organized as follows. We start by discussing related work and comparing LPCFS to it. In Section 2, we motivate use-once certificates, revocation, and the syntax of our logic BL^L through an example. Section 3 presents the proof theory of the logic BL^L briefly. Section 4 describes the design and implementation of our file system, LPCFS, that enforces policies written in BL^L. Section 5 presents experimental measurements of the overhead of tracking both use-once certificates and certificate revocations. Section 6 concludes the paper. The source code of LPCFS is available under a liberal license from the authors' webpages. A detailed description of the logic BL^L and proofs of its metatheorems are available in the second author's thesis [12, Chapter 9].

Related Work. We briefly discuss some closely related work. The idea of using logic for authorization goes back to the work of Lampson et al. [17] and has been adopted in several subsequent proposals. For a general description of the area, we refer the reader to two surveys [2,3].

Proof-carrying authorization (PCA), or the use of formal proofs for authorization, was first proposed by Appel and Felten [4] and evolved in two implemented systems [6,7], before two of the present authors applied it to a file

system, PCFS [15], which the present paper extends with support for use-once
and revocable certificates. To avoid the overhead of checking a proof and its certificates in the reference monitor at each access (as in PCA), PCFS offlines the
work of proof and certificate verification to a trusted verifier that issues a signed
capability in return, which is then used to authorize access at the file system's
reference monitor. The same architecture is inherited by our file system LPCFS,
except that we use the signed capability to also carry lists of both use-once and
persistent certificates used in a proof to the reference monitor, where the lists
are checked against the database (see Section 4 for details).

Our use of a *centralized* database for tracking use-once (and also revoked)
certificates contrasts from a fully distributed implementation, as in the work of
Bowers et al. [8]. In that work, Bowers et al. assume that each use-once certificate
is tracked by a remote trusted party called a ratifier, and use a contract signing
protocol between ratifiers to ensure that all use-once certificates in a proof are
marked consumed atomically. However, this is slow in practice, and unnecessary
for applications that are centralized, as is the case for our file system.

Linear logic was first proposed by Girard [16]. The use of linear logic for representing use-once certificates was first proposed by two of the authors [13] and
independently by Cederquist et al. [9]. Our policy logic BL^L is an amalgamation
of the logic BL used in PCFS and linearity from the work of the authors [13].
Barth and Mitchell [5] have used a fragment of linear logic to study monotonicity properties of algorithms for enforcement of digital rights (as in DRM
applications).

Some systems, e.g., Nexus [20], support use-once credentials by tracking their
use in the reference monitor, but do not distinguish them from persistent credentials in the policy logic. This approach has the disadvantage that proof construction and verification tools become oblivious to credential consumption and
seemingly correct proofs of authorization may be rejected by the reference monitor because they utilize a use-once credential more than once.

2   Motivating Example

In this section, we motivate the need for use-once certificates through the example of a fictitious online movie rental service's authorization policy. We also give
a brief overview of the syntax of our logic BL^L, describe a formalization of the
example policy in the logic, and motivate the need for certificate revocation.

Example: A Movie Rental Service. Consider the following policy for Web-
Film, a hypothetical online movie rental service. If principal K is a member of
the service, then she has access to view movie listings. If K is a member, and
K purchases a movie ticket, then K has the ticket which can be traded for the
right to download a movie M. If K exchanges a ticket in order to watch Ferris
Bueller's Day Off, then K no longer has the ticket but can read Ferris Bueller's
Day Off from the server for the next 30 days. Different principals are responsible
for different kinds of facts about the system: MovieServer controls access to

movies, UserDB keeps track of the user database, and TicketHolder keeps a list of tickets held by members and records of payment. Alice is a user of the rental service.

In order to formalize this policy within a logic, we need the notion of statements made by principals, consumable resources (such as money and tickets), and time-sensitive permissions (a principal can download a movie for 30 days after purchasing it with a ticket), all of which our logic BL^L supports.

A Brief Introduction to the Logic BL^L. BL^L is a logic for distributed access control, different principals making statements about access rights, together with the notion of consumable facts or resources which are consumed in deriving other facts. As in its precursor BL [15], facts may be time-sensitive: the proposition $A @ [u_1, u_2]$ means that proposition A holds between time points u_1 and u_2.

Statements made by principals in the system together form an access policy, or a list of hypotheses from which inferences about access to resources can be made. Because statements can be either *persistent*, in that they may be used arbitrarily many times through the course of reasoning, or *linear*, in that they may be used at most once, it is necessary to have two different connectives to represent statements. K once A means that the principal K asserts the proposition A *as a consumable resource*, which can be used only once in a proof of authorization. This contrasts from K says A, which means that principal K asserts the persistent fact A. For example, Bank once (HasMoney K) is a proposition which represents the bank stating that K has money; this fact may be exchanged for some other fact (e.g, that K owns a Ferrari), but it cannot be used more than once.

Two other connectives, implication and conjunction, have linear counterparts with meanings different from conventional logic. Linear implication, written $A \multimap B$, describes an implication which consumes the (linear) fact A and produces the linear fact B. The proposition $A \otimes B$ means that both A and B are true. Finally $!A$ represents that the proposition A may be used arbitrarily many times (i.e., A is persistent).

Example Formalized. Next, we formalize the authorization policies of Web-Film in BL^L. We start by describing the predicates needed for the formalization. The atomic proposition (may K F R) represents the authorization of permission R on file F to principal K, e.g., (may Alice FBDO read) gives Alice permission to read FBDO (Ferris Bueller's Day Off). Another atom used in the formalization is Member K, representing the assertion that K is a member of the service; in our example, the user database will state this *persistent* fact. HasTicket K represents that K has a ticket, which will be stated by the TicketHolder as a *linear* (use-once) fact. GetMovie M, the assertion of desire for a movie M, will be asserted by users of the system with the wish to purchase the movie M. Purchased K M represents the record of K having bought the movie M, which will be asserted by the TicketHolder as a persistent fact. HasMoneyForTicket K, that K has the money to purchase a ticket, will be asserted by K's bank as a linear fact

that can be used to purchase movie tickets. Finally, `BuyTicket` is asserted as a
linear fact by users wanting to purchase movie tickets.

Using these atoms, the policy of WebFilm described earlier can be represented
in BL^L as the following propositions. As a convention, any variables in uppercase
letters are implicitly assumed to be universally quantified inside the outermost
assertion K says $\bullet$.

$\gamma_1 =$ MovieServer says $((\text{UserDB says } (\text{member } K)) \multimap \,! \,(\text{may } K \, movieList \text{ read}))$
$\qquad @ \, [-\infty, \infty]$

$\gamma_2 =$ MovieServer says $(((\text{UserDB says } (\text{member } K))$
$\qquad\qquad \otimes (\text{TicketHolder once } (\texttt{HasTicket } K))$
$\qquad\qquad \otimes (\text{K once } (\texttt{GetMovie } M))) \multimap$
$\qquad\qquad !\,((\text{may } K \, M \text{ read}) @ \, [T, T+30])$
$\qquad\qquad \otimes (\text{TicketHolder says } (\texttt{Purchased } K \, M))) @ \, [T, T]$

$\gamma_3 =$ TicketHolder says $(((\text{UserDB says } (\text{member } K))$
$\qquad\qquad \otimes (\text{Bank once } (\texttt{HasMoneyForTicket } K))$
$\qquad\qquad \otimes (\text{K once } \texttt{BuyTicket}))$
$\qquad\qquad \multimap (\texttt{HasTicket } K)) @ \, [-\infty, \infty]$

$\gamma_4 =$ UserDB says $(\text{member Alice}) @ \, [-\infty, \infty]$

The first rule above means that the MovieServer states that if the UserDB states
that K is a member, then K can read the *movieList* any number of times. This
rule (like all others above) is persistent because it contains the says connective
at the top level. The permission granted by the rule is also persistent because
it contains a ! connective in front of it. The suffix $@ \, [-\infty, \infty]$ at the end of the
rule means that the rule is valid in all time intervals.

As another example, the second rule above means that if at time T, principal UserDB states that K is a member, K holds a ticket (TicketHolder once
(`HasTicket` K)), and K wants to buy the movie M (K once (`GetMovie` M)),
then K may read movie M any number of times in the interval $[T, T + 30]$ and
we record the fact that K has purchased the movie M. Note that the ticket and
K's desire to purchase the movie (K once (`GetMovie` M)) are consumed as part
of the rule, thus preventing the rule from firing again, unless K produces another
ticket and another certificate expressing the desire to purchase the movie.

In addition to these policy rules, we need several linear (use-once) propositions
to draw meaningful conclusions. For instance, the following use-once credentials
state respectively that at time T_0, Alice has enough money to buy a ticket, that
she wants to buy a ticket, and that she wants to obtain the movie FBDO.

$\delta_1 =$ Bank once $(\texttt{HasMoneyForTicket Alice}) @ \, [T_0, T_0]$
$\delta_2 =$ Alice once $(\texttt{BuyTicket}) @ \, [T_0, T_0]$
$\delta_3 =$ Alice once $(\texttt{GetMovie FBDO}) @ \, [T_0, T_0]$

Intuitively, we may expect that from the policy rules $\Gamma = \{\gamma_1, \gamma_2, \gamma_3, \gamma_4\}$ and
the use-once assumptions $\Delta = \{\delta_1, \delta_2, \delta_3\}$, we can construct a proof that Alice
can read the file FBDO in the interval $[T_0, T_0 + 30]$. The proof would *consume*

the use-once assumptions Δ. We now explain informally how this deduction is done in BL^{L}.

First, by modus ponens on the rule γ_3 and the premises γ_4, δ_1, and δ_2, we obtain the linear fact $\delta_4 =$ TicketHolder once (HasTicket Alice) @ $[T_0, T_0]$. Note that due to the use of the connective $\multimap$ in γ_3, this deduction consumes the linear assumptions δ_1 and δ_2, leaving only Γ, δ_3, and the new fact δ_4. Next, by modus ponens on the rule γ_2 with the premises γ_4, δ_4, and δ_3, we deduce that (!(may Alice FBDO read) @ $[T_0, T_0 + 30]$) $\otimes$ (TicketHolder says (Purchased Alice FBDO)) @ $[T_0, T_0]$. The first component of this tensor ($\otimes$) gives Alice the permission to read FBDO any number of times in the interval $[T_0, T_0 + 30]$, as expected. Also note that the second deduction step consumes both remaining linear facts δ_3 and δ_4.

Linear Proof-Carrying Authorization. How is deduction in BL^{L} related to policy enforcement in LPCFS? Consider a state of the system with persistent policy facts Γ and linear policy facts Δ. Suppose that a principal K constructs a proof M of authorization φ using a subset Δ' of the linear facts Δ and any subset of the persistent credentials Γ. When an access based on M is allowed, the reference monitor marks the subset Δ' consumed (in its central database), leaving only the linear facts $\Delta - \Delta'$ for use in future authorizations. All of Γ persists and can be used again.

Revocation. Revocation is a mechanism for canceling a previously issued certificate. For instance, assuming that WebFilm watermarks all its movies with identities of users who download them, the service may want to cancel Alice's membership if it discovers that Alice is illegally sharing movies downloaded from WebFilm. In our example and LPCFS, WebFilm can do this by telling the reference monitor that the certificate γ_4 that authorizes Alice's membership to the service has been revoked. The reference monitor stores this revocation in its database, thus rejecting any further authorizations that use γ_4.

It is important to note the distinction between use of a linear certificate, the revocation of a (persistent or linear) certificate, and time-based expiration of a certificate. A linear certificate is used when a proof based on it is successfully used to authorize access. Revocation takes place when a principal decides that a part P of her policy is flawed. She then adds the name of P to the revoked table in the reference monitor, so that no proof which relies on P will check successfully. A time-based expiration means that the certificate A @ $[u_1, u_2]$ cannot be used to deduce an authorization valid in an interval other than $[u_1, u_2]$, unless the policy explicitly allows this. Unlike linearity and time-based expiration, both of which have explicit representation in the logic, revocation has no representation in the logic and is an artifact of the enforcement architecture only.

3   The Policy Logic BL^{L}

This section describes the syntax and, briefly, the proof theory of BL^{L}. To keep the presentation simple, we omit a description of some standard connectives of linear logic, including $\mathbf{1}$, $\oplus$ and $\&$. We also do not describe BL^{L}'s treatment of stateful atoms and constraints, which are inherited from its predecessor BL [14]. Formulas (propositions) A, B have the following syntax. P denotes an atomic formula, which is a predicate applied to a list of terms, and σ denotes a type (sort) of terms.

$$\text{Formulas } A, B ::= P \mid A \otimes B \mid A \multimap B \mid \ !\, A \mid \forall x{:}\sigma.A \mid \exists x{:}\sigma.A \mid$$
$$K \text{ says } A \mid K \text{ once } A \mid A @ [u_1, u_2]$$

The intuitive meanings of the connectives were explained and illustrated in Section 2. Deduction is formally defined over judgments, which are assertions with formulas as subjects [11,19], and which may be established through proofs. We need four judgments to describe the constructs of BL^{L}: (1) $A \circ [u_1, u_2]$: Formula A holds throughout the interval $[u_1, u_2]$, and this fact can be used any number of times (2) $A \star [u_1, u_2]$: Formula A holds throughout the interval $[u_1, u_2]$, and this fact must be used once, (3) K claims $A \circ [u_1, u_2]$: Principal K asserts throughout the interval $[u_1, u_2]$ that formula A holds, and this fact may be used any number of times, and (4) K claims $A \star [u_1, u_2]$: Principal K asserts throughout the interval $[u_1, u_2]$ that formula A holds, and this fact must be used exactly once. Although inference is performed over judgments, the latter can also be represented equivalently (internalized) in the syntax of formulas. $A \star [u_1, u_2]$ is internalized as $A @ [u_1, u_2]$; $A \circ [u_1, u_2]$ is internalized as $!(A @ [u_1, u_2])$; K claims $A \star [u_1, u_2]$ is internalized as $(K \text{ once } A) @ [u_1, u_2]$; K claims $A \circ [u_1, u_2]$ is internalized as $(K \text{ says } A) @ [u_1, u_2]$.

Deduction is formalized with inference rules, which establish hypothetical judgments or sequents: $\Sigma; \Gamma; \Delta \xrightarrow{\nu} A \star [u_1, u_2]$, where

- Σ is a list of variables occurring free in the rest of the sequent, together with their types (sorts)
- Γ is a list of persistent assumptions of the form $A \circ [u_1, u_2]$ and K claims $A \circ [u_1, u_2]$
- Δ is a list of use-once assumptions of the form $A \star [u_1, u_2]$ and K claims $A \star [u_1, u_2]$
- $\nu = K', u_1', u_2'$, a triple containing a principal K' and a time interval $[u_1', u_2']$, is called the *view* of the sequent

The meaning of the entire sequent is: "Parametrically in the variables in Σ, the judgment $A \star [u_1, u_2]$ can be derived using the persistent assumptions Γ any number of times, and each of the use-once assumptions Δ exactly once. Further, this derivation is relative to the assumption that all statements made by principal K about the interval $[u_1', u_2']$ are true." In the following we describe some of the inference rules of the logic's proof system.

Axiom. The logic BL^{L} has one axiom that allows us to conclude that an atom P holds during an interval from the linear assumption that P holds on a larger interval. Further, to properly account for the use of resources, Δ must not contain any other assumption.

$$\frac{\Sigma; \Gamma \models u_1' \leq u_1 \qquad \Sigma; \Gamma \models u_2 \leq u_2'}{\Sigma; \Gamma; P \star [u_1', u_2'] \overset{\nu}{\rightarrow} P \star [u_1, u_2]} \text{init}$$

Copy. The following rule allows copying of a persistent assumption into the linear context Δ, where it can be analyzed by rules presented later. The persistent assumption is retained in the premise to allow it to be used again.

$$\frac{\Sigma; \Gamma, A \circ [u_1, u_2]; \Delta, A \star [u_1, u_2] \overset{\nu}{\rightarrow} B \star [u_1', u_2']}{\Sigma; \Gamma, A \circ [u_1, u_2]; \Delta \overset{\nu}{\rightarrow} B \star [u_1', u_2']} \text{copy}$$

Connective $\otimes$. The so-called linear multiplicative conjunction, $\otimes$, is defined by the following two inference rules:

$$\frac{\Sigma; \Gamma; \Delta_1 \overset{\nu}{\rightarrow} A_1 \star [u_1, u_2] \qquad \Sigma; \Gamma; \Delta_2 \overset{\nu}{\rightarrow} A_2 \star [u_1, u_2]}{\Sigma; \Gamma; \Delta_1, \Delta_2 \overset{\nu}{\rightarrow} A_1 \otimes A_2 \star [u_1, u_2]} \otimes \text{R}$$

$$\frac{\Sigma; \Gamma; \Delta, A_1 \star [u_1, u_2], A_2 \star [u_1, u_2] \overset{\nu}{\rightarrow} B \star [u_1', u_2']}{\Sigma; \Gamma; \Delta, A_1 \otimes A_2 \star [u_1, u_2] \overset{\nu}{\rightarrow} B \star [u_1', u_2']} \otimes \text{L}$$

The first rule says that to establish $A_1 \otimes A_2$ (in some interval), we must split the linear resources into Δ_1 and Δ_2, using the first set to prove A_1 and the other to prove A_2 (both in the same interval). Dually, the second rule means that the assumption $A_1 \otimes A_2$ is equivalent to having both A_1 and A_2. Note that the principal linear judgment $A_1 \otimes A_2 \star [u_1, u_2]$ is not included in the premise of the second rule, to prevent it from being used again.

Connective $\multimap$. Intuitively, the judgment $A_1 \multimap A_2 \star [u_1, u_2]$ means that there is a method to consume a proof of A_1 on any subset of $[u_1, u_2]$ and produce a proof of A_2 on the same subset. This is captured in the following rules of inference.

$$\frac{\Sigma, x_1{:}\text{time}, x_2{:}\text{time}; \Gamma, u_1 \leq x_1, x_2 \leq u_2; \Delta, A_1 \star [x_1, x_2] \overset{\nu}{\rightarrow} A_2 \star [x_1, x_2]}{\Sigma; \Gamma; \Delta \overset{\nu}{\rightarrow} A_1 \multimap A_2 \star [u_1, u_2]} \multimap \text{R}$$

$$\frac{\Sigma; \Gamma; \Delta_1 \overset{\nu}{\rightarrow} A_1 \star [u_1', u_2'] \quad \Sigma; \Gamma; \Delta_2, A_2 \star [u_1', u_2'] \overset{\nu}{\rightarrow} B \star [u_1'', u_2''] \quad \Sigma; \Gamma \models u_1 \leq u_1' \quad \Sigma; \Gamma \models u_2' \leq u_2}{\Sigma; \Gamma; \Delta_1, \Delta_2, A_1 \multimap A_2 \star [u_1, u_2] \overset{\nu}{\rightarrow} B \star [u_1'', u_2'']} \multimap \text{L}$$

Connective once. A proof of K once $A \star [u_1, u_2]$ is a proof of $A \star [u_1, u_2]$ in the view K, u_1, u_2 (rule onceR) using only assumptions of the forms K' claims $A' \circ [u_1', u_2']$ in Γ (notation $\Gamma|$) and K' claims $A' \star [u_1', u_2']$ in Δ (notation $\Delta|$). Note that to ensure that no linear resources are lost in moving from the conclusion of the rule to the premise, the linear assumptions in the conclusion are exactly

$\Delta|$. Dually, the assumption K once $A \star [u_1, u_2]$ can be used to deduce $A \star [u_1, u_2]$ if the view $\nu = K, u_b, u_e$ satisfies $[u_b, u_e] \subseteq [u_1, u_2]$ (rules onceL and lclaims).

$$\frac{\Sigma; \Gamma|; \Delta| \xrightarrow{K, u_1, u_2} A \star [u_1, u_2]}{\Sigma; \Gamma; \Delta| \xrightarrow{\nu} K \text{ once } A \star [u_1, u_2]}\text{onceR}$$

$$\frac{\Sigma; \Gamma; \Delta, K \text{ claims } A \star [u_1, u_2] \xrightarrow{\nu} B \star [u_1', u_2']}{\Sigma; \Gamma; \Delta, K \text{ once } A \star [u_1, u_2] \xrightarrow{\nu} B \star [u_1', u_2']}\text{onceL}$$

$$\frac{\Sigma; \Gamma; \Delta, A \star [u_1, u_2] \xrightarrow{\nu} B \star [u_1', u_2']}{\Sigma; \Gamma; \Delta, K \text{ claims } A \star [u_1, u_2] \xrightarrow{\nu} B \star [u_1', u_2']}\text{lclaims}$$

$$\nu = K, u_b, u_e \quad \Sigma; \Gamma \models u_1 \leq u_b \quad \Sigma; \Gamma \models u_e \leq u_2$$

Connective says. The connective says behaves similarly to once, except that in the rule saysR, we require the linear context to be empty. This is because K says A is a persistent fact, which may be used multiple times, so it cannot depend on any linear assumptions. Dually, in the rule (claims), we retain the principal formula in the premise to allow it to be used multiple times.

$$\frac{\Sigma; \Gamma|; \cdot \xrightarrow{K, u_1, u_2} A \star [u_1, u_2]}{\Sigma; \Gamma; \cdot \xrightarrow{\nu} K \text{ says } A \star [u_1, u_2]}\text{saysR}$$

$$\frac{\Sigma; \Gamma, K \text{ claims } A \circ [u_1, u_2]; \Delta \xrightarrow{\nu} B \star [u_1', u_2']}{\Sigma; \Gamma; \Delta, K \text{ says } A \star [u_1, u_2] \xrightarrow{\nu} B \star [u_1', u_2']}\text{saysL}$$

$$\frac{\Sigma; \Gamma, K \text{ claims } A \circ [u_1, u_2]; \Delta, A \star [u_1, u_2] \xrightarrow{\nu} B \star [u_1', u_2']}{\Sigma; \Gamma, K \text{ claims } A \circ [u_1, u_2]; \Delta \xrightarrow{\nu} B \star [u_1', u_2']}\text{claims}$$

$$\nu = K, u_b, u_e \quad \Sigma; \Gamma \models u_1 \leq u_b \quad \Sigma; \Gamma \models u_e \leq u_2$$

Metatheory. We have verified standard metatheoretic properties of the proof system of BL^{L}. For instance, we prove that the rules of cut and identity (which generalizes the init rule from atoms P to arbitrary formulas A) are both admissible in the logic.

Theorem 1 (Admissibility of cut). $\Sigma; \Gamma; \Delta_1 \xrightarrow{\nu} A \star [u_1, u_2]$ and $\Sigma; \Gamma; \Delta_2, A \star [u_1, u_2] \xrightarrow{\nu} B \star [u_1', u_2']$ imply $\Sigma; \Gamma; \Delta_1, \Delta_2 \xrightarrow{\nu} B \star [u_1', u_2']$.

Proof. By nested induction, first on the structure of the formula A and then on the heights of the two given derivations, as in prior work [15,18].

Theorem 2 (Identity). $\Sigma; \Gamma; A \star [u_1, u_2] \xrightarrow{\nu} A \star [u_1, u_2]$ for every formula A.

Proof. By induction on A.

4   The File System LPCFS

Like its predecessor PCFS, our file system LPCFS is implemented for the Linux operating system. Technically, both file systems are *virtual*, since they only add a layer of authorization checks to an existing file system, which is used for all disk I/O. The existing file system in all experiments reported in this paper is ext3. Both PCFS and LPCFS are implemented using the Fuse kernel module [1].

The general workflow in both file systems is the following. Users create policies, which are given to others in the form of certificates (in LPCFS, linear certificates are stored in a central database which can be read by all users). The certificates are used as assumptions to create proofs of authorization in a logic (BL for PCFS and BL^L for LPCFS). The proofs are verified by a trusted verifier (an independent program), and exchanged for signed capabilities called *procaps*, which are stored in an indexed store on the disk. During file system calls, the reference monitor looks up this store for appropriate procaps and checks them to authorize access and, in LPCFS, marks linear certificates as consumed. We explain each of these steps in more detail below but, briefly, policy enforcement in both PCFS and LPCFS follows the path:

$$\text{Policy} \rightarrow \text{Proof} \rightarrow \text{Procap} \rightarrow \text{File access}$$

Policy Creation. A policy is a set of logical formulas governing access rights to files. The policy consists of certificates, which contain formulas of BL^L signed with creators' (owners') private keys. Certificates may be persistent or linear (use-once).

A persistent certificate is stored in a file and given to others at the owner's discretion. Persistent certificates are created using the PCFS tool `pcfs-cert` that checks their syntax. There is no restriction on copying persistent certificates. New to LPCFS are linear certificates that are stored in a central SQLite database that is accessible to both users and the reference monitor. LPCFS provides a new tool `pcfs-parse-insert` to manage this database. The tool allows anyone to insert a well-formed, signed linear certificate into the database, and anyone to read certificates in the database, but only allows the reference monitor to mark a linear certificate consumed. To ensure the latter, the database file is accessible only to the superuser, and both the tool `pcfs-parse-insert` and the reference monitor run as superuser.

Revoked certificates are stored in a separate table in the same database that stores the linear certificates. This table can be manipulated using the LPCFS command-line tool `pcfs-view-remove` that allows listing of revoked certificates, and also allows the owner of a certificate to create an entry for revoking it.

Proof Construction. To authorize herself to access a file, a user must first construct a formal proof which shows that she has access. As discussed in Sections 2 and 3, this proof uses certificates as assumptions (the contexts Γ and Δ). Although users are free to construct proofs by any means they choose including heuristics and hard-coding, PCFS provides a tool called `pcfs-search` that uses backchaining to construct proofs automatically. In LPCFS, we have modified this tool to make it linearity-aware, i.e., it correctly ensures that linear certificates are used exactly once in the proof. This raises new challenges; for instance, when applying the $\otimes$R rule (Section 3), we need to choose a split for the linear assumptions from an exponential number of choices. We avoid this problem by using an approach to backchaining proof construction due to Cervesato et al. [10], which keeps track of unused resources in a branch and avoids this exponential choice during proof search.

Proof Verification. Once the user has constructed a proof M, this proof, together with the certificates used to construct it, is given to a proof verifier, invoked using another command line program, `pcfs-verify`. The verifier is a simple piece of code and must be trusted. In PCFS, the verifier checks that the logical structure of the proof M is correct, and that the digital signatures of all certificates used in the proof are correct. LPCFS adds two new checks: (1) that none of the certificates used in the proof have been revoked by their authors, and (2) that all linear certificates exist within the database and are unused. If all these checks succeed, the verifier gives back the user a *procap*, which is a capability that mentions the user, file, and permission (read, write, etc.) authorized. The procap also contains conditions related to time and system state under which the proof is valid (we have not discussed system state in this paper, but LPCFS inherits it from PCFS). In LPCFS, lists of unique identifiers of all persistent certificates (P) and linear certificates (L) on which the proof depends are also added to the procap. Finally, the procap is signed using a shared symmetric key that is known only to the verifier and the file system reference monitor. The signature is necessary to prevent users from forging capabilities. After receiving a procap, the user calls another command line tool which puts the procap in an indexed store on the disk.

File System Call and Access. LPCFS, like PCFS, respects the standard POSIX interface for file systems. During a file system call (read, write, open, etc.) the PCFS/LPCFS file system looks up the indexed procap store to authorize the operation. The number of procaps needed varies from 1 to 3 depending on the operation; these are unchanged from the prior work on PCFS. If all relevant procaps are found, they are checked. In PCFS, this check covers the procap's time and system state conditions; in LPCFS, the procap's certificate lists (P and L) are also checked as follows:

- An *exclusive transaction* with the database containing the linear certificates and the revoked certificates is started
- The revoked certificates table is queried to ensure it contains no elements in the persistent list, P
- The linear certificates table is queried to ensure it contains all elements of the linear list, L, and that none of them have been marked as "used" previously
- All the elements of L are marked as "used" in the database
- The transaction is committed
- File access is granted

The order of these operations is imperative. All other conditions in a procap must be checked before checking the certificate lists in it, as we do not want to unnecessarily mark linear certificates as used when access may not be granted. Also for that reason, we must check both the linear and the revoked certificates before consuming the linear certificates. It is also necessary that the linear certificates be marked as used *prior to giving file access*; if not, we risk a system failure preventing us from marking the certificates used despite an access having been made. Of course, this allows the possibility that a system failure after the certificates are marked but prior to access incorrectly causes the certificates to be marked. However, we maintain access logs and time of use within the database, so certificates marked consumed this way can be unmarked by an administrator during system recovery.

Summary of the Implementation. Our implementation of the LPCFS front end tools (proof search, proof verification, and certificate management) comprises approximately 9,000 lines of SML code. The original PCFS implementation of these tools was nearly 7,000 lines of code; our modifications and additions are spread throughout that code. Because the front end tools are used less frequently than the reference monitor, their efficiency is also less of a concern. The bottleneck for performance is the LPCFS reference monitor, which comprises approximately 11,000 lines of C++ code (the PCFS reference monitor was 10,000 lines long). We evaluate performance of the reference monitor in Section 5.

5   Experimental Results

In this section, we present the results of several experiments that measure the efficiency of the reference monitor (back end) of LPCFS. We are specifically interested in the costs of checking and consuming certificates when performing basic operations such as stat-ing a file (to which we address our microbenchmarks), and during a typical build cycle (to which we address our macrobenchmarks). All experiments reported here were performed on a 2.8 GHz 8-core machine with 3.8 GB RAM with a 500GB 7200 RPM hard drive running Linux kernel version 2.6.35-27-generic. We used the GNU C++ compiler (g++) to compile the reference monitor.

5.1   Macrobenchmarks

We performed two typical build-cycle benchmarks: (1) Untar-ing, compiling, and deleting the source code of the fuse kernel module 5 times (Fuse × 5), and (2) Untar-ing, configuring, compiling, and deleting the Poco C++ Base Library (Poco/Base). In running LPCFS, we gave read, write, execute permissions on the parent directory in which the tests were being run, first dependent upon no certificates, and then with each permission dependent upon one persistent certificate (which, of course, had not been revoked). No linear certificates were used in these benchmarks: we would not expect linear rights to be used in a build environment and so their effect is not a concern. The results of the benchmarks are shown below. All times are measured in seconds. Fuse/Null is a virtual file system with an architecture similar to that of LPCFS, except that it makes no access checks. This file system is our baseline for comparison.

Benchmark	LPCFS(0 certs)	LPCFS (1 cert/perm)	PCFS	Fuse/Null	Ext3
Poco/Base	614	638	614	611	538
Fuse × 5	97.55	98.64	96.41	91.18	85.48

In the absence of revocation checks (column 0 certs in the table), LPCFS overhead over Fuse/Null is 0.4% for Poco, and 7% for Fuse. These are similar to those of PCFS, which is to be expected, because in these cases the LPCFS and PCFS implementations behave similarly. The additional overhead of checking one certificate revocation per access (column 1 cert/perm in the table) is less than 1% for Fuse and less than 5% for Poco, which is not much. Interestingly, this overhead does not change with the size of the revoked certificate table, which is also supported by our microbenchmarks below.

5.2   Microbenchmarks

The purpose of microbenchmarking was to assess the cost of checking for existence of certificate revocations and linear certificates (and marking the linear certificates as used) in the database. In the first microbenchmark, we measured the amount of time taken to stat a file[1], when the permission to stat the file depended on $N = \{0, 1, 2, 10, 20, \ldots, 100\}$ linear certificates. Precisely, we created 10,000 files of size 1 byte each and procaps authorizing the execute permission to each of them (execute is the only permission needed to stat a file) with N linear certificates in each procap. The average time to stat a file for different values of N is shown in both tabular and graphical form in Figure 1. Note that stat-ing a file whose execute permission depends on N linear certificates requires N updates to the database (one update to mark each of the N certificates consumed).

With 0 certificates, the time taken by LPCFS per file (2.6ms) is similar to that taken by Fuse/Null (2.4ms) and PCFS (2.6ms). However, with even one linear certificate per procap, the time for access increases to 156ms. This is unsurprising because dependence on linear certificates implies that the database must be written to consume the linear certificates, which is an expensive operation. Note, however, that a linear certificate can be used only once after it is issued, so the *total* initial overhead due to linear certificates (156ms) across all system calls cannot exceed the number of such certificates issued. In practice, we may expect that not many linear certificates will be issued, so the overall cost should be manageable. As the chart in Figure 1 shows, after this initial overhead the time increases almost linearly with the number of linear certificates in each procap, and is approximately 1ms per certificate. Practical authorizations are unlikely to use more than one or two linear certificates each, so the incremental overhead (1ms/certificate) is unlikely to add up to a significant number for any access.

---

[1] The stat file system call reads a file's metadata, e.g., its length and owner.

Certs	0	1	2	10	20	30	40	50	60	70	80	90	100	PCFS	Fuse/Null
Time (ms)	2.6	156	155	157	190	205	228	231	235	243	250	261	279	2.6	2.4

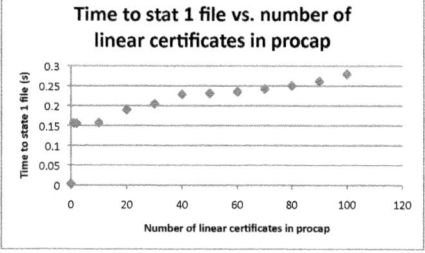

Fig. 1. Time to stat one file varying the number of linear certificates per procap

Our second microbenchmark measures the cost of checking for certificate revocations. This experiment is similar to the previous one, except that instead of linear certificates, we use persistent certificates in procaps, for which only revocations are checked. Again we varied the number of certificates in each procap in the set $N = \{0, 1, 2, 10, 20, \ldots, 100\}$. However, in addition, we also varied the number of certificates in the revocation table in the set $\{1000, 2000, \ldots, 10000\}$ to observe the impact, if any, of changing the size of this table. Our observations are shown in Figure 2. First, as is evident from the data, there is no sudden increase in access time when moving from 0 to 1 revocation checks per procap, as was the case for linear certificates. This is because a revocation check does not require writing the database and is, therefore, relatively inexpensive. Second, there is a uniform growth in the overhead with increase in the number of revocation checks per procap. The slope of this growth is approximately 0.02ms

Certs\DB Load	1000	2000	3000	4000	5000	6000	7000	8000	9000	10000
0	2.6	2.6	2.6	2.6	2.6	2.6	2.6	2.6	2.6	2.6
1	3.2	3.1	3.1	3.1	3.1	3.1	3.1	3.1	3.1	3.1
2	3.3	3.3	3.2	3.2	3.2	3.2	3.2	3.3	3.2	3.2
10	3.4	3.4	3.4	3.4	3.4	3.4	3.4	3.4	3.4	3.5
20	3.6	3.6	3.6	3.6	3.6	3.6	3.6	3.6	3.6	3.6
30	3.7	3.7	3.7	3.8	3.8	3.8	3.8	3.8	3.8	3.8
40	3.9	3.9	3.9	4.0	4.0	4.0	4.0	4.0	4.0	4.0
50	3.9	4 0	4.0	4.0	4.0	4.0	4.0	4.0	4.0	4.0
60	4.2	4.2	4.1	4.2	4.2	4.2	4.2	4.2	4.3	4.3
70	4.2	4.2	4.2	4.2	4.1	4.2	4.2	4.3	4.2	4.4
80	4.4	4.5	4.5	4.5	4.5	4.5	4.5	4.5	4.5	4.6
90	4.8	4.8	4.8	4.8	4.8	4.8	4.8	4.7	4.7	4.7
100	4.8	4.8	4.8	4.8	4.9	5.2	5.6	5.4	5.5	5.5

Fig. 2. Time to stat one file varying the number of required persistent certificates per procap (rows) and the size of the revocation list (columns). All times are reported in ms.

per certificate. Finally, the effect of changing the number of revoked certificates in the database is negligible. This is because the reference monitor reads the revocation table in accordance with the table's index.

5.3   Summary of Experimental Results

Our experiments show that increasing the size of the database does not significantly affect the cost of checking certificates at the time of file access. Increasing the number of certificates (linear or persistent) upon which permissions rely has a roughly linear correlation with the time required to gain a permission to a file. Linear certificates incur a significant, but constant, overhead because marking them consumed requires writing the database. Our macrobenchmarks show that there is not a significant overhead in maintaining a revocation list within a database and checking certificates against this list for a typical build cycle.

6   Conclusion

LPCFS extends previous work on the file system PCFS to support revocable and linear certificates within a proof-carrying authorization framework. Both extensions are implemented using a centralized database which maintains a list of revoked certificates and a table of linear certificates. Our experiments suggest that the cost of making additional checks to support these features is manageable.

An interesting future direction for this work is to consider linear and revocable certificates in a distributed setting: rather than requiring a centralized database, the certificates and revocation list could be kept at multiple nodes.

Further, we would like to study policy authoring and analysis. Owing to the complexity of the logic, policies may have unintended consequences if care is not taken in constructing them. It would be useful to develop tools for exploring possible consequences of a policy, or to aid in the proof of certain metatheorems about a particular policy. For example, for the policy in Section 2, it might be useful to prove that no statement made by Alice could affect the permissions available to Bob. Notions such as this are useful guidelines, both for individuals authoring the policy and for developers constructing policy verification tools.

Acknowledgments. Jamie Morgenstern and Frank Pfenning were partially supported by NSF grant number 0716469. Jamie Morgenstern was also supported by a Graduate Research Fellowship from the National Science Foundation. Deepak Garg was supported by the U.S. ARO contract "Perpetually Available and Secure Information Systems" (DAAD19-02-1-0389) to Carnegie Mellon's CyLab and the AFOSR MURI "Collaborative Policies and Assured Information Sharing".

References

1. FUSE: Filesystem in Userspace, http://fuse.sourceforge.net/
2. Abadi, M.: Logic in access control. In: 18th Annual Symposium on Logic in Computer Science (LICS 2003), pp. 228–233 (June 2003)
3. Abadi, M.: Logic in access control (tutorial notes). In: 9th International School on Foundations of Security Analysis and Design (FOSAD), pp. 145–165 (2009)
4. Appel, A.W., Felten, E.W.: Proof-carrying authentication. In: 6th ACM Conference on Computer and Communications Security (CCS), pp. 52–62 (1999)
5. Barth, A., Mitchell, J.C.: Managing digital rights using linear logic. In: 21st Annual IEEE Symposium on Logic in Computer Science (LICS), pp. 127–136 (2006)
6. Bauer, L.: Access Control for the Web via Proof-Carrying Authorization. Ph.D. thesis, Princeton University (2003)
7. Bauer, L., Garriss, S., McCune, J.M., Reiter, M.K., Rouse, J., Rutenbar, P.: Device-Enabled Authorization in the Grey System. In: Zhou, J., López, J., Deng, R.H., Bao, F. (eds.) ISC 2005. LNCS, vol. 3650, pp. 431–445. Springer, Heidelberg (2005)
8. Bowers, K.D., Bauer, L., Garg, D., Pfenning, F., Reiter, M.K.: Consumable credentials in logic-based access-control systems. In: Electronic Proceedings of the 14th Annual Network and Distributed System Security Symposium (NDSS 2007) (2007)
9. Cederquist, J.G., Corin, R., Dekker, M.A.C., Etalle, S., den Hartog, J.I., Lenzini, G.: Audit-based compliance control. International Journal of Information Security 6(2), 133–151 (2007)
10. Cervesato, I., Hodas, J.S., Pfenning, F.: Efficient resource management for linear logic proof search. Theoretical Computer Science 232, 133–163 (2000)
11. Chang, B.Y.E., Chaudhuri, K., Pfenning, F.: A judgmental analysis of linear logic. Tech. Rep. CMU-CS-03-131R. Carnegie Mellon University (2003)
12. Garg, D.: Proof Theory for Authorization Logic and Its Application to a Practical File System. Ph.D. thesis. Carnegie Mellon University (2009), available as Technical Report CMU-CS-09-168
13. Garg, D., Bauer, L., Bowers, K., Pfenning, F., Reiter, M.: A Linear Logic of Affirmation and Knowledge. In: Gollmann, D., Meier, J., Sabelfeld, A. (eds.) ESORICS 2006. LNCS, vol. 4189, pp. 297–312. Springer, Heidelberg (2006)
14. Garg, D., Pfenning, F.: Non-interference in constructive authorization logic. In: 19th Computer Security Foundations Workshop (CSFW), pp. 283–293 (2006)
15. Garg, D., Pfenning, F.: A proof-carrying file system. In: 31st IEEE Symposium on Security and Privacy (Oakland), pp. 349–364 (2010)
16. Girard, J.Y.: Linear logic. Theoretical Computer Science 50, 1–102 (1987)
17. Lampson, B., Abadi, M., Burrows, M., Wobber, E.: Authentication in distributed systems: Theory and practice. ACM Transactions on Computer Systems 10(4), 265–310 (1992)
18. Pfenning, F.: Structural cut elimination I. Intuitionistic and classical logic. Information and Computation 157(1/2), 84–141 (2000)
19. Pfenning, F., Davies, R.: A judgmental reconstruction of modal logic. Mathematical Structures in Computer Science 11, 511–540 (2001)
20. Schneider, F.B., Walsh, K., Sirer, E.G.: Nexus Authorization Logic (NAL): Design rationale and applications. Tech. rep. Cornell University (2009), http://ecommons.library.cornell.edu/handle/1813/13679

New Modalities for Access Control Logics: Permission, Control and Ratification

Valerio Genovese[1] and Deepak Garg[2]

[1] University of Luxembourg and University of Torino
[2] Max Planck Institute for Software Systems

Abstract. We present a new modal access control logic, ACL^+, to specify, reason about and enforce access control policies. The logic includes new modalities for permission, control, and ratification to overcome some limits of current access control logics. We present a Hilbert-style proof system for ACL^+ and a sound and complete Kripke semantics for it. We exploit the Kripke semantics to define Seq-ACL^+: a sound, complete and cut-free sequent calculus for ACL^+, implying that ACL^+ is at least semi-decidable. We point at a Prolog implementation of Seq-ACL^+ and discuss possible extensions of ACL^+ with axioms for subordination between principals.

1 Introduction

Logic plays a prominent role in the specification, reasoning and enforcement of access control policies in distributed systems. In the last two decades, several logic-based models have been proposed for access control policies, each with its own primitives, semantics and, in some cases, specific application domains (see [1,3] and [7] for surveys). The great variety (and complexity) of such systems makes it difficult to integrate, compare and objectively evaluate them. As is evident from recent research in access control [2,8,11,14,17], modal logic is a powerful framework to study expressiveness, complexity and semantics of access control logics. Although modal logic has proved useful for theoretical study of access control, it is not widely used in practice to enforce authorization policies (some notable exceptions are [5,6,13,21,22]).

The main reason for this gap is that although several epistemic modalities (e.g., says [18], said and knows [17]) have been studied in the context of access control, key access control concepts like permission, control or trust are not first-class citizens of modal access control languages and must be defined using epistemic modalities. This creates implicit relationships between the concepts and possibly leads to security risks (see [2] for some examples).

In this paper, we take a step towards addressing this shortcoming by proposing a constructive modal logic, ACL^+, which extends a standard access control logic with new connectives for permission, control and trust on principals' statements, and admits a semi-decidable calculus. We start by presenting a brief outline of the methodology of access control through logics in Section 2, and a specific connective says [18] that is central to almost all access control logics. In Section 3 we point at three shortcomings of says-based access control logics that, in our opinion, limit their applicability in practical

C. Meadows and C. Fernández-Gago (Eds.): STM 2011, LNCS 7170, pp. 56–71, 2012.

scenarios, thus motivating the need for the new modalities. In Section 4 we present the new modalities, their axioms and inference rules in a Hilbert-style calculus for ACL$^+$. Moreover, we show through examples how ACL$^+$ avoids the shortcomings reported in Section 3.

Section 5 presents sound and complete Kripke semantics for ACL$^+$. Kripke semantics, although useful for establishing several metatheorems of access control logics, are not operational and cannot be used directly in algorithms to reason about authorization. Accordingly, in Section 6 we present Seq-ACL$^+$, a sound, complete and cut-free sequent calculus for ACL$^+$ and then impose termination conditions on the sequent calculus that are derived from the Kripke semantics. We conjecture that the termination conditions do not lead to loss of completeness and point the reader to a working implementation of the calculus in Prolog.[1] In Section 7 we present extensions of ACL$^+$ with axioms that force subordination between principals. Section 8 discusses briefly some related work and Section 9 concludes the paper. A full version of the paper with proofs of theorems and and the Prolog implementation of ACL$^+$ are available from the authors' homepages.

2   Distributed Access Control Model

We consider a decentralized model of access control, where policy information is distributed among several principals. Principals support policy statements and credentials by writing them in certificates signed with their respective private keys. Since policy statements and credentials may be complex, and may assert facts conditional upon statements of other principals, formal logic is a natural choice to model policies. If principal A supports policy (or credential) φ, this is represented in the logic as the formula A says φ [18]. Technically, A says $\bullet$ is a family of principal-indexed modalities that has been included in several access control logics, albeit with slightly varying semantic interpretations.

An access is authorized (justified) if and only if it is entailed by available policy statements and credentials. The question of authorizing an access φ for principal A from a policy Γ can be cast formally as follows: Is it the case that Γ and A says φ entail φ? Or, in symbolic notation, is there a formal proof that Γ, A says $\varphi \vdash \varphi$?

Example 1. Consider the following policy:

1. If the *Admin* says that $file1$ can be read, then this must be the case.
2. *Admin* trusts *Bob* to decide whether or not $file1$ can be read.

In a propositional logic enriched with the says modality, we can express the above policy as follows [2]:

1. $(Admin$ says $read\_file1) \rightarrow read\_file1$
2. $Admin$ says $((Bob$ says $read\_file1) \rightarrow read\_file1)$

---

[1] In an earlier version of this paper we mentioned a proof of decidability of ACL$^+$, but subsequently we found a mistake in the proof that we have been unable to fix. However, we still believe that ACL$^+$ is decidable, hence the conjecture.

Further, *Bob* asking to read $file1$ can be represented as *Bob* says $read\_file1$. The reference monitor may authorize *Bob* on this request if and only if

$$(1), (2), Bob \text{ says } read\_file1 \vdash read\_file1$$

In most access control logics, the above entailment has a proof, so *Bob* will be able to read $file1$. We re-emphasize that the notion of authorization w.r.t. to a submitted request corresponds to the formal notion of derivability of the requested access from the available policy.

3   Limits of Access Control Logics: Permissions, Control and Information Flow

In this Section we point out three issues that, in our opinion, create a gap between existing work on logic-based approaches to access control as outlined above, and their deployment in practice. We call the first issue the problem of *implicit permissions*: If an action φ is entailed by a policy Γ, then *any* principal is authorized to perform it. The second issue concerns a logical separation of permission to perform an action from the ability to *control* the action, which also includes the permission to delegate the control further. The third issue is concerned with a fine-grained distinction between the *flow of information* (policy statements) from one principal to another, and its *acceptance* by the receiving principal or, in other words, the issue of separating (in the logic) hearsay from trust in the hearsay. We explain these issues one by one, and then present our proposal to address the issues by introducing new modalities into the logic.

Issue 1: Implicit Permissions

The standard definition of permission through entailment presented in Section 2 says that a principal A can perform action φ if from the prevailing policy Γ and A says φ, φ can be established. However, this creates a problem in practice: Once enough credentials exist to authorize an access for some principal, any principal is permitted the same access by the standard definition. For instance, in our earlier example, after *Bob* has created the credential *Bob* says $read\_file1$, any principal A will be authorized to read $file1$. This is because the existence of a proof of Γ, *Bob* says $read\_file1 \vdash read\_file1$ implies, by the law of weakening in the logic, that Γ, *Bob* says $read\_file1$, A says $read\_file1 \vdash read\_file1$ is also provable for any principal A.

The problem here is that the formula asserting the authorization — $read\_file1$ — does not include the identity of the principal who is authorized access. We propose to resolve this problem by introducing an explicit, principal-indexed modality for permissions, which we write $\mathbf{P}_A\varphi$ (Section 4). With this modality, policy Γ authorizes principal A to perform action φ iff $\Gamma \vdash \mathbf{P}_A\varphi$. By explicitly listing the principal authorized in the conclusion, we eliminate the problem of implicit permissions.

An alternate, related solution, not considered here, but often used in first-order logics for access control, is to treat the permission (e.g., $read\_file1$) as a relation over principals. Instead of writing $read\_file1$ we could write $read\_file1(A)$ to mean that principal A is authorized to read $file1$. However, since we are interested in implementing the logic, we avoid first-order logic.

Issue 2: Control or Delegatable Permissions

Often in access control, it is desirable to give an individual a permission and also the power to further delegate the permission. To this end we propose a new modality $\mathbf{C}_A\varphi$, read "A controls φ". The key axioms governing $\mathbf{C}_A\varphi$ are:

$$\vdash \mathbf{C}_A\varphi \to \mathbf{P}_A\varphi \tag{C2P}$$
$$\vdash (\mathbf{C}_A\varphi \wedge (A \text{ says } \mathbf{C}_B\varphi)) \to \mathbf{C}_B\varphi \tag{del-C}$$

The first axiom means that if principal A controls φ, then it is also permitted φ. This axiom relates control to permission and makes $\mathbf{C}_A\varphi$ strictly stronger than $\mathbf{P}_A\varphi$. The second axiom allows principal A, who controls φ, to delegate this control to a principal B simply by asserting this fact. This ability to delegate further distinguishes $\mathbf{C}_A\varphi$ from $\mathbf{P}_A\varphi$.

It is desirable that $(\mathbf{C}_A\varphi_1 \wedge \mathbf{C}_A\varphi_2) \to \mathbf{C}_A(\varphi_1 \wedge \varphi_2)$. For instance, if A has control over the deletion of files 1 and 2 individually, it should also have control over the deletion of the two files together, thus allowing it to delegate control over deletion of both files at once. A similar property for permissions may be harmful. For instance, if file 2 is the backup of file 1, we may not want to permit their simultaneous deletion ($\mathbf{P}_A(\varphi_1 \wedge \varphi_2)$), even if we allow their deletion individually ($\mathbf{P}_A\varphi_1 \wedge \mathbf{P}_A\varphi_2$). Formally, this difference is manifest in different logical treatments of the two modalities: while $\mathbf{C}_A$ is a normal *necessitation* modality, $\mathbf{P}_A$ is a *possibility* modality (see Section 4 for details).

Issue 3: Information Flow vs Acceptance

Besides the use of the modality $\mathbf{C}_A$, authority can also be delegated from one principal to another by nesting the says modality, as in the following statement from Example 1, which delegates the formula $read\_file1$ from principal $Admin$ to principal Bob:

2. $Admin$ says $((Bob$ says $read\_file1) \to read\_file1)$

Intuitively, we expect (as in Example 1) that this formula together with Bob says $read\_file1$ should imply that $Admin$ says $read\_file1$. However, performing this inference requires us to infer from Bob says $read\_file1$ that $Admin$ says Bob says $read\_file1$. To allow for this inference, most authorization logics include the following axiom, or a stronger axiom that implies it (this axiom was proposed by Abadi [1]):

A says $\varphi \to B$ says $(A$ says $\varphi)$ (I-SS)

However, this axiom also allows unwanted statements to flow from one principal to another. Here is an example. Suppose $Admin$ delegates to Bob the authority to $read\_file1$ through statement (2), under the conception that Bob will only allow $read\_file1$ under reasonable conditions. However, Bob, either mistakenly or maliciously, adds the following rule:

Bob says $(bad\_condition \to read\_file1)$

where $bad\_condition$ means that a certain bad condition (for reading $file1$) holds. Now, using the statements above and (I-SS), Bob says $bad\_condition$ implies that $Admin$ says $read\_file1$, which is undesirable.

The problem here is that the logic, so far, does not provide a construct to allow *Admin* to represent in statement (2) that it actually *trusts* the assumption (*Bob* says *read_file*1). We propose to rectify this situation by including the construct A ratified φ, which means that A says φ and that this statement is trusted by the principal in the enclosing scope. With this construct, *Admin* can revise its statement to say that:

2a. *Admin* says ((*Bob* ratified *read_file*1) → *read_file*1)

If *Bob* merely says *read_file*1, it will imply *Admin* says *Bob* says *read_file*1, but not *Admin* says *Bob* ratified *read_file*1, and not allow for the deduction of *Admin* says *read_file*1. To allow for the latter, *Admin* must make explicit rules to convert *Bob*'s statements to ratified statements, e.g., it may add the following two rules:

3. *Admin* says ((*Bob* says *good_condition*) → (*Bob* ratified *good_condition*))
4. *Admin* says ((*Bob* says (*good_condition* → *read_file*1)) → (*Bob* ratified (*good_condition* → *read_file*1)))

thus allowing deduction of *Admin* says *read_file*1 from the statements *Bob* says (*good_condition* → *read_file*1) and *Bob* says *good_condition*, but not from *Bob* says (*bad_condition* → *read_file*1) and *Bob* says *bad_condition*. The formal rules that allow these deductions and a more detailed example of the use of ratification are presented in Section 4.

4   The New Modalities

In this section we formally describe ACL$^+$, our access control logic with the modalities $\mathbf{P}_A$, $\mathbf{C}_A$ and A ratified •. To summarize,

1. Permission and control can be represented directly in ACL$^+$ using the modalities $\mathbf{P}_A\varphi$ (principal A is authorized (permitted) φ) and $\mathbf{C}_A\varphi$ (principal A controls φ).
2. ACL$^+$ contains the operator A ratified φ, which means that principal A states φ and this statement has been ratified (or, is trusted) by the principal in whose context the formula is interpreted.

We introduce ACL$^+$ piecewise, starting with a simple access control logic containing the modality says defined by the following rules and axioms (φ and ψ denote logical formulas):

All axioms of intuitionistic propositional logic   (IPC)

$$\frac{\vdash \varphi \quad \vdash \varphi \to \psi}{\vdash \psi}$$ (MP)

$$\frac{\vdash \varphi}{\vdash A \text{ says } \varphi}$$ (nec-S)

$\vdash (A \text{ says } (\varphi \to \psi)) \to (A \text{ says } \varphi) \to (A \text{ says } \psi)$ (K-S)

$\vdash A \text{ says } \varphi \to B \text{ says } (A \text{ says } \varphi)$ (I-SS)

We note that our logic is intuitionistic (constructive). The use of intuitionistic logic for access control has been motivated in prior work [12]; briefly, constructivism disallows proofs by contradiction, thus eliminating authorization if it is merely not denied. Axioms (nec-S) and (K-S) express that says is a normal necessitation modality and are standard in access control literature.

New Modalities for Access Control Logics   61

4.1 Permission and Control

To this basic logic we add the modalities $\mathbf{P}_A$ and $\mathbf{C}_A$, characterized by the following rules and axioms:

$$\frac{\vdash \varphi}{\vdash \mathbf{C}_A\varphi} \tag{nec-C}$$

$$\vdash \mathbf{C}_A(\varphi \to \psi) \to (\mathbf{C}_A\varphi \to \mathbf{C}_A\psi) \tag{C-Deduce}$$

$$\vdash \mathbf{C}_A\varphi \to \mathbf{P}_A\varphi \tag{C2P}$$

$$\vdash \mathbf{P}_A(\varphi \vee \psi) \to \mathbf{P}_A\varphi \vee \mathbf{P}_A\psi \tag{or-P}$$

$$\vdash (\mathbf{C}_A\varphi \wedge (A \text{ says } \mathbf{C}_B\varphi)) \to \mathbf{C}_B\varphi \tag{del-C}$$

Axiom (C-Deduce) expresses that control is closed under logical deduction while rule (nec-C) means that all valid formulas of the logic are controlled by every principal A. Together, (nec-C) and (C-Deduce) make $\mathbf{C}_A$ a normal necessitation modality (similar to $\square$ in standard modal logics). As motivated in Section 3, we model permission with a possibility modality, i.e., it is not closed under logical consequence, but we require it to distribute over disjunction (or-P). Axiom (C2P) relates the notion of control to that of permission and reads: "If principal A controls φ, then it is authorized (permitted) on φ". This implies that control of a formula is stronger than permission on the formula. Axiom (del-C) allows a principal A in control of φ to delegate that control to another principal B (see Example 2).

Definition 1 (Authorization). *Given a policy Γ, we say that A is authorized on access φ if and only if $\Gamma \vdash \mathbf{P}_A\varphi$.*

Example 2. The policy of Example 1 can be re-represented with the new modalities as follows

    (1) $\mathbf{C}_{Admin}(read\_file1)$
    (2) $Admin$ says $(\mathbf{C}_{Bob}(read\_file1))$

From (del-C), (MP) and (C2P) we can prove that Bob is authorized to read $file1$, i.e., $(1),(2) \vdash \mathbf{P}_{Bob}(read\_file1)$.

Example 3. A principal can selectively delegate privileges it controls to other principals. Consider a policy in which A controls the deletion of files 1 and 2. A can delegate to B the authority to delete file 1 only by asserting that B controls it. Formally,

$$\mathbf{C}_A(delete\_file1 \wedge delete\_file2), A \text{ says } (\mathbf{C}_B(delete\_file1)) \vdash \mathbf{C}_B(delete\_file1)$$

Proof. From the assumption $\mathbf{C}_A(delete\_file1 \wedge delete\_file2)$ infer using (nec-C) and (C-deduce) that $\mathbf{C}_A(delete\_file1)$. $\mathbf{C}_B(delete\_file1)$ follows using (del-C) and the assumption A says $(\mathbf{C}_B(delete\_file1))$.

4.2 The Modality (A ratified φ)

Next, we add to our logic the modality A ratified φ, which means not only that A says φ, but also that the latter has been checked, ratified, or is trusted by the principal in whose scope it occurs (Section 3). For instance, the formula B says $(A$ ratified $\varphi)$ means that: "A says φ and B ratified (trusts) this statement".

Like $\mathbf{C}_A$ and A says $\bullet$, we model A ratified $\bullet$ as a normal modality:

$$\frac{\vdash \varphi}{\vdash A \text{ ratified } \varphi} \qquad \text{(nec-R)}$$

$$\vdash (A \text{ ratified } (\varphi \to \psi)) \to (A \text{ ratified } \varphi) \to (A \text{ ratified } \psi) \qquad \text{(K-R)}$$

Further, the modality A ratified φ implies A says φ, but the converse is not true in general:

$$\vdash (A \text{ ratified } \varphi) \to (A \text{ says } \varphi) \qquad \text{(RS)}$$

The axiom (RS) makes A ratified φ stronger than A says φ. Statement φ directly signed by a principal can be taken as an evidence of A says φ, not A ratified φ. (I-SS) and (RS) together imply that:

$$\vdash (A \text{ ratified } \varphi) \to B \text{ says } A \text{ says } \varphi$$

but it is not possible to derive in general that

$$\vdash (A \text{ says } \varphi) \to B \text{ says } A \text{ ratified } \varphi$$

which would be unjustified because if A says φ, then B has not necessarily ratified it.

Example 4. The purpose of introducing the modality A ratified $\bullet$ is to allow a principal control over what statements and proofs of another principal it will admit as trusted. Assume that a hospital administrator PA controls access to sensitive patient records. The main policy is that "a doctor has access to all patient records" and the determination of who constitutes a doctor comes from the principal HR, representing the human resources database. Let $\mathbf{C}_A(access\_records)$ mean that principal A has control over the access to patient records and $isDoctor\_A$ mean that A is a doctor. Let $\mathcal{P}$ be the set of all relevant principals. The main policy can be encoded as the formula[2]:

$$PA \text{ says } \bigwedge_{A \in \mathcal{P}}[(HR \text{ ratified } isDoctor\_A) \to (\mathbf{C}_A(access\_records))] \qquad \text{(P1)}$$

Observe that we are using (HR ratified $\ldots$) inside the policy instead of (HR says $\ldots$) to ensure that consequences of the policy depend only on statements of HR that have been ratified by PA.

Now, PA can choose to trust the policies of HR selectively. For instance, if PA trusts all deductions of the form $isDoctor\_A$ that HR may make, it can have the policy:

$$PA \text{ says } \bigwedge_{A \in \mathcal{P}}((HR \text{ says } isDoctor\_A) \to (HR \text{ ratified } isDoctor\_A)) \qquad \text{(P2)}$$

Then, for any principal A, we have that

$$(P1), (P2), HR \text{ says } (isDoctor\_A) \vdash PA \text{ says } \mathbf{C}_A(access\_records)$$

If, on the other hand, PA only trusts HR's statements about two principals $Alice$ and Bob, it can selectively assert (in place of (P2)) that:

---

[2] Because we are using a propositional language, we assume principals to range over a *finite* set $\mathcal{P}$. Accordingly, $\bigwedge_{A \in \mathcal{P}} \varphi$ reads "For all principals A in $\mathcal{P}$, φ holds".

PA says $((HR$ says $isDoctor\_Alice) \rightarrow (HR$ ratified $isDoctor\_Alice))$
PA says $((HR$ says $isDoctor\_Bob) \rightarrow (HR$ ratified $isDoctor\_Bob))$

As a last illustration, suppose that the HR has two policies, one of which states that every administrator is a doctor and the other of which (mistakenly) states that every hospital employee is a doctor:

$$HR \text{ says } \bigwedge_{A \in \mathcal{P}}(isAdmin\_A \rightarrow isDoctor\_A) \tag{P3}$$
$$HR \text{ says } \bigwedge_{A \in \mathcal{P}}(isEmployee\_A \rightarrow isDoctor\_A) \tag{P4}$$

PA can choose to ratify the first of these, but not the second, by asserting in place of (P2) that:

$$PA \text{ says } ((HR \text{ says } \bigwedge_{A \in \mathcal{P}}(isAdmin\_A \rightarrow isDoctor\_A)) \rightarrow (HR \text{ ratified}$$
$$\bigwedge_{A \in \mathcal{P}}(isAdmin\_A) \rightarrow isDoctor\_A))) \tag{P5}$$

$$PA \text{ says } \bigwedge_{A \in \mathcal{P}}((HR \text{ says } isAdmin\_A) \rightarrow (HR \text{ ratified } isAdmin\_A)) \tag{P6}$$

Suppose that HR says $isAdmin\_Alice$. Then, we can deduce PA says $\mathbf{C}_{Alice}(access\_records)$ from (P1), (P3), (P5) and (P6) as follows:

1. From (P3) and (I-SS), deduce that

$$PA \text{ says } (HR \text{ says } (\bigwedge_{A \in \mathcal{P}}(isAdmin\_A \rightarrow isDoctor\_A)))$$

2. From (1), (K-S) and (P5) deduce that

$$PA \text{ says } (HR \text{ ratified } (\bigwedge_{A \in \mathcal{P}}(isAdmin\_A \rightarrow isDoctor\_A)))$$

3. From $(HR$ says $isAdmin\_Alice)$ and (I-SS) deduce that $(PA$ says HR says $isAdmin\_Alice)$
4. From (3), (K-S) and (P6) deduce that $(PA$ says HR ratified $isAdmin\_Alice)$
5. From (2), (4), (K-S), and (K-R) deduce that $(PA$ says HR ratified $isDoctor\_Alice)$
6. From (5), (P1), and (K-S) deduce that $(PA$ says $\mathbf{C}_{Alice}(access\_records))$

If we replace the assumption $(HR$ says $isAdmin\_Alice)$ with the assumption $(HR$ says $isEmployee\_Alice)$, then we cannot deduce $(PA$ says $(\mathbf{C}_{Alice}(access\_records)))$ because we cannot deduce (5) above. In place of (5), we can deduce only the weaker statement $(PA$ says $(HR$ says $isDoctor\_Alice))$, which does not imply $(PA$ says $\mathbf{C}_{Alice}(access\_records))$ in our theory.

5   Semantics

In this section, we define sound and complete semantics for ACL$^+$. Our semantics uses graph-based structures called Kripke models, that are standard in modal logic. The technical challenge here, as for every modal logic, lies in identifying a suitable class of Kripke structures that correspond exactly to the calculus of Section 4. Although Kripke semantics are not necessarily intuitive, they lead directly to a proof theory for the logic, a semi-decidability result for it and an implementation of the proof theory (Section 6).

Definition 2. *An intuitionistic model,* $\mathcal{M}$, *of* ACL^+ *is a tuple*

$$(W, \leq, \{S_A\}_{A \in \mathcal{P}}, \{C_A\}_{A \in \mathcal{P}}, \{R_A\}_{A \in \mathcal{P}}, \{P_A\}_{A \in \mathcal{P}}, h)$$

where

- $\mathcal{P}$ *is a set of principals.*
- $(W, \leq)$ *is a preorder, where elements of W are called states or worlds, and $\leq$ is a binary relation over W which satisfies the following conditions*

$$\forall x.(x \leq x) \tag{refl}$$
$$\forall x, y, z.((x \leq y) \wedge (y \leq z) \rightarrow (x \leq z)) \tag{trans}$$

- S_A, C_A, R_A *and* P_A *are binary relations on W that satisfy the following conditions:*

$$\forall x, y, z, w.(((x \leq y) \wedge (yS_Az) \wedge (z \leq w)) \rightarrow (xS_Aw)) \tag{mon-S}$$
$$\forall x, y, z, w.(((x \leq y) \wedge (yC_Az) \wedge (z \leq w)) \rightarrow (xC_Aw)) \tag{mon-C}$$
$$\forall x, y, z, w.(((x \leq y) \wedge (yR_Az) \wedge (z \leq w)) \rightarrow (xR_Aw)) \tag{mon-R}$$
$$\forall x, y, z, w.(((x \leq y) \wedge (zP_Ay) \wedge (z \leq w)) \rightarrow (wP_Ax)) \tag{mon-P}$$

- h *is an assignment which, for each atom q, assigns the subset of worlds $h(q) \subseteq W$ where q holds. Moreover, we require h to be monotone w.r.t. $\leq$, i.e., if $x \in h(q)$ and $x \leq y$ then $y \in h(q)$.*

Conditions above ensure monotonicity *of the logic (Lemma 1), which is a standard property of Kripke semantics for constructive logics. Moreover, to force ACL^+ models to admit the axioms (I-SS), (C2P), (del-C) and (RS) we require the following to hold for any two principals A and B.*

$$\forall x, y, z.(((xS_By) \wedge (yS_Az)) \rightarrow (xS_Az)) \tag{s-I-SS}$$
$$\forall x \exists y.(xC_Ay \wedge xP_Ay) \tag{s-C2P}$$
$$\forall x, y.((xC_By) \rightarrow ((xC_Ay) \vee \exists z((xS_Az) \wedge (zC_By)))) \tag{s-del-C}$$
$$\forall x, y.((xS_Ay) \rightarrow (xR_Ay)) \tag{s-RS}$$

An *interpretation* for the logic is a pair $\mathcal{M}, t$ where $\mathcal{M}$ is a model and t is a world in $\mathcal{M}$.

Definition 3 (Satisfaction Relation). *The satisfaction relation "$\models$" between interpretations and formulae of the logic is defined below. (The letter q denotes an atomic formula.)*

- $\mathcal{M}, t \models q$ iff $t \in h(q)$
- $\mathcal{M}, t \not\models \bot$
- $\mathcal{M}, t \models \varphi \vee \psi$ iff $\mathcal{M}, t \models \varphi$ or $\mathcal{M}, t \models \psi$
- $\mathcal{M}, t \models \varphi \wedge \psi$ iff $\mathcal{M}, t \models \varphi$ and $\mathcal{M}, t \models \psi$
- $\mathcal{M}, t \models \varphi \rightarrow \psi$ iff for all $s, t \leq s$ and $\mathcal{M}, s \models \varphi$ imply $\mathcal{M}, s \models \psi$
- $\mathcal{M}, t \models \neg\varphi$ iff for all $s, t \leq s$ implies $\mathcal{M}, t \not\models \varphi$
- $\mathcal{M}, t \models A$ says φ iff for all s such that tS_As we have $\mathcal{M}, s \models \varphi$
- $\mathcal{M}, t \models \mathbf{C}_A\varphi$ iff for all s such that tC_As we have $\mathcal{M}, s \models \varphi$
- $\mathcal{M}, t \models A$ ratified φ iff for all s such that tR_As we have $\mathcal{M}, s \models \varphi$
- $\mathcal{M}, t \models \mathbf{P}_A\varphi$ iff there exists an s such that tP_As and $\mathcal{M}, s \models \varphi$

Lemma 1 (Monotonicity). *For any formula φ and any interpretation $\mathcal{M}, t$, if $\mathcal{M}, t \models \varphi$ and $t \leq s$ then $\mathcal{M}, s \models \varphi$.*

We say that $\mathcal{M} \models \varphi$ if for all $t \in \mathcal{M}$, it is the case that $\mathcal{M}, t \models \varphi$. Further, $\Gamma \models \varphi$ if for every intuitionistic model $\mathcal{M}$, $\mathcal{M} \models \Gamma$ implies $\mathcal{M} \models \varphi$.

Theorem 1 (Soundness). *If $\vdash \varphi$ then $\models \varphi$*

Theorem 2 (Completeness). *If $\Gamma \models \varphi$ then $\Gamma \vdash \varphi$*

We note that the conditions (s-I-SS), (s-C2P), (s-del-C) and (s-RS) are *canonical* for the axioms (I-SS), (C2P), (del-C) and (RS), respectively, i.e., a logic with any subset of these axioms is sound and complete with respect to models that satisfy the conditions corresponding to the chosen axioms.

6   A Semantics-Based Calculus for ACL⁺

In this section we briefly present Seq-ACL⁺, a sound, complete and cut-free sequent calculus for ACL⁺. The calculus is inspired by the work of Negri [19][3] and follows the so-called labeled approach [4,20], which directly uses the Kripke semantics. The use of labeled sequent calculi for access control is relatively new and has been introduced in [15,16] to define proof theory of a specific says-based access control logic. Our sequent calculus directly leads to a semi-decision procedure for the logic ACL⁺.

Seq-ACL⁺ manipulates two types of labeled formulas:

1. *World formulas*, denoted by $x : \varphi$, where x is a world and φ is a formula of ACL⁺, intuitively meaning that φ holds in world x.
2. *Transition formulas* representing semantic accessibility relationships. These formulas have one of the forms $xS_Ay, xC_Ay, xR_Ay, xP_Ay$ and $x \leq y$.

A sequent is a tuple $\langle \Sigma, \mathbb{M}, \Gamma, \Delta \rangle$, usually written $\Sigma; \mathbb{M}; \Gamma \Rightarrow \Delta$ where $\mathbb{M}, \Gamma$ and Δ are multisets of labeled formulas and Σ is the set of labels (worlds) appearing in the rest of the sequent. Intuitively, the sequent $\Sigma; \mathbb{M}; \Gamma \Rightarrow \Delta$ means that "every model which satisfies all labeled formulas of $\Gamma \cup \mathbb{M}$ satisfies at least one labeled formula in Δ". This is made precise by the notion of *validity* in the following definition.

Definition 4 (Sequent validity). *Given a model*

$$\mathcal{M} = (W, \leq, \{S_A\}_{A \in \mathcal{P}}, \{C_A\}_{A \in \mathcal{P}}, \{R_A\}_{A \in \mathcal{P}}, \{P_A\}_{A \in \mathcal{P}}, h)$$

and a label alphabet $\mathcal{A}$, consider a mapping $I : \mathcal{A} \to W$. Let F denote a labeled formula, whose labels are contained in $\mathcal{A}$. Define $\mathcal{M} \models_I F$ as follows:

- *$\mathcal{M} \models_I x : \alpha$ iff $\mathcal{M}, I(x) \models \alpha$*
- *$\mathcal{M} \models_I xC_Ay$ iff $I(x)C_AI(y)$ (Similarly for S_A, R_A, P_A and $\leq$).*

---

[3] In particular, proofs of metatheorems about Seq-ACL⁺ use methods developed in [19].

Axiom Rules

$$\frac{}{\Sigma; \mathbb{M}, x \leq y; \Gamma, x : p \Rightarrow y : p, \Delta}\text{init} \qquad \frac{}{\Sigma; \mathbb{M}; \Gamma, x : \bot \Rightarrow \Delta}\bot\text{L} \qquad \frac{}{\Sigma; \mathbb{M}; \Gamma \Rightarrow x : \top, \Delta}\top\text{R}$$

Logical Rules

$$\frac{\Sigma; \mathbb{M}; \Gamma \Rightarrow_\mathcal{T} x : \alpha, \Delta \quad \Sigma; \mathbb{M}; \Gamma \Rightarrow_\mathcal{T} x : \beta, \Delta}{\Sigma; \mathbb{M}; \Gamma \Rightarrow_\mathcal{T} x : \alpha \wedge \beta, \Delta}\wedge\text{R} \qquad \frac{\Sigma; \mathbb{M}; \Gamma, x : \alpha, x : \beta \Rightarrow_\mathcal{T} \Delta}{\Sigma; \mathbb{M}; \Gamma, x : \alpha \wedge \beta \Rightarrow_\mathcal{T} \Delta}\wedge\text{L}$$

$$\frac{\Sigma; \mathbb{M}; \Gamma \Rightarrow_\mathcal{T} x : \alpha, x : \beta, \Delta}{\Sigma; \mathbb{M}; \Gamma \Rightarrow_\mathcal{T} x : \alpha \vee \beta, \Delta}\vee\text{R} \qquad \frac{\Sigma; \mathbb{M}; \Gamma, x : \alpha \Rightarrow_\mathcal{T} \Delta \quad \Sigma; \mathbb{M}; \Gamma, x : \beta \Rightarrow_\mathcal{T} \Delta}{\Sigma; \mathbb{M}; \Gamma, x : \alpha \vee \beta \Rightarrow_\mathcal{T} \Delta}\vee\text{L}$$

$$\frac{\Sigma; \mathbb{M}, x \leq y; \Gamma, x : \alpha \rightarrow \beta \Rightarrow_\mathcal{T} y : \alpha, \Delta \quad \Sigma; \mathbb{M}, x \leq y; \Gamma, x : \alpha \rightarrow \beta, y : \beta \Rightarrow_\mathcal{T} \Delta}{\Sigma; \mathbb{M}, x \leq y; \Gamma, x : \alpha \rightarrow \beta \Rightarrow \Delta}\rightarrow\text{L}$$

$$\frac{\Sigma, y; \mathbb{M}, x \leq y; \Gamma, y : \alpha \Rightarrow y : \beta, \Delta}{\Sigma; \mathbb{M}; \Gamma \Rightarrow x : \alpha \rightarrow \beta, \Delta}\rightarrow\text{R}_{\; y \text{ new}}$$

$$\frac{\Sigma; \mathbb{M}, xS_A y; \Gamma, x : A \text{ says } \alpha, y : \alpha \Rightarrow \Delta}{\Sigma; \mathbb{M}, xS_A y; \Gamma, x : A \text{ says } \alpha \Rightarrow \Delta}\text{says L} \qquad \frac{\Sigma, y; \mathbb{M}, xS_A y; \Gamma \Rightarrow_\mathcal{T} y : \alpha, \Delta}{\Sigma; \mathbb{M}; \Gamma \Rightarrow_\mathcal{T} x : A \text{ says } \alpha, \Delta}\text{says R}_{\; y \text{ new}}$$

$$\frac{\Sigma; \mathbb{M}, xC_A y; \Gamma, x : \mathbf{C}_A \alpha, y : \alpha \Rightarrow \Delta}{\Sigma; \mathbb{M}, xC_A y; \Gamma, x : \mathbf{C}_A \alpha \Rightarrow \Delta}\text{CL} \qquad \frac{\Sigma, y; \mathbb{M}, xC_A y; \Gamma \Rightarrow y : \alpha, \Delta}{\Sigma; \mathbb{M}; \Gamma \Rightarrow x : \mathbf{C}_A \alpha, \Delta}\text{CR}_{\; y \text{ new}}$$

$$\frac{\Sigma; \mathbb{M}, xR_A y; \Gamma, x : A \text{ ratified } \alpha, y : \alpha \Rightarrow \Delta}{\Sigma; \mathbb{M}, xR_A y; \Gamma, x : A \text{ ratified } \alpha \Rightarrow \Delta}\text{ratified L} \qquad \frac{\Sigma, y; \mathbb{M}, xR_A y; \Gamma \Rightarrow y : \alpha, \Delta}{\Sigma; \mathbb{M}; \Gamma \Rightarrow x : A \text{ ratified } \alpha, \Delta}\text{ratified R}_{\; y \text{ new}}$$

$$\frac{\Sigma; \mathbb{M}, xP_A y; \Gamma \Rightarrow x : \mathbf{P}_A \alpha, y : \alpha, \Delta}{\Sigma; \mathbb{M}, xP_A y; \Gamma \Rightarrow x : \mathbf{P}_A \alpha, \Delta}\mathbf{PR} \qquad \frac{\Sigma, y; \mathbb{M}, xP_A y; \Gamma, y : \alpha \Rightarrow \Delta}{\Sigma; \mathbb{M}; \Gamma, x : \mathbf{P}_A \alpha \Rightarrow \Delta}\mathbf{PL}_{\; y \text{ new}}$$

Semantical Rules

$$\frac{\Sigma; \mathbb{M}, x \leq y, yS_A z, z \leq w, xS_A w; \Gamma \Rightarrow \Delta}{\Sigma; \mathbb{M}, x \leq y, yS_A z, z \leq w; \Gamma \Rightarrow \Delta}\text{mon-S} \quad \frac{\Sigma; \mathbb{M}, x \leq y, yC_A z, z \leq w, xC_A w; \Gamma \Rightarrow \Delta}{\Sigma; \mathbb{M}, x \leq y, yC_A z, z \leq w; \Gamma \Rightarrow \Delta}\text{mon-C}$$

$$\frac{\Sigma; \mathbb{M}, x \leq y, yR_A z, z \leq w, xR_A w; \Gamma \Rightarrow \Delta}{\Sigma; \mathbb{M}, x \leq y, yR_A z, z \leq w; \Gamma \Rightarrow \Delta}\text{mon-R} \quad \frac{\Sigma; \mathbb{M}, x \leq y, zP_A y, z \leq w, wP_A x; \Gamma \Rightarrow \Delta}{\Sigma; \mathbb{M}, x \leq y, zP_A y, z \leq w; \Gamma \Rightarrow \Delta}\text{mon-P}$$

$$\frac{\Sigma; \mathbb{M}, x \leq x; \Gamma \Rightarrow \Delta}{\Sigma; \mathbb{M}; \Gamma \Rightarrow \Delta}\text{refl}_{\; x \in \Sigma} \qquad \frac{\Sigma; \mathbb{M}, x \leq y, y \leq z, x \leq z; \Gamma \Rightarrow \Delta}{\Sigma; \mathbb{M}, x \leq y, y \leq z; \Gamma \Rightarrow \Delta}\text{trans}$$

Access Control Rules

$$\frac{\Sigma; \mathbb{M}, xS_B y, yS_A z, xS_A z; \Gamma \Rightarrow \Delta}{\Sigma; \mathbb{M}, xS_B y, yS_A z; \Gamma \Rightarrow \Delta}\text{s-I-SS} \qquad \frac{\Sigma, y; \mathbb{M}, xC_A y, xP_A y; \Gamma \Rightarrow \Delta}{\Sigma; \mathbb{M}; \Gamma \Rightarrow \Delta}\text{s-C2P}_{\; y \text{ new}}$$

$$\frac{\Sigma; \mathbb{M}, xC_B y, xC_A y; \Gamma \Rightarrow \Delta \quad \Sigma, z; \mathbb{M}, xC_B y, xS_A z, zC_B y; \Gamma \Rightarrow \Delta}{\Sigma; \mathbb{M}, xC_B y; \Gamma \Rightarrow \Delta}\text{s-del-C}_{\; z \text{ new}}$$

$$\frac{\Sigma; \mathbb{M}, xS_A y, xR_A y; \Gamma \Rightarrow \Delta}{\Sigma; \mathbb{M}, xS_A y; \Gamma \Rightarrow \Delta}\text{s-RS}$$

Fig. 1. Seq-ACL$^+$ Rules

We say that $\Sigma; \mathbb{M}; \Gamma \Rightarrow \Delta$ *is valid in* $\mathcal{M}$ *if, for every mapping* $I : \Sigma \to W$, *if* $\mathcal{M} \models_I F$ *for every* $F \in \mathbb{M} \cup \Gamma$, *then* $\mathcal{M} \models_I G$ *for some* $G \in \Delta$. *We say that* $\Sigma; \mathbb{M}; \Gamma \Rightarrow \Delta$ *is valid in Seq-ACL$^+$ if it is valid in every* $\mathcal{M}$.

Figure 1 lists the rules of the calculus Seq-ACL$^+$, divided into four groups.

- *Axiom rules* do not have premises and describe valid sequents.
- *Logical rules* operate on connectives of the logic.
- *Semantic rules* define the properties that hold for relationships $\leq, S_A, R_A, C_A$ and P_A in all ACL$^+$ models.
- *Access control rules* codify axioms that differentiate ACL$^+$ from other constructive normal modal logics, i.e., (I-SS), (C2P), (del-C) and (RS).

Note that semantic and access control rules are in one-to-one correspondence with semantic conditions of Definition 2.

We say that a sequent $\Sigma; \mathbb{M}; \Gamma \Rightarrow \Delta$ is *derivable* in Seq-ACL$^+$ if it admits a *derivation*. A derivation is a tree whose nodes are sequents. A branch is a sequence of nodes $\Sigma_1; \mathbb{M}_1; \Gamma_1 \Rightarrow \Delta_1, \Sigma_2; \mathbb{M}_2; \Gamma_2 \Rightarrow \Delta_2, \ldots, \Sigma_n; \mathbb{M}_n; \Gamma_n \Rightarrow \Delta_n, \ldots$ Each node $\Sigma_i; \mathbb{M}_i; \Gamma_i \Rightarrow \Delta_i$ is obtained from its immediate successor $\Sigma_{i-1}; \mathbb{M}_{i-1}; \Gamma_{i-1} \Rightarrow \Delta_{i-1}$ by applying *backward* a rule of Seq-ACL$^+$, having $\Sigma_{i-1}; \mathbb{M}_{i-1}; \Gamma_{i-1} \Rightarrow \Delta_{i-1}$ as the conclusion and $\Sigma_i; \mathbb{M}_i; \Gamma_i \Rightarrow \Delta_i$ as one of its premises. A branch is closed if one of its nodes is an instance of axiom rules, otherwise it is open. We say that a tree is closed if all of its branches are closed. A sequent $\Sigma; \mathbb{M}; \Gamma \Rightarrow \Delta$ has a derivation in Seq-ACL$^+$ if there is a closed tree having $\Sigma; \mathbb{M}; \Gamma \Rightarrow \Delta$ as the root. As an example we show a derivation of the axiom (C2P) in Seq-ACL$^+$.

$$\cfrac{\cfrac{\cfrac{\cfrac{\cfrac{\cfrac{\overline{x,y,z; x \leq y, z \leq z, yC_Az, yP_Az; y : \mathbf{C}_Ap, z : p \Rightarrow y : \mathbf{P}_Ap, z : p}^{\text{ init}}}{x,y,z; x \leq y, yC_Az, yP_Az; y : \mathbf{C}_Ap, z : p \Rightarrow y : \mathbf{P}_Ap, z : p}^{\text{ refl}}}{x,y,z; x \leq y, yC_Az, yP_Az; y : \mathbf{C}_Ap, z : p \Rightarrow y : \mathbf{P}_Ap}^{\text{ PR}}}{x,y,z; x \leq y, yC_Az, yP_Az; y : \mathbf{C}_Ap \Rightarrow y : \mathbf{P}_Ap}^{\text{ CL}}}{x,y,z; x \leq y, yC_Az, yP_Az; y : \mathbf{C}_Ap \Rightarrow y : \mathbf{P}_Ap}^{\text{ s-C2P}}}{x,y; x \leq y; y : \mathbf{C}_Ap \Rightarrow y : \mathbf{P}_Ap}}{x; ; \Rightarrow x : \mathbf{C}_Ap \to \mathbf{P}_Ap}^{\to \text{R}}$$

Theorem 3 (Admissibility of cut). $\Sigma; \mathbb{M}; \Gamma \Rightarrow x : \alpha, \Delta$ *and* $\Sigma; \mathbb{M}; \Gamma, x : \alpha \Rightarrow \Delta$ *imply* $\Sigma; \mathbb{M}; \Gamma \Rightarrow \Delta$.

Theorem 4 (Soundness of Seq-ACL$^+$). *If a sequent* $\Sigma; \mathbb{M}; \Gamma \Rightarrow \Delta$ *is derivable then it is valid in the sense of Definition 4.*

Theorem 5 (Completeness of Seq-ACL$^+$). *If a formula* α *is valid in ACL$^+$ (i.e.,* $\models \alpha$*), then* $x; ; \Rightarrow x : \alpha$ *is derivable in Seq-ACL$^+$.*

Theorems 4 and 5 imply that ACL$^+$ is semi-decidable because the rules of Figure 1 can be implemented backwards with iterative deepening to always find a proof of any provable formula.

6.1 Termination

Next, we propose several conditions on application of rules of the sequent calculus Seq-ACL$^+$, which together ensure that a backward search in the calculus always terminates. The conditions are based on similar conditions in the work of Negri [19] for the unimodal case. Although the conditions are known to preserve completeness in the unimodal case, we do not know whether they preserve completeness in Seq-ACL$^+$ also. We strongly suspect that this is the case and state this belief as an unproved conjecture. We do prove that *some* of our termination conditions preserve completeness of proof search.

The first source of non-termination in backward proof search is that the rules saysL, ratifiedL, CL, and PR may increase the complexity of sequents in a backward proof search. However, as the following (provable) Lemma shows, such "critical" rules can be applied in a controlled way. (Without loss of generality we assume that the root of each proof has the form $x; ; \Rightarrow x : \varphi$).

Lemma 2 (Controlled use of rules). *In each branch of a backward proof search, it is useless to: (1) apply CL on the same transition relation $xC_Ay \in \mathbb{M}$ more than once, (2) apply PR on the same transition relation $xP_Ay \in \mathbb{M}$ more than once, (3) apply rule χ for $\chi \in \{$mon-S,mon-R,mon-C,mon-P,sym,trans,s-I-SS,s-del-C,s-C2P,s-RS$\}$ on the same transition formula (or label as in s-RS) more than once.*

However, there are other reasons why a backward proof search may not terminate. In particular:

1. Interaction of the rule (trans) with →L adds new accessible worlds, and we can build chains of accessible worlds on which →L can be applied *ad infinitum*.
2. Application of rules s-del-C and s-C2P generates transition relations with new labels that can be used for repeated application of the same rules.

We propose to bound the number of such interactions using a counting argument, as in the work of Negri [19]. Let $depth(F)$ be the height of the parse tree of formula F.

Definition 5 (Label distance). *Given a sequent $\Sigma, \mathbb{M}, \Gamma \Rightarrow \Delta$ and two labels x and y such that $x \leq y \in \mathbb{M}$, we define the distance $d(x,y)$ between two labels as 0 when $x = y$ and n when $x \neq y$, where n is the length of the longest sequence of transitions in $\mathbb{M}$ "connecting" the two labels, i.e., $x \overset{\sim}{\bigcirc} x_1, x_1 \overset{\sim}{\bigcirc} x_2, \ldots, x_{n-1} \overset{\sim}{\bigcirc} y$ where $\overset{\sim}{\bigcirc} \in \{S_A, C_A, R_A, P_A, \leq\}$ (for any principal A). As an example, if $\{x \leq y, yC_Az, zP_Ak, xS_Ak\} \in \mathbb{M}$, then $d(x,k) = 3$.*

Conjecture 1 (Bounded application of rules). The following bounding heuristic preserves completeness of proof search. In any backward proof search starting with the root $x; ; \Rightarrow x : F$, for any label x_1 occurring in the search such that $d(x,x_1) > depth(F)$, it is useless to: (1) apply →L on a transition formula $x_1 \leq x_2$, (2) apply s-C2P on the label x_1, (3) apply s-del-C on a transition formula $x_1C_Bx_2$.

If this conjecture holds, we easily obtain decidability for ACL$^+$.

Conjecture 2 (Decidability). The logic ACL$^+$ is decidable.

A Prolog implementation of Seq-ACL$^+$ with the above termination conditions is available from our homepages.

7 Extending Seq-ACL$^+$ with Constructs for Subordination

The correspondence between semantic conditions and axioms allows us to modularly extend ACL$^+$ with new axioms, and new (corresponding) sequent calculus rules. As a specific case, we show here how we may extend the logic with new *subordination axioms* of any of the following forms, and obtain completeness with respect to the semantics. (In these axioms A and B are specific principals, not metavariables, but φ is a metavariable standing for all formulas.)

$$\vdash A \text{ says } \varphi \to B \text{ says } \varphi \qquad\qquad (\text{sub-S})_B^A$$
$$\vdash A \text{ ratified } \varphi \to B \text{ ratified } \varphi \qquad\qquad (\text{sub-R})_B^A$$
$$\vdash \mathbf{P}_A\varphi \to \mathbf{P}_B\varphi \qquad\qquad (\text{sub-P})_B^A$$
$$\vdash \mathbf{C}_A\varphi \to \mathbf{C}_B\varphi \qquad\qquad (\text{sub-C})_B^A$$

We call these axioms subordination axioms because each axiom suggests that one of the two principals A and B is subordinate to the other. The first (second) axiom means that statements (ratifications) of A are echoed by B, so B is, in a sense, subordinate to A. The third (fourth) axiom means that if A has a permission (ability to control), then so does B, so B is more powerful than A.

Definition 6. *The semantic conditions on models corresponding to the axioms above are, respectively:*

$$\forall x, y.(xS_By \to xS_Ay) \qquad\qquad (\text{s-sub-S})_B^A$$
$$\forall x, y.(xR_By \to xR_Ay) \qquad\qquad (\text{s-sub-R})_B^A$$
$$\forall x, y.(xP_Ay \to xP_By) \qquad\qquad (\text{s-sub-P})_B^A$$
$$\forall x, y.(xC_By \to xC_Ay) \qquad\qquad (\text{s-sub-C})_B^A$$

Corresponding access control rules for the sequent calculus are shown in Figure 2.

Lemma 3. *Extension of Seq-ACL$^+$ with any subset of the rules in Figure 2 preserves admissibility of cut. Further, the calculus is sound and complete with respect to intuitionistic models that satisfy the corresponding conditions from Definition 6.*

$$\frac{\Sigma; \mathbb{M}, xS_Ay, xS_By; \Gamma \Rightarrow \Delta}{\Sigma; \mathbb{M}, xS_By; \Gamma \Rightarrow \Delta}\text{s-sub-S}_B^A \qquad \frac{\Sigma; \mathbb{M}, xR_Ay, xR_By; \Gamma \Rightarrow \Delta}{\Sigma; \mathbb{M}, xR_By; \Gamma \Rightarrow \Delta}\text{s-sub-R}_B^A$$

$$\frac{\Sigma; \mathbb{M}, xP_Ay, xP_By; \Gamma \Rightarrow \Delta}{\Sigma; \mathbb{M}, xP_Ay; \Gamma \Rightarrow \Delta}\text{s-sub-P}_B^A \qquad \frac{\Sigma; \mathbb{M}, xC_By, xC_Ay; \Gamma \Rightarrow \Delta}{\Sigma; \mathbb{M}, xC_By; \Gamma \Rightarrow \Delta}\text{s-sub-C}_B^A$$

Fig. 2. Access Control Rules for Subordination

8   Related Work

The study of formal properties of says and other constructs in modal logic is a relatively new research trend. Prior work by the second author [10] adopts a modified version of constructive modal logic S4 called DTL_0 and shows how existing access control logics can be embedded (via translation) into DTL_0. Other work [11] translates existing access control logics into S4 by relying on a slight simplification of Gödel's translation from intuitionistic logic to S4, and extending it to formulas of the form A says φ. The first author has developed conditional logics as a general framework for modular sequent calculi for standard access control logics with the says connective [15,16]. Dinesh et al. [9] present an access control logic based on says and extended with obligation and permissions, but their treatment of permissions is different from ours and is closely tied to says. The use of canonical properties for access control axioms was first considered in [8] where standard access control axioms (e.g. (unit) and (hand-off)) are characterized in terms of first-order conditions on Kripke models.

The says modality also appears in several languages for writing access control policies, notably SecPAL [7] and DKAL [17]. But there are several differences in these languages and ACL^+. For example, ACL^+ is propositional, whereas both SecPAL and DKAL have first-order quantification over principals and other objects, which is often useful to compact policy representation. However, these languages remove other features to maintain decidability: In both SecPAL and DKAL, the says modality can only be applied over atoms. In particular, the use of says over a disjunction is prohibited by both SecPAL and DKAL, although it may be useful in distributed scenarios where communication is not guaranteed. For instance, if the reference monitor knows that A says $(\varphi \vee \psi)$, but principal A is not available to verify which of φ or ψ it supports, it might still be possible to infer a useful fact from A says $(\varphi \vee \psi)$ alone. In both SecPAL and DKAL such a fact cannot be expressed and hence this situation cannot be modeled.

9   Conclusion

We have presented ACL^+, a constructive multi-modal logic for access control that introduces three new modalities $\mathbf{P}_A$ (permission), $\mathbf{C}_A$ (control), and ratified (trusted statement) to fix practical problems in reasoning with policies using logic. The connectives of the logic are defined by a sound and complete Kripke semantics for ACL^+ together with a correspondence between conditions on models and the logic's axioms. The semantics lead to Seq-ACL^+, a sound, complete, cut-free calculus for ACL^+ and a semi-decision procedure for it. Finally, ACL^+ can be extended with new axioms, as illustrated by examples of axioms for specific kinds of subordination among principals.

Acknowledgments. Valerio Genovese was supported by the National Research Fund, Luxembourg. This work was performed while Deepak Garg was at Carnegie Mellon University and supported by the U.S. Army Research Office contract "Perpetually Available and Secure Information Systems" (DAAD19-02-1-0389) to Carnegie Mellon CyLab and the AFOSR MURI "Collaborative Policies and Assured Information Sharing".

References

1. Abadi, M.: Logic in access control. In: Proceedings of the 18th Annual IEEE Symposium on Logic in Computer Science (LICS), pp. 228–233 (2003)
2. Abadi, M.: Variations in Access Control Logic. In: van der Meyden, R., van der Torre, L. (eds.) DEON 2008. LNCS (LNAI), vol. 5076, pp. 96–109. Springer, Heidelberg (2008)
3. Abadi, M.: Logic in access control (tutorial notes). In: Proceedings of the 9th International School on Foundations of Security Analysis and Design (FOSAD), pp. 145–165 (2009)
4. Basin, D., D'Agostino, M., Gabbay, D.M., Matthews, S., Viganó, L.: Labelled Deduction. Springer, Heidelberg (2000)
5. Bauer, L.: Access Control for the Web via Proof-Carrying Authorization. Ph.D. thesis, Princeton University (2003)
6. Bauer, L., Garriss, S., McCune, J.M., Reiter, M.K., Rouse, J., Rutenbar, P.: Device-Enabled Authorization in the Grey System. In: Zhou, J., López, J., Deng, R.H., Bao, F. (eds.) ISC 2005. LNCS, vol. 3650, pp. 431–445. Springer, Heidelberg (2005)
7. Becker, M.Y., Fournet, C., Gordon, A.D.: SecPAL: Design and semantics of a decentralized authorization language. Journal of Computer Security 18(4), 619–665 (2010)
8. Boella, G., Gabbay, D.M., Genovese, V., van der Torre, L.: Fibred security language. Studia Logica 92(3), 395–436 (2009)
9. Dinesh, N., Joshi, A.K., Lee, I., Sokolsky, O.: Permission to speak: A logic for access control and conformance. Journal of Logic and Algebraic Programming 80(1), 50–74 (2011)
10. Garg, D.: Principal centric reasoning in constructive authorization logic. In: Informal Proceedings of Intuitionistic Modal Logic and Application (IMLA) (2008), Full version available as Carnegie Mellon Technical Report CMU-CS-09-120
11. Garg, D., Abadi, M.: A Modal Deconstruction of Access Control Logics. In: Amadio, R.M. (ed.) FOSSACS 2008. LNCS, vol. 4962, pp. 216–230. Springer, Heidelberg (2008)
12. Garg, D., Pfenning, F.: Non-interference in constructive authorization logic. In: Proceedings of the 19th IEEE Computer Security Foundations Workshop (CSFW), pp. 283–293 (2006)
13. Garg, D., Pfenning, F.: A proof-carrying file system. In: Proceedings of the 31st IEEE Symposium on Security and Privacy, Oakland, pp. 349–364 (2010)
14. Genovese, V., Giordano, L., Gliozzi, V., Pozzato, G.L.: A constructive conditional logic for access control: A preliminary report. In: Proceedings of the 19th European Conference on Artificial Intelligence (ECAI), pp. 1073–1074 (2010)
15. Genovese, V., Giordano, L., Gliozzi, V., Pozzato, G.L.: Logics for access control: A conditional approach. In: Informal Proceedings of the 1st Workshop on Logic in Security (LIS), pp. 78–92 (2010)
16. Genovese, V., Giordano, L., Gliozzi, V., Pozzato, G.L.: A Conditional Constructive Logic for Access Control and its Sequent Calculus. In: Brünnler, K., Metcalfe, G. (eds.) TABLEAUX 2011. LNCS, vol. 6793, pp. 164–179. Springer, Heidelberg (2011)
17. Gurevich, Y., Neeman, I.: Logic of infons: The propositional case. ACM Transactions on Computational Logic 12(2), 1–28 (2011)
18. Lampson, B.W., Abadi, M., Burrows, M., Wobber, E.: Authentication in distributed systems: Theory and practice. ACM Transactions on Computer Systems 10(4), 265–310 (1992)
19. Negri, S.: Proof analysis in modal logic. Journal of Philosophical Logic 34, 507–544 (2005)
20. Negri, S., von Plato, J.: Proof Analysis. Cambridge University Press (2011)
21. Schneider, F.B., Walsh, K., Sirer, E.G.: Nexus Authorization Logic (NAL): Design rationale and applications. ACM Transcations on Information and System Security 14(1), 1–28 (2011)
22. Wobber, E., Abadi, M., Burrows, M.: Authentication in the taos operating system. ACM Transactions on Computer Systems 12(1), 3–32 (1994)

Security Notions of Biometric
Remote Authentication Revisited

Neyire Deniz Sarier

B-IT, Cosec
Dahlmannstr. 2, D-53113 Bonn Germany
denizsarier@yahoo.com

Abstract. In this paper, we describe a new biometric-based remote authentication (BRA) system by combining distributed biometric authentication and cancelable biometrics. The motivation of this construction is based on our new attacks against the BRA schemes designed according to the security model of Bringer et al. Specifically, we prove that identity privacy cannot be achieved for the schemes in this model, if biometrics is assumed as public data and a publicly stored sketch is employed for improved accuracy. Besides, a statistical attack is shown that is effective even if the sketch is stored as encrypted. To prevent statistical attacks, we propose a weaker notion of identity privacy, where the adversary has limited power. Next, we design a BRA protocol in cancelable biometric setting, which is also applicable for biometrics represented as a set of features. For this setting, we define a stronger security notion, which is guaranteed for the BRA schemes that are vulnerable to our attacks if they are implemented in cancelable biometric setting.

Keywords: Security Notions, Biometric-based Remote Authentication, Identity Privacy, Secure Sketch, Cancelable Biometrics.

1 Introduction

Biometric-based authentication systems can be classified as remote or local authentication, where the former system authenticates a user over a network by performing the matching of his transmitted fresh biometrics to his stored biometric data at the remote server. A special type of biometric-based remote authentication (BRA) system and a new security model is introduced by Bringer et al. in ACISP'07, where security against insider attacks is considered. In this model, the server-side functionalities are performed in a distributed fashion using a detached biometric database and non-colluding system components. Basically, this system is composed of three entities, the authentication server $\mathcal{AS}$, the sensor $\mathcal{S}$ capturing the biometrics and the detached biometric database $\mathcal{DB}$. $\mathcal{AS}$ only stores the identity information of the users and provides the communication between $\mathcal{S}$ and $\mathcal{DB}$. Besides, $\mathcal{AS}$ does not have access to the reference biometrics that is stored as encrypted using homomorphic encryption, thus all the computations performed by $\mathcal{AS}$, $\mathcal{S}$ and $\mathcal{DB}$ stay in the encrypted domain. This leads to

C. Meadows and C. Fernández-Gago (Eds.): STM 2011, LNCS 7170, pp. 72–89, 2012.

a new security notion called identity privacy that guarantees the privacy of the link between the identity (name) and the biometrics of the user although biometrics is assumed as public data. The intuition of this notion is that a malicious $\mathcal{AS}$ that generates two templates for a user, cannot identify from the protocol runs, which of the two biometric templates is registered to the $\mathcal{DB}$ as encrypted with probability significantly better than that of random guessing. Moreover, $\mathcal{AS}$ performs the matching after a Private Information Retrieval (PIR) protocol that prevents a curious $\mathcal{DB}$ from tracking the user that authenticates to the system. Thus, transaction anonymity against a (malicious) database is satisfied which is the second notion for biometric remote authentication.

1.1 Related Work

Existing distributed biometric remote authentication schemes differ from each other based on the homomorphic encryption scheme chosen, incorporation of a secure sketch scheme, the biometric storage mechanism and whether an additional security factor is required as in the case of multi-factor biometric authentication. The distributed biometric remote authentication schemes that are designed according to the security model of Bringer et al. [2,4,16,13] combine homomorphic encryption, secure sketches and Private Information Retrieval (PIR) to achieve the security notions of identity privacy and transaction anonymity. The first biometric system in this model [3] employs Goldwasser-Micali encryption and a special PIR in order to compare two binary biometric strings in encrypted domain using hamming distance. Next, the systems of [4,16] require a secure sketch scheme to error-correct the biometric string such as an 2048 bits Iris code and use ElGamal encryption for equality testing [7] together with an efficient PIR scheme. Similarly, the work of [2] combines a secure sketch, Goldwasser-Micali and Paillier encryption in Lipmaa's PIR protocol to prevent the attacks against the scheme in [3]. Besides, in [13], elliptic curve ElGamal and a PIR scheme is employed together with a special secure sketch scheme applicable to an ordered biometric feature set. Another work that assumes biometrics as a set of features [1] provides a secure biometric identification scheme using a Support Vector Machine and Paillier encryption by adapting the security notions for biometric features (usually an k-tuple of numbers). A survey of these systems is given in [12]. Recently, [15] presents a survey of attacks against the schemes of [3,1] and some other biometric schemes. No attacks are known for the schemes presented in [2,4,16], which require the use of secure sketches. Except for the works of [1,13,11,14], the biometrics is assumed as a binary string such as an 2048 bits iris code, whereas the general representation of biometrics is a set of features that can be either ordered such as face, voice, iris, handwritten signatures or unordered such as fingerprint minutia.

1.2 Motivation and Contributions

The contributions of our paper is twofold. First, we consider the biometric remote authentication (BRA) schemes that require a fuzzy sketch scheme for improved accuracy. We analyze the security based on the model of Bringer et al., where we prove that if biometrics is assumed as public data and the fuzzy sketch required for error-correction is stored publicly, the notion of identity privacy against a malicious authentication server $\mathcal{AS}$ can never be satisfied. Basically, this notion guarantees the secrecy of identity-biometrics relation through a security game between the (malicious) $\mathcal{AS}$ and a simulator (i.e. challenger) $\mathcal{C}$. If $\mathcal{AS}$ can correctly distinguish the registered reference template $\sim$that is one of the two templates output by $\mathcal{AS}\sim$ by listening to the protocol runs, $\mathcal{AS}$ wins this game, thus breaks the scheme in the sense of identity privacy.

In identity privacy game, the malicious $\mathcal{AS}$ has to output two biometric templates describing the user U. Since the definition of this notion does not restrict $\mathcal{AS}$ on how he chooses the two biometric templates, $\mathcal{AS}$ can output a pair of templates (b_1, b_2) for U, where the distance between the two templates is either $\mathsf{dis}(b_1, b_2) < t$ or $\mathsf{dis}(b_1, b_2) > t$. Here, t is the error correction threshold of the secure sketch scheme that is used to correct the errors given a similar biometrics and a public helper data PAR. For the two cases, we prove separately that the adversary can easily compute the exact biometric template that is registered by the challenger $\mathcal{C}$ of the game using the helper data PAR of the secure sketch that is publicly available. Thus, the schemes of [4,16] and any biometric remote authentication scheme that assumes biometrics and the required secure sketch as public data are vulnerable to this attack and cannot satisfy identity privacy. Although the scheme of [2] stores the helper data PAR as encrypted, we propose a statistical attack to break identity privacy, where the adversary uses the (known) distribution of U's biometrics and outputs the two templates (b_1, b_2) for U in a special way. To our knowledge, no concrete attack has been presented against the sketch-based schemes of [2,4,16].

Thus, we observe that the security model of Bringer et al. does not consider the attacks that reveal the cleartext of the stored reference biometrics with the help of the public sketch. Besides, if the sketch is stored secretly, then identity privacy game should be modified so that there is a restriction on the templates generated by the adversary $\mathcal{AS}$ to prevent $\mathcal{AS}$ breaking the notion with statistical attacks. Thus, we describe a new notion called Weak-Identity privacy that does not allow the adversary to generate the possible templates for a particular user, instead the templates are given to him by the challenger. Under this new notion, the scheme of [2] is resistant against our statistical attacks.

Secondly, we discuss alternative solutions to guarantee the security of BRA schemes requiring public sketches. The trivial solution for the schemes [4,16] is to store the sketch PAR secretly, namely, in the tamper-proof smartcard of the user. This will result in a two-factor authentication scheme, thus, the system is not anymore a pure biometric-based authentication scheme. Besides, if these systems are implemented for biometrics that are represented as a set of features, this solution still does not cover brute-force attacks for biometrics with a small feature space. We note that current provably secure schemes are only defined for biometrics represented as a fixed length binary string such as an 2048 bits long Iris code except for the schemes of [13,1] that assume biometrics as a set of features, i.e. k-tuple of integers.

As a first solution, we describe a new BRA protocol where we combine cancelable biometrics and distributed remote authentication. Briefly, cancelable biometrics perform a distortion of the biometric image or features before matching. The variability in the distortion parameters provides the cancelable nature of the scheme. Distortion (i.e masking) is performed either using a one-way transformation or a high entropy randomness that is stored in the user's smart card to be used later for authentication in the transformed space. Our protocol is applicable for biometrics represented as a set of features and resistant against brute-force attacks if the feature space is small. Next, we define a stronger notion as 'Identity privacy for cancelable biometrics', where breaking this notion implies breaking the underlying encryption scheme in the sense of indistinguishability. The schemes of [4,16] that are vulnerable to our attack are secure in cancelable biometric setting based on this new notion.

Finally, we employ the detached biometric storage in distributed biometric authentication systems, which is not considered in current cancelable biometric systems and in their security analysis. Thus, a trusted biometric database can serve different service providers due to its distributed structure. Besides, a major difference of our model to existing schemes of Bringer et al. [3,2,4,16] is the use of bilinear pairings, which allows the $\mathcal{AS}$ to compute the final authentication decision without any decryption operation. Thus, $\mathcal{AS}$ does not need to store a secret key, whose leakage endangers the system's security drastically.

2   Preliminaries

In order to analyze the differences between existing biometric remote authentication systems, we briefly define the necessary components of the biometric remote authentication systems designed according to the model of Bringer et al.

Definition 1. *A function $\epsilon(k) : \mathbb{N} \to \mathbb{R}$ is defined as negligible if for any constant c, there exists $k_0 \in N$ with $k > k_0$ such that $\epsilon < (1/k)^c$.*

Definition 2. *A Private Information Retrieval (PIR) protocol allows a party to retrieve the i-th bit (more generally, the i-th item) from the $\mathcal{DB}$ consisting of m bits while keeping the value i private.*

2.1   Architecture of the System

The system structure for biometric-based remote authentication schemes designed according to the security model of Bringer et al. consists of four components. Here, the user U and the sensor S denote the client side and the remaining components denote the server-side of the system.

-*Human user U*, which uses his biometrics to authenticate himself to an authentication server. The user may possess a smart card for storing additional data such as error correcting information or user specific data other than biometrics if a multi-factor authentication scheme is designed.

-*Sensor client* S, which captures the raw biometric data and extracts a biometric template, and communicates with the authentication server by performing cryptographic operations such as public key encryption. We also assume a liveness link between the sensor and the server-side components, to provide confidence that the biometric data received on the server-side is from a living person.

-*Authentication server* AS, which deals with human user's authentication request by communicating with the user and organizing the entire server-side procedure. The data stored at the AS consists of a list $\mathcal{L} = \{ID_1, ..., ID_N\}$ of user identities $ID_l \in \{0,1\}^*$. The index of the user in this list will be $j \in \{1, ..., N\}$. In a successful authentication the AS will obviously learn the user's identity, which means that it should learn nothing about the biometric data being submitted.

-*Database* DB, which stores biometric information for users either in cleartext or as in encrypted form. Since the DB is aware of privileged biometric data, it should learn nothing about the user's identity, or even be able to correlate or trace authentication runs from a given (unknown) user.

A biometric authentication system consists of the two following phases:

- *Enrollment phase*: The user U registers his reference biometrics at the database DB and his personalized username ID at the authentication server AS. The user may have multiple registrations at the same AS under different usernames.
- *Verification phase*: The user U issues an authentication request to the authentication server AS through the sensor client S. AS decides based on U's biometrics with help from the database DB.

2.2   Secure Sketches

Let $\mathcal{H}$ be a metric space with distance function dis. A secure sketch scheme allows recovery of a hidden value $w \in \mathcal{H}$ from any value $w' \in \mathcal{H}$ close to this hidden value with the help of some public value PAR, which does not leak too much information about w. A $(\mathcal{H}, m, m', t)$- sketch is a pair of functions (SS,Rec):

-The sketching function SS takes $w \in \mathcal{H}$ as input and returns the public parameter PAR in $\{0,1\}^*$ such that for all random variables W over $\mathcal{H}$ with min-entropy $\mathbf{H}_\infty(W) \geq m$, the conditional min-entropy is $\tilde{\mathbf{H}}_\infty(W|SS(W)) \geq m'$.

-The Rec function takes a vector w' and PAR as input and computes w if and only if $\mathrm{dis}(b, b') \leq t$ for any PAR $= SS(w)$.

The fuzzy sketch for iris biometrics based on the code-offset construction is used in the biometric authentication schemes of [2,16]. Let C be an $(n, k, 2t+1)$ binary linear error correcting code in Hamming space. Let PAR $= c \oplus b$, where c is a random codeword in C. From the corrupted codeword $c' = \text{PAR} \oplus b' = c \oplus (b \oplus b')$, one can recover c if the hamming distance $\mathrm{dis}_\mathcal{H}$ between b and b' is $\mathrm{dis}_\mathcal{H}(b, b') < t$. An important requirement for such a scheme is that the value PAR should not reveal too much information about the biometric template b.

2.3 Cancelable Biometrics

The idea of cancelable biometrics is to transform biometric data with an irreversible transformation and to perform the matching directly on the transformed data allowing the use of existing feature extraction and matching algorithms. Formally, given two biometric data w and w', the matching score will be computed directly on transformed data by $m(f(w), f(w'))$, where m denotes the similarity measure and f be a transformation that does not degrade the matching performances too much. The three properties of f are: (1) w and $f(w)$ do not match together; (2) For two different transformations f_1 and f_2, $f_1(w)$ and $f_2(w)$ do not match together; (3) A pre-image of $f(w)$ is hard to compute.

Besides, [10,8,5] proposes another method for cancelable biometrics, where the biometric information is masked by a random number, and then, the masked information is stored in the server as a template. The random number used for masking is needed to have a certain level of entropy, and to be stored in a smart card carried by authorized user. Biometric information presented at the authentication phase is also masked by the same random number, and compared with the template (i.e. biometric information masked by the random number) [10]. This way, biometric data stored at the server is protected through this transformation and biometrics can be updated by changing the transformation function or the randomness. This system also prevents the user's traceability across different biometric databases. Example systems employing a high entropy randomness stored in a smart card for cancelable biometrics are given in [8,5,10]. Even if the (masked) templates are compromised, no biometric information will leak out. Also, in this method, no information except for the random number is stored in a smart card, which is assumed as a tamper proof smart card.

2.4 ElGamal Encryption Scheme

- Setup: An authority chooses and publishes a cyclic group $\mathbb{G}$ of prime order q together with a generator g of the group. Also, ElGamal encryption can be implemented on an elliptic curve.
- Keygen: Each user chooses the private key $x \leftarrow \mathbb{Z}_q$ and publishes the corresponding public key $y = g^x$.
- Encrypt: To encrypt a message $m \in \mathbb{G}$, one randomly selects $r \leftarrow \mathbb{Z}_q$ and computes $(u, v) = (g^r, y^r m)$. The ciphertext is $c = (u, v) \in C$.
- Decrypt: To decrypt $c = (u, v)$, one computes $m = vu^{-x}$.

ElGamal cryptosystem [7] is one-way secure based on the CDH problem, IND-CPA secure based on the DDH problem and OW-PCA secure if the GDH problem is hard. In many practical protocols $\mathbb{G}$ would be the group of multiples of a point P on an elliptic curve defined over a finite field.

The multiplicative homomorphic property is that $\mathsf{Enc}(a) \times \mathsf{Enc}(b) = \mathsf{Enc}(a \times b)$. ElGamal encryption can also be additively homomorphic if we generate the ciphertext $c = \mathsf{Enc}_{pk}(m) = (g^r, pk^r g^m)$ instead of $c = (g^r, pk^r m)$. Thus, $\mathsf{Enc}(a) \times \mathsf{Enc}(b) = \mathsf{Enc}(a + b)$.

3   Security Model

The security model of the biometric remote authentication systems designed according to the model of Bringer et al. [3,4,2,16,13,1] have the following properties. Firstly, sensor client S and authentication server AS are assumed to be independent components. In [16], this is considered to be an appropriate assumption in the remote authentication environment, where human users access AS through different S's, which are not owned by AS but have a business agreement with it. Additionally, we have the following properties.

-Liveliness Assumption: This is an indispensable assumption on S for any biometric system as it guarantees with high probability that the biometrics is coming from a live human user.
-Security link Assumption: To provide the confidentiality and integrity of sensitive information, the communication channel between U, S, AS and DB should be encrypted using standard protocols.
-Collusion Assumption: Due to the distributed system structure, we assume that U, DB and AS are malicious but they do not collude. Also, S is always honest.

3.1   Identity Privacy

The security notions for biometric remote authentication are introduced in [3] and further analyzed in [2,4,16,1]. Informally, this notion guarantees the privacy of the sensitive relationship between the user identity and its biometrics against a malicious authentication server AS even in case of multiple registrations of the same user with different personalized usernames. Briefly, it means that the authentication server or the database (or an attacker that has compromised one of them) cannot recover the biometric template of the user [3,16]. Here, l denotes the security parameter of the protocol and the symbol $\emptyset$ means that there is no explicit output (besides the state information) for the adversary.

Given an adversary A running against the biometric authentication scheme and a challenger C that simulates the registration phase of the scheme, we consider the following game between A and C.

Experiment $Exp_A(l)$
For $(i, ID_i, b_i^0, b_i^1, (ID_j, b_j)_{\{j \neq i\}}) \leftarrow A(1^l)$
$b_i^\beta \xleftarrow{\text{R}} \{b_i^0, b_i^1\}$
$b_i = b_i^\beta$
$\emptyset \leftarrow Enrollment((ID_j, b_j)_j)$
$\beta' \leftarrow A(Challenger; Verification)$
if $\beta' = \beta$ return 1 else return 0

A biometric authentication scheme satisfies the notion of Identity Privacy if

$$Adv_A(l) = Pr[Exp_A = 1 | \beta = 1] - Pr[Exp_A = 1 | \beta = 0] \quad (1)$$

is negligible. Here, the adversary A generates the authentication data for the users U_j ($j \neq i$) together with two biometric (binary) templates b_i^0, b_i^1 for an additional user U_i in the system. The challenger $\mathcal{C}$ picks at random biometrics $b_i = b_i^\beta$ of U_i and simulates the enrollment phase by registering the encryption of the biometrics of each user in the system at the $\mathcal{DB}$. After running the verification protocol polynomially many times, $\mathcal{A}$ outputs a guess for the biometrics of U_i that $\mathcal{C}$ has chosen. The intuition of this notion is that a malicious authentication server, who knows that the registered biometric template is one of the two templates that he has generated, cannot identify the random choice β of the challenger from listening to the protocol runs with probability significantly better than that of random guessing.

A second notion is defined as transaction anonymity, which means that a malicious database cannot learn anything about the personal identity of the user for any authentication request made to the authentication server [3,16]. This notion is based on the security of the PIR protocol (i.e. user privacy of the PIR) instead of the secrecy of the identity-biometrics relation.

4   Schemes Based on Secure Sketches

In [2], [4] and [16], the authors present distributed biometric remote authentication schemes requiring secure sketches. The main difference of these biometric systems is the integration of a secure sketch scheme for error correcting a biometric (binary) string such as an 2048 bits Iris code and the use of homomorphic encryption. This way, there is no need for a similarity metric (i.e. hamming distance) for the final decision, instead the system is used for equality testing. Here, each biometric string is stored at the $\mathcal{DB}$ as encrypted with the public key pk of the $\mathcal{AS}$ as opposed to the scheme of [3], where each biometrics is stored in clear.

The first scheme of [4] and the scheme of [16] are based on ElGamal encryption, where $\mathcal{AS}$ generates an ElGamal key pair (pk, sk) during the setup phase of the protocol with $pk = y = g^x$ and $sk = x$.

In the enrollment phase, the user U registers at the $\mathcal{DB}$ by sending $R = (R^1, R^2) = \mathsf{Enc}(g^b, pk) = (g^r, y^r g^b)$, namely the ElGamal encryption of its biometrics b to $\mathcal{DB}$ and the parameter PAR is publicly available for reconstruction of the same biometrics b using the secure sketch scheme. The user U also registers his pseudorandom identifier ID at the $\mathcal{AS}$. Verification phase is as follows:

- $\mathcal{S}$ sends U's identity ID to the $\mathcal{AS}$ and the error-corrected and encrypted fresh biometrics $X = (X^1, X^2) = \mathsf{Enc}(g^{b'}, pk)$ to the $\mathcal{DB}$ using the PAR for error-correction and ElGamal encryption.
- For each entry $j \in [1, N]$, $\mathcal{DB}$ selects random $r_j, r_j' \in \mathbb{Z}_q$ and computes
$$C_j = ((g^{r_j'}(X^1(R_j^1)^{-1})^{r_j},\ (y^{r_j'}(X^2(R_j^2)^{-1})^{r_j})) = (g^{r_j'}(g^r(R_j^1)^{-1})^{r_j},$$
$y^{r_j'}(y^r g^{b'}(R_j^2)^{-1})^{r_j})$, where R_j, $j \in [1; N]$ is the ElGamal encryption of each user U_j's biometrics stored in the $\mathcal{DB}$ during enrollment.
- Finally, $\mathcal{AS}$ runs an efficient PIR protocol to obtain the value C corresponding to the user U from the $\mathcal{DB}$ and decrypts it using his secret key sk. If $\mathsf{Dec}(C){=}1$, $\mathcal{AS}$ authenticates U, else rejects.

Secondly, [2] uses Goldwasser-Micali encryption and a different PIR scheme for storing biometrics as encrypted sketches, which we summarize as below.

In the enrollment phase, the user U registers at the $\mathcal{DB}$ by sending $R = (R^1, R^2) = \mathsf{Enc}(\mathsf{PAR}, pk)$ and $H(c)$, namely the encryption of its biometric sketch $\mathsf{PAR} = c \oplus b$ using Goldwasser-Micali encryption scheme and the hash of the codeword c, i.e. $H(c)$ to $\mathcal{DB}$, where the parameter PAR is not publicly available as in [4,16]. The user also registers his pseudorandom identifier ID and $H(c)$ at the $\mathcal{AS}$. For authentication, the following steps are performed.

- $\mathcal{S}$ sends the user identity ID to the $\mathcal{AS}$ and the encryption of the fresh biometrics $X = (X^1, X^2) = \mathsf{Enc}(b', pk)$ using Goldwasser-Micali encryption.
- $\mathcal{S}$ integrates the encrypted biometrics of the user into the PIR request that is sent to the $\mathcal{DB}$, which returns the encryption of $c \oplus b' \oplus b$ and the encryption of $H(c)$ to the $\mathcal{AS}$.
- Finally, $\mathcal{AS}$ decrypts the values with the help of the hardware security model that stores the secret keys of the system and obtains $c' = c \oplus b' \oplus b$ and $H(c)$. If $\mathsf{dis}(b, b') < t$, then $\mathcal{AS}$ is able to decode c' and obtains a codeword c''. Next, it checks $H(c) = H(c'')$ to accept/reject the authentication request of U.

As one can notice from the first step of the authentication phase of [4] and [2], the sensor client $\mathcal{S}$ communicates with the $\mathcal{DB}$ to send the fresh encryption of the biometrics, which could be impractical. In practice, there might be only very few organizations that can be trusted by human users to store their biometric information though they may want to use their biometrics for the authentication purpose at many authentication servers. Therefore, in [16], the authors suggest a scenario like that of Single Sign-On systems, where biometric information for all authentication servers are centrally stored and managed. Thus, human users access the authentication server through sensor clients, which are not owned by the authentication server but have a business agreement with the authentication server. Hence, the sensor does not need to communicate with the $\mathcal{DB}$ during the verification phase as in [4,2], instead $\mathcal{S}$ only communicates with the $\mathcal{AS}$. Considering this fact, [16] presents a slightly modified version of the first scheme of [4] by simplifying the randomization step of the $\mathcal{DB}$.

5   A New Attack

Considering the security model for identity privacy as described in section 3.1, we first assume that the adversary produces two biometric templates (b_i^0, b_i^1) for the target user U_i with ID_i such that $\mathsf{dis}(b_i^0, b_i^1) < t$, where t is the error correction threshold of the secure sketch scheme. We call this first attack as $Atk1_\mathcal{A}$, which successfully distinguishes the template that was registered for the challenge user ID_i using the public helper data PAR_i, which is the output of the secure sketch in order to be used to error correct the biometrics.

For the attack $Atk1_\mathcal{A}$, the adversary can easily distinguish which template was chosen by the challenger to be registered for U_i by looking at the output of the decoding function of the secure sketch. If he correctly guessed the template

Attack $Atk1_\mathcal{A}$	Attack $Atk2_\mathcal{A}$
For $(i, ID_i, b_i^0, b_i^1, (ID_j, b_j)_{\{j \neq i\}}) \leftarrow \mathcal{A}(1^l)$.	For $(i, ID_i, b_i^0, b_i^1, (ID_j, b_j)_{\{j \neq i\}}) \leftarrow \mathcal{A}(1^l)$
$b_i^\beta \xleftarrow{\text{R}} \{b_i^0, b_i^1\}$	$b_i^\beta \xleftarrow{\text{R}} \{b_i^0, b_i^1\}$
$b_i = b_i^\beta$	$b_i = b_i^\beta$
$\emptyset \leftarrow Enrollment((ID_j, b_j)_j)$	$\emptyset \leftarrow Enrollment((ID_j, b_j)_j)$
Use public data of ID_i: $\mathsf{PAR}_i = c \oplus b_i^\beta$	Use public data of ID_i: $\mathsf{PAR}_i = c \oplus b_i^\beta$
$\quad$ Compute $b_i^1 \oplus \mathsf{PAR}_i = c'$	$\quad$ Compute $b_i^1 \oplus \mathsf{PAR}_i = c'$
$\quad$ If $\mathsf{Decode}(c') = c'$	$\quad$ If $\mathsf{Decode}(c') = \perp$
$\quad\quad$ Return $\beta = 1$	$\quad\quad$ Return $\beta = 0$
$\quad$ Else if $\mathsf{Decode}(c') = b_i^0 \oplus \mathsf{PAR}_i$	$\quad$ Else If $\mathsf{Decode}(c') = b_i^1 \oplus \mathsf{PAR}_i$
$\quad\quad$ Return $\beta = 0$	$\quad\quad$ Return $\beta = 1$

b_i^1, then the computation of $b_i^1 \oplus \mathsf{PAR}_i$ will result in a correct codeword, which does not need to be error corrected. Otherwise, he returns $\beta = 0$.

The second case we consider is that the adversary produces two biometric templates (b_i^0, b_i^1) for the target user ID_i with $\mathsf{dis}(b_i^0, b_i^1) > t$, which we call as $Atk2_\mathcal{A}$. We note that this pair of templates still describe the same user U_i, since the variation of the biometrics can be larger then the error-correction capacity of the secure sketch. Our attack successfully distinguishes the template that was registered for the challenge user ID_i using the public helper data PAR_i. The difference to the previous attack is that, if b_i^1 is not the template that was registered by the challenger $\mathcal{C}$, then, since the distance between the two templates (b_i^0, b_i^1) is above the error-correction capacity, the decoding procedure will not work. Thus, the registered template is b_i^0, and $\mathcal{A}$ returns $\beta = 0$.

The reason that the public data PAR of the secure sketch scheme helps the adversary in the identity privacy game is due to the fact that for secure sketch construction the standard notions of security do not fit. The statement "PAR leaks no information about the biometric template b" is normally formalized by requiring that b and PAR be almost statistically independent. Even the analogue requirement for computationally bounded adversaries, semantic security, is impossible here: if Eve knows that b is one of two similar strings (b_1, b_2), then she can compute b from PAR and b_1. The difficulty, then, is that the standard definitions of security require secrecy even when Eve knows a lot about b, which is in contrast to the security of sketches, where Eve is sufficiently uncertain about b, since biometrics is assumed as secret data. In [6], it is shown that secure sketches can only guarantee entropic security, which assumes that the adversary is sufficiently uncertain about the user's biometrics, which implies that secure sketches can never guarantee the notion of indistinguishability for computationally bounded adversaries. Thus, the schemes of [4,16] and any biometric remote authentication scheme that assumes biometrics and the required secure sketch as public data are vulnerable to this attack and cannot satisfy identity privacy.

As opposed to the schemes of [4,16], the scheme of [2] stores the sketch as encrypted in the $\mathcal{DB}$. Thus, a malicious $\mathcal{AS}$ has only access to different corrupted codewords $c_{ik}' = \mathsf{PAR}_i \oplus b_{ik}'$, where b_{ik}' is the fresh biometrics of the user U_i at the kth authentication run. However, this data can also help the malicious $\mathcal{AS}$

when playing the identity privacy game, since there is no restriction on the two
templates the adversary generates for the challenge user U_i. Assume that the
adversary knows that biometrics of U_i behave according to some distribution,
and has determined the mean of this distribution after taking enough samples;
a well-motivated adversary can take more measurements, and thus determine
the mean more accurately. Let the adversary set one of the two templates he
generates in the game as equal to the mean value of this distribution, i.e. $b_i^0 = \mu$
and the second template he has to output equal to the value that is the maximum
(allowable) distance to the mean, i.e. $b_i^1 = \mu + \delta$, where 2δ denotes the variability
of the biometrics of U_i with identity ID_i, namely the range of U_i's biometrics.
Enough number of samples $\{b_{ir}^S\}_{1<r<M}$ of U_i's biometric data b_i allows the
adversary to compute this range information. Since the malicious $\mathcal{AS}$ performs
the decoding of the corrupted codeword c_i' for user U_i and obtains the correct
codeword c_i that was used in $\mathsf{PAR}_i = c_i \oplus b_i^\beta$, $\mathcal{AS}$ has access to c_{ik}''s for $1 < k < M$
obtained at the kth authentication run of U_i and the unique codeword c_i after
decoding each corrupted codeword c_{ik}'. The attack is denoted by $Atk3_{\mathcal{A}}^*$.

Attack $Atk3_{\mathcal{A}}^*$

For $(i, ID_i, b_i^0, b_i^1, (ID_j, b_j)_{\{j \neq i\}}) \leftarrow \mathcal{A}(1^l)$ s.t. $b_i^0 = \mu$ and $b_i^1 = \mu + \delta$
$b_i^\beta \xleftarrow{R} \{b_i^0, b_i^1\}$
$b_i = b_i^\beta$
$\emptyset \leftarrow Enrollment((ID_j, b_j)_j)$
At the kth authentication run of ID_i ,where $1 < k < M$
$\quad$ Obtain the data of ID_i, $\mathsf{PAR}_i \oplus b_{ik}' = c_i \oplus b_i^\beta \oplus b_{ik}' = c_{ik}'$
$\quad$ If $\mathsf{Decode}(c_{ik}') = c_i$, store $e_{ik} = c_{ik}' \oplus c_i$.
Compute $a = Mean(HW(e_{ik}))$, $b = Mean(HW(b_{ir}^S \oplus b_i^0))$ and $c = Mean(HW(b_{ir}^S \oplus b_i^1))$
If $a \approx b$ return $\beta = 0$, else if $a \approx c$ return $\beta = 1$

The intuition of this attack is that by setting one of the templates to the mean
of the distribution of U_i's biometrics, and the other template to the maximum
value of its range, listening to enough protocol runs of U_i allows the adversary to
distinguish which template was registered using a statistical attack on the errors.
Since the hamming weight HW of the error $e_{ik} = b_i^\beta \oplus b_{ik}'$ when $b_i^\beta = b_i^0$ will
be significantly less than the hamming weight of the error when $b_i^\beta = b_i^1$, we can
apply various statistical analysis methods by comparing the errors obtained from
the authentication runs of U_i to the simulated errors based on the distribution
of the U_i's biometrics and determine the value of β.

$\quad$ An alternative way to analyze the error and determine the value of β could be
described by the following algorithm. Similar to the attack $Atk3_{\mathcal{A}}^*$, in this attack
we expect that the majority of the fresh templates presented to the sensor to
be concentrated around the mean template b_i^0 of user U_i. Thus, computing an
intermediate value b_i^2 can help us to determine the value of β. The exact value of
b_i^2 could be set based on the distribution of the biometrics and other experiments.

$\quad$ Thus, the condition on the two templates generated by $\mathcal{A}$ must be specified
in a concrete way to avoid such statistical attacks. However, with this current

---

Attack $Atk3_{\mathcal{A}}^{**}$

For $(i, ID_i, b_i^0, b_i^1, (ID_j, b_j)_{\{j \neq i\}}) \leftarrow \mathcal{A}(1^l)$ s.t. $b_i^0 = \mu$ and $b_i^1 = \mu + \delta$

$b_i^{\beta} \xleftarrow{\text{R}} \{b_i^0, b_i^1\}$

$b_i = b_i^{\beta}$

$\emptyset \leftarrow Enrollment((ID_j, b_j)_j)$

Compute $b_i^2 \approx \mu + \delta/2$

At the kth authentication run of ID_i ,where $1 < k < M$

      Obtain the data of ID_i, $\mathsf{PAR}_i \oplus b_{ik}' = c_i \oplus b_i^{\beta} \oplus b_{ik}' = c_{ik}'$

      If $\mathsf{Decode}(c_{ik}') = c_i$, store $e_{ik} = c_{ik}' \oplus c_i$

Compute $a = Mean(HW(e_{ik}))$, $b = (HW(b_i^2 \oplus b_i^0))$

If $a < b$ return $\beta = 0$, else return $\beta = 1$

---

definition of identity privacy, this is not possible since the generation of the two templates is controlled by the adversary. Thus, one should modify the identity privacy notion to avoid statistical attacks. One possible solution is adapting a weaker security notion of public key encryption to our setting. This weaker notion is called as Weak-Indistinguishability where the adversary cannot select challenge plaintexts (m_0, m_1), instead the challenger computes (m_0, m_1) and returns them to the adversary [17]. The same idea could be applied to identity privacy notion, where the two possible templates for U_i are computed by the challenger using the biometric template space BtSp associated to the user U_i. Then, one of the two templates presented by the challenger to the adversary is registered to the database. If the two templates $\{b_i^0, b_i^1\}$ are chosen close to each other, then we may refer to the notion of *Indistinguishability of Errors*, which prevents an insider adversary to obtain some information about the reference template of U_i based on the errors he collects.

Thus, Weak-Identity Privacy is defined as follows:

    Experiment $Exp_{\mathcal{A}}(l)$

    For $(i, ID_i, (ID_j, b_j)_{\{j \neq i\}}) \leftarrow \mathcal{A}(1^l)$

    $\{b_i^0, b_i^1\} \leftarrow \mathsf{BtSp}(U_i)$

    $b_i^{\beta} \xleftarrow{\text{R}} \{b_i^0, b_i^1\}$

    $b_i = b_i^{\beta}$

    $\emptyset \leftarrow Enrollment((ID_j, b_j)_j)$

    $\beta' \leftarrow \mathcal{A}(Challenger; Verification)$

    if $\beta' = \beta$ return 1 else return 0

A biometric authentication scheme satisfies Weak-Identity Privacy if equation (1) is negligible. Under this weaker notion, [2] is secure against statistical attacks. The security analysis based on this weaker notion is identical to the analysis presented in [2].

6   Preventing the Attacks

As we show in the previous section, for each different scheme, we have a different attack based on the properties/architecture of the system. For statistical attacks against schemes with encrypted sketches, we suggest to evaluate the security of the scheme based on our new notion called Weak-Identity privacy. Other sketch-based schemes used for equality testing can be made resistant against our attacks through the following solutions. The first solution is to store the sketch PAR secretly for the schemes of [4,16], for instance in the tamper-proof smartcard of the user. This will result in a multi-factor authentication scheme, thus, the system is not anymore a pure biometric based authentication scheme. Still, this solution does not cover a brute-force attack if these systems are employed for biometrics that can be represented as a set of features with a small feature space. Since encryption of each feature is performed individually, an insider adversary can try different feature sets to obtain some information on the stored template of the user from the authentication result. For a large feature space, he can mount an attack similar to the statistical attack of the previous section. Specifically, if the biometrics is represented as an ordered set of features as in face biometrics, the adversary can generate the two templates in such a way that the first template includes some particularly chosen features, whereas the second template does not. By observing the matching/non-matching of these particular features, the malicious server can distinguish which template is registered by the challenger. It is cancelable biometrics that can prevent this attack, if the stored template is somehow distorted, where the distortion parameters are unknown to the insider adversary. Specifically, if we define identity privacy in a different setting, then biometric remote authentication schemes assuming biometrics as public data can achieve Identity privacy if they are combined with cancelable biometrics. The cancelable biometrics system we use requires a high entropy randomness that is stored in the user's smart card to be used later for authentication in the transformed space. This way, biometric data stored at the server is protected through this transformation and biometrics can be updated by changing the transformation function or the randomness. This system also prevents the user's traceability across different biometric databases, even if the (distorted) biometric templates are stored in clear. Example systems employing a high entropy randomness stored in a smart card for cancelable biometrics are given in [8,5,10].

Our proposed design is a multi-factor solution that requires each user to possess a smartcard to store some high entropy randomness that will be hashed with the biometrics before the encryption (and storage in the $\mathcal{DB}$). So the same randomness is used during verification by hashing it with the fresh biometrics and after that, the encryption of the result is transmitted to the server side for matching. If a secure sketch is applied, then first biometrics are corrected with the help of PAR, then the randomness is hashed with the corrected biometrics and encryption is performed afterwards. Also, our proposal allows for the integration of a secure sketch without endangering the security of the scheme, since the value PAR is only stored in the tamper-proof smart card of the user. This way, the secrecy of the relationship between the identity and the stored (distorted) biometrics of the user is maintained based on the privacy of the randomness used in the distortion of the biometrics, which is stored in the tamper-proof smartcard of the user. This solution guarantees the two security notions even if we employ a secure sketch and biometrics with small feature space. Finally, we use a cryptographic hash function for the computation of the distorted biometrics, thus, statistical attacks are not possible as even one bit of change of the input of the hash function leads to a complete different hash value.

6.1   A New Protocol

In this section, we describe an example scheme that achieves weak-identity privacy for biometrics represented as an ordered set of features and (standard) identity privacy for biometrics represented as a binary string. The new scheme is defined in cancelable biometrics setting, where we assume biometrics as public data but the randomness used in the distortion of the biometric features is kept as secret. We assume biometrics as an ordered set of features such as face, iris, voice, handwritten signatures [9], however, the system also works for biometrics defined as a binary string such as an 2048-bit Iris code. The matching of the fresh biometrics and the stored template is performed as in [13] with the help of bilinear pairings, where the authentication server $\mathcal{AS}$ does not need a secret key for its operations. This is an important difference to the existing schemes [4,16,2], which store the biometrics as encrypted with the public key of the $\mathcal{AS}$. Thus, if the secret key of the $\mathcal{AS}$ is leaked, then each user in the system has to re-register in the best case scenario, i.e. before the compromise of the $\mathcal{DB}$, whereas the compromise of the $\mathcal{AS}$ does not affect the security of our system as $\mathcal{AS}$ does not need its secret key for its computations due to the use of bilinear pairings, hence, does not store any secret key. Finally, we assume the general representation of biometrics, where a biometric template B_e consists of k features, i.e. $B_e = \{w_i\}_{1 \leq i \leq k}$. A possible attack for this type of biometrics occurs when the feature space is small. A malicious $\mathcal{AS}$ may compare the encryption of different features to the authentication data and using pairings, he decides whether he correctly guessed the feature. Since we concatenate a different random string to each feature, based on the secrecy of these distortion values applied to each feature, the adversary cannot launch this brute-force attack. In our scheme, we use the same architecture of [16] as summarized in section 4, which does not require a detached verification unit $\mathcal{VU}$ and the sensor does not communicate with the biometric database as in many real-life applications.

Enrollment Phase

- $\mathcal{S}$ generates his key pair $(pk_\mathcal{S}, sk_\mathcal{S})$ and publishes the two keys. In addition, $\mathcal{AS}$ is given an elliptic curve ElGamal public key $pk_{\mathcal{AS}} = g^y$ without the associated secret key, for instance, a trusted third party can generate this public key. Finally, a cryptographic hash function $H : \{0,1\}^* \to \mathbb{G}$ and a bilinear pairing $\hat{e} : \mathbb{G} \times \mathbb{G} \to \mathbb{F}$ are required.
- The user U generates his personalized username ID and registers it at the $\mathcal{AS}$, computes his distorted biometrics by picking at random $r_i \in \mathbb{Z}_q$ for $i \in [1; k]$ to compute $H(w_i, r_i)$ and registers his distorted biometric features as

$R_i = (R_i^1, R_i^2) = (g^{r_i}, g^{y r_i} H(w_i, r_i))$ for $i \in [1; k]$ at the $\mathcal{DB}$. The distortion numbers $\{r_1, ..., r_k\}$ are stored at the tamper-proof smartcard of U.

Remark 1. To further increase the accuracy, a secure sketch for ordered biometrics can be used, whose public parameter PAR is only stored in the tamperproof smartcard of the user together with the distortion numbers, thus PAR is not publicly available as in the schemes of [4,16,2]. This is required to guarantee the identity privacy notion if a secure sketch is employed.

Verification Phase

- $\mathcal{S}$ sends the user U's identity ID and the encrypted fresh biometrics for $i \in [1; k]$, $X_i = (X_i^1, X_i^2) = \mathsf{Enc}(H(w_i', r_i), pk_{\mathcal{AS}}) = (g^{x_i}, g^{y x_i} H(w_i', r_i))$ to the $\mathcal{AS}$ using ElGamal encryption and the distortion values r_i's stored in the smartcard. $\mathcal{S}$ sends his signature σ on $X = \{X_i : i \in [1; k]\}$ to $\mathcal{AS}$.
- $\mathcal{AS}$ verifies the signature of $\mathcal{S}$ and communicates with the $\mathcal{DB}$.
- $\mathcal{DB}$ computes for each entry $j \in [1, N]$ the rerandomization of R_{ji},where R_{ji} is the encryption of the ith feature of the jth user's distorted biometrics. For instance, the rerandomization for U's biometric template is computed as $C_i = (C_i^1, C_i^2) = (g^{\beta_i} R_i^1, g^{y \beta_i} R_i^2) = (g^{\beta_i + r_i}, g^{y \beta_i + y r_i} H(w_i, r_i))$ for $i \in [1; k]$.
- $\mathcal{AS}$ first retrieves the index for ID and runs an efficient PIR protocol to obtain the user U's rerandomized biometrics denoted as C_i for each feature of U. Next, $\mathcal{AS}$ selects a random $s_i \in \mathbb{Z}_q$ and computes for each biometric feature of U, $Z_i = (X_i \oslash C_i)^{s_i}$, where, for any integer x and two ElGamal ciphertexts (c_1, c_2) and (c_3, c_4), the operator $\oslash$ is defined as follows: $((c_1, c_2) \oslash (c_3, c_4))^x = ((\frac{c_1}{c_3})^x, (\frac{c_2}{c_4})^x)$. Thus, for the matching features, we obtain $Z_i = (Z_i^1, Z_i^2) = ((g^{x_i} \cdot (g^{\beta_i + r_i})^{-1})^{s_i}, (g^{y x_i} \cdot (g^{y \beta_i + y r_i})^{-1})^{s_i})$.
  Finally, $\mathcal{AS}$ finds the total number of matched features using bilinear pairings. Here, $\mathcal{AS}$ obtains $\hat{e}(pk_{\mathcal{AS}}, Z_i^1) = \hat{e}(g, Z_i^2)$ for the matching features by computing in total $2k$ bilinear pairings. If the number of Z_i's satisfying this equation is above the threshold, $\mathcal{AS}$ authenticates U, else rejects.

Lemma 1. *The proposed scheme achieves identity privacy against the $\mathcal{AS}$, based on the Gap DH problem and the tamper-proofness of the user smartcard.*

Lemma 2. *The proposed scheme achieves transaction anonymity against a malicious $\mathcal{DB}$, based on the security (user privacy) of the PIR protocol.*

Due to the page limitations, the proofs will be presented in the full version of this paper.

6.2 Identity Privacy for Cancelable Biometrics: A New Notion

Our first solution presented in the previous section guarantees identity privacy due to the one-wayness property of the cancelable biometrics and the secrecy of the helper data PAR. Thus, in order to distinguish one of the biometric templates, the adversary playing the identity privacy game as described in [3] has to break the one-wayness of the cancelable biometrics, where one-wayness is a weaker security notion than indistinguishability. To overcome this limitation, we define the following notion, where breaking this new notion implies breaking the underlying encryption scheme in the sense of indistinguishability, which is a stronger security notion.

Given an adversary $\mathcal{A}$ running against the biometric authentication scheme and a challenger $\mathcal{C}$ that simulates the registration phase of the scheme, we consider the following game between $\mathcal{A}$ and $\mathcal{C}$.

Experiment $Exp_A(l)$
For $((ID_j, b_j, r_j, PAR_j)_{\{j \neq e\}}) \leftarrow \mathcal{A}(1^l)$
$(e \neq j, ID_e, b_e, r_e^0, r_e^1, PAR_e) \leftarrow \mathcal{A}(1^l)$
$r_e^\beta \xleftarrow{\text{R}} \{r_e^0, r_e^1\}$
$r_e \leftarrow r_e^\beta$
$\emptyset \leftarrow Enrollment^*(Distortion(b_j, r_j)_j)$
$\beta' \leftarrow \mathcal{A}(Challenger; Verification)$
if $\beta' = \beta$ return 1 else return 0

A biometric authentication scheme satisfies the notion of "Identity Privacy for Cancelable Biometrics" if equation (1) is negligible. Here, the adversary $\mathcal{A}$ generates the authentication data for $N - 1$ users together with the reference biometrics b_j, the secure sketch PAR, and two different distortion parameters for an additional user U_e. $\mathcal{C}$ picks at random a distorion parameter $r_e = r_e^\beta$. Next, the chosen distortion parameter is applied to the reference biometric template and the enrollment phase is completed. The difference of our notion to the Bringer et al.'s identity privacy notion [3,2,16] is that the $\mathcal{C}$ does not need to choose randomly one of the two similar biometrics generated by the adversary $\mathcal{A}$, since with the public value PAR, the error-corrected template can be easily computed and a unique reference template b_e is obtained. Thus, $\mathcal{C}$ only needs to apply the random distortion r_j^β to this reference template b_j and then register the encryption of this distorted biometrics in the $Enrollment^*$ phase. This application could be performed as in the protocol described in section 6.1, by simply picking at random $r_e^1, r_e^2 \in \mathbb{Z}_q$ as input to the hash function. After running the verification protocol, $\mathcal{A}$ outputs a guess for the distortion parameter that $\mathcal{C}$ has chosen. One can easily show that the schemes of [4,16] achieve identity privacy for cancelable biometrics against a malicious $\mathcal{AS}$, based on the semantic security of the ElGamal encryption although the sketch PAR is public. The proof is identical to the proofs presented in [4,16] for biometrics represented as a fixed length binary string. If biometrics is represented as a set of features, a set of randomly picked distortion parameters is applied instead of a single parameter.

7   Comparison

In this section, we present an overview of the protocols designed according to the model of Bringer et al. We compare the schemes based on the security notions they achieve and whether the schemes are still secure even if the secret key of the verification unit in [3,1] or the secret key of the authentication server in [16,4] is leaked, where this key is required for the matching stage and the final decision. In our scheme the authentication server does not know his secret key and uses bilinear pairings for the matching in the encrypted domain, thus, our scheme is resistant against this attack. $^+$ denotes the first biometric scheme.

Table 1. Comparison of distributed biometric remote authentication schemes

Scheme	Identity Privacy	Transaction Anonymity	Security against Key Compromise	Current Attacks
Sys. 1 [3]	No	No	No	Attack of [15]
Sys. 2 [1]	Yes	Yes	No	Attack of [15]
Sys.$^+$3 [4]	No	Yes	No	$Atk1_A, Atk2_A$
Sys. 4 [2]	No	Yes	No	$Atk3^*_A, Atk3^{**}_A$
Sys. 5 [16]	No	Yes	No	$Atk1_A, Atk2_A$
New Sys.	Yes	Yes	Yes	-

8   Conclusion

In this paper, we present three new attacks that reveal the reference biometric template of the user to the malicious server. The first type of attack applies to any system that assumes biometrics and the sketch as public data since a secure sketch can only guarantee a weak level of security. However, if the sketch is stored secretly, i.e. in a tamper-proof smartcard, then the systems are secure for biometrics represented as a fixed length binary string. The second type of attack is a statistical attack, which works even if the sketch is stored as encrypted at the database. Consequently, the security of pure biometric remote authentication schemes is questionable if they are evaluated in the framework of a realistic and strong security model. Thus, we suggest that BRA systems should be implemented as a two-factor authentication system, which employs a tamper-proof smartcard for storing additional data as the second factor. Besides, the current systems are not suitable for other biometric traits that are represented as an ordered/unordered feature set, whereas our new protocol for cancelable biometric setting is both secure against the three types of attacks and resistant for attacks as a result of different representations of biometrics. Finally, if identity privacy is redefined in cancelable biometric setting, the schemes vulnerable to the first type of attack are secure for public sketches.

Acknowledgement. This work was supported in part by the B-IT Research School within the NRW (North Rhine-Westphalia) Research Schools of Excellence. The author is grateful to her supervisor Prof. Dr. Joachim von zur Gathen for his valuable support, encouragement and guidance. Also, the author is grateful to Prof. Michael Huth and the reviewers of STM for their valuable comments.

References

1. Barbosa, M., Brouard, T., Cauchie, S., de Sousa, S.M.: Secure Biometric Authentication with Improved Accuracy. In: Mu, Y., Susilo, W., Seberry, J. (eds.) ACISP 2008. LNCS, vol. 5107, pp. 21–36. Springer, Heidelberg (2008)

2. Bringer, J., Chabanne, H.: An Authentication Protocol with Encrypted Biometric Data. In: Vaudenay, S. (ed.) AFRICACRYPT 2008. LNCS, vol. 5023, pp. 109–124. Springer, Heidelberg (2008)
3. Bringer, J., Chabanne, H., Izabachène, M., Pointcheval, D., Tang, Q., Zimmer, S.: An Application of the Goldwasser-micali Cryptosystem to Biometric Authentication. In: Pieprzyk, J., Ghodosi, H., Dawson, E. (eds.) ACISP 2007. LNCS, vol. 4586, pp. 96–106. Springer, Heidelberg (2007)
4. Bringer, J., Chabanne, H., Pointcheval, D., Tang, Q.: Extended Private Information Retrieval and its Application in Biometrics Authentications. In: Bao, F., Ling, S., Okamoto, T., Wang, H., Xing, C. (eds.) CANS 2007. LNCS, vol. 4856, pp. 175–193. Springer, Heidelberg (2007)
5. Cambier, J., von Seelen, U.C., Moore, R., Scott, I., Braithwaite, M., Daugman, J.: Application specific biometric templates. In: IEEE Workshop on Automatic Identification Advanced Technologies, pp. 167–171. IEEE (2002)
6. Dodis, Y., Smith, A.: Correcting errors without leaking partial information. In: STOC 2005, pp. 654–663. ACM (2005)
7. El Gamal, T.: A Public Key Cryptosystem and a Signature Scheme Based on Discrete Logarithms. In: Blakely, G.R., Chaum, D. (eds.) CRYPTO 1984. LNCS, vol. 196, pp. 10–18. Springer, Heidelberg (1985)
8. Hirata, S., Takahashi, K.: Cancelable Biometrics with Perfect Secrecy for Correlation-Based Matching. In: Tistarelli, M., Nixon, M.S. (eds.) ICB 2009. LNCS, vol. 5558, pp. 868–878. Springer, Heidelberg (2009)
9. Li, Q., Sutcu, Y., Memon, N.D.: Secure Sketch for Biometric Templates. In: Lai, X., Chen, K. (eds.) ASIACRYPT 2006. LNCS, vol. 4284, pp. 99–113. Springer, Heidelberg (2006)
10. Sakashita, T., Shibata, Y., Yamamoto, T., Takahashi, K., Ogata, W., Kikuchi, H., Nishigaki, M.: A Proposal of Efficient Remote Biometric Authentication Protocol. In: Takagi, T., Mambo, M. (eds.) IWSEC 2009. LNCS, vol. 5824, pp. 212–227. Springer, Heidelberg (2009)
11. Sarier, N.D.: A New Approach for Biometric Template Storage and Remote Authentication. In: Tistarelli, M., Nixon, M.S. (eds.) ICB 2009. LNCS, vol. 5558, pp. 909–918. Springer, Heidelberg (2009)
12. Sarier, N.D.: A survey of distributed biometric authentication systems. In: BIOSIG 2009. LNI, vol. 155, pp. 43–55. GI (2009)
13. Sarier, N.D.: Improving the accuracy and storage cost in biometric remote authentication schemes. J. Network and Computer Applications 33(3), 268–274 (2010)
14. Sarier, N.D.: Practical Multi-factor Biometric Remote Authentication. In: BTAS 2010, pp. 1–6. IEEE (2010)
15. Simoens, K., Bringer, J., Chabanne, H., Seys, S.: Analysis of biometric authentication protocols in the blackbox model. CoRR, abs/1101.2569 (2011)
16. Tang, Q., Bringer, J., Chabanne, H., Pointcheval, D.: A Formal Study of the Privacy Concerns in Biometric-Based Remote Authentication Schemes. In: Chen, L., Mu, Y., Susilo, W. (eds.) ISPEC 2008. LNCS, vol. 4991, pp. 56–70. Springer, Heidelberg (2008)
17. Yang, G., Tan, C.H., Huang, Q., Wong, D.S.: Probabilistic Public Key Encryption with Equality Test. In: Pieprzyk, J. (ed.) CT-RSA 2010. LNCS, vol. 5985, pp. 119–131. Springer, Heidelberg (2010)

Hiding the Policy in Cryptographic Access Control

Sascha Müller and Stefan Katzenbeisser

Technische Universität Darmstadt &
Center for Advanced Security Research Darmstadt (CASED)
Security Engineering Group
{mueller,katzenbeisser}@seceng.informatik.tu-darmstadt.de

Abstract. Recently, cryptographic access control has received a lot of attention, mainly due to the availability of efficient *Attribute-Based Encryption (ABE)* schemes. ABE allows to get rid of a trusted reference monitor by enforcing access rules in a cryptographic way. However, ABE has a privacy problem: The access policies are sent in clear along with the ciphertexts. Further generalizing the idea of policy-hiding in cryptographic access control, we introduce *policy anonymity* where – similar to the well-understood concept of k-anonymity – the attacker can only see a large set of possible policies that might have been used to encrypt, but is not able to identify the one that was actually used. We show that using a concept from graph theory we can extend a known ABE construction to achieve the desired privacy property.

Keywords: Access control, privacy, tree majors, abe, anonymity, hidden policies.

1 Introduction

In the last years, new primitives like Attribute-Based Encryption (ABE) and Predicate Encryption (PE) that enable cryptographic access control have been developed in the cryptographic community. Using these ideas, access controls systems can now be constructed that do not rely on a trusted reference monitor to enforce access rules. Instead, the information is encrypted in a way that allows decryption only by parties that are eligible to decrypt them. Specifically, in Ciphertext-Policy Attribute-Based Encryption (CP-ABE), every user receives a private key that corresponds to an individual set of attributes, each attribute attesting a certain property that the user has. Each ciphertext is encrypted with a policy over these attributes in the form of a Boolean formula, and everyone whose attributes satisfy that policy can decrypt the ciphertext. The encrypted data cannot be decrypted and thus is invisible to all other users.

This approach allows to enforce access rules in many practical scenarios. For example, in the popular *Role-based Access Control (RBAC)* approach, users are assigned to *roles* and each user's roles determine which rights he has. CP-ABE can be used to efficiently enforce access rights in an RBAC scenario: For each role there is an attribute, and for each role a user possesses, he receives the corresponding attribute. Access rights are described as logical formulas over the universe of attributes. For example, if data is encrypted with a policy `RoleA AND (RoleB OR RoleC)`, every user who is active in the role `RoleA` and either `RoleB` or `RoleC` can decrypt the data.

C. Meadows and C. Fernández-Gago (Eds.): STM 2011, LNCS 7170, pp. 90–105, 2012.

As another example, consider a company that hosts DRM protected media files. Users can purchase licenses from various content providers that issue usage licenses containing keys required to decrypt the protected files. Let us assume that two such content providers are `contprov1` and `contprov2`. A usage license could be expressed as a Boolean formula over attributes. For example, the policy could state that the protected file should only be decrypted by someone who has purchased licenses from at least one of the given content providers and is authenticated as an adult. Policy P_2 in Figure 2 is an example of such a DRM policy. It is also possible to automatically extract such policies from policies written in the Open Digital Rights Language (ODRL) [10].

Note that in both examples, rules are enforced automatically by the cryptographic construction. Also, the access rules may be very complex allowing for elaborate, fine-grained access control if so desired by the scenario. Numerous CP-ABE schemes have been proposed with varying features that support different types of policy languages.

While CP-ABE today is well-developed and can be considered practical, there are still some desirable features missing, one of which we are concerned with in this work: In most CP-ABE constructions, the policy is sent along with the ciphertext. This appears sensible as the decryptor needs to know which of his attributes are needed to access the data. However, the policy itself might be considered worth to protect as it might reveal clues to the content of the encrypted data. For example, consider a patient report in a hospital setting that is encrypted with a policy that allows encryption only by parties with the role *neurologist* or *gerontologist*. This policy alone reveals some information about the content, i.e., the patient seems to be advanced in years and might have a neurological condition. Thus, policy privacy can be an essential feature.

1.1 Towards Policy Privacy

Currently, there are two approaches to realize policy privacy. The first and most well-understood approach is predicate encryption (PE), which can be seen as a generalization of ABE in which policies are hidden. Unfortunately, while some PE constructions today are very expressive, they are still quite limited: No particular PE instance is able to support every possible Boolean formula and PE policies are often formulated in unintuitive or inefficient ways. (We will elaborate on this important aspect later on.) This is contrary to our goal of high expressiveness and intuitive policies.

The second approach, which we are concerned with here, is to modify common CP-ABE constructions to somehow hide the policy while still allow an eligible user to decrypt. We first examine that a policy can never been *completely* hidden in a ciphertext, as it has to be stored in a finite space and a known format, so there is always a limited, finite set of possible policies that can be encoded in a particular ciphertext. This motivates to introduce the notion of *policy anonymity*, which is similar to the established notion of anonymity sets [18] and k-anonymity [5]: Given a number of candidates for a policy, the anonymity set, an attacker cannot determine which actual policy was used for the encryption.

Extending a CP-ABE construction to have a hiding feature has been attempted by Nishide et al. [13] and Yu et al. [23], both of which extend the CP-ABE scheme of [4], where the policy consists of a single AND-gate. Simply speaking, in these extensions the policy is still an AND-gate, but the decryptor does not now the particular configuration and has to apply all his attribute keys to decrypt. In both cases the anonymity set consists of all policies that consists of a single AND-gate over a subset of all attributes of the system.

In this paper we show that one of Nishide's CP-ABE constructions [13] can be modified in order to support the encryption with every Boolean formula by combining several AND-gates in a specific way and using a novel idea from graph theory. This in turn allows the encryptor to choose a particular anonymity set which contains – among with the original policy – many others.

The idea of the construction is as follows: Given a policy, represented by a syntax tree with ∧ and ∨-gates, we construct a *major* of this tree, i.e., a supertree that is built by expanding nodes of the original tree into new subtrees. Such a major can be used to express many different policies by assigning different expressions to its leaves. The set of all such policies makes up the anonymity set. The decryptor knows only that the used policy is among all policies that can be encoded by the supertree. The leaves of this major are encryptions of blinded partial secrets that represent ∧-gates. As these ∧-gates are hidden, an adversary does not know which of the possible policies of the anonymity set is used in the encryption, but by our construction he is still able to decrypt the message if he fulfills the hidden policy. He will determine which of the leaves he is able to satisfy, obtain some of the encoded partial secrets, combine them according to the tree structure using his private key, and unblind the resulting combination to retrieve the secret. Our application of Nishide's construction takes collusion attacks into account, so no group of users (who fulfill different parts of a policy) can decrypt the policy unless one member of the group fulfills the complete policy.

Example. To give an intuition of the hiding property of our system, examine Figure 1, which represents the structure of a policy anonymity set which is sent along with a ciphertext. The form of this tree is known to everyone, but the leaves are hidden using the ideas of Nishide's construction. Each leaf hides an ∧-gate with an unknown con-

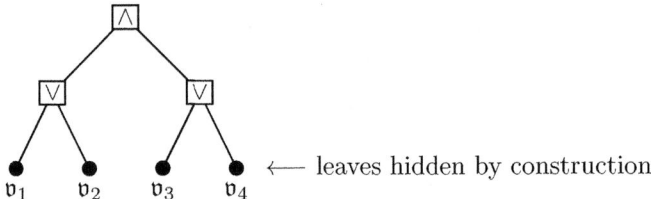

$\longleftarrow$ leaves hidden by construction

Fig. 1. Sample obfuscated policy

figuration. Each ∧-gate could also represent the constant values ⊥ (false) or ⊤ (true). Figure 2 shows some policies that might be encoded with this tree. Consider, for example, policy P_4. In our construction, each of $x_1, \ldots, x_{10}$ may represent an expression of the form $A = x$ for an attribute A and an attribute value x. Here, the leaf $\mathfrak{v}_1$ could encode the expression $\mathfrak{v}_1 \equiv x_1 \wedge x_2 \wedge x_3$, $\mathfrak{v}_2$ could encode $\mathfrak{v}_2 \equiv x_4$, $\mathfrak{v}_3 \equiv x_5 \wedge x_6$, and $\mathfrak{v}_4 \equiv x_7 \wedge x_8 \wedge x_9 \wedge x_{10}$. There are various ways to encode simpler policies like $x_1 \wedge x_2$

P_1 :   RoleA ∧ (RoleB ∨ RoleC)
P_2 :   (adult ∨ cc = verified) ∧
            ((contprov1.article1 = purchased ∧ account1 = balanced) ∨
            (contprov2.article1 = purchased ∧ account2 = balanced))
P_3 :   userrole = surgeon ∧ employer = hospitalx
P_4 : $((x_1 \wedge x_2 \wedge x_3) \vee x_4) \wedge ((x_5 \wedge x_6) \vee (x_7 \wedge x_8 \wedge x_9 \wedge x_{10}))$

Fig. 2. Example policies for Fig. 1

or $x_1 \wedge (x_2 \vee x_3)$. For example, the former policy can be encoded by mapping, $\mathfrak{v}_1 \equiv \bot$, $\mathfrak{v}_2 \equiv x_1 \wedge x_2$ $\mathfrak{v}_3 \equiv \top$, and $\mathfrak{v}_4$ to a random ∧-gate, or by mapping $\mathfrak{v}_1 \equiv x_1$, $\mathfrak{v}_2 \equiv \bot$, $\mathfrak{v}_3 \equiv x_2$, and $\mathfrak{v}_4 \equiv \bot$. Several other mappings are possible. This shows that the policies encoded in a simple tree can be very complex and diverse.

An attacker cannot know the concrete semantics of the leaves, but he can determine if an attribute set satisfies the partial policy of a leaf. We will use this ability in the decryption algorithm.

1.2 Related Work

In predicate encryption schemes [8,7,19,3], decryption is possible if a predicate over the user attributes and the ciphertext attributes is fulfilled. Current PE constructions are very powerful and support rather expressive predicates. Currently the most versatile solutions seem to be those that use inner product queries [8,7]. It has been shown [7] that such a scheme can be used to construct a scheme that supports, for example, DNFs or CNFs of some bounded degree, or a predicate that can be expressed by a polynomial over the attributes. However, this predicate (for example a predicate for DNFs of some degree d) is encoded in the user keys, so it is fixed after the key generation algorithm. The complexity of the system is dependent on the size of that predicate. This means that no single PE scheme is able to express every possible policy in polynomial size and due to the bounded size of the predicate can only support a limited set of policies. Speaking in terms of anonymity, there is a fixed anonymity set that applies to all ciphertexts of an instantiation of a PE system.

In our approach, there is no fixed anonymity set. Instead, each encrypting party decides on the anonymity set when encrypting. All policies are expressed as syntax trees, so every Boolean formula can be expressed in polynomial size. As we will show in Section 4.1, the anonymity set is exponential in the size of the tree major that was used to encode the policy.

Furthermore it should be noted that predicate encryption schemes require very large groups and are only efficient for small attribute sets thereby making them unfeasible for many applications.

Aside from PE schemes, policy privacy has also been examined in the context of trust negotiation [6]. Here, large scrambled circuits are used to obfuscate the underlying policy, which is similar to our idea of using large tree majors. Trust negotiation is an interactive process whereas in this paper we are concerned with an off-line access control mechanism. Recently, Seyalioglu and Sahai [17] proposed an encryption scheme which also uses garbled circuits and hides the policy. However, in their scheme, the public key of a recipient must be used for the encryption, making it infeasible in the CP-ABE setting where the identities of the recipients are not known.

Literature on smallest common supertrees and related topics is extensive [16,21,15], however the constraints we are dealing with in our scenario have to our knowledge not yet been discussed. For a good, though somewhat dated, survey see [2]. There are several CP-ABE schemes [8,11,22,1], but only [13], which we modify in this paper, and [23] support policy hiding.

Outline. In the following section we discuss how to obfuscate policies by creating syntax tree majors. The syntax tree majors are then used in our CP-ABE system described in Section 3. Section 4 discusses various security aspects of this system. Section 5 concludes.

2   Syntax Tree Majors

The basic idea of our system is to take a policy, encoded as a monotonic syntax tree, and find another policy that semantically contains many different policies, including the original one. An attacker is not able to decide which policy was actually used for the encryption.

Definition 1 (monotonic syntax tree). *A monotonic syntax tree T is a tree where all inner nodes are labeled with either $\wedge$ or $\vee$ and the leaves represent either Boolean variables or the constant values $\perp$ or $\top$. If the root of T is labeled $\wedge$, then every inner node of odd depth is labeled $\vee$, and every inner node of even depth is labeled $\wedge$. We call such a tree $\wedge$-rooted. Analogously, a $\vee$-rooted tree is a tree whose root is labeled $\vee$ and where every inner node of odd depth is labeled $\wedge$, and every inner node of even depth is labeled $\vee$.*

It is easy to see that any syntax tree over the operands $\wedge$ and $\vee$ can be transformed into a monotonic syntax tree by contracting adjacent $\wedge$- and $\vee$-nodes. As the labeling of all inner nodes follows from the labeling of the root node, we usually omit the labels of the inner nodes, calling the resulting tree *implicitly labeled.*

As explained in the introduction, we will use a CP-ABE scheme that encrypts the leaves, which correspond to attributes, but the construction will hide the concrete correspondence between leaves and attributes. Also note that our construction supports only monotonic syntax trees, but as there might be negative attributes (i.e., attributes that attest that the possessor does *not* have a certain property), even non-monotonic policies can be represented by monotonic syntax trees by applying DeMorgan's laws until all negations are atomic.

In order to further obfuscate the policy, we compute a larger policy such that by mapping some of its leaves to the values $\top$ and $\perp$ we are able to encode the original policy. For example, the monotonic syntax tree in Figure 3a represents the formula $x \wedge \bar{z}$. As an adversary does not know which leaves (if any) are mapped to $\top$ and $\perp$, there are many possible forms the encoded policy might have, and as the configuration of the leaves is hidden, he is not able to access the concrete policy. We say that the larger policy *semantically contains* many smaller policies. More formally:

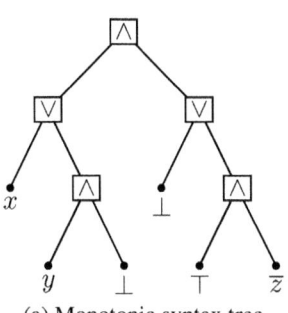

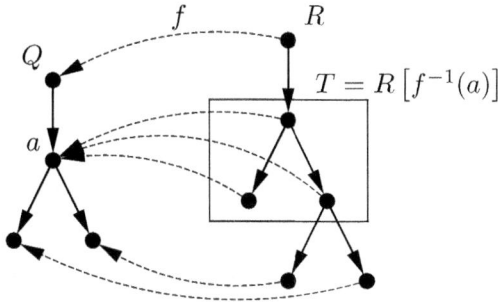

(a) Monotonic syntax tree   (b) A mapping f of a major to a minor (leaves omitted)

Fig. 3. Examples

Definition 2 (semantic containment). *Let F and G be Boolean formulas over vectors of Boolean variables $x = (x_1, \ldots, x_n)$, resp. $y = (y_1, \ldots, y_m)$ where $m \leq n$. We call F semantically contained in G if there exists a function ϕ that maps the variables of x to either variables of y or to constant values $\top$ or $\bot$, such that $G(\psi(\phi(x))) = F(\psi(x))$ for all configuration mappings $\psi : x \mapsto \{\bot, \top\}^n$.*

We can apply this definition to syntax trees as follows: Let Q be a monotonic syntax tree with leaves $\mathbb{L}(Q) = \{u_1, \ldots, u_{|\mathbb{L}(Q)|}\}$ and R a monotonic syntax tree with leaves $\mathbb{L}(R) = \{v_1, \ldots, v_{|\mathbb{L}(R)|}\}$. We say that R *semantically contains* Q, if there is a function $\phi : \mathbb{L}(R) \to \mathbb{L}(Q) \cup \{\bot, \top\}$ such that for all configurations $\psi : \mathbb{L}(Q) \to \{\top, \bot\}$, it holds that $\psi(\phi(R)) \equiv \psi(Q)$, i.e., after applying ϕ to R, it computes the same value as Q for every possible configuration of the variables.

The type of supertree we examine is closely related to the notion of *tree majors*. Informally, a tree R is a major of a tree Q, if Q can be obtained from R by contracting a number of edges. Equally, a major of Q can be constructed by expanding some nodes into subtrees. A major can be characterized by a mapping $f : V(R) \to V(Q)$ of vertexes of a tree R to Q. We call R a *syntax tree major* of Q if we can find a mapping f with the following properties: Given a node $a \in Q$, the nodes of $f^{-1}(a)$ form a connected subtree T of R, which we denote $T = R[f^{-1}(a)]$. This is illustrated in Figure 3b. Different subtrees must not overlap and all edges of Q must be preserved in R. This is similar to the definition of a tree major.

However, in our scenario we additionally require the expanded tree to preserve the labeling of all nodes, as it needs to have the same semantics as the original tree. To understand the implications of this, let the label of a in Figure 3b be $\vee$. All other labels of Q follow from this by Definition 1. Now consider the subtree T of R. As our definition does not allow adjacent $\vee$-nodes, some nodes of T must be labeled $\wedge$. However, as both the direct predecessor of T in R and all direct successors of T in R are labeled with $\wedge$, no node of T can have the label $\wedge$. From this consideration, it follows that all subtrees introduced in a tree major of a syntax tree must have even height.

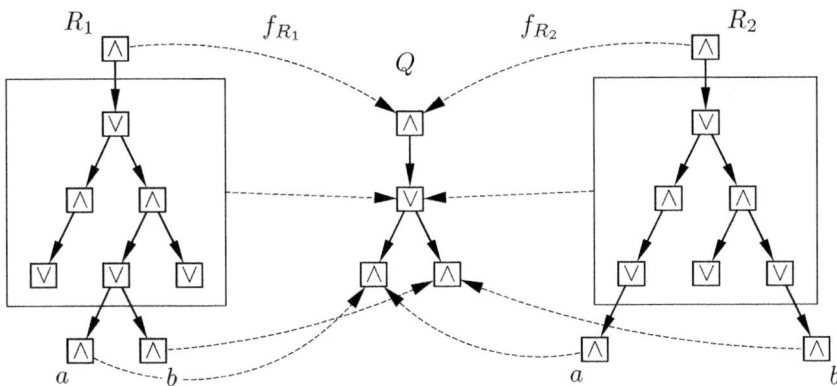

Fig. 4. Two valid syntax tree majors

Both R_1 and R_2 of Figure 4 are examples of such majors. Note the placements of the leaves a and b. In both cases, the root of the smallest subgraph that contains both nodes has a root labeled with $\vee$. This node will take on the role that the parent of $f(a)$ and $f(b)$ in Q has (which is also an $\vee$-node).

Generally, all syntax tree majors must follow the rule that if two nodes a and b have a common parent in Q, then their unique common ancestor in R must have the same label as that parent. As a counter example consider the tree major R_3 (Figure 5), where the root of the smallest subtree containing a and b is an $\wedge$-node, thus not qualifying as a syntax tree major. The original graph contained a formula $f(a) \vee f(b)$, but this cannot be encoded in the given major, as a and b are only connected by an $\wedge$-node. It is now easy to see that in these cases the smallest subtrees containing a and b must have odd height.

More formally, we adapt the definition of tree minors from [14] to implicitly labeled monotonic syntax trees and define *syntax tree majors* as follows:

Definition 3 (syntax tree major). *A tree R is a syntax tree major of a tree Q if there exists a surjection $f : V(R) \to V(Q)$ such that*

1. *for each $a \in V(Q), T = R\left[f^{-1}(a)\right]$ is a connected subtree of R, and every path from the root of T to a leaf of T consists of an even number of edges;*
2. *for each pair $a, b \in V(Q), f^{-1}(a) \cap f^{-1}(b) = \emptyset$;*
3. *for $S = \{(u, v) \in E(R) \mid f(u) \neq f(v)\}$, there exists a bijection $\xi : S \to E(Q)$ such that for each $e(s, t) \in S, \xi(e) = (f(s), f(t))$.*
4. *For each pair of edges $(x, a) \in E(Q)$ and $(x, b) \in E(Q)$, let U be the smallest subtree of R that has both a and b as leaves. Then the paths from the root of U to the roots of the subtrees $f^{-1}(a)$ and $f^{-1}(b)$ have odd length.*

We call f the *characteristic function* of the major.

If R is a syntax tree major of Q according to this definition, it semantically contains Q, and it is straightforward to configure R such that it computes the same function as Q. A proof for this statement along with complete algorithms for finding a suitable configuration of R is given in the full version of this paper [12].

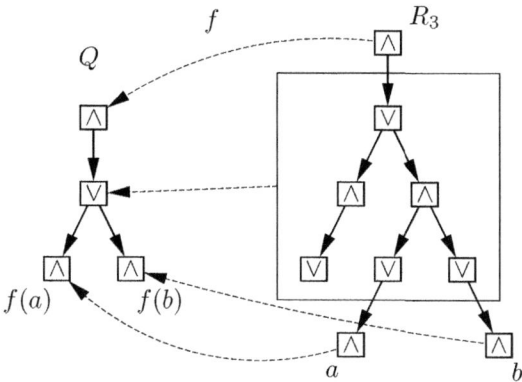

Fig. 5. An invalid syntax tree major

3 Building the System

We now describe a CP-ABE system with hidden policies, where policies are represented as syntax trees. It is based on [13], but extended to support any Boolean formula by utilizing syntax tree majors. The leaves of the syntax tree are expressions of the form $A = x$, where A identifies an attribute and x the value that this attribute must have. See Figure 2 for some example policies. Our construction supports n attributes, denoted $L_1, \ldots, L_n$. Each attribute can take on one of a number of symbolic values. We denote the number of possible values of an attribute L_i by n_i and the symbolic values of the attribute by $v_{i,1}, \ldots, v_{i,n_i}$. Thus, each leaf of the tree encodes an expression $L_i = v_{i,t}$. Using this approach, we are able to support every policy that can be expressed as a Boolean formula.

Note that we can also emulate numeric attributes using a bag of bits representation [1], where each number is represented by a bit string and there are two attributes for each bit. To use this, the policy would first be formulated in a more abstract form, using comparisons with numbers in the leaves like $A = x$, $A \leq x$, or $A \geq x$. These leaves would then be expanded into subtrees that evaluate the expressions using the bit representations, as outlined in [1].

3.1 Setup and KeyGen

Setup. An asymmetric bilinear group $e : \mathbb{G}_1 \times \mathbb{G}_2 \to \mathbb{G}_T$ of order p with generators $g_1 \in \mathbb{G}_1$ and $g_2 \in \mathbb{G}_2$ is chosen. The trusted authority randomly selects random values for $\omega, \overline{\omega}, \beta, \overline{\beta} \in \mathbb{Z}_p^*$ and for each value $v_{i,t}$ of each attribute he also selects a random $\{a_{i,t} \in \mathbb{Z}_p^*\}_{1 \leq t \leq n_i, 1 \leq i \leq n}$. The public key PK consists of the bilinear group with generators g_1, g_2 and the values $\left\{A_{i,t} = g_1^{a_{i,t}}\right\}_{1 \leq t \leq n_i, 1 \leq i \leq n}$, as well as $Y = e(g_1, g_2)^{\omega}$, $\overline{Y} = e(g_1, g_2)^{\overline{\omega}}$, $B = g_1^{\beta}$, and $\overline{B} = g_1^{\overline{\beta}}$. The master key MK is

$$MK = \left\langle \omega, \beta, \overline{\omega}, \overline{\beta}, \{\{a_{i,1}\}_{1 \leq t \leq n_i}\}_{1 \leq i \leq n} \right\rangle.$$

Intuitively we hereby construct two parallel cryptosystems that use the same group structure and the same secret attribute keys but differ in the values of the secret key components ω and β. We will the denote the cryptosystem that uses ω and β the *primary* cryptosystem and the one that uses $\overline{\omega}$ and $\overline{\beta}$ the *secondary* cryptosystem. The primary cryptosystem will be used to encrypt the actual secret message, while the secondary one will help the decryptor to decide which nodes he can access with his attribute set. To this end, we encrypt the fixed value 1 using the secondary cryptosystem. The decryptor will try to decrypt this value from the ciphertext to see if he can satisfy the policy of the gate.

KeyGen. Let $L = [L_1, L_2, \ldots, L_n] = [v_{1,t_1}, v_{2,t_2}, \ldots, v_{n,t_n}]$ be the attribute list for the user who wishes to obtain the secret key. If the user is not eligible of the requested attributes, the trusted authority returns $\perp$. Otherwise, it picks random values $s, \lambda_i \in \mathbb{Z}_p^*$ for $1 \leq i \leq n$, and computes $D_0 = g_2^{\beta^{-1}(\omega-s)}$ and $\overline{D_0} = g_2^{\overline{\beta}^{-1}(\overline{\omega}-s)}$. For $1 \leq i \leq n$, the authority also computes $[D_{i,1}, D_{i,2}] = [g_2^{s+a_{i,t_i}\lambda_i}, g_2^{\lambda_i}]$ where $L_i = v_{i,t_i}$. The secret key SK_L is $\langle D_0, \overline{D_0}, \{D_{i,1}, D_{i,2}\}_{1 \leq i \leq n} \rangle$.

3.2 Encryption

After the encryptor has decided on the encryption policy and constructed a monotonic syntax tree Q, he creates a syntax tree major R of Q which is used to hide the actual policy Q.

Constructing a Tree Major. There are three ways to construct a syntax tree major of a syntax tree Q that represents a policy: One way is to randomly expand edges of Q into trees of even height. This will result in a random major R.

Another, more interesting approach is to "mix" Q with other trees, constructing a common major that from an adversary's point of view could encode all of the input trees as well as numerous combinations of them. This is discussed in the full version of this paper [12]. Note that while the resulting tree could encode all of the input trees, we will configure the leaves such that only the desired tree Q is encoded, so satisfying any of the other trees used as input to the algorithm does not allow decryption unless Q is satisfied, too.

A third approach to construct suitable syntax tree majors could be to initially decide on a large generic tree R_0 that semantically contains all possible policies that are used in a given setting. For example, an encryptor may find that all policies that he normally uses are syntax tree minors of a 3-ary tree of height 4. Then he could always set R to that tree and use it as a syntax tree major for all encryptions. Using such an approach for a policy represented by a syntax tree Q, a mapping $f : V(R) \rightarrow V(Q)$ must be found that adheres to Definition 3. If Q is indeed a minor of R, such a mapping can be found in $O(|V(R)|)$ by a brute force algorithm that tries to match vertices of Q to vertices of R starting from the leaves of both trees. In this case, after initially selecting the generic tree R_0, the process of constructing a tree major is omitted for all further encryptions, and instead the encryptor simply sets $R := R_0$.

The result of any of these the possible approaches is a syntax tree major R and a mapping $f : V(R) \rightarrow V(Q)$ that characterizes the relationship between Q and R. We will configure R such that it computes exactly the same function as Q, but keep this configuration invisible to an attacker.

Encoding the Formula. After constructing a syntax tree major R with root T and mapping f, the encryptor randomly chooses an $r \in \mathbb{Z}_p^*$ and executes $\texttt{EncodeSecret}(T, r)$ (see Algorithm 1). This algorithm encodes the secret value $r \in \mathbb{Z}_p$ into the tree. Beginning from the root of the tree, the algorithm recursively traverses downwards to the leaves. If a node is an $\wedge$-node, the secret r is split into partial secrets, one for each child of the node (the decryptor must satisfy all children to recover the secret), so that the sum of all partial secrets equals r. If a node is an $\vee$-node, the secret is propagated to all child nodes. The output is a labeling $m(c)$ of all nodes of $c \in R$ to partial secrets in $\mathbb{Z}_p^*$. The idea is that a decryptor needs to be able decrypt a sufficient set of partial secrets to recover the main secret r. In the next step, the encryptor chooses which of the leaves of R should be used to compute the desired formula and which ones should be set to $\bot$ or $\top$ such that R computes the same function as Q. Let $\tilde{M} : \mathbb{L}(R) \rightarrow \{\mathscr{F}, \bot, \top, \mathrm{rand}\}$ be the result of this, i.e., if $\tilde{M}(\mathfrak{v}) = \mathscr{F}$, encode a genuine part of Q, if $\tilde{M}(\mathfrak{v}) = \bot$, encode $\bot$, $\tilde{M}(\mathfrak{v}) = \top$, encode $\top$, or else randomly choose what to compute. There are various ways to find such a mapping. We explain one such way in the full version of this paper [12] (see Algorithms 2 and 3 in Appendix A). After this process, each leaf $\mathfrak{v}$ is marked with $\tilde{M}(\mathfrak{v})$, a partial secret $m(\mathfrak{v})$, and there is a mapping $f(\mathfrak{v})$ that maps $\mathfrak{v}$ to a leaf of Q that represents an expression of the form $L_i = v_{i,t}$. (Note that the algorithms mark all nodes of R, but from now on we will only need the marks of the leaves.)

The first part of the ciphertext is $\tilde{C} = MY^r$ and $C_0 = B^r$, which encodes the value r and the secret message M.

The basic idea of our approach is to encrypt every leaf's partial secret $m(\mathfrak{v})$ with either the constant value represented by $\tilde{M}(\mathfrak{v})$ or — if $\tilde{M}(\mathfrak{v}) = \mathscr{F}$ — with the attribute $f(\mathfrak{v})$. Wlog, assume that the last inner nodes of every path to a leaf are $\wedge$-gates (if such a last inner node is an $\vee$, replace every leaf $\mathfrak{v}$ of that gate with an $\wedge$-gate having the sole child $\mathfrak{v}$). For each of these last inner $\wedge$-gates $\mathfrak{v}$, the encryptor computes ciphertext components $CT^{(\mathfrak{v})}$ for the primary cryptosystem as follows:

Case 1: If all children of $\mathfrak{v}$ are either $\top$ or $\mathscr{F}$, encode a genuine $\wedge$-gate as follows: Pick random values $r_i^{(\mathfrak{v})}$, $\forall i = 1 \ldots n$, such that $m(\mathfrak{v}) = \sum_i r_i^{(\mathfrak{v})}$. For each attribute $1 \leq i \leq n$ set $C_{i,1}^{(\mathfrak{v})} = g_1^{r_i^{(\mathfrak{v})}}$ and compute $\{C_{i,t,2}^{(\mathfrak{v})}\}_{1 \leq t \leq n_i}$ as follows: if the ith attribute is not found in the children of $f(\mathfrak{v})$ (i.e., the value is *don't care*) or the attribute value $v_{i,t}$ is found in the children, set $C_{i,t,2}^{(\mathfrak{v})} = A_{i,t}^{r_i^{(\mathfrak{v})}}$; otherwise (i.e., the value $v_{i,t}$ is forbidden for this attribute), select $C_{i,t,2}^{(\mathfrak{v})}$ randomly.

Case 2: If one of the children is $\bot$, the decryption must never succeed. In this case, all $C_{i,1}^{(\mathfrak{v})}$ and $C_{i,t,2}^{(\mathfrak{v})}$ are set to random values.

Algorithm 1: EncodeSecret(T,r)

Input : Tree R, Subtree T of R (represented by its root), number r
Output : $m : V(R) \rightarrow \mathbb{Z}_p^*$

$m(T) \longleftarrow r$;
if T *is no leaf* **then**
    if T *is* $\wedge$-*rooted* **then**
        Let the number of child nodes be n.
        $r_i \xleftarrow{\text{R}} \mathbb{Z}_p^*, 1 \leq i \leq n$, such that $\sum_i r_i = r$.
        forall *children c* **do** EncodeSecret(c, r_i)
    else
        forall *children c* **do** EncodeSecret(c, r)
    end
end

Case 3: If all children are marked rand, flip a coin to decide whether to proceed with Case 1 (encrypting with a random $\wedge$-gate) or with Case 2.

Finally, compute the ciphertext components $H^{(\mathfrak{v})} = \overline{Y}^{m^{(\mathfrak{v})}}$ and $\overline{C_0}^{(\mathfrak{v})} = \overline{B}^{m^{(\mathfrak{v})}}$. This encrypts an additional ciphertext in the secondary cryptosystem which equals to 1.

Combining these components, the ciphertext for leaf $\mathfrak{v}$ is

$$CT^{(\mathfrak{v})} = \left\langle \overline{C_0}^{(\mathfrak{v})}, H^{(\mathfrak{v})}, \left\{ C_{i,1}^{(\mathfrak{v})}, \left\{ C_{i,t,2}^{(\mathfrak{v})} \right\}_{1 \leq t \leq n_i} \right\}_{1 \leq i \leq n} \right\rangle.$$

The final ciphertext is

$$CT = \left\langle \tilde{C}, C_0, \left\{ CT^{(\mathfrak{v})} \vee \text{leaves } \mathfrak{v} \right\} \right\rangle,$$

along with a topological description of the tree (including the labels but excluding any other marks).

3.3 Decryption

In order to decrypt, the decryptor determines which leaves his attribute set satisfies. This is done by decrypting the second encrypted value using the second cryptosystem with all attributes that he has and comparing the result to the value 1. If the decryptor's attribute set does not fulfill the policy, he gets a value different from 1. For each leaf $\mathfrak{v} \in \mathbb{L}(R)$ set $C'^{(\mathfrak{v})}_{i,2} = C^{(\mathfrak{v})}_{i,t_i,2}$, where $1 \leq i \leq n$ and $L_i = v_{i,t_i}$ and compute

$$M^{(\mathfrak{v})} = \prod_{i=1}^{n} \frac{e(C_{i,1}^{(\mathfrak{v})}, D_{i,1})}{e(C'^{(\mathfrak{v})}_{i,2}, D_{i,2})} \qquad \text{and} \qquad \tau^{(\mathfrak{v})} = \frac{H^{(\mathfrak{v})} \cdot M^{(\mathfrak{v})}}{e(\overline{C_0}^{(\mathfrak{v})}, \overline{D}_0)}.$$

For each $\mathfrak{v}$, $M^{(\mathfrak{v})} = e(g_1, g_2)^{s \cdot m^{(\mathfrak{v})}}$, where s is specific to the used attribute set and was set in the KeyGen algorithm, and $\tau^{(\mathfrak{v})} = 1$ if the leaf can be satisfied by the decryptor, and otherwise a random value. Note that if the decryptor can not satisfy the leaf, $\tau^{(\mathfrak{v})}$ might also be equal to 1. However, the probability for this occurring is $1/p$ for p the order of the bilinear group, which is negligible.

Note that while the decryptor now knows which parts of the tree he satisfies, he does not know the policies of the respective leaves since their configuration is hidden by the construction. However, with all $\tau^{(\mathfrak{v})}$, he is able to decrypt as follows: First he removes some of the leaves that he does not satisfy (i.e., where $\tau^{(\mathfrak{v})} \neq 1$) as they do not contain any information that he can use. For all $\tau^{(\mathfrak{v})} \neq 1$, replace $\mathfrak{v}$ with the constant value $\bot$ and simplify the tree by substituting subtrees with their obvious results using the formulas $A \wedge \bot = \bot$ and $A \vee \bot = A$. The remaining tree either contains only leaves that can be satisfied or is a single node $\bot$. In the latter case, return $\bot$ (as the attribute set does not satisfy the policy). For each remaining $\vee$-node N, randomly choose a subtree of N and substitute N with it. (This works because Algorithm 1 encoded the same value in all subtrees of an $\vee$ node, so we can use any of them to retrieve it.)

Finally, collapse all remaining $\wedge$-nodes to a single one. The message M can now be retrieved as

$$M = \frac{\tilde{C} \prod_{\mathfrak{v}} M^{(\mathfrak{v})}}{e(C_0, D_0)},$$

where $\mathfrak{v}$ are all remaining leaves of that single $\wedge$-node. By multiplying a valid combination of $M^{(\mathfrak{v})}$ together, the partial secrets $m(\mathfrak{v})$ add up to the secret value r which then is unblinded by the above formula.

Correctness. Using a secret key SK_L that satisfies the tree, we have

$$\frac{\tilde{C} \prod_{\mathfrak{v}} M^{(\mathfrak{v})}}{e(C_0, D_0)} = M \cdot \frac{Y^r}{e(C_0, D_0)} \prod_{\mathfrak{v}} \prod_{i} \frac{e(C_{i,1}^{(\mathfrak{v})}, D_{i,1})}{e(C'_{i,2}^{(\mathfrak{v})}, D_{i,2})}$$

$$= M \cdot e(g_1, g_2)^{\omega r - \beta r \beta^{-1}(\omega - s) + \Sigma_{\mathfrak{v}} \left(\Sigma_i (r_i^{(\mathfrak{v})} \cdot (s + a_{i,t_i} \lambda_i) - (a_{i,t} r_i^{(\mathfrak{v})} \lambda_i)) \right)}$$

$$= M \cdot e(g_1, g_2)^{-rs + \Sigma_{\mathfrak{v}} \left(\Sigma_i r_i^{(\mathfrak{v})} s \right)}.$$

The tree is constructed such that for a leaf $\mathfrak{v}$ that is satisfied, $\Sigma_i r_i^{(\mathfrak{v})} = m(\mathfrak{v})$ and for a sufficient subset of the leaves, $\Sigma_{\mathfrak{v}} m(\mathfrak{v}) = r$, so $\Sigma_{\mathfrak{v}} \left(\Sigma_i r_i^{(\mathfrak{v})} s \right) = rs$ and the equation yields $M \cdot e(g_1, g_2)^{rs - rs} = M$. Note that if the equation is computed using a key SK_L that does not satisfy the tree, then some $C'_{i,2}^{(\mathfrak{v})}$ will be random values instead of $g_1^{a_{i,t} r_i^{(\mathfrak{v})}}$. In this case, some $m(\mathfrak{v})$ will not be computed correctly, so the exponents do not cancel out and the result will be different from M (with overwhelming probability).

4   Discussion

In this section we discuss the properties of our extended construction. For sake of space, the formal security proof is given in the full version of this paper [12].

4.1 Anonymity of the Policy

In our construction the ciphertext is encrypted with a major of the syntax tree. As the leaves of this tree are hidden from an adversary, he cannot decide which of the possible policies was actually used. The anonymity set $\mathbb{A}(E,L)$ is determined by the ciphertext E and the attribute set of the decryptor $L = [L_1, \ldots, L_n]$. We will now briefly discuss the size of $\mathbb{A}(E,L)$. As a lower bound, assume $n_i = 2$ for all $1 \le i \le n$, i.e., every attribute has only two possible symbolic values. If the decryptor can access an $\wedge$-gate with his attribute set L, he can conclude that each ith attribute encoded in the policy of the $\wedge$-gate is either set to the value L_i that he owns or is a "don't care". Similarly, if he cannot decrypt an $\wedge$-gate, he can conclude that there is at least one attribute i in the policy of the $\wedge$-gate that is unequal to his attribute value L_i. In both cases the number of possible $\wedge$-gates is $O(2^n)$. For a tree R with leaves $\mathbb{L}(R)$, the number of possible policies is in $O(2^{n \cdot |\mathbb{L}(R)|})$.

In some scenarios, it might suffice if the attacker knows only the general form of the policy, i.e., he wants to know, which nodes of the tree belong to the actual policy and which ones are dummy gates introduced in order to obfuscate the policy. In our construction, the form of the policy is determined by the leaves. Some of these are set to a constant value ($\top$ or $\bot$) to render unused inner nodes inoperative, some are genuine $\wedge$-gates encoding parts of the policy. Thus, to find out which form the original policy has, an attacker must know which $\wedge$-gates are constant values and which ones are not, which for a tree R with leaves $\mathbb{L}(R)$ gives $O(2^{|\mathbb{L}(R)|})$ combinations. However, for reasons of symmetry, some of these forms may be topologically identical, so the number of forms might be smaller than that. The most symmetries are found in a complete n-ary tree. However, in [9] it is shown that even in such a tree, the number of topologically different subtrees is exponential in the number of nodes, so it is at least exponential in the number of leaves. Thus, even taking into account symmetries, the number of possible forms of a policy encoded in a syntax tree major is exponential in the number of leaves.

We show that an attacker cannot distinguish between policies within his anonymity set in Appendix D in the full version of this paper [12].

4.2 Comparison with Nishide's Construction

The partial ciphertext $CT^{(\mathfrak{v})}$ of a leaf $\mathfrak{v}$ has roughly the same size as a complete encryption of Nishide's original construction from [13]. In the case where the tree consists only of a single leaf, the ciphertext of our construction is even a bit larger than it would be in the original one, because we store additional values that enable the decryptor to determine whether he is eligible to decrypt. It is natural to ask if this is an improvement.

Concretely, one could transform a policy to DNF form with n conjunctions and encrypt each conjunction separately, creating n ciphertext instances of Nishide's construction. This requires approximately as much memory as using our construction for a tree with n leaves. This is of course only feasible if the policy in question has a small DNF representation, i.e., one with a small number of conjunctions. The leaves in our scheme represent conjunctions, but only of parts of the encoded policy, and they can be combined in various ways following the description of the major which is sent along with

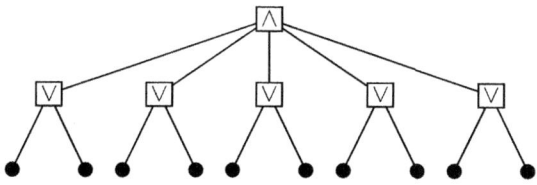

Fig. 6. 2-CNF of size 5

the ciphertext. For example, the 2-CNF formula shown in Figure 6 can be encoded with 10 leaves, but its DNF representation consists of $2^5 = 32$ conjunctions, so 32 instances of Nishide's construction would be needed to encode it. This is not a problem in our construction as the original 2-CNF form can be used for the encryption. (Note that when using the 2-CNF syntax tree as a major for encryptions, the policy automatically supports ∧-gates as leaves, so it is actually stored as a conjunction of DNFs. This form has been called CDNF in [20] and is considered very expressive.)

4.3   Reducing the Size of the Ciphertext

For each leave's encryption every attribute of the system is used. This is the only way to maximize the anonymity set, because when some attribute A is not used for the decryption of a leaf $\mathfrak{v}$, then the decryptor can obviously conclude that the partial policy of $\mathfrak{v}$ does not contain A. However, if the universe of attributes of a given system is very large, it might be feasible to use only a comparatively small set of attributes for the encryption of each leaf while still using enough attributes to get a sufficiently large anonymity set. Similarly to [13], each leaf $\mathfrak{v}$ may be encrypted with its own set of attributes $\mathscr{A}_\mathfrak{v}$. $\mathscr{A}_\mathfrak{v}$ can be a random superset of the set attributes actually used in the leaf. However, in order to hide as much of the semantics of each partial policy, some care must be taken, as it should be understood which information an attacker gains by the knowledge of $\mathscr{A}_\mathfrak{v}$. It must also be considered that $\mathscr{A}_\mathfrak{v}$ must be sent along with each leaf, which slightly increases the size of the ciphertext.

As a more systematic approach, the universe of attributes could be partitioned into different domains $\mathbb{D}_i, 1 \leq i \leq n_D$ with n_D the number of domains. For example one domain $\mathbb{D}_1$ could contain all user-specific attributes, $\mathbb{D}_2$ could contain all device-specific attributes, $\mathbb{D}_3$ all location-specific attributes, etc. If each domain $\mathbb{D}_i$ consists of $|\mathbb{D}_i|$ attributes, then the anonymity set of a respective leaf $\mathscr{A}_\mathfrak{v}$ with $\mathscr{A}_\mathfrak{v} = \mathbb{D}_i$ is $O(2^{|\mathbb{D}_i|})$. With this approach, an advisor knows that a leaf $\mathfrak{v}$ with $\mathscr{A}_\mathfrak{v} = \mathbb{D}_1$ might encode a partial policy over some user-specific properties (or as always an encoding of ⊥ or ⊤), but he does not know which one or which ones. This gives the encryptor precise control over what information is disclosed with an encrypted leaf. Moreover, instead of listing each element of $\mathscr{A}_\mathfrak{v}$, with this approach only the index i of $\mathbb{D}_i$ needs to be sent along with the partial ciphertext of $\mathfrak{v}$, $CT^{(\mathfrak{v})}$.

5 Conclusion

We introduced the notion of policy anonymity in cryptographic access control. To this end, we proposed the idea to obfuscate the policy used in an encryption by constructing a syntax tree major of the syntax tree that encodes the desired policy. The leaves are then hidden from an adversary using a cryptographic primitive. We discussed how these majors can be characterized and how to configure the leaves to encode a specific, given policy in one of its majors. The majors can be chosen arbitrarily large, and the larger a major is the larger becomes the anonymity set. From the anonymity set, an adversary gains only very general informations about the encoded policy; for example he knows an upper bound of its complexity and that some of his attribute sets satisfy certain parts of the major. We then used these primitives to modify a CP-ABE scheme with partially hidden policies to support every policy that can be expressed as a Boolean formula and enable an encryptor to obfuscate that policy.

Our construction compares favorably to [13] as it is able to efficiently encode any policy that can be expressed as a Boolean formula and is not limited to policies with small DNF represenations and to the various Predicate Encryption schemes. However, it may be possible to construct a scheme that hides even more properties of the encoded policy by using a different encoding of the it, like garbled circuits which presently have been utilized to solve different problems [6,17]. We leave this as future work. Also, our approach may be applicable to other CP-ABE system that like Nishide's support only $\wedge$-conjunctions.

References

1. Bethencourt, J., Sahai, A., Waters, B.: Ciphertext-policy attribute-based encryption. In: IEEE Symposium on Security and Privacy, pp. 321–334 (2007)
2. Bille, P.: A survey on tree edit distance and related problems. Theor. Comput. Sci. 337(1-3), 217–239 (2005)
3. Boneh, D., Waters, B.: Conjunctive, Subset, and Range Queries on Encrypted Data. In: Vadhan, S.P. (ed.) TCC 2007. LNCS, vol. 4392, pp. 535–554. Springer, Heidelberg (2007)
4. Cheung, L., Newport, C.C.: Provably secure ciphertext policy ABE. In: Ning, P., di Vimercati, S.D.C., Syverson, P.F. (eds.) ACM Conference on Computer and Communications Security, pp. 456–465. ACM (2007)
5. Ciriani, V., di Vimercati, S.D.C., Foresti, S., Samarati, P.: k-anonymity. In: Yu, T., Jajodia, S. (eds.) Secure Data Management in Decentralized Systems. Advances in Information Security, vol. 33, pp. 323–353. Springer, Heidelberg (2007)
6. Frikken, K.B., Li, J., Atallah, M.J.: Trust negotiation with hidden credentials, hidden policies, and policy cycles. In: NDSS. The Internet Society (2006)
7. Katz, J., Sahai, A., Waters, B.: Predicate Encryption Supporting Disjunctions, Polynomial Equations, and Inner Products. In: Smart, N.P. (ed.) EUROCRYPT 2008. LNCS, vol. 4965, pp. 146–162. Springer, Heidelberg (2008)
8. Lewko, A., Okamoto, T., Sahai, A., Takashima, K., Waters, B.: Fully Secure Functional Encryption: Attribute-Based Encryption and (Hierarchical) Inner Product Encryption. In: Gilbert, H. (ed.) EUROCRYPT 2010. LNCS, vol. 6110, pp. 62–91. Springer, Heidelberg (2010)
9. Matula, D.W.: On the number of subtrees of a symmetric n-ary tree. SIAM Journal on Applied Mathematics 18(3), 668–703 (1970)

10. Müller, S., Katzenbeisser, S.: Hiding the policy in cryptographic access control. Technical report (2011), http://eprint.iacr.org/2011/255.pdf
11. Müller, S., Katzenbeisser, S.: A new DRM architecture with strong enforcement. In: ARES, pp. 397–403. IEEE Computer Society (2010)
12. Müller, S., Katzenbeisser, S., Eckert, C.: On multi-authority ciphertext-policy attribute-based encryption. Bulletin of the Korean Mathematical Society (B-KMS) 46(4), 803–819 (2009)
13. Nishide, T., Yoneyama, K., Ohta, K.: Attribute-based encryption with partially hidden ciphertext policies. IEICE Transactions 92-A(1), 22–32 (2009)
14. Nishimura, N., Ragde, P., Thilikos, D.M.: Finding Smallest Supertrees under Minor Containment. In: Widmayer, P., Neyer, G., Eidenbenz, S. (eds.) WG 1999. LNCS, vol. 1665, pp. 303–312. Springer, Heidelberg (1999)
15. Riesen, K., Bunke, H.: Approximate graph edit distance computation by means of bipartite graph matching. Image Vision Comput. 27(7), 950–959 (2009)
16. Rosselló, F., Valiente, G.: An algebraic view of the relation between largest common subtrees and smallest common supertrees. CoRR, abs/cs/0604108 (2006)
17. Sahai, A., Seyalioglu, H.: Worry-free encryption: functional encryption with public keys. In: Al-Shaer, E., Keromytis, A.D., Shmatikov, V. (eds.) ACM Conference on Computer and Communications Security, pp. 463–472. ACM, New York (2010)
18. Serjantov, A., Danezis, G.: Towards an Information Theoretic Metric for Anonymity. In: Dingledine, R., Syverson, P.F. (eds.) PET 2002. LNCS, vol. 2482, pp. 41–53. Springer, Heidelberg (2003)
19. Shi, E., Bethencourt, J., Chan, H.T.-H., Song, D.X., Perrig, A.: Multi-dimensional range query over encrypted data. In: IEEE Symposium on Security and Privacy, pp. 350–364 (2007)
20. Smart, N.P.: Access Control using Pairing Based Cryptography. In: Joye, M. (ed.) CT-RSA 2003. LNCS, vol. 2612, pp. 111–121. Springer, Heidelberg (2003)
21. Valiente, G.: Constrained tree inclusion. J. Discrete Algorithms 3(2-4), 431–447 (2005)
22. Waters, B.: Ciphertext-policy attribute-based encryption: An expressive, efficient, and provably secure realization. In: The 14th IACR International Conference on Practice and Theory of Public Key Cryptography, PKC (March 2008)
23. Yu, S., Ren, K., Lou, W.: Attribute-based content distribution with hidden policy. In: Secure Network Protocols, NPSEC 2008 (2008)

Location Privacy in Relation to Trusted Peers

Klaus Rechert[1] and Benjamin Greschbach[2]

[1] Faculty of Engineering, Albert-Ludwigs University Freiburg i. B., Germany
[2] School of Computer Science and Communication, KTH - Royal Institute of
Technology, Stockholm, Sweden

Abstract. One common assumption when defining location privacy metrics is that one is dealing with attackers who have the objective of re-identifying an individual out of an anonymized data set. However, in today's communication scenarios, user communication and information exchange with (partially) trusted peers is very common, e.g., in communication via social applications. When disclosing voluntarily a single observation to a (partially) trusted communication peer, the user's privacy seems to be unharmed. However, location data is able to transport much more information than the simple fact of a user being at a specific location. Hence, a user-centric privacy metric is required in order to measure the extent of exposure by releasing (a set of) location observations. The goal of such a metric is to enable individuals to estimate the privacy loss caused by disclosing further location information in a specific communication scenario and thus enabling the user to make informed choices, e.g., choose the right protection mechanism.

1 Introduction

Location information has recently become a popular but also valuable communication item. Ubiquitous and affordable mobile communication paired with a new generation of so-called Smartphones has given rise to a large variety of location based applications. However, exploitation of mobile location information also brings new challenges to the users' privacy.

Providing a proper definition of location privacy has proven to be a difficult task. Many different definitions were published, all covering specific aspects. One abstract definition, first defined by Westin [1] and modified by Duckham & Kulik [2], describes location privacy as:

> "[...] a special type of information privacy which concerns the claim of individuals to determine for themselves *when, how,* and to *what extent* location information about them is communicated to others."

According to this definition the user should be in control of the dissemination of his location information. Location sharing usually involves location data as coordinates related to a sphere or map. Depending on the source, this information might be error prone. For instance, the accuracy of GPS location determination using a consumer device (Smartphone) might range from 1 to 50 meters; location

C. Meadows and C. Fernández-Gago (Eds.): STM 2011, LNCS 7170, pp. 106–121, 2012.
© Springer-Verlag Berlin Heidelberg 2012

determination utilizing a GSM/3G infrastructure might have an error range of 50-250 meters.

In today's communication scenarios user communication and information exchange with (partially) trusted peers is very common, e.g., in communication via social applications. In disclosing voluntarily a single observation to a (partially) trusted communication peer, the user's privacy seems to be unharmed (using the aforementioned definition). However, location data is able to transport much more information than the simple fact of a user being at a specific location. In the long run, location data is able to describe what a user has done and what he is currently doing.

For instance, a single location observation might have a different impact on the user's privacy depending on time and place but also on the *observer*. The observer might be able to make exact conclusions about the user's state and intention, if the observer has good background knowledge about the user (e.g., wife, friends). Even observers with little or no background knowledge are able to gain knowledge about the user. For example, by observing a user's frequently visited places, one can make conclusions about the user's workplace or other preferences. Using Westin's definition, it is difficult for a user to measure the *extent* of his location disclosure, especially with trusted communication peers where an anonymity approach is unsuitable. Hence, a user-centric privacy metric is required to measure the extent of exposure caused by releasing (a set of) location observations. From a user's perspective, with the goal of minimizing exposure, only as little information as possible should be disclosed.

2   Related Work

Privacy metrics is an important field in research on mobile communication and location based services, since they provide the fundamental model to evaluate a privacy protecting scheme. One way of characterizing a (location) privacy metric is the underlying adversary model: the metric describes how successfully one's privacy is protected against the defined adversary.

A popular model is an adversary that observes in some way generalized location data and tries to reconstruct this data based on connected traces of a single individual. In a second step the adversary may re-identify the traced individual through his workplace or home by incorporating external knowledge (e.g. [3]). For instance, Shorki et al. defined a location privacy metric that measures the (in)ability of an adversary to accurately track a mobile user over space and time [4]. A popular privacy metric is *k-anonymity*, developed in [5] and further extended for a location context (e.g. [6,7]). A single variable is able to determine a user's privacy level, i.e., being indistinguishable from $k-1$ other agents. However, this metric may be misleading if all k users are within a region with only a few plausible positions. *l*-diversity and road segment *s*-diversity avoid this issue by only taking plausible positions into account [8]. Furthermore, *k*-anonymity and similar methods imply that a suitable number of cooperative agents are available for a specific service or listening group and global knowledge about the state of other agents is required. Thus, a user cannot determine or preserve a desired privacy level in an autonomous manner. Neither does this metric cover the sensitivity of a location at a given time [4], nor is it able to fully protect specific movement patterns [9].

A different method for measuring location privacy is to make use of the uncertainty of an adversary to assign a new observation to a trace of a specific individual, e.g., by assigning probabilities to movement patterns and thus compensating changed pseudonyms [10]. A similar measurement was proposed as *time-to-confusion* metric, the tracking time of an individual until the adversary cannot determine the next position with sufficient certainty [3].

The aforementioned privacy metrics usually require full insight into the set of all users to determine the level of privacy for a single user within this set, and they usually are based on the assumption that the user requires full anonymity. Hence, such measures are not suitable for communication with (semi-)trusted peers (e.g., social contacts) or in ubiquitous communication networks which require a confirmed user identity. Furthermore, such models assume that for every available service there is a sufficient number of cooperative agents nearby and such an approach is usually applicable for a subset of location based service.

Cranshaw et al. developed an entropy-based approach for analyzing the social context of a geographic region. The proposed model assigns a high entropy to a place if a large variety of users was observed at that location, a low entropy value if the place was visited by only a few users [11]. Based on the location diversity measurement above, a user-study was conducted on presence-sharing preferences. Toch et al. found that people are more comfortable sharing their location in places which are visited by a large and diverse group of people in contrast to places which are highly frequented but by a homogeneous group [12]. Diaz et al. introduced a measure of entropy to quantify the degree of anonymity a mix-network provides [13]. Kamiyama et al. extended the entropy measure to quantify information disclosure through various media [14]. The described measurement quantifies the privacy loss caused by the disclosure of several (sensitive) attributes.

3   User-Centric Location Privacy Metric

For a user-centric location privacy model, location privacy has to be seen from a different angle. As the user is not always able to hide or remain anonymous, she could still achieve insight on the possible knowledge base of the communication peers involved and thus could achieve or increase location privacy (w.r.t. the aforementioned definition) through informed decisions on *when*, *how* and to *what extent* she discloses her location information. Hence, an evaluation of the user's location in the context of each listener group is necessary.

3.1   Adversary Model

In terms of (location) privacy, all communication peers are considered only as partially trusted, because once data is exchanged, this information usually cannot be recalled by the user. Even when considering explicit (legal contract) or implicit (social contract) based privacy policies, the control problem remains. Hence, all partially trusted peers are also considered as adversaries. Furthermore, from a user's perspective, there is no certain knowledge on the capabilities of the observing/listening adversary, especially how disclosed or observed location data is used and what kind of conclusion the adversary is able to make based on the information collected. Hence, the adversary model is limited to information an adversary may have collected during a defined observation period. We assume that an adversary A has a memory $O = \{o_1, \ldots, o_m\}$ of observations on the user's movement history based on time-stamped location observations $o_t = (c, \varepsilon)_t \in \mathbb{O}$, which are tuples of a geographic coordinate $c \in \mathbb{C}$ and an error estimate $\varepsilon \in \mathbb{E}$ of this coordinate. The index t is a timestamp describing when the location observation was made, with o_m being the latest observation. The function $loc : \mathbb{O} \to \mathbb{C}$ extracts the location information from the tuple and $err : \mathbb{O} \to \mathbb{E}$ returns the error estimate. The choice of the geographic coordinate system ($\mathbb{C}$) and the concrete representation of the error ($\mathbb{E}$) is not important in the context of this paper.

In our scenario the user's utility is positive in a communication relation with communication peer (adversary) A. Otherwise a rational agent would not share information. We make a similar assumption for the adversary's utility ($U_A(o_t) \geq 0$). A separation of the user's utility disclosing information and the user's level of privacy is required, as the utility of location information naturally conflicts with the user's privacy level. In order to benefit from location-aware services, the user's location disclosure is required. Thus, for any location disclosure the user's privacy might decrease. Hence, the adversary's utility is negatively correlated with the user's privacy level in a communication relation with adversary A denoted as $P^A \in [0, -\infty)$, with $P^A = 0$ as the maximal achievable privacy level:

$$U_A(O) \simeq -P^A(O), \tag{1}$$

For instance, if the user does not disclose any location information, the user's privacy is maximal but the adversary's utility is zero. Thereafter there is a utility gain if the adversary extends his knowledge either on the user's preferences or on his (periodic) behavior. Accordingly, $U_A(O') \geq U_A(O)$, with $O' := O \cup o'$, iff. o' reveals previously unknown information to the adversary A. Hence the user's privacy w.r.t. adversary A can only decrease by disclosing additional information: $P^A(O') \leq P^A(O)$.

An increase in the user's privacy level is only possible if the user is intentionally lying about his location, because providing false information may degrade the adversary's knowledge base or may lead to false conclusions. However, by providing false location information the user's utility decreases as well. For instance, in the case of location-based services a decrease in the user's utility might be caused by a decreased quality of service. In a communication scenario with social contacts, getting caught lying might lead to negative social consequences. For the rest of this paper we therefore assume that location observations reflect the true positions of the user.

Furthermore, the adversary's utility as well as the user's privacy depends on the nature and magnitude of the error estimate ε. First, with more accurate information more information might possibly be disclosed and thus, $err(o') < err(o) \Rightarrow U_A(o') \geq U_A(o)$, whereas the actual information gain is dependent, e.g., on landscape and application characteristics. Second, the error value ε for a given location sample is evaluated differently depending on the adversary and the kind of observation. If the adversary determines the location by direct observation (o^{adv}), e.g., through a WiFi/GSM/3G infrastructure, the adversary knows the size and distribution of the expected error for the observed location sample. If location information is given by the user (o^{usr}), the adversary has no information about the quality and thus the magnitude of the error ε of the observed sample. The user might have altered the spatial and/or temporal accuracy of the location information before submission. In general we can assume that $err(o^{adv}) \leq err(o^{usr})$ and therefore $U_A(o^{adv}) \geq U_A(o^{usr})$, since a robust error estimation reduces the adversary's uncertainty and thus increases the potential information gain for the same given error ε. But more importantly the adversary chooses time and frequency of location observations.

3.2   Measuring Location Privacy

To measure the user's privacy or privacy loss, the objective measurable components defining P^A w.r.t. location observations have to be identified. Taking into account the aforementioned privacy definition and adversary model, the evaluation of observations regarding new information about the user is required. This information can be split into two parts: (1) gaining *knowledge* on the user's regular behavior and preferences (e.g., his neighborhood, occupation, leisure activities or social contacts) and (2) deriving *sensitive* private information on his current context (e.g., his activity or intention at an observed place).

We define the change of the user's privacy level due to a new location observation o' made by an adversary A who already has a location record O about the user straightforwardly by $\Delta P^A(O, o') := P^A(O \cup o') - P^A(O)$. According to the requirements from the adversary model with $U_A(O') \geq U_A(O)$ and $U_A \simeq -P^A$ it follows that $\Delta P^A(O, o') \leq 0$.

Knowledge. In order to reflect the duration, density and quality of an observation, a model of all past disclosures, i.e., history or knowledge K, to a given adversary is required. The user's privacy is threatened by the discovery of his regular behavior and preferences (i.e., movement pattern). Since a user cannot change the knowledge an adversary already has, the user may evaluate the level of completeness of an adversary's information and the information gain as well as privacy loss for disclosing a further location sample.

Based on the adversary's utility function, we require that $\Delta K(O, o') = K(O \cup o') - K(O) \geq 0$. If no new information is released, $\Delta K = 0$ and thus no privacy loss is experienced by the user. Section 4 presents an example implementation of K.

Sensitivity. The second component threatening the user's privacy w.r.t. his current location is the sensitivity S of an observation o_t. Due to diverse preferences the individual subjective sensitivity of a certain location cannot be expressed in a generic way. However, an objective measure of location sensitivity is the level of the potential exposure caused by disclosing the user's location at a given time and date. The user is *exposing* himself by allowing or providing location observations. As in daily life, such behavior may provide new, possibly sensitive knowledge to any observer. However, in a crowded shopping or business district during business hours the user's exposure is limited. Even with knowledge of his current location, the user is hard to spot and therefore it is hard to observe his current activities or guess the user's intention, because the number and diversity of possible places where a user could be are rather high.

Similarly, S describes how difficult it is for an observer to observe or derive the user's real-life activity for a given (set of) location observation(s). Note that the observer may have good background knowledge about the user and therefore be able to derive the user's activity with little or rough and error prone location data. More formally $S(O, o_t) \in [0,1]$ expresses the probability of an adversary being able to derive the current activity of the user, i.e., the reason for her visiting location $loc(o_t)$, taking previously visited locations O into account (especially the latest, $o_m \in O$). For $S(O, o_t) = 0$ the adversary does not learn anything about the user's activity or motivation for being located at o_t, while in the case of $S(O, o_t) = 1$ the adversary can derive this information from the location data without any doubts. Due to the spatiotemporal error $\varepsilon \in \mathbb{E}$, o_t describes only an area in $\mathbb{C}$ where the user might be located. Let c'_t be the actual precise location of the user at time t. If c_t^{ae} is the adversary's estimate of the location of the user at time t (making use of background knowledge of the user and external map knowledge), then $S(O, o_t) = Pr(c'_t = c_t^{ae})$. Hence, with a growing spatiotemporal error and/or a dense and diverse landscape, the number of possible locations where a user could be increases and thus also the adversary's uncertainty regarding the user's action.

In section 5 an example implementation of location sensitivity is discussed.

Trust Relation. Third, the level of trust (denoted as θ) for a given adversary has to be modeled. In our communication scenario, the level of trust is defined as the estimated personal background knowledge a specific adversary already has about the user, based on the assumption that the user has trusted a peer to a certain extent, such that he has previously disclosed a certain amount of personal information, possibly through a different channel.

For instance, while communicating with social peers θ is more important, as with growing personal trust social contacts already have a good knowledge from other sources than mobile or social applications of the user's behavior in particular. Hence, the sensitivity of the current location might cause the individual to be more exposed, e.g., it might trigger uncomfortable questions, since these peers are able to infer subjectively sensitive places by using their background knowledge. In a communication relation with less trusted adversaries, e.g., location based services without (or with pseudonymous) registration, the protection of the user's daily routines is more important as there is usually little or no personal background knowledge. By disclosing regular patterns, the user might be identified (cf. [15,16]). By contrast, a single location sample without context on the observed individual has only little or no information value regarding the user's preferences or habits. The value of θ can be either predefined per classification of the listener class A or can be used as a user-parameter.

Definition of Privacy Loss. To formalize the discussion above, the privacy loss ΔP^A w.r.t. an adversary A, a set of m past location observations O of this adversary and a new location sample o' is

$$-\Delta P^A(O, o') = (1 - \theta_A)\Delta K_A(O, o') + \theta_A S_A(O, o') \tag{2}$$

which is the weighted knowledge gain on the user's preferences ΔK_A and the location sensitivity S_A. This proposed location privacy metric captures the relative privacy loss, instead of measuring a privacy level. Especially in environments with (partially) trusted peers, the comparison of privacy levels is difficult because of the different relations and knowledge between users. By measuring only the relative privacy loss, different adversaries can be compared. Furthermore, the sensitivity measure is bound to a certain context. Thus, there is no absolute level of location sensitivity over time.

Comparison with Anonymity Metrics. In the case of a full anonymity scenario, we assume no trust relation at all to be existent between the user and the observer. Therefore we expect no background knowledge about the user on the observer's side and choose $\theta = 0$ accordingly. That implies that only the level of K matters for the privacy (or anonymity) level. By definition K describes the length, density and quality of the adversary's observations. In the case of an anonymity metric it describes the length of the observation of a single pseudonym and the level of knowledge gained about the user by observation. Thus, for any $\Delta K > 0$ the probability of being anonymous decreases. For instance, a simple user-centric estimation on the level of anonymity could be calculated based on the results by Golle and Partridge [15].

4   Example Implementation of K

In order to calculate the user's privacy level the adversary's knowledge (gain) has to be modeled. We assumed a knowledge gain / privacy loss only if the adversary learns some previously unknown information. For a user it is important to know what extra information the disclosure of a single location sample o' gives to an adversary A w.r.t. the adversary's observation history.

In a study on movement patterns of mobile phone users, Gonzalez et al. found a characteristic strong tendency of humans to return to places they visited before. Furthermore, the probability of returning to a location depends on the number of location samples for that location. A rough estimation can be denoted as $Pr(l_k) \sim k^{-1}$ where k is the rank of the location l based on the number of observations [17]. In a similar study it was shown that the number of significant places is limited ($\approx$ 8-15). A user spends about 85% of the time at these places. However, there is a long tail area with several hundred places which are visited less than 1% of the time but make up about 15% of the user's total observation time [18]. For the proposed privacy model we concentrate on the top-L popular places (with L being in the range of about 8-15), as these places are likely to be revisited and therefore are considered as significant places in a user's routine. If we assume that the attacker's a-priori knowledge about the observed location sample o' is limited to the generic probability distribution describing human mobility patterns and the accumulated knowledge so far, then we can model the adversary's knowledge as the uncertainty assigning the observed location information to a top-L place. Entropy can be used to express the uncertainty of the adversary and therefore the user's privacy. In the following we consider a location $l \in \mathbb{C}^*$ to be an arbitrarily shaped area in $\mathbb{C}$ and denote the spatial inclusion of a precise coordinate $c \in \mathbb{C}$ in area l by writing $c \cong l$. To comply with the characteristics of human mobility patterns, we define the probability of an observed location sample o' belonging to one of the top-L locations (l_i, $i \in \{1, \ldots, L\}$) as $p_{l_i} := Pr(loc(o') \cong l_i) = \frac{\tau}{i}$ where $\tau \in (0, 1]$ is chosen in a way such that $\left(\sum_{i=1}^{L} p_{l_i}\right) + \gamma = 1$ with $\gamma \in [0, 1)$ representing the summed probability for o' belonging to one of the many seldom visited places in the long tail distribution observed by Bayir et al. [18]. Assuming that the adversary A has already discovered the top k locations of the user (by making use of the previously observed user locations in O), we make a distinction between two cases: (A) o' belongs to a frequently visited location already known to the adversary ($\exists i \in \{1, \ldots, k\} : loc(o') \cong l_i$), or (B) the adversary is not able to unambiguously connect the location observation to an already detected top-L location.

In case (A) no information about new frequently visited places is revealed. For case (B) we measure privacy as the uncertainty (i.e., entropy) on assigning o' to one of the remaining unknown top L locations. We denote with $p_{sk} := \sum_{i=1}^{k} p_{l_i}$ the summed probability for the k top locations *known* to the adversary and accordingly $p_{su} := \sum_{i=k+1}^{L} p_{l_i}$ the summed probability for the *unknown* top locations. Given that o' does not belong to one of the k known places, the probability for the remaining places $l_{k+1} \ldots l_L$ changes to $p_{l_i}^k = p_{l_i} \cdot (1 + \frac{p_{sk}}{p_{su}})$, which yields the following entropy calculation:

$$K_A^{L(B)}(O, o') = -\left(\sum_{i=k+1}^{L} p_{l_i}^k \log p_{l_i}^k \right) - \gamma \log \gamma \quad , \tag{3}$$

where γ denotes the summed probability of location samples which do not belong to the top L locations. The overall uncertainty level of the adversary is the weighted sum of the two cases (A) and (B) described above:

$$K_A^L(O, o') = p_{(A)} \cdot K_A^{L(A)}(O, o') + p_{(B)} \cdot K_A^{L(B)}(O, o') \quad , \tag{4}$$

where $p_{(A)} = p_{sk}$ is the probability of case (A) and $p_{(B)} = 1 - p_{(A)}$ the probability of case (B). Integrating the two formulas of the two cases, the overall uncertainty of an adversary for connecting o' with a top location is:

$$K_A^L(O, o') = (1 - p_{sk}) \cdot \left(-(\sum_{i=k+1}^{L} p_{l_i}^k \log p_{l_i}^k) - \gamma \log \gamma \right) \quad . \tag{5}$$

4.1   Uncertainty of a Location Observation

In order to get a robust reflection of a user's frequently visited places, using a clustering approach leads to an efficient but also abstract representation of the user's regular behavior. Several studies (e.g. [3,19]) have demonstrated that clustering is an effective tool for identification of a user's significant places.

However, the estimated or given horizontal positioning error has to be taken into account. Location information is usually expressed as inaccurate data, regardless of the error source, which is either data degraded on purpose or due to technical issues like an error prone positioning determination. Until now, we assumed a simple binary decision as to whether a location sample belongs to a regularly visited place (i.e., cluster) or not, hence $\varepsilon \cong 0$ and a function $C_O(l) = |\{o \in O \mid loc(o) \cong l\}|$ counting the number of times a user was observed at a given location $l \in \mathbb{C}^*$ (see section 4 above), making it possible to rank the places by their popularity $(l_1, l_2, \ldots l_L$, with $C_O(l_i) \geq C_O(l_{i+1})$ – which means that l_1 is the most frequently visited location). In a more realistic setting location information is error prone. Depending on the nature of the observation, the effect of $\varepsilon > 0$ is different. If the user performs the location determination, the estimated error based on the technology used is known to the user but not to the adversary. Furthermore, users might deliberately increase ε to protect their privacy.

If the location is directly observed by the adversary, both user and adversary have knowledge on the possible error distribution depending on the technology used. Depending on the communication infrastructure used, users can make assumptions about the physical limitations of the technology involved and thus can estimate a best case value for ε. In order to model the adversary's uncertainty we introduce p_c as the probability of function C^E assigning o' correctly to a location $l \in \mathbb{C}^*$, taking $\varepsilon = err(o')$ into account (and $\overline{p_c} := 1 - p_c$). As the precise definition of p_c depends on the implementation of C^E, we only assume a correlation between the error and this probability: $p_c \sim \varepsilon^{-1}$.

Modeling the adversary's uncertainty based on ε is in practice both difficult and possibly harmful to the user, since the adversary's capabilities might be underestimated, resulting in a higher and misleading privacy level. Due to limited user knowledge, a default value of $\varepsilon = 0$ is used to simulate worst case knowledge and to avoid a possibly dangerous false sense of privacy. Still, ε remains an optional variable to the user.

4.2   Determining an Adversary's Knowledge Gain

With the uncertainty value before and after disclosure of o', an adversary only gains new information if a new frequently visited location is uncovered and can be calculated as $\Delta K_A^L(O, o') = K_A^L(O, o') - K_A^L(O \setminus \{o_m\}, o_m)$, where o_m is the latest location observation in O (and therefore the direct predecessor of o').

If o' can be assigned to a known location $l_i \in L$, then $\Delta K_A^L = 0$, as by definition no information about new frequently visited places is revealed. However, the weight of already determined frequently visited places can change due to such an observation. People's preferences are not static and hence neither are their preferences regarding frequently visited places. For instance, people change employer (or workplace) and/or move from time to time. Such changes in regular behavior cause private information to be disclosed and thus harm the user's privacy. To model these changes, the observation horizon can be limited and any information older than a certain amount of time is discarded.

To model changes in the frequency of the user's top locations and a user's regular behavior, we measure the change in distribution made by a new observation. The adversary's a-priori knowledge is the distribution of the time spent at all known locations and hence their relative importance to the user. Thus, an adversary gains extra knowledge if the distribution of time spent has changed, i.e., the user's preferences have changed. For every detected location we assume that the true probability $q(O, o', l_i) := Pr_O(loc(o') \cong l_i)$ is the relative observed importance of location l_i derived from the previous observations in O (e.g. $Pr_O(loc(o') \cong l_i) \sim C_O(l)$). We define the information gain as the difference between the observed distribution before and after the disclosure of additional data. One simple method to measure the information gain is the relative entropy using KL-divergence [20]

$$K_A^C(O, o') = -\sum_{i=1}^{k} q(O, o', l_i) \log \frac{q(O, o', l_i)}{q((O \cup o'), o', l_i)} \quad , \tag{6}$$

where $q(O, o', l_i)$ denotes the probability of returning to l_i before and $q((O \cup o'), o', l_i)$ the new probability after the new observation o'. Finally, we express the privacy loss as

$$\Delta K_A(O, o') = \Delta K_A^L(O, o') + K_A^C(O, o'). \tag{7}$$

The privacy metric component ΔK_A, expressing knowledge about the user's preferred places, only measures the relative distribution of the times a user was observed at a specific place. Thus it is applicable for location based services without continuous observation or traces (e.g., location updates through an SNS are usually not continuous traces and appear infrequently).

4.3   Example

For our experiments we implemented a location cluster function based on a radius filter. For periodic and gap based location data (e.g., GSM) such a filter simply reflects how often a user was observed at a specific place. Additionally, for GPS data a gap filter was used to cover periods without GPS reception. Throughout the experiments a value of $\tau = 0.3$ was used, which roughly represents the results from the aforementioned studies on human mobility patterns. Furthermore, 12 clusters were expected. Figure 1(a) and 1(b) show 10 detected clusters from a 17-day GPS trace from a single user with a total of 17744 recorded GPS points. To measure the knowledge gain the data was segmented into daily data sets. After about 11 days the values of the final result of 10 clusters were discovered and remained constant afterwards.

The user's privacy level, based on the K_A^L, decreases almost linearly with the detection or disclosure of regularly visited places. The privacy loss caused by disclosing a low ranked place and thus with a low probability of being revisited is almost equal to that caused by disclosing a high ranked place. Especially for a setting with semi-trusted adversaries, this result reflects the (commercial) importance of lower ranked clusters w.r.t. the completeness of a user's profile. Since lower ranked clusters are harder to detect, uncovering such a place reflects the density and/or the length of observation of an adversary and thus the user's exposure.

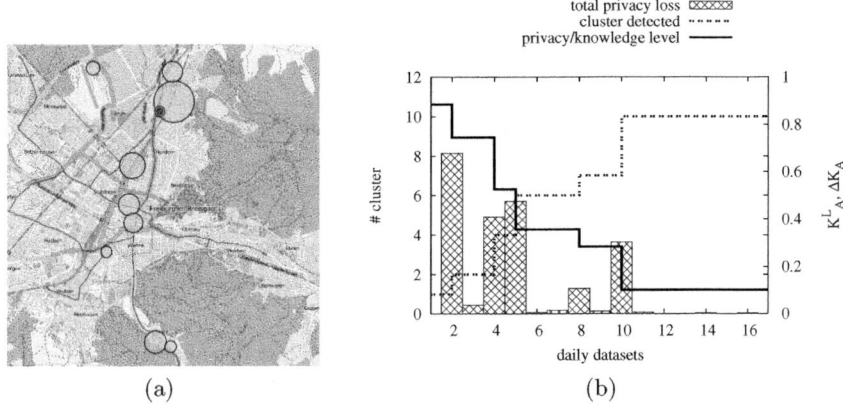

Fig. 1. A user's privacy profile to a single adversary A based on a 17-day GPS trace. The data for K_A^L was normalized to 1.0. (a) shows the cluster result after 17 days; radius of each cluster denotes its relative importance; (b) shows detected clusters and calculated privacy gain/level.

5   Example Implementation of S

The last component of a user-centric privacy metric is the sensitivity of a given location and time. In contrast to the knowledge about the user's regular behavior which an adversary could extract from frequently visited places, users might evaluate the sensitivity of certain locations w.r.t. location privacy differently at different times, depending both on the type of place and the actual listener group.

However, the sensitivity of a location at a certain time can only be measured in objective terms. Personal preferences are too diverse and a generic formalization of possible subjective measures is difficult.

5.1   Static Location Sensitivity

Based on the ideas of location l-diversity [8] and related variants we define the sensitivity of a location $l \in \mathbb{C}^*$ as the user's plausible deniability of being at a (possible) subjectively sensible location $\hat{l}$, w.r.t. the knowledge of time t and the estimated location error ε. This definition can also be rewritten as the probability of an individual being at location l^* but observed at location l. Thereby l^* is an alternative plausible location in $\mathbb{C}^*$, which is not considered as subjectively sensitive.

However, taking only into account the number of plausible positions is not always sufficient. The number, distribution and especially the nature of the possible locations matter as well. For instance, if a person is in an area with a high density of landmarks (points of interest (POIs)), an adversary's uncertainty is high regarding the user's motivation in visiting the observed area. Furthermore, with a greater number of people nearby or visiting an area, a user's privacy increases (cf. [12]). Therefore, a discounting factor $\rho \in (0..1]$ is introduced, describing the nature of a given area, i.e., decreasing the "plausibility" depending on the listener and/or time of day. The static location sensitivity is defined as

$$S_A^S(o_t) = \frac{1}{\text{numloc}(o_t)\rho(o_t)}. \tag{8}$$

The size of the area is defined by the maximum possible horizontal (deliberate or technical) location error ε and the maximum velocity at which a user can move. Function $numloc : \mathbb{O} \rightarrow \mathbb{N}$ returns the number of plausible positions for a given location sample, based on map-data. While $numloc$ is a static measurement (i.e., the geographic features are considered static), ρ is time dependent, because the use cases for the landscape change depending, for example, on the time of the day, the day of the week, the season, etc..

5.2   Dynamic Location Sensitivity

A static measurement only captures an isolated observation. In most cases people move and submit their location continuously or frequently. Therefore, the sensitivity evaluation should also contain a dynamic, time-dependent component. For instance, the adversary only knows the published positions but not the exact route in between. The adversary may use a routing algorithm to determine a likely route a user could have taken. If there is only a single route, the adversary gains perfect knowledge. Consequently, the user gains privacy if the ambiguity of possible routes increases and thus the uncertainty of the adversary regarding the locations where a user could have been between two consecutive location disclosures.

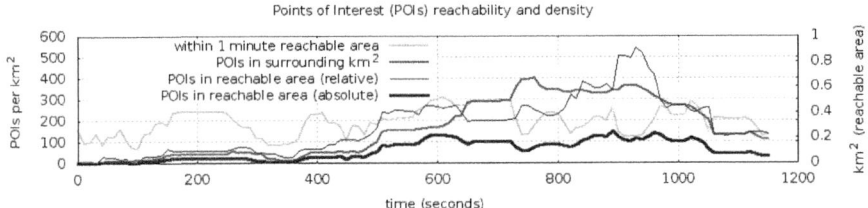

Fig. 2. A user trace of 1160 seconds, traveling 8.24 km showing the number of plausible locations and reachable POIs within one minute

We extend the static definition by including the time frame between two consecutive location disclosures as

$$S_A^D(O, o_t) = \frac{1}{\mathrm{numreach}(o_m, o_t)\rho(o_m, o_t)},\qquad(9)$$

with a function $numreach : \mathbb{O} \times \mathbb{O} \rightarrow \mathbb{N}$ calculating the number of plausible locations in the reachable area between two consecutive location disclosures $o_m \in O$ (the latest in O) and o_t, and at a given velocity. Thus, the sensitivity component reflects the objectively measurable sensitivity of the user's current position by incorporating accuracy of the location determination, time, density of measurements and landscape.

5.3   Example

The sensitivity metric measures the information gain of an adversary knowing the user's current location. In contrast to the metric on cyclic behavior, we assume the adversary's information gain is derived from direct inference of the current location and the incorporation of external knowledge (e.g., map data). For our experiments we used data from OpenStreetmap (OSM). [1] The project provides accurate and deep map data for the evaluated region and allows the characterization of possibly sensible locations (e.g., public buildings, medical facilities, banks, etc. are marked through various attributes). Furthermore, the data can be downloaded and stored on a mobile device in order to make autonomous decisions without network access.

Two simple example components of calculating ρ by exploiting map features are the density of reachable landmarks or POIs and the expected population density for a given location and time. Figure 2 shows a sample trace of about 19 minutes traveling 8.24 km through the city. The trace was started in a business/industrial area, went through a residential area (around 150-250 and from 500) before entering the city center (around 750-1000). While the number of reachable plausible positions remains roughly at the same level, the number of reachable POIs increases in the city center significantly.

---

[1] The OpenStreetmap Project, http://openstreetmap.org, [1/15/2011].

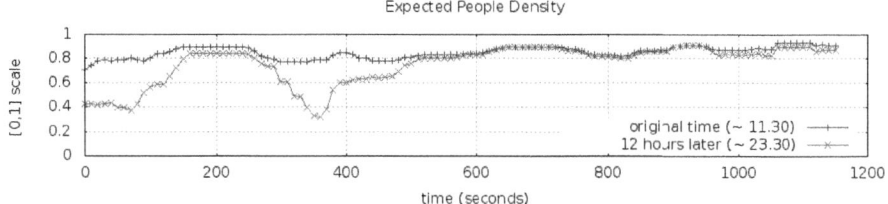

Fig. 3. Day-time dependent expected person density for a user trace of 1160 seconds, traveling 8.24 km. Calculation based on area classification based on OpenStreetmap data.

As a second example for the same trace, the expected person density was calculated. For each OSM *landuse*-tag[2] attribute a non-empirical estimation of expected person density was made. For instance, residential areas were assigned a high value for every time of day; for commercial and industrial areas a high value during business hours but otherwise a low value seems appropriate. For future work, empirical values need to be adopted. Figure 3 shows that during the day there is little variation, basically due to the fact that the trace never left city boundaries. However, at night there is a noticeable drop while crossing a business/industrial area (to 150 from 350).

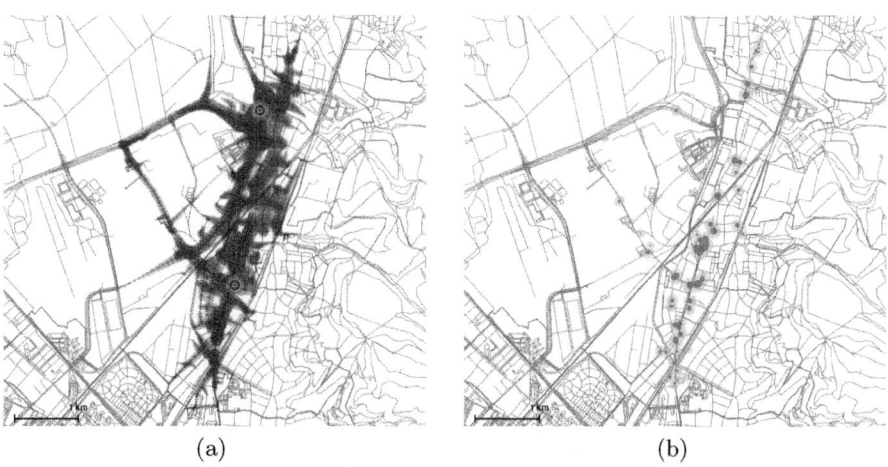

(a)   (b)

Fig. 4. (a) Reachable area between two published locations (4 min 56 sec). The radius of the circles indicate the possible waiting time to reach the final goal in time. The red line shows the actual route the user took. (b) The marked areas indicate possible visited POIs; the radius indicates the possible length of stay.

---

[2] http://wiki.openstreetmap.org/wiki/Map_Features#Landuse, [1/15/2011].

The dynamic measurement can be refined by incorporating all possible reachable plausible positions within a given timespan and velocity. Another possibility is to include all reachable POIs and the maximum possible length of stay. Figure 4(a) illustrates a possible implementation of *numreach*(), i.e., calculating all reachable plausible positions between two consecutive location disclosures. In this example the assumption about the potential travel speed was held static. This restriction can be lifted by using a more sophisticated route-planning algorithm and further external information. Figure 4(b) shows possible reachable POIs and the possible duration of stay.

6   Conclusion and Outlook

As today's communication scenarios get more diverse, the assumption of the anonymity of a user when sharing location data seems inadequate in many cases. As location information gains in importance, every entity involved in the communication process has to be considered as an adversary, since communication peers are usually considered as partially trusted.

We have proposed a theoretical user-centric privacy metric to allow a user to uncover the extent of information disclosure and to evaluate autonomously his privacy level in a communication relation with semi-trusted listener groups. The model makes no assumptions about the adversary's knowledge, capabilities or intention. The goal of such a metric is to enable an individual to estimate the knowledge gain caused by disclosing further location information in a specific communication scenario and thus enabling the user to make informed choices, e.g., choose the right protection mechanism. We divided the location privacy level into different subcomponents, reflecting the user's trust level, periodic habits leading to re-identification or to uncovering personal preferences, the evaluation of the user's exposure at a given time and differentiated between different kinds of location samples. Finally, some examples of an implementation for the main components were discussed.

For future work an implementation in a real-world application has to be developed together with a simple visualization of the privacy metric result. Therewith (location) privacy becomes for the user a more concrete fact instead of simply an abstract definition.

References

1. Westin, A.F.: Privacy and Freedom, 1st edn., Atheneum, New York (1967)
2. Duckham, M., Kulik, L.: Location privacy and location-aware computing, pp. 35–51. CRC Press, Boca Rator (2006)
3. Hoh, B., Gruteser, M., Xiong, H., Alrabady, A.: Achieving guaranteed anonymity in gps traces via uncertainty-aware path cloaking. IEEE Transactions on Mobile Computing 9(8), 1089–1107 (2010)
4. Shokri, R., Freudiger, J., Jadliwala, M., Hubaux, J.P.: A distortion-based metric for location privacy. In: WPES 2009: Proceedings of the 8th ACM workshop on Privacy in the Electronic Society, pp. 21–30. ACM, New York (2009)

5. Sweeney, L.: k-anonymity: a model for protecting privacy. Int. J. Uncertain. Fuzziness Knowl.-Based Syst. 10(5), 557–570 (2002)
6. Gruteser, M., Grunwald, D.: Anonymous usage of location-based services through spatial and temporal cloaking. In: MobiSys 2003: Proceedings of the 1st International Conference on Mobile Systems, Applications and Services, pp. 31–42. ACM, New York (2003)
7. Gedik, B., Liu, L.: Protecting location privacy with personalized k-anonymity: Architecture and algorithms. IEEE Transactions on Mobile Computing 7(1), 1–18 (2008)
8. Liu, L.: Privacy and location anonymization in location-based services. SIGSPATIAL Special 1, 15–22 (2009)
9. Bettini, C., Wang, X.S., Jajodia, S.: Protecting Privacy Against Location-Based Personal Identification. In: Jonker, W., Petković, M. (eds.) SDM 2005. LNCS, vol. 3674, pp. 185–199. Springer, Heidelberg (2005)
10. Beresford, A., Stajano, F.: Location privacy in pervasive computing. IEEE Pervasive Computing 2(1), 46–55 (2003)
11. Cranshaw, J., Toch, E., Hong, J., Kittur, A., Sadeh, N.: Bridging the gap between physical location and online social networks. In: Ubicomp 2010: Proceedings of the 12th ACM International Conference on Ubiquitous Computing, pp. 119–128. ACM, New York (2010)
12. Toch, E., Cranshaw, J., Drielsma, P.H., Tsai, J.Y., Kelley, P.G., Springfield, J., Cranor, L., Hong, J., Sadeh, N.: Empirical models of privacy in location sharing. In: Ubicomp 2010: Proceedings of the 12th ACM International Conference on Ubiquitous Computing, pp. 129–138. ACM, New York (2010)
13. Díaz, C., Seys, S., Claessens, J., Preneel, B.: Towards Measuring Anonymity. In: Dingledine, R., Syverson, P.F. (eds.) PET 2002. LNCS, vol. 2482, pp. 54–68. Springer, Heidelberg (2003)
14. Kamiyama, K., Ngoc, T.H., Echizen, I., Yoshiura, H.: Measuring Accumulated Revelations of Private Information by Multiple Media. In: Cellary, W., Estevez, E. (eds.) Software Services for e-World. IFIP AICT, vol. 341, pp. 70–80. Springer, Heidelberg (2010)
15. Golle, P., Partridge, K.: On the Anonymity of Home/Work Location Pairs. In: Tokuda, H., Beigl, M., Friday, A., Brush, A.J.B., Tobe, Y. (eds.) Pervasive 2009. LNCS, vol. 5538, pp. 390–397. Springer, Heidelberg (2009)
16. Ma, C.Y., Yau, D.K., Yip, N.K., Rao, N.S.: Privacy vulnerability of published anonymous mobility traces. In: Proceedings of the Sixteenth Annual International Conference on Mobile Computing and Networking, MobiCom 2010, pp. 185–196. ACM, New York (2010)
17. Gonzalez, M.C., Hidalgo, C.A., Barabasi, A.-L.: Understanding individual human mobility patterns. Nature 453(7196), 779–782 (2008)
18. Bayir, M., Demirbas, M., Eagle, N.: Discovering spatiotemporal mobility profiles of cellphone users. In: IEEE International Symposium on a World of Wireless, Mobile and Multimedia Networks & Workshops, WoWMoM 2009, pp. 1–9 (2009)
19. Ashbrook, D., Starner, T.: Using gps to learn significant locations and predict movement across multiple users. Personal Ubiquitous Comput. 7, 275–286 (2003)
20. Kullback, S., Leibler, R.A.: On information and sufficiency. The Annals of Mathematical Statistics 22(1), 79–86 (1951)

Fairness in Non-Repudiation Protocols

Wojciech Jamroga, Sjouke Mauw, and Matthijs Melissen

Computer Science and Communication
University of Luxembourg

Abstract. We indicate two problems with the specifications of fairness that are currently used for the verification of non-repudiation and other fair-exchange protocols. The first of these problems is the implicit assumption of perfect information. The second problem is the possible lack of effectiveness. We solve both problems in isolation by giving new definitions of fairness, but leave the combined solution for further work. Moreover, we establish a hierarchy of various definitions of fairness, and indicate the consequences for existing work.

Keywords: Security protocols, verification, non-repudiation and fair exchange protocols, alternating-time temporal logic, imperfect information.

1   Introduction

The correctness of a security protocol depends in general on the precise formulation of its security requirements. Consequently, the development of appropriate security requirements is at least as important as the proper design of security protocols. Classical requirements, such as *confidentiality* and *authentication*, are well understood and have been exhaustively investigated [1,2,3]. Research on more recent requirements, such as *receipt-freeness* in electronic voting protocols [4,5], seems to converge, while for other properties, such as *ownership transfer* in RFID protocols, discussions have only recently started [6].

In this paper, we study the development of the requirement of *fairness* for *non-repudiation protocols*. The main goal of a non-repudiation protocol is to allow two (or more) parties to exchange goods or messages without any of the parties being able to falsely deny having taken part in the exchange. Such a protocol is designed so that the sender of the message obtains a *non-repudiation of receipt* (NRR) evidence and the receiver of the message a *non-repudiation of origin* (NRO) evidence. The main security requirement is *fairness*, which roughly states that if the receiver obtains NRO, then the sender can obtain NRR, and vice versa. An example of a non-repudiation protocol is a *certified e-mail* protocol [7].

Although other requirements, such as *abuse-freeness*, also apply to non-repudiation protocols (and the wider class of *fair-exchange protocols*), we will only investigate fairness and its relation to *effectiveness* and *strategic timeliness*. Effectiveness (sometimes also called *viability*) is not a security requirement, but a functional requirement, stating that the protocol can actually achieve the exchange of an NRR and an NRO evidence. Strategic timeliness requires that an agent always has an honest strategy to stop execution of the protocol.

C. Meadows and C. Fernández-Gago (Eds.): STM 2011, LNCS 7170, pp. 122–139, 2012.
© Springer-Verlag Berlin Heidelberg 2012

In the literature on non-repudiation protocols, a variety of different interpretations of the fairness requirement have been described. Most of these were formalized in the modal logic ATL [8] as to allow for the automated verification of protocols through model checking, for example in the Mocha model checker [9]. The observed variations seem to be due to differences in the assumed execution models of the agents involved, to differences in the adversary model, and to differences in the intended application of the protocol. Some authors already provided insight in the relation between some of the fairness definitions [10].

Nevertheless, we observe two limitations of the existing definitions. The first concerns the implicit assumption of *perfect information*, as it is called in game theory. By this we mean that, at each moment, all agents have full knowledge of the global state of the system. In practice this does not seem a realistic assumption for a security protocol. One would expect an agent to only know his own state and use a protocol to infer knowledge of the other agents' states. This assumption has a significant impact on the formulation of fairness in ATL.

The second limitation concerns the combination of fairness and effectiveness. In the game-theoretical setting, both properties are expressed in terms of the existence of strategies. By taking the conjunction of the two properties, one does not necessarily obtain a single strategy that enforces both fairness and effectiveness. Here, we propose a new property which blends fairness and effectiveness properly.

The contribution of this paper is as follows. *(i)* We revisit existing notions of fairness (Sec. 3.1). *(ii)* We introduce a notion of fairness based on the assumption of imperfect information (Sec. 3.2). *(iii)* We combine fairness and effectiveness (Sec. 3.3). *(iv)* We develop the hierarchy of fairness requirements and prove correctness and strictness of the inclusions (Sec. 4). *(v)* We consider implications for the practical use of various notions of fairness in the literature (Sec. 5). These contributions are preceded by a short introduction to non-repudiation protocols and an overview of the logic ATL (Sec. 2).

2   Preliminaries

2.1   Non-Repudiation Protocols

Non-repudiation guarantees that an agent cannot deny having taken part in a message exchange, if it has actually done so in the course of the protocol [11]. To achieve this, protocol participants usually collect evidences that can later be presented to a judge. If Alice sends a message m to Bob, we can distinguish a *non-repudiation of origin* (NRO) evidence, which proves that Alice cannot deny having sent m, and a *non-repudiation of receipt* (NRR) evidence, which proves that Bob cannot deny having received m. Both Alice and Bob have an incentive to cheat. This means that, e.g., Bob may try to obtain m without providing an NRR. Evidences are typically implemented with cryptographic signatures over the message (and possibly some other data).

It is often desirable to have the guarantee of fair exchange [12] of non-repudiation. For example, when Alice sends message m to Bob, it should hold that Alice receives NRR if and only if Bob receives NRO.

Fairness cannot be ensured without at least one external agent, which is trusted by both parties, and is called a Trusted Third Party (TTP) [13]. The TTP can be *inline, online* or *offline*. An inline TTP handles the items to be exchanged. An online TTP does *not* handle the items to be exchanged, but is necessary in each invocation of the main protocol. An offline TTP is only invoked in dispute resolution.

The communication channels between the TTP and the other agents are assumed to be *resilient*, i.e. all data is delivered after a finite, but unknown amount of time. The communication channels between the other agents are assumed to be *unreliable*, i.e. data may be lost. We assume a standard Dolev-Yao attacker who has full control over the unreliable channels of the network and who may co-operate with any of the possibly dishonest parties to disrupt the protocol.

In this paper, we assume that all messages and evidences that are being transmitted are labeled with the type of the message or evidence, the name of the sender, the name of the intended recipient, the name of the TTP which is agreed upon, and an identifier linking the message to the protocol session. Further, as to focus on non-repudiation, we assume in the example protocols that all exchanged messages are cryptographically protected, thereby preventing possible attacks on confidentiality and authenticity of the exchanged messages.

Protocol 1.	Protocol 2.
1. $A \rightarrow B$: m, NRO	1. $A \rightarrow T$: m, NRO
2. $B \rightarrow A$: NRR	2. $T \rightarrow B$: m
	3. $B \rightarrow T$: NRR
	4. $T \rightarrow B$: NRO
	5. $T \rightarrow A$: NRR

Protocol 1 is an example of a simple non-repudiation protocol, where Alice and Bob exchange non-repudiation of origin and receipt of message m. The protocol specifies that first Alice sends message m and NRO to Bob, and then Bob sends NRR to Alice. Here, NRO could be implemented as $[f_{NRO}, A, B, m]_A$ and NRR as $[f_{NRR}, A, B, m]_B$, where $[M]_C$ is the signature of agent C over message M, and f_{NRR} and f_{NRO} are flags indicating the type of the evidence. Note that this protocol is not fair, as Bob can abort after step 1, leaving Alice without NRR. Protocol 2 is an example of a fair NR-protocol (with inline TTP). Fairness is intuitively guaranteed because the TTP will not send out NRO and NRR before he has collected both evidences.

Non-repudiation protocols with inline TTP are generally inefficient, as the TTP becomes easily a bottleneck. Protocols with offline TTP do not suffer from this problem, but also tend to be more complex, as they typically comtain non-determinism and various sub-protocols. This means that it is less easy to check by hand that fairness is satisfied.. Therefore, a formal way of verifying fairness is needed.

2.2   Alternating-Time Temporal Logic

We use alternating-time temporal logic (ATL) [8] to specify requirements of fair exchange. ATL is very suitable for specification of security protocols, because it allows to express that there exists *a strategy* with which an agent obtains a desired property, instead of requiring that all protocol runs have to satisfy the property, independent of the agent's behavior. We only give a brief introduction to ATL; we refer to [8] for the full definition.

An ATL formula is one of the following:

- p, for propositions $p \in \Pi$
- $\neg \varphi$ or $\varphi_1 \vee \varphi_2$, where φ, φ_1 and φ_2 are ATL formulas.
- $\langle\!\langle A \rangle\!\rangle \bigcirc \varphi$, $\langle\!\langle A \rangle\!\rangle \Box \varphi$ or $\langle\!\langle A \rangle\!\rangle \varphi_1 \, \mathcal{U} \, \varphi_2$, where $A \subseteq \Sigma$ is a set of agents, and φ, φ_1 and φ_2 are ATL formulas.

The *strategic operator* $\langle\!\langle A \rangle\!\rangle$ can be seen as a path quantifier that ranges over all paths that the agents in A can force the game into, irrespective of how the other agents proceed. Furthermore, $\bigcirc$ ("next"), $\Box$ ("always") and $\mathcal{U}$ ("until") are *temporal operators*. Sometimes we write $\langle\!\langle a_1, \ldots, a_n \rangle\!\rangle$ instead of $\langle\!\langle \{a_1, \ldots, a_n\} \rangle\!\rangle$. Additional Boolean connectives are defined in the usual manner. We also define $\Diamond$ ("eventually") as $\Diamond\varphi \equiv \mathsf{true} \, \mathcal{U} \, \varphi$.

ATL formulas are interpreted in a *concurrent games structure* (*CGS*), which is a tuple $S = \langle \mathrm{Agt}, Act, Q, \Pi, \pi, d, \delta \rangle$ with the following components: a finite set Agt of *agents*; a finite set Q of *states*; a finite set Π of *propositions*; for each state $q \in Q$, a set $\pi(q) \subseteq \Pi$ of propositions true at q; for each agent $A \in \mathrm{Agt}$ and each state $q \in Q$, a set $d_A(q) \subseteq Act$ of actions available at state $q \in Q$ to agent $A \in \mathrm{Agt}$; and a transition function δ that assigns a new state $\delta(q, j_1, \ldots, j_k) \in Q$ to every combination of state q and actions $j_1, \ldots, j_k$, one per agent in Agt.

A *path* in S is an infinite sequence $\lambda = q_0, q_1, q_2, \ldots$ of states such that for all positions $i \geq 0$, we have $q_{i+1} = \delta(q, j_1, \ldots, j_k)$ for some actions $j_1, \ldots, j_k$. We refer to a path starting at state q as a *q-path*. For a path λ and a position $i \geq 0$, we use $\lambda[i]$ and $\lambda[0, i]$ to denote the i-th state of λ and the finite prefix $q_0, q_1, \ldots, q_i$ of λ, respectively. A *strategy* f_A for agent A determines, for every finite sequence of states s, an action $f_A(s)$ for agent A. A collective strategy F_A is simply a tuple of strategies f_A, one for each agent $A \in \mathcal{A}$. We define the *outcome* of F_A from $q \in Q$ as the set $out(q, F_A)$ of q-paths that the agents in $\mathcal{A}$ enforce when executing F_A. The semantics of ATL is defined as follows:

- $S, q \models p$ for propositions $p \in \Pi$, iff $p \in \pi(q)$.
- $S, q \models \neg\varphi$ iff $S, q \not\models \varphi$.
- $S, q \models \varphi_1 \vee \varphi_2$ iff $S, q \models \varphi_1$ or $S, q \models \varphi_2$.
- $S, q \models \langle\!\langle A \rangle\!\rangle \bigcirc \varphi$ iff there exists a collective strategy F_A such that for all paths $\lambda \in out(q, F_A)$, we have $S, \lambda[1] \models \varphi$.

- $S, q \models \langle\!\langle A \rangle\!\rangle \Box \varphi$ iff there exists F_A such that for all $\lambda \in out(q, F_A)$ and all positions $i \geq 0$, we have $S, \lambda[i] \models \varphi$.
- $S, q \models \langle\!\langle A \rangle\!\rangle \varphi_1 \: \mathcal{U} \: \varphi_2$ iff there exists F_A such that for all $\lambda \in out(q, F_A)$ there exists $i \geq 0$ with $S, \lambda[i] \models \varphi_2$ and for all $0 \leq j < i$ we have $S, \lambda[j] \models \varphi_1$.

The universal path quantifier of the branching-time temporal logic CTL can be captured in ATL as $\forall \equiv \langle\!\langle \emptyset \rangle\!\rangle$. The existential path quantifier $\exists$ will be interpreted as usual in CTL. The expressiveness of ATL can be illustrated by the following examples. The formula $\neg\langle\!\langle A \rangle\!\rangle \Diamond\varphi$ means that A does not have a strategy to ever obtain φ. The formula $\forall\Box(\langle\!\langle B \rangle\!\rangle\Box\neg\varphi \vee \exists\Diamond\psi)$ means that in every reachable state, either B has a strategy that always avoids φ, or there exists a path that eventually results in a state where ψ holds.

The following properties will be used later. Proofs are straightforward.

Fact 1. $q \models \neg\exists\varphi$ *implies* $q \models \neg\langle\!\langle \mathbb{Agt} \rangle\!\rangle\varphi$.

Fact 2. $S, q \models \langle\!\langle A \rangle\!\rangle(\varphi \: \mathcal{U} \: \psi)$ *implies* $S, q \models \langle\!\langle A \rangle\!\rangle\Diamond\psi$.

3   Capturing Fairness of Exchange in ATL

Various ATL definitions of fairness have been proposed in the literature on non-repudiation protocols and other fair exchange protocols. In this section, we give an overview of the proposed definitions. Then, we have a look at two fundamental problems with the existing formalizations and propose how they can be repaired.

3.1   Existing Formalizations

When Alice sends a message to Bob, one can distinguish *fairness for Alice* (whenever Bob receives NRO, Alice is guaranteed to receive NRR), and *fairness for Bob* (whenever Alice receives NRR, Bob is guaranteed to receive NRO). We only consider fairness for Alice; fairness for Bob can be formulated symmetrically.

Fairness for an agent only needs to be guaranteed when the agent complies with the protocol: if an agent does not follow the protocol, he does that at his own risk. An agent that complies with the protocol is called *honest*. Fairness should be guaranteed for honest agents even if the other agents are *dishonest*, i.e., behave in a way that is not foreseen by the protocol. Therefore, when studying fairness for Alice, we assume that Alice is honest and that Bob might be dishonest. We do not require recovery of fairness after unintended dishonest behavior caused by system failures, as has been considered in [14,15].

To check fairness of a protocol using ATL, the protocol is modeled as a concurrent game structure [10]. We set agents $\mathbb{Agt} = \{A_h, B, T\}$, where A stands for Alice, B stands for Bob, X_h signifies that agent X is restricted to honest behavior, and T stands for the TTP (which is always honest). Furthermore we set propositions $\Pi = \{\mathsf{NRO}, \mathsf{NRR}\}$. The proposition NRO is true in these states where Bob possesses non-repudiation of origin, and the proposition NRR is true in these states where Alice possesses non-repudiation of receipt. We assume that the model is *turn-based* (i.e., agents do not act simultaneously), and that the behavior of the TTP is deterministic (given the current state of the system). We do not model the communication channel explicitly to simplify the notation and avoid the necessity to formalize channel resilience, which cannot be done in "pure" ATL.

Strong Fairness. One of the definitions of fairness proposed by Kremer and Raskin [16] is *strong fairness*. It can be formulated as follows:

$$\textsc{StrongFair} \equiv \forall\Box(\mathsf{NRO} \to \forall\Diamond\mathsf{NRR})$$

Strong fairness for Alice states that in every reachable state where Bob has NRO, Alice should eventually obtain NRR, whatever the agents do. Strong fairness can be seen as *enforced fairness*: if due to underspecification the protocol is non-deterministic and thus gives Alice multiple available strategies, each of these strategies should guarantee her NRR.

Non-enforced Fairness. If we assume that Alice is rational, StrongFair is stronger than necessary. A weaker form of fairness, which requires Alice to play rational, has also been proposed by Kremer and Raskin [16] through the following ATL formula:

$$\textsc{NEFair} \equiv \neg\langle\!\langle B \rangle\!\rangle\Diamond(\mathsf{NRO} \land \neg\langle\!\langle A_h \rangle\!\rangle\Diamond\mathsf{NRR})$$

This formula states that Bob should not have a strategy to reach a state where he has NRO while Alice at the same time does not have a strategy to obtain NRR. We will call this notion *non-enforced fairness*, because a protocol that satisfies this requirement does not *enforce* fairness: if Alice has multiple strategies, one "good" strategy is sufficient; the other strategies might still result in an unfair situation.

Strategic Fairness. An intermediate notion of fairness, called *strategic fairness*, has been proposed by Chadha et al. [10].

$$\textsc{StratFair} \equiv \forall\Box(\mathsf{NRO} \to \langle\!\langle A_h \rangle\!\rangle\Diamond\mathsf{NRR})$$

A protocol satisfies *strategic fairness* for Alice if and only if in every reachable state, it holds that whenever Bob has received NRO, there exists a strategy for honest Alice that gives her NRR.

It seems to us, however, that this definition is counterintuitive, as it combines the enforced and non-enforced approach. If one assumes that Alice has enough rationality to resolve non-determinism in the correct way, then it is not necessary to require that she obtains the fair situation $\mathsf{NRO} \to \langle\!\langle A_h \rangle\!\rangle\Diamond\mathsf{NRR}$ independently of her strategy; it would suffice if there *exists* a strategy for Alice that guarantees the fair situation. On the other hand, if one does not assume that Alice is able to resolve non-determinism in the correct way, then it is not enough to require that there *exists* a strategy that gives her NRR; she might still never receive NRR when she never plays the right strategy. Therefore, strategic fairness is too strong for rational agents, and too weak for agents without rationality.

Weak Fairness. Another definition of fairness, proposed by Chadha et al. [10] to simplify verification, is *weak fairness*.

$$\textsc{WeakFair} \equiv \forall\Box(\mathsf{NRO} \to \exists\Diamond\mathsf{NRR})$$

A protocol satisfies weak fairness for Alice if and only if in every reachable state, it holds that whenever Bob has received NRO, if all agents cooperate, Alice will eventually get NRR.

Invariant Fairness. One disadvantage with the above formulations of fairness is that counterexamples cannot always be expressed as single paths. An alternative definition of fairness is proposed based on invariants. *Invariant fairness* [10] for Alice only tests those states in which Alice has stopped the protocol, allowing counterexamples to be expressed as traces. We define the proposition Stop_A to be true exactly when Alice has stopped executing the protocol. It is assumed that as soon as Alice has stopped executing the protocol, she cannot receive NRR anymore, i.e., $\forall\Box((\mathrm{Stop}_A \wedge \neg\mathsf{NRR}) \to \forall\Box\neg\mathsf{NRR})$. Now invariant fairness is defined as follows:

$$\textsc{InvFair} \equiv \forall\Box(\mathrm{Stop}_A \to (\mathsf{NRO} \to \mathsf{NRR}))$$

This formula states that in all states where Alice has stopped executing the protocol, Alice should possess NRR whenever Bob possesses NRO.

3.2   Fair Exchange and Imperfect Information

ATL formulas are normally evaluated in a model that assumes *perfect information*, that is, agents are assumed to know precisely the current global state of the system, including the local states of the other agents [8]. This is also the way in which Mocha evaluates ATL formulas. This assumption is unrealistic for communication protocols: if all agents knew the local state of all other agents, no communication would be needed. We will look at NEFAIR, and see that assuming perfect information, as is done in [16], leads to counterintuitive results.

A perfect information strategy for Alice can be *non-executable* under imperfect information: the strategy might require executing different actions in situations that look the same to Alice. Furthermore, even if she has an executable strategy, she may be unaware of having it, and unable to identify it [17]. For example, one can construct a protocol in which the message that Alice needs to send depends on whether Bob did or did not receive some other message. Alice does not know which messages have been received by Bob, so although she has a strategy to send the right message if she had perfect information, she is not able to follow this strategy under imperfect information.

An example of this is Protocol 3, in which Alice sends message m to Bob, and NRO and NRR are exchanged. First, Alice sends m and NRO to the TTP. The TTP forwards m to Bob, who replies by sending NRR and a boolean p back to the TTP. Then the TTP sends NRO to Bob. Alice continues by sending a boolean p' to the TTP. Only if Bob's boolean p equals Alice's boolean p', the TTP sends NRR to Alice.

Protocol 3.	Protocol 4.

Protocol 3.
1. $A \to T$: m, NRO
2. $T \to B$: m
3. $B \to T$: NRR, bool p
4. $T \to B$: NRO
5. $A \to T$: bool p'
6. If $p = p'$:
   (a) $T \to A$: NRR

Protocol 4.
1. $T \to A$: start
2. $T \to B$: start
3. Choose between:
   (a) 1. $A \to T$: NRO, request_id
      2. $B \to T$: NRR, id
      3. $T \to B$: NRO
      4. $A \to T$: re-request_id
   (b) 1. $B \to T$: NRR, id
      2. $A \to T$: NRO, request_id
      3. $T \to B$: NRO
4. $T \to A$: NRR, id

Intuitively, Protocol 3 is not a fair protocol, as Alice can only obtain NRR by sending p' in step 5 such that p' equals p. However, she does not have a way of knowing p, and therefore does not know the correct value of p'. Nevertheless, the protocol satisfies NEFAIR, as $\langle\langle A_h \rangle\rangle \Diamond$NRR is true in step 5, since Alice has a correct (perfect information) strategy: if $p = $ false, she sends false, and if $p = $ true, she sends true. The problem is that this strategy is not executable if Alice has imperfect information.

In the previous example, it is immediately obvious that Alice's lack of uinformation causes the protocol to be broken. Protocol 4 is a less contrived example (to simplify the presentation, it is assumed that the TTP stops sending messages to agents from which he receives messages that do not correspond to the protocol). Here, the non-determinism is caused by the order of arrival of messages, instead of by a boolean chosen by the other agent. In this protocol, first the TTP sends the message start to Alice and Bob. Then Alice sends NRO and a message request_id to request Bob's id to the TTP, and Bob sends NRR and his id to the TTP. However, the behavior of the TTP depends on the order in which these messages arrive. If the request arrives before the id, as in branch (a), the TTP sends NRO to Bob, but Alice's request is ignored until Alice sends an additional message re-request_id, on which the TTP sends her the id and NRR. If the request arrives after the id, as in branch (b), the TTP sends NRO to Bob and, immediately, NRR and the id to Alice.

This implies that Alice will never receive NRR in case she does not send re-request_id in branch (a). On the other hand, in branch (b) Alice will never receive NRR if she does send re-request_id. Alice cannot know or make sure that request_id arrives before or after Bob's id, and neither does she know how long the TTP will wait before answering her. Therefore, Alice does not know which branch of the protocol is executed by the TTP, which means that she does not know whether she needs to send request_id or not. Still, this protocol satisfies NEFAIR, as Alice has a perfect information strategy to obtain NRR, namely sending re-request_id in branch (a) and not sending it in (b).

The problem can be solved by interpreting specifications in *ATL with imperfect information* [18], where agents can only observe a part of the global state, and their strategy is required to choose the same action in states they cannot distinguish. That version of ATL is interpreted in an *imperfect information con-current game structure* (*iCGS*)), which is a concurrent game structure extended with an *indistinguishability relation* $\sim_A$ for every agent $A \in \text{Agt}$. Strategies are required to be *uniform*, that is, if sequences s, s' are indistinguishable for agent A, written $s \sim_A s'$, then the strategy for agent A assigns the same action to s and s', i.e., $f_A(s) = f_A(s')$. Now, the semantics of $\langle\!\langle A \rangle\!\rangle\Box$ is changed as follows: $q \models \langle\!\langle A \rangle\!\rangle\Box\varphi$ if and only if there exists a uniform collective strategy F_A such that for all agents $A \in \mathcal{A}$, states $q' \sim_A q$, paths $\lambda \in out(q', F_A)$ and positions $i \geq 0$, we have $\lambda[i] \models \varphi$. The semantics of "next" and "until" are changed in the same way. Note that: (1) the set of uniform strategies in S is always a subset of perfect information strategies in S; (2) perfect information semantics of ATL is well-defined in iCGS (it simply ignores the indistinguishability relations); (3) each CGS can be seen as an iCGS where for every agent a, $\sim_a$ is the minimal reflexive relation.

Imperfect information semantics is sufficient to give an intuitive interpretation to STRATFAIR, WEAKFAIR, STRONGFAIR and INVFAIR (for the latter too, the choice of semantics only matters if the initial state is unknown). However, it is not enough to "repair" NEFAIR. If Alice wants to be sure that she can obtain NRR, it is also necessary to use *non-enforced controled fairness* (NECFAIR) instead of NEFAIR.

$$\text{NECFAIR} \equiv \langle\!\langle A_h \rangle\!\rangle\Box\neg(\text{NRO} \wedge \neg\langle\!\langle A_h \rangle\!\rangle\Diamond\text{NRR})$$

To see the difference between NEFAIR and NECFAIR, we define an *unfair situation* (in which Bob has NRO and Alice does not have a strategy to obtain NRR) as UNFAIR $\equiv$ (NRO $\wedge \neg\langle\!\langle A_h \rangle\!\rangle\Diamond$NRR). Then we can write:

$$\text{NEFAIR} \equiv \neg\langle\!\langle B \rangle\!\rangle\Diamond\text{UNFAIR},$$
$$\text{NECFAIR} \equiv \langle\!\langle A_h \rangle\!\rangle\Box\neg\text{UNFAIR}.$$

Note also that for models with Agt $= \{A, B, T\}$ and deterministic T, the NEFAIR requirement is equivalent to $\neg\langle\!\langle \text{Agt}\backslash A_h \rangle\!\rangle\Diamond$UNFAIR. That is, NEFAIR requires that all agents but Alice have no common strategy to reach an unfair situation, while NECFAIR states that Alice has a strategy to always avoid an unfair situation, i.e., Alice is *in control* over the outcome. These two formulas are equivalent assuming perfect information and turn-based models [8]. However, in imperfect information models, both NEFAIR and the negation of NECFAIR can hold, as for example in Protocol 3 (on the other hand, NECFAIR does imply NEFAIR, even in imperfect information models). Because Protocol 3 is intuitively unfair, we have that under imperfect information, NEFAIR is not sufficient for Alice to avoid an unfair situation and NECFAIR should be required.

In some situations, Alice might accept that she cannot avoid an unfair situation, as long as Bob does not have a strategy to bring Alice in an unfair situation. In that case, NEFAIR, the weaker form of fairness, is sufficient. Consider for example the case where Bob wants to rob Alice's locker by opening the lock with the right code. Bob could be lucky in guessing the right code and therefore Alice has no strategy to avoid an unfair situation. Alice might accept this, as long as

Bob does not have a (imperfect information) strategy that guarantees that he opens the locker, and the number of possible codes is sufficiently large.

From now on, we will follow Schobbens [18] and use subscripts I (respectively i) to denote that the specification is interpreted in the perfect (resp. imperfect) information semantics of ATL whenever the type of semantics has impact on the truth of the specification. We will also write that φ_x *implies* ψ_y iff, for every iCGS S and state q in it, we have that $S, q \models_x \varphi$ implies $S, q \models_y \psi$.

Fact 3. *If φ includes no strategic operators then $(\langle\!\langle A \rangle\!\rangle \varphi)_i$ implies $(\langle\!\langle A \rangle\!\rangle \varphi)_I$. The converse does not hold in general.*

3.3   Effective Fairness

Now we show that fairness is not sufficient for a fair-exchange protocol, and discuss an additional requirement, called *effectiveness* (in some papers also *viability*). It turns out that combine these two requirements is not trivial.

To see the need for effectiveness, consider the *empty protocol*, i.e., the (admittedly useless) protocol, that specifies that no message will be sent. It is obvious that this protocol satisfies all definitions of fairness discussed above, as no unfair situation can possibly occur. Still the protocol is clearly not a good fair-exchange protocol, because even if the agents want to, they cannot exchange evidences.

To prevent protocols like this, we need to impose a second requirement (besides fairness), that states that the protocol is *effective*. This means that Alice and Bob have a collective strategy to run the protocol such that both agents obtain their evidence. This requirement can be formulated in ATL as follows:

$$\text{EFFECTIVE} \equiv \langle\!\langle A_h, B_h \rangle\!\rangle \Diamond (\text{NRO} \wedge \text{NRR})$$

Requiring effectiveness excludes the empty protocol. However, requiring both effectiveness and non-enforced fairness is not sufficient to rule out bad protocols. To see this, let us consider Protocol 5.

Protocol 5.

---
1. Choice for A:
   - (a) 1. $A \rightarrow B$: NRO
       2. $B \rightarrow A$: NRR
   - (b) End of protocol.

In this protocol, Alice can choose to either send NRO to Bob and wait for NRR to be sent to her, or immediately stop the protocol.

This protocol is effective (if Alice chooses 1a and both parties continue the protocol, they get their evidence. Furthermore, the protocol satisfies non-enforced fairness, because Alice has a strategy to achieve fairness (by choosing 1b). Thus, the protocol satisfies both (non-enforced) fairness and effectiveness. However, intuitively, it is still not a good protocol, as Bob might be dishonest and stop the protocol after 1(a)1, leaving Alice without her evidence. This problem arises because A's strategy that guarantees effectiveness is different from A's strategy that guarantees fairness. To solve this problem, we need to require that there exists a strategy for Alice that satisfies both effectiveness and fairness at the same time. The following ATL formula accomplishes this:

$$\langle\!\langle A_h, B_h \rangle\!\rangle(\text{NEFair } \mathcal{U} \ (\text{NRO} \wedge \text{NRR}))$$

This formula expresses that A and B have a collective strategy that guarantees NEFair for Alice until both Bob and Alice have their evidence.

The formula requires that Bob is honest in the outer quantifier, but allows Bob to be dishonest in the quantifier inside NEFair. This is a problem, as agents need to be either modeled as honest or dishonest. Therefore, we introduce an additional proposition Honest$_B$, which is true as long as Bob has only sent messages allowed by the protocol. Now we can reformulate the requirement for Bob's honesty so that it applies only to effectiveness and not fairness:

$$\text{EffFair} \equiv \langle\!\langle A_h, B \rangle\!\rangle(\text{NECFair } \mathcal{U} \ (\text{NRO} \wedge \text{NRR} \wedge \text{Honest}_B))$$

Now we show that effective fairness indeed guarantees both effectiveness and non-enforced fairness.

Theorem 1. EffFair$_I$ *implies* Effective$_I$ *and* NECFair$_I$, *and* EffFair$_i$ *implies* Effective$_i$ *and* NECFair$_i$.

Proof. That EffFair$_I$ implies Effective$_I$ follows directly from Fact 2. To prove that EffFair$_I$ implies NECFair$_I$, we show first that NRO $\wedge$ NRR implies NECFair$_I$. Assume $S, q \models_I$ NRO $\wedge$ NRR. Let λ be a q-path and $i \geq 0$. Then we have that $S, \lambda[i] \models_I$ NRR (as NRR is a property that stays true after it has been true for the first time). Then it holds that $S, \lambda[i] \models_I \langle\!\langle A_h \rangle\!\rangle\text{true } \mathcal{U}$ NRR and thus $S, \lambda[i] \models_I \langle\!\langle A_h \rangle\!\rangle\Diamond$NRR, and therefore $S, \lambda[i] \not\models_I$ NRO $\wedge \neg\langle\!\langle A_h \rangle\!\rangle\Diamond$NRR. This implies that $S, q \models_I \forall\Box\neg(\text{NRO}\wedge\neg\langle\!\langle A_h \rangle\!\rangle\Diamond\text{NRR})$, and thus $S, q \models_I \langle\!\langle A \rangle\!\rangle\Box\neg(\text{NRO}\wedge \neg\langle\!\langle A_h \rangle\!\rangle\Diamond\text{NRR}) = \text{NECFair}$.

That EffFair$_I$ implies Effective$_I$ follows directly from Fact 2. In order to prove that EffFair$_I$ implies NEFair$_I$, we show first that NRO $\wedge$ NRR implies NEFair$_I$. Assume $S, q \models_I$ NRO $\wedge$ NRR. Let λ be a q-path and $i \geq 0$. Then we have that $S, \lambda[i] \models_I$ NRR (as NRR is a property that stays true after it has been true for the first time). Then it holds that $S, \lambda[i] \models_I \langle\!\langle A_h \rangle\!\rangle\text{true } \mathcal{U}$ NRR and thus $S, \lambda[i] \models_I \langle\!\langle A_h \rangle\!\rangle\Diamond$NRR, and therefore $S, \lambda[i] \not\models_I$ NRO $\wedge \neg\langle\!\langle A_h \rangle\!\rangle\Diamond$NRR. Therefore, it holds that $S, q \models_I \neg\langle\!\langle B \rangle\!\rangle\Diamond(\text{NRO} \wedge \neg\langle\!\langle A_h \rangle\!\rangle\Diamond\text{NRR}) = \text{NEFair}$.

Now assume EffFair$_I$. Then there exists $F = \{F_A, F_B\}$ for A_h, B_h such that for all $\lambda \in out(q, F)$ there is $i \geq 0$ with $S, \lambda[i] \models_I$ NRO $\wedge$ NRR, and for all $0 \leq j < i$, we have $S, \lambda[j] \models_I$ NECFair. If $i = 0$, we have that $S, \lambda[0] \models_I$ NECFair as NRO $\wedge$ NRR implies NECFair$_I$. Otherwise, we have $S, \lambda[j] \models_I$ NECFair directly.

The proof for imperfect information is analogous.

Note that the converse implications do not hold. For example, Protocol 5 satisfies both Effective and NEFair, but not EffFair.

We observe that EFFFAIR$_I$ suffers from the problems concerning imperfect information mentioned in Sec. 3.2. Moreover, even if a protocol satisfies EFFFAIR$_i$, it can still be the case that the strategies for Alice behind the outer and the nested strategic operators cannot be combined into a single uniform strategy (cf. [19]). Consider the situation where Alice can either stop, resulting in fairness but not effectiveness, or continue, only resulting in fairness (and effectiveness) if Bob plays honest and neither fairness nor effectiveness otherwise. This is problematic if Alice does not know whether Bob plays honest: in that case, EFFFAIR$_I$ is satisfied, but Alice does not have a strategy that results in both fairness and effectiveness.

We have shown that fairness is not sufficient for fair-exchange protocols, and that effectiveness is also needed. Moreover, non-enforced fairness and effectiveness cannot be combined trivially. We give a new specification, EFFFAIR, that handles this combination. This problem does not occur for weak, strategic, strong or invariant fairness and effectiveness. For these specifications, it is sufficient to require the conjunction of fairness and effectiveness.

4   Hierarchy of Fairness Requirements

We proceed by studying the relations between the different definitions of fairness. Fig. 1 contains a graphical view of these relations. Below we include proof sketches for some of the relations. The other cases are relatively straightforward. Unless explicitly stated otherwise, the same reasoning applies to both semantic variants of ATL.

Strong, Strategic, Weak and Invariant Fairness Chadha et. al [10] prove that

$$\text{STRONGFAIR}_I \Rightarrow \text{STRATFAIR}_I \Rightarrow \text{WEAKFAIR}_I \Rightarrow \text{INVFAIR}_I.$$

The latter three implications extend to imperfect information. Furthermore, they show that STRATFAIR$_I$, WEAKFAIR$_I$ and INVFAIR$_I$ are equivalent under *strategic timeliness*. Strategic timeliness states that Alice always has an honest strategy that eventually allows her to stop executing the protocol: TIMELY $\equiv \forall\Box(\langle\!\langle A_h \rangle\!\rangle\Diamond\text{Stop}_A)$. Furthermore, INVFAIR$_I$, WEAKFAIR$_I$ and STRONGFAIR$_I$ are clearly equivalent with INVFAIR$_i$, WEAKFAIR$_i$ and STRONGFAIR$_i$, respectively, as they do not contain strategic modalities.

These are the only implications that hold between STRONGFAIR, STRATFAIR, WEAKFAIR and INVFAIR. We show this by providing a number of counterexamples, see Fig. 2. Protocol 6 satisfies STRATFAIR, but not STRONGFAIR. Protocol 7 (a protocol lacking strategic timeliness) satisfies WEAKFAIR but not STRATFAIR. Protocol 8 (another protocol lacking strategic timeliness) satisfies INVFAIR, but not WEAKFAIR. Finally, STRONGFAIR$_i$ $\Rightarrow$ STRATFAIR$_i$ and WEAKFAIR$_i$ $\Rightarrow$ STRATFAIR$_i$ are not valid, even under strategic timeliness, as they do not hold in a model where the initial state with ¬NRO is indistinguishable from an unreachable state with NRO ∧ ¬NRR holds.

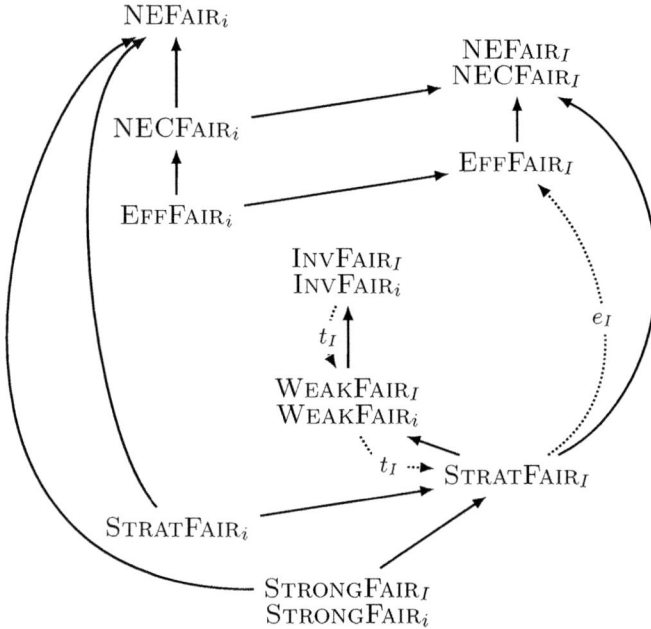

Fig. 1. Relationships between different notions of fairness. Solid arrows stand for implications, i.e., lead from stronger to weaker definitions of fairness. Dashed arrows represent implications that hold only under additional assumptions of effectiveness (e) or strategic timeliness (t). Missing arrows correspond to implications that do not hold. *Note:* we did not include arrows that follow from transitivity of implication.

Non-enforced Fairness. Now we study how STRONGFAIR, STRATFAIR, WEAK-FAIR and INVFAIR relate to NEFAIR.

Theorem 2. STRATFAIR *implies* NEFAIR.

Proof. Assume $\forall\Box(\text{NRO} \rightarrow \langle\!\langle A_h \rangle\!\rangle \Diamond \text{NRR})$. Because $\forall\Box\varphi \rightarrow \neg\exists\Diamond\neg\varphi$ is a CTL validity, we have $\neg\exists\Diamond(\text{NRO} \wedge \neg\langle\!\langle A_h \rangle\!\rangle \Diamond \text{NRR})$. Therefore, by Fact 1 it holds that $\neg\langle\!\langle B \rangle\!\rangle \Diamond(\text{NRO} \wedge \neg\langle\!\langle A_h \rangle\!\rangle \Diamond \text{NRR})$.

Similarly, STRONGFAIR implies NEFAIR as well. Also, because STRATFAIR, WEAKFAIR and INVFAIR are equivalent given strategic timeliness, WEAKFAIR and INVFAIR imply NEFAIR given strategic timeliness. Now we show that the other implications do not hold. Protocol 9 satisfies NEFAIR, but not STRONG-FAIR, STRATFAIR, WEAKFAIR or INVFAIR. Protocol 7, a protocol that does not satisfy strategic timeliness, satisfies INVFAIR and WEAKFAIR, but not NE-FAIR. Finally, $\text{STRATFAIR}_i \Rightarrow \text{NECFAIR}_i$ is not valid, as it does not hold in a model with a state q with a next state where $\text{NRO} \wedge \neg\text{NRR}$ holds such that q is indistinguishable from the initial state.

Protocol 6.
1. $B \to T$: NRR
2. $T \to A$: continue
3. $A \to B$: NRO
4. Choice for A:
   (a) 1. $A \to T$: true
       2. $T \to A$: NRR
   (b) 1. $A \to T$: false
       2. Go to 4.

Protocol 7.
1. $A \to B$: NRO
2. Choice for B:
   (a) 1. $B \to A$: NRR
   (b) 1. $B \to A$: cont.
       2. Go to 2.

Protocol 8.
1. $A \to B$: NRO
2. $B \to A$: continue
3. Go to 2.

Protocol 9.
1. $B \to T$: NRR
2. $A \to B$: NRO
3. Choice for A:
   (a) 1. End of proto-
       col.
   (b) 1. $A \to T$: cont.
       2. $T \to A$: NRO

Fig. 2. Counterexample protocols

Moreover, as shown in Section 3.2, NEFAIR and NECFAIR are equivalent under perfect information, while under imperfect information, NECFAIR implies NECFAIR, but not vice versa.

Effective Fairness. We proceed by studying the relations between EFFFAIR and the other definitions of fairness. EFFFAIR implies NEFAIR, as shown in Theorem 1. The following theorem states that in effective protocols, STRATFAIR$_I$ implies EFFFAIR$_I$. This theorem does only hold assuming perfect information. Under imperfect information, Alice is not guaranteed to know whether Bob plays honest, and cannot decide whether she should continue the cooperation with Bob or not.

Theorem 3. *Whenever* EFFECTIVE$_I$ *holds,* STRATFAIR$_I$ *implies* EFFFAIR$_I$.

Proof. Assume that EFFECTIVE$_I$ and STRATFAIR$_I$ hold. We set $\varphi = \neg(\text{NRO} \land \neg\langle\langle A_h \rangle\rangle \Diamond \text{NRR})$ and $\psi = \text{NRO} \land \text{NRR}$. STRATFAIR$_I = \forall \Box(\text{NRO} \to \langle\langle A_h \rangle\rangle \Diamond \text{NRR})_I$ is equivalent to $\forall \Box \neg(\text{NRO} \land \neg\langle\langle A_h \rangle\rangle \Diamond \text{NRR})_I$ and can thus be written as $(\forall \Box \varphi)_I$. This means that for all paths $\lambda \in out(q, \emptyset)$ and all positions $i \geq 0$, we have $\lambda[i] \models_I \forall \Box \varphi$ as well (1). EFFECTIVE$_I$ can be written as $(\langle\langle A_h, B_h \rangle\rangle \Diamond \psi)_I$. By definition of $\Diamond$, there exists a pair F of strategies for agents A_h and B_h, respectively, such that for all $\lambda \in out(q, F)$ there exists $i \geq 0$ with $\lambda[i] \models_I \psi$ (2). Let F be a pair of strategies for A and B satisfying this condition. Then we have that for all $\lambda \in out(q, F)$ there exists $i \geq 0$ with $\lambda[i] \models_I \psi$ by (2), and for all $0 \leq j < i$, we have $\lambda[j] \models_I \langle\langle A_h \rangle\rangle \Box \varphi$ by (1). By definition of $\mathcal{U}$, we obtain $q \models_I \langle\langle A_h, B_h \rangle\rangle((\langle\langle A_h \rangle\rangle \Box \neg(\text{NRO} \land \neg\langle\langle A_h \rangle\rangle \Diamond \text{NRR})) \mathcal{U} (\text{NRO} \land \text{NRR}))$, i.e., EFFFAIR$_I$.

Again, these results, and the transitive closures of them, are all the implications that hold. Protocol 5 satisfies NEFAIR, but not EFFFAIR. Furthermore, the empty protocol, which obviously does not satisfy effectiveness, satisfies STRONG-FAIR, STRATFAIR, WEAKFAIR and INVFAIR, but not EFFFAIR. Finally, Protocol

7, not satisfying strategic timeliness, satisfies WEAKFAIR and INVFAIR, but not
EFFFAIR.

5   Related Work

Various definitions of non-repudiation and fair exchange have been formalized
and verified with LTL, cf. e.g. [2,3]. However, as we argue in this paper, these
definitions are often either too strong or too weak because they do not take into
account the agents' ability to choose the right strategy. In this section, we discuss
how our results relate to existing proposals about verification of non-repudiation
protocols and other fair-exchange protocols with the strategic logic ATL.

Kremer and Raskin [16] use NEFAIR to verify various non-repudiation
protocols. They find flaws in the Zhou-Gollmann optimistic protocol [20], the
Asokan-Shoup-Waidner certified mail protocol [7] and the Markowitch-Kremer
multi-party non-repudiation protocol [21]. An improved version of the latter
protocol, as well as the Kremer-Markowitch non-repudiation protocol [22], are
shown to satisfy NEFAIR. However, as we have seen in Sec. 3.2, the protocols
that are shown to satisfy NEFAIR might still be unfair if the agents' strategies are not executable due to imperfect information. Furthermore, all strategies
that guarantee fairness in these protocols might be ineffective, as we proved in
Sec. 3.3.

Chadha et al. [10] demonstrate that the GM protocol [23], a multi-party contract signing protocol, does not satisfy INVFAIR, WEAKFAIR, STRATFAIR and
STRONGFAIR for four participants. However, as we have seen, non-enforced fairness might still hold. It can be argued that non-enforced fairness is sufficient, if it
is assumed that Alice has the ability to resolve the choices in a non-deterministic
protocol in the way that is the most advantageous for her.

Liu et al. [24] propose an extended CEM (certified e-mail) protocol with TTP
transparency and use STRATFAIR to prove fairness. However, strategic timeliness
is only checked in a perfect information model, which means that the protocol
may be intuitively unfair in the presence of imperfect information, as we saw
in Sec. 3.2. Furthermore, the extended CEM protocol does not necessarily have
strong fairness, as STRATFAIR does not imply STRONGFAIR. This means that it
is still important that the agents resolve the non-determinism of the protocol in
the correct way.

Finally, Zhang et al. [25] analyze a number of multi-party contract signing
protocols. WEAKFAIR and INVFAIR are used to prove that the MR protocol [26]
is fair with up to 5 signers, and that the MRT protocol [27] with 3 signers has
a flaw. Furthermore, a corrected MRT protocol for 3 and 4 signers is presented,
which is shown to satisfy WEAKFAIR and INVFAIR. Because strategic timeliness
is proven, the results carry over to STRATFAIR. We saw in Sec. 4 that STRATFAIR
does not imply STRONGFAIR, and that NEFAIR does not imply STRATFAIR.
Therefore, it could be that both the original and the corrected version of the MRT
protocol satisfy NEFAIR, i.e., are fair assuming agents have enough rationality
to take the correct choices. On the other hand, it could be that both the original

and corrected version of the MRT protocol lack STRONGFAIR, i.e., that in both protocols, not every way of resolving non-determinism leads to fairness. In the same way does the successful verification of STRATFAIR in the MR protocol not guarantee NEFAIR. Furthermore, as strategic timeliness is only checked in a perfect information model, the MR protocol and the corrected MRT protocol might be only fair under the unrealistic assumption of perfect information (see Sec. 4).

6   Conclusions and Future Work

We have shown that there are a number of problems involved with the specifications of fairness that are currently used for the verification of non-repudiation and other fair-exchange protocols. First, one of the definitions of fairness, non-enforced fairness, accepts intuitively unfair protocols, because it has been overlooked that agents can have imperfect information. This makes it clear that formal verification should take imperfect information into account. We have proposed a new definition of fairness that can be used in models with imperfect information. Furthermore, we have shown that fairness is not a sufficient requirement for fair-exchange protocols, as protocols are also required to be effective. We have shown that if both fairness and effectiveness are expressed in terms of strategies, the two requirements cannot be combined easily. We have proposed a new definition of fairness that combines the requirements correctly. Moreover, we have given a hierarchy of the various definitions of fairness, and have proven that this hierarchy is correct. Finally, we have indicated the consequences of our results for existing results from literature. We have shown two problems with the specifications of fairness that are currently used for verification of non-repudiation and other fair-exchange protocols, namely the implicit assumption of perfect information and the possible lack of effectiveness. We have also proposed new definitions of fairness that handle the issues appropriately. Moreover, we have established a hierarchy of fairness definitions, and indicated the consequences of our results for existing work.

Depending on the assumptions about the agents, different definitions of fairness would be advisable to use. If the agents are not rational and should be protected against taking bad decisions, then STRONGFAIR is clearly the best option. If the agents are rational, the situation is more sophisticated, as we know how to specify fairness and effectiveness under imperfect information but *not* both at the same time. To find as many flaws as possible, we recommend to verify EFFFAIR in imperfect information semantics. However, even protocols that satisfy this specification might be flawed: EFFFAIR guarantees the existence of a strategy that is both fair and executable with imperfect information, and the existance of a strategy that is both fair and effective, but not the existance of a strategy that is both executable, fair and effective. More research is required to find directions to solve this problem.

In the future, we hope to find a specification that imposes *both* fairness and effectiveness under imperfect information. Furthermore, it would be interesting to study ATL specifications of *abuse-freeness*, a property that guarantees that no signer can prove to an outside observer that he is able to determine the result of the protocol. Moreover, we hope to verify the concepts of fairness for existing non-repudiation protocols. This may require a fundamental extension of verification techniques as there are no ATL model checkers for imperfect information. There was an attempt in one of the older versions of MCMAS [28], but because of conceptual as well as computational problems the extension was subsequently abandoned. Also, the ALPAGA model checker [29] can only solve a limited fragment of imperfect information games.

Acknowledgements. The authors would like to thank Jun Pang, Jean-François Raskin and Leon van der Torre for valuable comments and suggestions. This work was supported by the FNR (National Research Fund) Luxembourg under projects S-GAMES, C08/IS/03 and GMASec - PHD/09/082.

References

1. Roscoe, A.: Intensional Specifications of Security Protocols. In: Proc. CSFW 1996, pp. 28–38. IEEE (1996)
2. Lowe, G.: A hierarchy of authentication specifications. In: 10th Computer Security Foundations Workshop (CSFW 1997), June 10-12, pp. 31–44. IEEE Computer Society, Rockport (1997)
3. Cremers, C., Mauw, S., de Vink, E.: Injective synchronisation: an extension of the authentication hierarchy. Theoretical Computer Science 367, 139–161 (2006); Special issue on ARSPA 2005, (P. Degano and L. Viganò, eds.)
4. Benaloh, J., Tuinstra, D.: Receipt-free secret ballot elections (extended abstract). In: Proc. 26th ACM Symposium on the Theory of Computing (STOC), pp. 544–553. ACM (1994)
5. Delaune, S., Kremer, S., Ryan, M.: Coercion-resistance and receipt-freeness in electronic voting. In: Proceedings of the 19th IEEE Computer Security Foundations Workshop (CSFW 2006). IEEE Computer Society Press, Venice (2006)
6. van Deursen, T., Mauw, S., Radomirović, S., Vullers, P.: Secure Ownership and Ownership Transfer in RFID Systems. In: Backes, M., Ning, P. (eds.) ESORICS 2009. LNCS, vol. 5789, pp. 637–654. Springer, Heidelberg (2009)
7. Asokan, N., Shoup, V., Waidner, M.: Asynchronous Protocols for Optimistic Fair Exchange. In: Proc. of the IEEE Symp. in Security and Privacy, pp. 86–99 (1998)
8. Alur, R., Henzinger, T.A., Kupferman, O.: Alternating-time temporal logic. Journal of the ACM 49, 672–713 (2002)
9. Alur, R., Henzinger, T., Mang, F., Qadeer, S., Rajamani, S., Tasiran, S.: MOCHA: Modularity in Model Checking. In: Vardi, M.Y. (ed.) CAV 1998. LNCS, vol. 1427, pp. 521–525. Springer, Heidelberg (1998)
10. Chadha, R., Kremer, S., Scedrov, A.: Formal Analysis of Multiparty Contract Signing. Journal of Automated Reasoning 36, 39–83 (2006)
11. Dashti, M.T.: Keeping Fairness Alive. PhD thesis, Vrije Universiteit, Amsterdam (2008)
12. Ben-Or, M., Goldreich, O., Micali, S., Rivest, R.: A fair protocol for signing contracts. IEEE Transactions on Information Theory T-36, 40–46 (1990)
13. Even, S., Yacobi, Y.: Relations among public key signature systems (1980)

14. Ezhilchelvan, P.D., Shrivastava, S.K.: Systematic Development of a Family of Fair Exchange Protocols. In: Proc. of the 17th Annual IFIP WG 11.3 Working Conference on Database and Applications Security, pp. 243–258. Kluwer Academic Press (2003)
15. Liu, P.: Avoiding loss of fairness owing to failures in fair data exchange systems. Decision Support Systems 31, 337–350 (2001)
16. Kremer, S., Raskin, J.F.: A game-based verification of non-repudiation and fair exchange protocols. Journal of Computer Security 11 (2003)
17. Jamroga, W., van der Hoek, W.: Agents that know how to play. Fundamenta Informaticae 63, 185–219 (2004)
18. Schobbens, P.Y.: Alternating-time logic with imperfect recall. Electronic Notes in Theoretical Computer Science 85, 82–93 (2004)
19. Jamroga, W., Bulling, N.: Comparing variants of strategic ability. In: Proceedings of EUMAS 2010 (2010)
20. Zhou, J., Gollmann, D.: An efficient non-repudiation protocol. In: Proceedings 10th Computer Security Foundations Workshop, pp. 126–132 (1997)
21. Markowitch, O., Kremer, S.: A Multi-Party Optimistic Non-Repudiation Protocol. In: Won, D. (ed.) ICISC 2000. LNCS, vol. 2015, pp. 109–122. Springer, Heidelberg (2001)
22. Kremer, S., Markowitch, O.: Optimistic non-repudiable information exchange. In: Biemond, J. (ed.) 21th Symp. on Information Theory in the Benelux, Werkgemeenschap Informatie- en Communicatietheorie, Enschede, pp. 139–146 (2000)
23. Garay, J., MacKenzie, P.: Abuse-free multi-party contract signing. Distributed Computing, 846–846 (1999)
24. Liu, Z., Pang, J., Zhang, C.: Verification of A Key Chain Based TTP Transparent CEM Protocol. UNU-IIST 60 (2010)
25. Zhang, Y., Zhang, C., Pang, J., Mauw, S.: Game-Based Verification of Multi-Party Contract Signing Protocols. In: Degano, P., Guttman, J.D. (eds.) FAST 2009. LNCS, vol. 5983, pp. 186–200. Springer, Heidelberg (2010)
26. Mukhamedov, A., Ryan, M.: Fair multi-party contract signing using private contract signatures. Information and Computation 206, 272–290 (2008)
27. Mauw, S., Radomirovic, S., Dashti, M.T.: Minimal Message Complexity of Asynchronous Multi-party Contract Signing. IEEE (2009)
28. Lomuscio, A., Qu, H., Raimondi, F.: MCMAS: A Model Checker for the Verification of Multi-Agent Systems. In: Bouajjani, A., Maler, O. (eds.) CAV 2009. LNCS, vol. 5643, pp. 682–688. Springer, Heidelberg (2009)
29. Berwanger, D., Chatterjee, K., De Wulf, M., Doyen, L., Henzinger, T.A.: Alpaga: A Tool for Solving Parity Games with Imperfect Information. In: Kowalewski, S., Philippou, A. (eds.) TACAS 2009. LNCS, vol. 5505, pp. 58–61. Springer, Heidelberg (2009)

Risk-Aware Role-Based Access Control

Liang Chen and Jason Crampton

Information Security Group and Department of Mathematics
Royal Holloway, University of London
{liang.chen.2005,jason.crampton}@rhul.ac.uk

Abstract. The increasing need to share information in dynamic environments has created a requirement for risk-aware access control systems. The standard RBAC model is designed to operate in a relatively stable, closed environment and does not include any support for risk. In this paper, we explore a number of ways in which the RBAC model can be extended to incorporate notions of risk. In particular, we develop three simple risk-aware RBAC models that differ in the way in which risk is represented and accounted for in making access control decisions. We also propose a risk-aware RBAC model that combines all the features of three simple models and consider some issues related to its implementation. Compared with existing work, our models have clear authorization semantics and support richer types of access control decisions.

1   Introduction

Access control mechanisms are typically policy-based, meaning that attempts to access resources are allowed or denied based on whether the access is authorized by some policy. Traditionally, the job of an access control system is to decide whether an access is authorized and to allow only those access attempts that are authorized.

Risk-aware access control is a novel access control paradigm that was proposed to meet the increasing need to share information in "agile" and ephemeral organizations such as coalitions and collaborations [7,14,16,18,24]. The core goal of developing risk-aware access control is to provide a mechanism that can manage the trade-off between the risk of allowing an unauthorized access with the cost of denying access when the inability to access resources may have profound consequences. When a user makes a request to access some resources, a risk-aware access control mechanism will evaluate the request by estimating the expected costs and benefits of granting access: the request might be denied if the risk is above some system-defined threshold; alternatively, the request might be denied if the cost exceeds the expected benefit.

This approach to deciding access requests is completely different from earlier access control models in which access control decisions are made on the basis of predefined policies that explicitly distinguish between allowed and denied access. In other words, risk-aware access control systems are designed to be more permissive than traditional access control mechanisms, in the sense that some

C. Meadows and C. Fernández-Gago (Eds.): STM 2011, LNCS 7170, pp. 140–156, 2012.
© Springer-Verlag Berlin Heidelberg 2012

risky or exceptional accesses are allowed, provided the risk of allowing such access can be accounted for and is not unacceptably high. Therefore, an important step for modeling risk-aware access control is to identify appropriate ways of estimating and managing risk. Most existing work in the literature attempts to achieve this in the context of multi-level security [7,8,18].

Role-based access control (RBAC) has been the subject of considerable research in the last decade [3,12,23], resulting in the release of the ANSI RBAC standard [1]. A number of commercial products, such as Windows Authorization Manager and Oracle 9, implement some form of RBAC. The basic idea of RBAC is that users and permissions are associated with roles, and that there are significantly fewer roles than there are users or permissions. In other words, a role provides a convenient way of associating a group of users with some set of permissions. This feature of role abstraction greatly simplifies the management of access control policies. Some other features that make RBAC attractive include the support for role hierarchies and the specification of separation of duty constraints [1].

To make use of RBAC in dynamic environments, we believe that there is a pressing need to develop appropriate risk-aware RBAC models, and it is this need we address in this paper. However, existing work in this area has one common limitation: existing models for risk-aware RBAC [2,5,11,19] only support the type of binary decisions, where the accesses with acceptable risk are allowed (and denied otherwise). We believe that risk-aware RBAC models should be able to make access control decisions on the basis of estimates of risk, system-defined risk thresholds, and risk mitigation strategies. In addition, existing models usually assess risk of granting access requests in terms of the trustworthiness of users [5,11]. However, the question of whether we could assess risk in terms of other components of RBAC model, to the best of our knowledge, has not yet been adequately investigated. Such considerations are the focus of this paper. More specifically, the contributions of this paper are as follows.

- We argue that the risk of granting an access request in an RBAC system depends on one or more of the following factors: user trustworthiness, the degree of competence of a user with respect to a particular user-role assignment, and the degree of appropriateness of a permission-role assignment for a given role.

- We propose a novel approach to the management and coordination of risk in an RBAC system. Our approach requires that each permission is associated with a risk mitigation strategy that is a list of risk interval and obligation pairs, where each risk interval is associated with an obligation. This approach of defining risk management at the permission level is much more fine-grained than most existing approaches that typically adopt a global mitigation and risk management strategy [7].

- We develop three simple risk-aware RBAC models, varying in the way of measuring and computing risk. These three models augment the standard RBAC96 model with a risk-aware authorization decision function.

– We introduce a risk-aware RBAC model that combines all the features of three simple models, and propose a strategy for the implementation of the model in practice.

The rest of the paper is organized as follows. In the next section we introduce relevant background material, including a graph-based formalism of RBAC96 and our recent work on spatio-temporal RBAC models; this prior work forms the basis for our risk-aware model. In Sect. 3 we discuss how to determine the risk of granting access requests in an RBAC system. In Sect. 4 we formally define the RBAC_T, RBAC_C, RBAC_A models. In Sect. 5 we introduce the full risk-aware RBAC model. Section 6 compares our work with related work in the literature. Section 7 concludes the paper with some suggestions for future work.

2   Background

There are several role-based access control models in the literature, but the best known is undoubtedly the RBAC96 family of models due to Sandhu *et al* [23]. RBAC96 defines four access control models: RBAC_0, RBAC_1, RBAC_2 and RBAC_3. The material in this paper is developed in the context of RBAC_1, which is the most widely used model and corresponds to the hierarchical model in the ANSI RBAC standard; hereafter we write RBAC96 to mean RBAC_1 only.

The RBAC96 model defines a set of roles R, a role hierarchy $RH \subseteq R \times R$, a user-role assignment relation $UA \subseteq U \times R$ (where U is a set of users), and a permission-role assignment relation $PA \subseteq P \times R$ (where P is a set of permissions[1]). We write $\leqslant$ to denote the transitive, reflexive closure of the RH relation; $(R, \leqslant)$ is a partially ordered set (since the directed graph of the role hierarchy relation is assumed to be acyclic). We represent an RBAC96 state (an instance of the RBAC96 model) as a tuple (UA, PA, RH). The RBAC96 state is used to determine whether an access control request (modeled as a user-permission pair) is authorized.

2.1   RBAC96 State as a Directed Graph

We noted that it is convenient to represent an RBAC96 state as an acyclic directed graph [6]. In particular, it provides a simple way of evaluating access requests in an RBAC96 system. In this paper, we will develop our risk-aware RBAC models based on this graph-based representation.

An RBAC96 state (UA, PA, RH) is represented by an acyclic, directed graph $G = (V, E)$, where $V = U \cup R \cup P$, and $E = UA \cup PA \cup RH$. In other words, each vertex v represents an entity, such as a user u, a role r or a permission p in an

---

[1] The RBAC96 model treats permissions as "uninterpreted symbols", because the precise natural of permissions is "implementation and system dependent". In the ANSI RBAC standard [1], which is based on the RBAC96 model, permissions are defined by an object and an action. For the sake of consistency with the ANSI RBAC standard, we define permissions as object-action pairs in this paper.

RBAC96 system, and each directed edge $e = (v_i, v_j)$ represents a relationship between two entities v_i and v_j; specifically, $(v_i, v_j) \in E$ if and only if (precisely) one of the following conditions holds

$$(v_i, v_j) \in UA, \quad (v_j, v_i) \in RH, \quad (v_j, v_i) \in PA.$$

An *authorization path* (or *au-path*) between v_1 and v_n is a sequence of vertices $v_1, \ldots, v_n$ such that $(v_i, v_{i+1}) \in E$, $i = 1, \ldots, n-1$. In particular, a user u can ("is authorized to") activate a role r if there is an au-path between u and r; a role r is authorized for permission p if there is an au-path between r and p; and a user u is authorized for permission p if there is an au-path between u and p. In other words, determining whether a user u is authorized to invoke a permission p reduces to finding a path from u to p that includes a role activated by u. A central notion in RBAC96 is that of sessions. For ease of exposition, we do not consider sessions until Section 5.1.

2.2   Spatio-Temporal Constraints and Inheritance in RBAC

Recently, we developed a family of spatio-temporal RBAC models [6]. The syntax of these models uses a simple extension of the RBAC96 model with two spatio-temporal constraint specification functions. The semantics of these models are based on the graph-based formalism of RBAC96 described above, and vary in the extent to which RBAC entities and relations are constrained by spatio-temporal restrictions. The state of a spatio-temporal RBAC model is a labeled directed graph, in which $\lambda : V \to D$ and $\mu : E \to D$, for some spatio-temporal domain D. More specifically, the semantics of the *standard model* ($\mathrm{RBAC}_{ST}^{=}$) are determined by the values of λ for nodes on the au-path; the semantics of the *strong model* (RBAC_{ST}^{+}) are determined by λ and μ for nodes and edges on the au-path; the semantics of the *weak model* (RBAC_{ST}^{-}) are determined by the values of λ for the two end-points of the au-path.

We believe that our examination of spatio-temporal RBAC models provides useful insights into the way of developing risk-aware RBAC models. In particular, based on the lessons learned from our study of the complex interactions between constraints and inheritance, we decide not to associate risk with roles and relationships within the role hierarchy. Indeed, it is not clear to us how risk can meaningfully be associated with roles and the role hierarchy. In the next section, we describe how we choose to define risk in RBAC.

3   Defining Risk in RBAC

In the field of information security, the notion of *risk* is often defined in terms of a combination of the likelihood that a threat will occur, and the severity of the resulting impact of the threat [17]. In the context of RBAC, we take the view that the risk of granting a request to perform some permission can be generally determined by the cost that will be incurred if the permission is authorized and subsequently misused, and the likelihood of the permission being misused.

One of the key steps to deploying a risk-aware RBAC system is to estimate the cost of permissions being misused, where the cost of a permission misuse depends on the value of the object associated with that permission and the action that is taken on the object. In the context of multi-level security models, for example, the cost of a read permission being misused is determined by the value of the information requested to be read, where the value of the information is represented by a sensitivity label to which the information is assigned [7]. There exist approaches to determine the cost of permission misuse [15], although choosing an appropriate approach for estimating the cost of permission misuse is likely to be a delicate task.

On the other hard, determining the likelihood of misuse of permissions is inherently hard, since it requires an ability to predict future actions of the requestors. In RBAC, we believe that there are at least three ways in which permission misuse might arise and the likelihood of misuse might therefore be quantified.

Firstly, there is a natural correspondence between *trustworthiness* and the likelihood of misuse of permissions. In earlier RBAC models (and access control models in general), authorized users are always trusted not to misuse the permissions for which they are authorized. Clearly, however, some authorized users are not *trustworthy*. It is reasonable to define different degrees of trustworthiness of users which directly reflects the likelihood of those users to misuse their granted permissions. Intuitively, a user who has a high likelihood of misusing her permissions can be simply regarded as being less trustworthy.[2] In Sect. 4.2 we consider an RBAC model in which user trustworthiness is an explicit part of the model.

In RBAC, a user is authorized for a permission by virtue of role assignments, where roles typically correspond to various job functions within an organization. Users are assigned to roles based on their qualification or competence, whereas permissions are associated with roles based on work-related or functional considerations. In Sect. 4.3, we propose an approach in which the user's competence to perform a role to which she is assigned is explicitly qualified.

Based on the above observations, we assume that if a role is assigned to a less competent user, then this user has a higher likelihood of misusing permissions associated with the role than some more competent user. Conversely, we can try to quantify the degree to which it is appropriate to assign a permission to a role. In some situations, it may be useful to associate a role with permissions for which the role is not obviously appropriate. In a healthcare system, for example, we might wish to restrict authorization to read medical records to doctors and consultants. However, we may choose to authorize the nurse role to read patients' medical records, not because it is appropriate, but because in an emergency it may be vital that there is some healthcare professional who is able to access medical records. Given a role that is associated with some less appropriate permissions with regard to the role's job duties, we take the view

---

[2] Trust-management and reputation-management system are tools that might be used to compute the trustworthiness of users [9].

that any user who is authorized for this role has a relatively high likelihood of misusing those permissions. We introduce an RBAC model in Sect. 4.4 which explicitly quantifies the appropriateness of a permission-role assignment.

4   Simple Models for Risk-Aware RBAC

In this section, we develop three simple models for risk-aware RBAC that support richer types of policy decisions beyond the usual "deny" and "grant" ones. In particular, the access control decision function in our models is able to make its access decisions based on the RBAC policies and the risk of granting access requests. As discussed in Sect. 3, the risk of granting a request (u, p) is defined using the cost of p misuse, and the likelihood of u to misuse p. There are three distinct possibilities that can be used to measure the likelihood of misuse of permissions, which are embodied in our different models.

4.1   Risk Mitigation

To devise a risk-evaluation strategy for RBAC, we need to determine a *risk threshold* that the RBAC system is willing to accept when granting access requests, and what kind of risk mitigations should occur if a risky access is allowed. In this paper, we define risk thresholds and risk mitigation strategies on a per-permission basis, which provides far more control than the common alternative of setting risk thresholds that apply to all permissions.

We assume the existence of a risk domain $\mathcal{D} = [0, 1] \stackrel{\text{def}}{=} \{d \in \mathbb{R} : 0 \leqslant d \leqslant 1\}$. We write $[t, t')$ to denote the *risk interval* $\{x \in \mathcal{D} : t \leqslant x < t'\}$. Let B denote a set of obligations, where an obligation $b \in B$ is some action(s) that must be taken by the Policy Enforcement Point (PEP) when enforcing an access control decision (as in XACML [20]). For uniformity of exposition, we write $\perp$ to denote the "null" obligation; the PEP is not required to do anything for the null obligation.

Informally, we associate a permission p with a list of interval-obligation pairs: if the risk associated with access request (u, p) is t then we enforce the obligations corresponding to the interval containing t. More formally, we define a *risk mitigation strategy* to be a list $[(0, \perp), (t_1, b_1), \ldots, (t_{n-1}, b_{n-1}), (t_n, \perp)]$, where $0 < t_1 < t_2 < \cdots < t_n \leqslant 1$ and $b_i \in B$. Each permission p is associated with a risk mitigation strategy. Then,

- the request (u, p) is permitted (unconditionally) if the risk of allowing (u, p) is less than t_1;
- the request (u, p) is permitted but the PEP must enforce obligation b_i if the risk of allowing (u, p) belongs to $[t_i, t_{i+1})$;
- the request (u, p) is denied if the risk of allowing (u, p) is greater than or equal to t_n.

It can be seen that the first element of the risk mitigation strategy is redundant; we include it for clarity of exposition.

Although our approach increases the complexity of risk management at the permission level, it is much more fined-grained than most existing approaches that usually adopt a global mitigation and risk management strategy [7,14,16]. In other words, unlike our approach, the occurrence of errors in the management of the global risk thresholds will have an impact on the correctness of deciding all relevant access requests.

In addition, by associating risk thresholds with permissions we simplify the computation of risk of granting requests. In particular, we can ignore the cost of a permission p being misused when considering the risk of granting p. This is because system administrators have "valued" the cost of p's misuse by defining risk thresholds and risk mitigations for p. In contrast, existing approaches that manage risk globally have to be aware of the cost of permissions being misused when evaluating requests for those permissions. Henceforth, we are only concerned with the likelihood of p's misuse in the computation of the risk of granting p.

4.2   The RBAC$_T$ Model

The trustworthiness- and role-based access control (or RBAC$_T$) model augments the standard RBAC96 model with two functions $\alpha : U \to (0,1]$ and $\lambda : P \to M$, where $\alpha(u)$ denotes the degree of trustworthiness of u, M denotes the set of risk mitigation strategies and $\lambda(p)$ denotes the risk mitigation strategy associated with p's usage. To compute the risk of granting a request (u, p), we define a risk function $risk_T : U \times P \to [0, 1]$ as

$$risk_T(u, p) = \begin{cases} 1 - \alpha(u) & \text{if there exists an au-path from } u \text{ to } p \\ 1 & \text{otherwise.} \end{cases}$$

In other words, $risk_T(u, p)$ is 1 for request (u, p) if there does not exist an au-path from u to p. By definition, for any permission p, the request (u, p) will be denied if the risk of granting it equal to 1; that is, if there is no au-path from u to p. In contrast, if there exists an au-path from u to p, the risk of granting (u, p) is determined by u's trustworthiness. For example, given two requests (u_1, p) and (u_2, p), $risk_T(u_1, p) < risk_T(u_2, p) < 1$ means that allowing u_2 to perform p is more risky than allowing u_1 to access (because u_1 is more trustworthy than u_2). Note that $risk_T(u, p)$ is determined, in part, by the existence of an au-path from u to p. In other words, our approach to risk computation in RBAC$_T$ incorporates the standard RBAC method of checking whether a request is authorized. This will be a common feature of our risk-aware models.

We now define an authorization decision function $Auth_T$ which, given an RBAC$_T$ state (V, E, α, λ), an access request (u, p) and a risk mitigation strategy $\lambda(p) = [(0, \perp), (t_1, b_1), \ldots, (t_{n-1}, b_{n-1}), (t_n, \perp)]$ for p, returns an authorization decision and an obligation. Specifically,

$$Auth_T((V, E, \alpha, \lambda), (u, p), \lambda(p)) = \begin{cases} (\texttt{allow}, \bot) & \text{if } risk_T(u, p) < t_1, \\ (\texttt{allow}, b_i) & \text{if } risk_T(u, p) \in [t_i, t_{i+1}), \\ (\texttt{deny}, \bot) & \text{if } risk_T(u, p) \geqslant t_n. \end{cases}$$

In other words, a request by u to perform p is allowed if there exists an au-path from u to p in the $RBAC_T$ graph and the risk of granting (u, p) is less than a specified risk threshold t_n of p (and denied otherwise). In addition, some system obligations b_i will be forced to execute with the allow access if the risk is perceived as being relatively high (within some interval $[t_i, t_{i+1})$, where $1 \leqslant i < n$).

We believe that the concept of trustworthiness and the risk-assessment methodology we developed in $RBAC_T$ can be naturally integrated into other access control models, enabling them to become risk-aware. In the next section, we introduce risk-aware RBAC models with consideration of competence and appropriateness in the user-role assignments and the permission-role assignments respectively.

4.3   The RBAC$_C$ Model

The competence- and role-based access control (or $RBAC_C$) model augments the standard RBAC96 model with two functions $\beta : U \times R \to (0, 1]$ and $\lambda : P \to M$, where $\beta(u, r)$ denotes u's degree of competence to perform role r, and $\lambda(p)$ denotes the risk mitigation strategy associated with p's usage. Note that, for all $(u, r) \in UA$, we require $\beta(u, r) > 0$; this is because it is not meaningful to assign u to r if u has no competence to perform the role r. Unlike $RBAC_T$, $RBAC_C$ defines the concept of competence on the user-role assignments, which leads to a different way of computing the risk of granting requests.

Given an $RBAC_C$ state $G = (V, E, \beta, \lambda)$, we write $(v, *)$ for the set of entities that are connected *from* v by edges; that is, $(v, *) = \{v' \in V : (v, v') \in E\}$. We also write $(*, v)$ for the set of entities that connected *to* v by edges; that is, $(*, v) = \{v' \in V : (v', v) \in E\}$. For brevity, we write $v*$ for $(v, *)$ and $*v$ for $(*, v)$. Given $v \in V$, we write $\downarrow v$ to denote the set of entities for which v is RBAC96-authorized; that is $\downarrow v = \{v' \in V : \text{there exists an au-path from } v \text{ to } v'\}$. Analogously, we define $\uparrow v = \{v' \in V : \text{there exists an au-path from } v' \text{ to } v\}$.

Given a request (u, p), there may be multiple paths between u and p in the $RBAC_C$ graph. Obviously, we are interested in finding the set of roles for which u is explicitly authorized and that lie on an au-path from u to p, that is $u* \cap \uparrow p$. To compute the risk of granting (u, p), we need to consider the degree of competence that u has to perform each role in $u* \cap \uparrow p$. Given a request (u, p), there might exist one or more au-paths from u to p, the risk of granting (u, p) is determined by finding an au-path $u, r, \ldots, p$ such that $\beta(u, r)$ is maximum. In other words, u is competent to perform all roles in $u* \cap \uparrow p$ to some extent, and there is a role for which she is most competent, therefore this role is the one that is considered when evaluating the access request. Formally, we define a risk function $risk_C : U \times P \to [0, 1]$ as

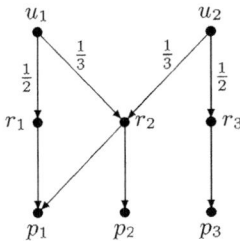
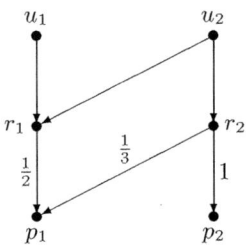

(a) A simple RBAC$_C$ state   (b) A simple RBAC$_A$ state

Fig. 1. A graphical representation of RBAC$_C$ and RBAC$_A$ states

$$
risk_C(u,p) = \begin{cases} 1 & \text{if } u* \cap {\uparrow}p = \emptyset, \\ 1 - \max\{\beta(u,r) : r \in u* \cap {\uparrow}p\} & \text{otherwise.} \end{cases}
$$

Consider the directed graph of an RBAC$_C$ configuration shown in Fig. 1(a), where $\beta(u_1, r_1) = \beta(u_2, r_3) = \frac{1}{2}$, and $\beta(u_1, r_2) = \beta(u_2, r_2) = \frac{1}{3}$. Then u_1 is able to perform p_1 through the role r_1 for which u_1 is most competent. Hence, $risk_C(u_1, p_1) = 1 - \frac{1}{2} = \frac{1}{2}$. However, $risk_C(u_1, p_3) = 1$ as $u* \cap {\uparrow}p_3 = \{r_1, r_2\} \cap \{r_3\} = \emptyset$ which means there is no au-path from u_1 to p_3.

Given an RBAC$_C$ state (V, E, β, λ), an access request (u, p) and a risk mitigation strategy $\lambda(p)$ for p, we can define an authorization decision function $Auth_C$ (as we did for $Auth_T$):

$$
Auth_C((V, E, \beta, \lambda), (u, p), \lambda(p)) = \begin{cases} (\texttt{allow}, \perp) & \text{if } risk_C(u, p) < t_1, \\ (\texttt{allow}, b_i) & \text{if } risk_C(u, p) \in [t_i, t_{i+1}), \\ (\texttt{deny}, \perp) & \text{if } risk_C(u, p) \geqslant t_n. \end{cases}
$$

4.4 The RBAC$_A$ Model

The appropriateness- and role-based access control (or RBAC$_A$) model augments the standard RBAC96 model with two functions $\gamma : P \times R \to (0, 1]$ and $\lambda : P \to M$, where $\gamma(p, r)$ denotes the degree of appropriateness with which p is assigned to r, and $\lambda(p)$ denotes the risk mitigation strategy associated with p's usage. Similarly, for all $(p, r) \in PA$, we require $\gamma(p, r) \neq 0$.

Like RBAC$_C$, RBAC$_A$ introduces a similar approach to computing the risk of granting requests, although the notion of appropriateness is defined on the permission-role assignments. Given (u, p), we write $*p$ to denote the set of roles to which p is explicitly assigned. We write $*p \cap {\downarrow}u$ for the set of roles in $*p$ for which u is authorized. In other words, $*p \cap {\downarrow}u$ is the set of roles that are explicitly authorized for p and that lie on an au-path between u and p.

Given $p \in P$, p might be explicitly assigned to multiple roles, and each of these assignments is associated with a certain degree of appropriateness. A user u can use p by activating the most appropriate role to which p is assigned, and certainly this role is the one that is considered when evaluating the risk of granting the access request. Hence, we define the risk function $risk_A : U \times P \to [0, 1]$ to be

$$
risk_A(u, p) = \begin{cases} 1 & \text{if } *p \cap \downarrow u = \emptyset, \\ 1 - \max\{\gamma(p, r) : r \in *p \cap \downarrow u\} & \text{otherwise.} \end{cases}
$$

Take an example of an RBAC$_A$ state in Fig. 1(b). We can see that u_2 is able to perform p_1 through r_1 or r_2. However, the role r_1 is the most appropriate one to which p_1 is assigned, therefore, the γ value of $\frac{1}{2}$ could be taken, and $risk_A(u_2, p_1) = \frac{1}{2}$.

Given an RBAC$_A$ state (V, E, γ, λ), an access request (u, p) and a risk mitigation strategy $\lambda(p)$ for p, the authorization decision function $Auth_A$ is defined as:

$$
Auth_A((V, E, \gamma, \lambda), (u, p), \lambda(p)) = \begin{cases} (\texttt{allow}, \bot) & \text{if } risk_A(u, p) < t_1, \\ (\texttt{allow}, b_i) & \text{if } risk_A(u, p) \in [t_i, t_{i+1}), \\ (\texttt{deny}, \bot) & \text{if } risk_A(u, p) \geqslant t_n. \end{cases}
$$

5 A Risk-Aware RBAC Model

A risk-aware RBAC model may combine the features of two or more of the RBAC$_T$, RBAC$_C$ and RBAC$_A$ models. For the sake of completeness, we consider the risk-aware RBAC (or R^{2}BAC) model that supports all the features of the RBAC$_T$, RBAC$_C$ and RBAC$_A$ models. In other words, we now work with the directed, labeled graph $G = (V, E, \alpha, \beta, \gamma, \lambda)$.

As in RBAC$_C$ and RBAC$_A$, to compute the risk of granting a request (u, p) in G, we firstly need to decide how to compute the risk associated with an au-path from u to p based on $(\alpha, \beta, \text{and } \gamma)$. Unlike our simpler models, we must then decide how to combine the risk of all au-paths between u and p into an appropriate risk value. We believe that there are at least two approaches to computing the risk associated with an au-path from u to p.

Given an au-path $u, r, \ldots, r', p$, one possibility is to define the risk associated with this path to be

$$
1 - \min\{\alpha(u), \beta(u, r), \gamma(r', p)\}.
$$

In other words, the risk of the au-path $u, r, \ldots, r', p$ is determined by the minimum value in the set comprising u's trustworthiness, the degree of competence for u to perform r, and the degree of appropriateness for p to be assigned to r'. Intuitively, an untrustworthy user still has a high likelihood of misusing her granted permission, even if she can invoke the permission through a role for which she is entirely competent and for which the permission is entirely appropriate. Similarly, a trustworthy user still has a high likelihood of misusing a permission if she can only perform the permission through a role for which she has little competence or for which the role is rather inappropriate for the permission.

An alternative way of computing the risk associated with a path is to compute

$$\min\{1, (1 - \alpha(u)) + (1 - \beta(u, r)) + (1 - \gamma(r', p))\}.$$

This computation acknowledges that there are risks associated with each part of the path and accumulates those risks.

Of course, it may be appropriate to compute the risk associated with a path as a more complex function of $\alpha(u)$, $\beta(u, r)$ and $\gamma(r', p)$. We defer the exploration of this matter, which would require substantial experimental validation, to future work. The purpose of this paper is to provide a risk-aware RBAC model that will provide a robust framework for the investigation of these issues.

We now consider how to combine the risks associated with multiple paths. Given $u, p \in V$, let $\Pi(u, p)$ denote the set of au-paths between u and p, and for each $\pi \in \Pi(u, p)$, let $risk(\pi)$ denote the risk associated with au-path π. We define $risk : U \times P \to [0, 1]$, where

$$risk(u, p) = \begin{cases} 1 & \text{if } \Pi(u, p) = \emptyset, \\ \min\{risk(\pi) : \pi \in \Pi(u, p)\} & \text{otherwise.} \end{cases}$$

Note that, as in RBAC_C and RBAC_A, the way of computing the risk of allowing u to perform p in R^2BAC is to choose the minimum value from the risk of all au-paths between u and p.

Consider the directed graph of an R^2BAC configuration shown in Fig. 2(a), where β and γ values are indicated by labels attached to edges, and assume that $\alpha(u) = 1$. There exist two au-paths from u to p_1, that is $u \to r_1 \to r_3 \to p_1$ and $u \to r_2 \to p_1$. If we use the first approach to compute the risk of those two au-paths, then $risk(u, r_1, r_3, p_1) = 1 - \frac{1}{2} = \frac{1}{2}$, and $risk(u, r_2, p_1) = 1 - \frac{1}{3} = \frac{2}{3}$. Therefore, the risk of granting u to perform p_1 is determined by the risk associated with the au-path $u \to r_1 \to r_3 \to p_1$, that is, $risk(u, p_1) = \frac{1}{2}$. If we use the second approach to compute the risk of those two au-paths, then $risk(u, r_1, r_3, p_1) = 1$, and $risk(u, r_2, p_1) = \frac{2}{3}$. Hence the risk of granting (u, p_1) is $\frac{2}{3}$, which is determined by the risk associated with the au-path $u \to r_2 \to p_1$.

Given an R^2BAC state $G = (V, E, \alpha, \beta, \gamma, \lambda)$, an access request (u, p) and a risk mitigation strategy $\lambda(p)$ for p, an authorization decision function $Auth$ is defined in the same way as before, that is:

$$Auth((V, E, \alpha, \beta, \gamma, \lambda), (u, p), \lambda(p)) = \begin{cases} (\texttt{allow}, \bot) & \text{if } risk(u, p) < t_1, \\ (\texttt{allow}, b_i) & \text{if } risk(u, p) \in [t_i, t_{i+1}), \\ (\texttt{deny}, \bot) & \text{if } risk(u, p) \geqslant t_n. \end{cases}$$

5.1   On the Advantages of Flat Risk-Aware RBAC

Given an R^2BAC state $G = (V, E, \alpha, \beta, \gamma, \lambda)$ and a request (u, p), we could use a breadth-first search algorithm to find all au-paths between u and p, and then

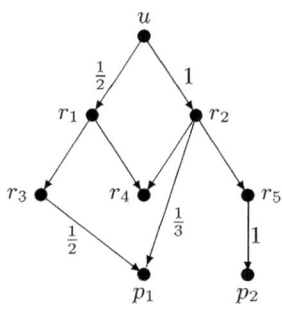

(a) Hierarchical R²BAC state

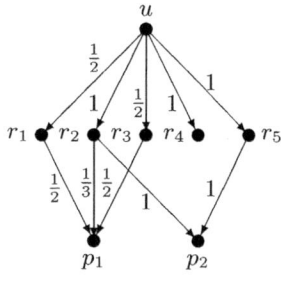

(b) Equivalent flat R²BAC state

Fig. 2. A graphical representation of R²BAC states

apply the risk function $risk(u, p)$ on all auth-paths to obtain a risk value. In many applications, we require a rapid response from the access decision function. In a risk-aware, hierarchical RBAC system with many users and permissions, this decision function, which depends on the computation of risk for multiple paths, may have unacceptably high overheads.

Based on this observation we discuss one way in which these performance issues might be addressed. In particular, we transform a hierarchical R²BAC state into an equivalent flat R²BAC state $G' = (V, E', \alpha, \beta', \gamma', \lambda)$ (in the sense that the risk of each request remains the same and, therefore, the authorization decision function returns the same decision) using the following procedure.

1. For all $u \in U$ and for all $r \in \downarrow u \cap R$, we define $(u, r) \in UA'$;
2. For all $p \in P$ and for all $r \in \uparrow p \cap R$, we define $(p, r) \in PA'$;
3. For all $(u, r) \in UA'$, define $\beta'(u, r) = \max\{\beta(u, r') : (u, r') \in UA, r' \geqslant r\}$;
4. For all $(p, r) \in PA'$, define $\gamma'(p, r) = \max\{\gamma(p, r') : (p, r') \in PA, r' \leqslant r\}$;
5. Define $E' = UA' \cup PA'$.

In the first two steps, we make explicit the user- and permission-role assignments that were previously implied by the role hierarchy. In the next four steps we ensure that each user- and permission-role assignment is associated with an appropriate β or γ value.

We now show how the transformation works by taking the example of the R²BAC state illustrated in Fig. 2(a). The first two steps remove the need for the role hierarchy by explicitly assigning u to roles r_3, r_4 and r_5, the permission p_1 to roles r_1 and r_2 and p_2 to r_2. Then $\beta'(u, r_4)$ takes the maximum of the two values 1 and $\frac{1}{2}$, so $\beta'(u, r_4) = 1$ using Step 3. Similarly, Step 4 allows us to compute γ values for p_1 and p_2. Finally, we output the flat R²BAC state shown in Fig. 2(b).

Having "flattened" our hierarchical RBAC state, all au-paths have length 2. We can then use our chosen method for computing the risk associated with an au-path to compute the risk associated with a request, as before. We can now use this risk value as part of the input to our risk-aware authorization decision function.

Of course, the likely reduction in time taken to decide access requests is offset by the fact that greater storage is required for the RBAC relations. Perhaps more important, however, is the increased difficulty in ensuring consistent updates to the RBAC state: one of the great virtues of hierarchical RBAC is that it simplifies the management of user- and permission-role assignments, since many such assignments are implied by the role hierarchy. It is likely that different trade-offs will be tolerated for different applications and different contexts. An investigation of these trade-offs would be an interesting subject for future work.

5.2 On Sessions in Risk-Aware RBAC

The RBAC96 model introduces the notion of *sessions* to achieve the principle of *least privilege* [22] in RBAC systems. Until this point we have ignored sessions, which are an important part of the RBAC96 model.

A user may create one or more sessions: in each session the user only activates a set of roles that are required to accomplish her task. Conceptually, a session is associated with a user and is a subset of the roles for which a user is authorized. A request (u, p) is authorized if there exists a session s associated with u and a role r in s such that there is an au-path from r to p.

In terms of our graph-based formalism, we may introduce a new graph $G_{\mathrm{Dyn}} = (V_{\mathrm{Dyn}}, E_{\mathrm{Dyn}})$ to represent the run-time state. This graph is derived from the RBAC96 graph in the following way. Writing S to denote the set of sessions, $V_{\mathrm{Dyn}} = S \cup R \cup P$ and $(s, r) \in E_{\mathrm{Dyn}}$ if role r has been activated in session s. A request is now modeled as a pair (s, p),[3] where s is a session, and is authorized only if there exists an au-path from s to p.

We can very easily extend the above approach to our risk-aware formalism. Specifically, risk is calculated over paths in G_{Dyn}, rather than G. In other words, the risk computation now applies to a session, rather than a user, so the end-user may find different mitigations being applied, depending on the session she chooses to activate.

6 Related Work

There has been significant research on risk-aware access control for enabling the secure sharing of information within or across multiple organizations [7,8,14,16,18,24,25]. However, most works attempt to achieve this goal by proposing approaches based on risk estimation and economic mechanisms [7,14,16,18,24]. On the other hand, there are only a few papers on extending RBAC models with risk semantics [2,5,11,19]. Unlike our models, none of them is concerned with the *authorization* semantics of risk-aware RBAC models. In this section, we review some work that are most related to ours, and illustrate the importance of our risk-aware RBAC models.

---

[3] A session is analogous to a subject in models based on a protection matrix.

Cheng *et al* [7] recently introduced a Fuzzy MLS system that controls the user's read access to information. The risk of granting a user to read a data object is estimated based on the security label of the object and the degree of the trustworthiness of the user. A number of explicit formulae is provided to compute the trustworthiness of the user based on the security clearance and category set of the user. On the other hand, Srivatsa *et al* [24] proposed a trust and key management paradigm for securing information flows across organizations, where the trustworthiness of a user is computed using a dynamic trust metric that depends on user's behavior. We believe that these approaches to computing trustworthiness of users can be used to specify the α function in our risk-aware RBAC models.

In addition, Cheng *et al* [7] suggested a global approach to risk management in the Fuzzy MLS model. They define a "hard" boundary, above which all accesses are denied, and a "soft" boundary, below which all accesses are allowed. Between the hard and the soft boundaries, an access request is allowed only if a risk mitigation mechanism can be applied to the access. In our work, we apply similar techniques to RBAC. However, we adopt a more sophisticated treatment of risk mitigation.

There has also been some work on incorporating risk semantics in the RBAC model. Nissanke and Khayat [19] assumed the existence of a partially ordered set of risk levels, and assigned these risk levels to permissions in an RBAC system. Therefore, the usage of one permission might be more risky than the other according to the risk levels to which these permissions are assigned. They also suggested an approach to reorganize the role hierarchy using risk analysis of permissions. In contrast to their work, we are concerned with how much risk will be incurred by allowing users to perform permissions, and provide explicit methods of computing such risk. Dimmock *et al* [11] extended the OASIS RBAC model [3] to make decisions on the basis of trustworthiness of users and cost of actions for certain outcomes. Unlike our models, the extended OASIS model returns binary decisions: a user's request to take an action with certain outcome is denied if the trustworthiness of the user is too low for the outcome's cost, and allowed otherwise. Furthermore, Aziz *et al* [2] introduced a refined RBAC model with the consideration of risk associated with operational semantics of permissions, collective usage of permissions, and conflicts of interest respectively. Celiker *et al* [5] introduced a probabilistic risk management framework to measure and evaluate users' risk in an RBAC system. Unlike our models, neither of these approaches support a risk-aware evaluation mechanism that is able to return richer types of access control decisions.

In summary, although all above work attempted to study risk in the context of RBAC, none of them has considered the possible ways of quantifying risk in the components of the RBAC model, and examined the way of extending the access control decision function in RBAC to become risk-aware.

7   Concluding Remarks

In this paper we have examined a number of possible ways to define risk in different components of the RBAC model. In particular, we observed that the risk of granting a request in the RBAC model could be rephrased in terms of user trustworthiness, the degree of competence of a user-role assignment, or the degree of appropriateness of a permission-role assignment. We assume that there exist appropriate software components that are able to evaluate these factors, and dynamically adjust the degree of these factors when context is changed.

Moreover, we developed three simple risk-aware RBAC models that consider those three quantitative factors respectively. We used a graph-based formalism of RBAC96 as a basis for defining the semantics of these models, and suggested the association of risk mitigation strategies with permissions. The resulting models have clear authorization semantics and accommodate the awareness of risk in deciding access requests.

Finally, we proposed a full risk-aware RBAC model that combines all the features of three simple models, and considered some of the practical issues that might arise when implementing such a model. To our knowledge, this is the first model that defines quantitative factors on various components of the RBAC model, and studies the way of combining these factors in order to acquire an appropriate method of computing the risk of allowing access.

There are several interesting directions for future work. As described above, we introduced the β and γ functions to quantify the competence of user-role assignments and appropriateness of permission-role assignments respectively. However, we did not provide an explicit way of specifying these two functions. We are currently working on an approach that constructs β and γ from the structure of the RBAC96 graph. In particular, we propose a formula for β, for example, that is able to compute the competence values for all user-role relations including those that are not encoded in the RBAC96 graph.

One interesting possibility for future work is to develop context- and risk-aware RBAC models. In particular, we would like to define a matrix of risk mitigation strategies to be associated with each permission, where each row represents a different context. The context could be as simple as emergency or non-emergency situations (as used in break-glass policies [4]) or we could monitor whether there are alternative more senior users available to invoke the permission (as used in the auto-delegation mechanism [10]).

We also would like to extend our models to include user obligations [13], and use the idea of "charging for risk" to enforce those obligations. The risk charge is removed from the user's "risk account" if the user fulfils the obligation. However, if the obligation is not fulfilled, the risk charge increases the risk associated with any subsequent requests made by the user. A user who is unable or unwilling to fulfil her obligations will eventually be denied all access requests. In other words, the honest user has an incentive to fulfil her obligations.

We would also like to extend our model to include usage control [21]. Of particular interest would be the way in which obligations might be used as a feedback mechanism to modify risk mitigation strategies themselves. In this way, risk-awareness and risk mitigation might become responsive to previous access requests and system activity.

Finally, we hope to develop a metamodel that captures the different ways of interactions between authorization and obligation. We could then construct a series of role-based models that instantiate one or more features of the metamodel. In particular, the metamodel enables us to develop new risk-aware RBAC models that provide more flexible and sophisticate ways of associating obligations with risk-aware authorization decisions.

Acknowledgements. We would like to thank the anonymous reviewers for their helpful feedback.

This research was sponsored by US Army Research laboratory and the UK Ministry of Defence and was accomplished under Agreement Number W911NF-06-3-0001. The views and conclusions contained in this document are those of the authors and should not be interpreted as representing the official policies, either expressed or implied, of the US Army Research Laboratory, the U.S. Government, the UK Ministry of Defense, or the UK Government. The US and UK Governments are authorized to reproduce and distribute reprints for Government purposes notwithstanding any copyright notation hereon.

References

1. American National Standards Institute: American National Standard for Information Technology – Role Based Access Control (2004), ANSI INCITS 359-2004
2. Aziz, B., Foley, S.N., Herbert, J., Swart, G.: Reconfiguring role based access control policies using risk semantics. Journal of High Speed Networks 15(3), 261–273 (2006)
3. Bacon, J., Moody, K., Yao, W.: A model of OASIS role-based access control and its support for active security. ACM Transactions on Information and System Security 5(4), 492–540 (2002)
4. Brucker, A.D., Petritsch, H.: Extending access control models with break-glass. In: Proceedings of the 14th ACM Symposium on Access Control Models and Technologies, pp. 197–206 (2009)
5. Celikel, E., Kantarcioglu, M., Thuraisingham, B.M., Bertino, E.: A risk management approach to RBAC. Risk and Decision Analysis 1(1), 21–33 (2009)
6. Chen, L., Crampton, J.: On spatio-temporal constraints and inheritance in role-based access control. In: Proceedings of the 2008 ACM Symposium on Information Computer and Communications Security, pp. 356–369 (2008)
7. Cheng, P.C., Rohatgi, P., Keser, C., Karger, P.A., Wagner, G.M., Reninger, A.S.: Fuzzy multi-level security: An experiment on quantified risk-adaptive access control. In: Proceedings of the 2007 IEEE Symposium on Security and Privacy, pp. 222–230 (2007)
8. Clark, J.A., Tapiador, J.E., McDermid, J.A., Cheng, P.C., Agrawal, D., Ivanic, N., Slogget, D.: Risk based access control with uncertain and time-dependent sensitivity. In: Proceedings of the International Conference on Security and Cryptography, pp. 5–13 (2010)
9. Crampton, J., Huth, M.: Detecting and countering insider threats: Can policy-based access control help? In: Proceedings of the 5th International Workshop on Security and Trust Management (2009)

10. Crampton, J., Morisset, C.: An Auto-Delegation Mechanism for Access Control Systems. In: Cuellar, J., Lopez, J., Barthe, G., Pretschner, A. (eds.) STM 2010. LNCS, vol. 6710, pp. 1–16. Springer, Heidelberg (2011)
11. Dimmock, N., Belokosztolszki, A., Eyers, D.M., Bacon, J., Moody, K.: Using trust and risk in role-based access control policies. In: Proceedings of the 9th ACM Symposium on Access Control Models and Technologies, pp. 156–162 (2004)
12. Ferraiolo, D.F., Kuhn, D.R.: Role-based access controls. In: Proceedings of the 15th National Computer Security Conference, pp. 554–563 (1992)
13. Irwin, K., Yu, T., Winsborough, W.H.: On the modeling and analysis of obligations. In: Proceedings of the 13th ACM Conference on Computer and Communications Security, pp. 134–143 (2006)
14. JASON Program Office: Horizontal integration: Broader access models for realizing information dominance. Technical Report JSR-04-132, MITRE Corporation (2004)
15. Landoll, D.J.: The Security Risk Assessment Handbook: A Complete Guide for Peforming Security Risk Assessments. CRC Press (2005)
16. Molloy, I., Cheng, P.C., Rohatgi, P.: Trading in risk: Using markets to improve access control. In: Proceedings of the 2008 Workshop on New Security Paradigms, pp. 107–125 (2008)
17. National Institute of Standards and Technology: Risk Management Guide for Information Technology Systems (2002), NIST Special Publication 800-30
18. Ni, Q., Bertino, E., Lobo, J.: Risk-based access control systems built on fuzzy inferences. In: Proceedings of the 5th ACM Symposium on Information Computer and Communications Security, pp. 250–260 (2010)
19. Nissanke, N., Khayat, E.J.: Risk based security analysis of permissions in RBAC. In: Proceedings of the 2nd International Workshop on Security in Information Systems, pp. 332–341 (2004)
20. Moses, T. (ed.): OASIS: eXtensible Access Control Markup Language (XACML) Version 2.0, OASIS Standard (February 1, 2005)
21. Park, J., Sandhu, R.S.: The UCON$_{ABC}$ usage control model. ACM Transactions on Information and System Security 7(1), 128–174 (2004)
22. Saltzer, J.H., Schroeder, M.D.: The protection of information in computer systems. Proceeding of the IEEE 63(9), 1278–1308 (1975)
23. Sandhu, R.S., Coyne, E.J., Feinstein, H.L., Youman, C.E.: Role-based access control models. IEEE Computer 29(2), 38–47 (1996)
24. Srivatsa, M., Balfe, S., Paterson, K.G., Rohatgi, P.: Trust management for secure information flows. In: Proceedings of the 15th ACM Conference on Computer and Communications Security, pp. 175–188 (2008)
25. Zhang, L., Brodsky, A., Jajodia, S.: Toward information sharing: Benefit and risk access control (BARAC). In: Proceedings of the 7th IEEE International Workshop on Policies for Distributed Systems and Networks, pp. 45–53 (2006)

Automated Analysis of Infinite State Workflows with Access Control Policies

Alessandro Armando[1,2] and Silvio Ranise[2]

[1] DIST, Università degli Studi di Genova, Italia
[2] Security and Trust Unit, FBK, Trento, Italia

Abstract. Business processes are usually specified by workflows extended with access control policies. In previous works, automated techniques have been developed for the analysis of authorization constraints of workflows. One of main drawback of available approaches is that only a bounded number of workflow instances is considered and analyses are limited to consider intra-instance authorization constraints. Instead, in applications, several workflow instances execute concurrently, may synchronize, and be required to ensure inter-instance constraints. Performing an analysis by considering a finite but arbitrary number of workflow instances can give designers a higher confidence about the quality of their business process. In this paper, we propose an automated technique for the analysis of both intra- and inter-instance authorization constraints in workflow systems. We reduce the analysis problem to a model checking problem, parametric in the number of workflow instances, and identify a sub-class of workflow systems with a decidable analysis problem.

1 Introduction

Workflows specify the behaviour of an application as the execution of inter-dependent units of work, called tasks. Several applications, such as business processes and E-services, use workflow management to achieve certain goals in the context of an organization which imposes additional constraints for authorizing employees to execute certain tasks in order to prevent insider frauds. For example, business processes consist of a collection of web services spawning several workflow instances that can be dynamically created or deleted, and execute concurrently while exchanging messages or synchronizing. The control-flow of the instances is dependent of the data-flow, and *vice versa*, to guarantee that the criteria for the successful application of the underlying business model are correctly applied. Given this complexity, it is not surprising that the analysis of this type of applications is a substantial problem and that available analysis techniques are not completely satisfactory. The main reason for this is two-fold. First, applications are designed to be parametric in the number of workflow instances and the analysis must be conducted regardless of their number. This amounts to the verification of an infinite family; namely one for each size (i.e. number of workflow instances) in the application. Most existing approaches fix the size to some number k (usually, $k = 1$), so that the dynamic nature of the

C. Meadows and C. Fernández-Gago (Eds.): STM 2011, LNCS 7170, pp. 157–174, 2012.

application is not taken into account at all (see, e.g., [12] for a discussion of this and related issues). This has also a negative impact on the authorization level where, not only intra-instance authorization constraints should be considered, but also inter-instance ones (see, e.g., [15]). The second reason is that the data-flow is crudely abstracted (e.g., by making finite the domains over which the variables range) or is completely neglected. In fact, the analyses which are capable of handling parametrized systems impose the restriction that each instance is finite-state (see, e.g., [1] for a discussion on this issue). Even those analysis techniques considering just a single workflow instance, often neglect the data-flow although there are some exceptions, such as [4]. This implies also a lack of precision in the modelling of some authorization policies, which require to take into account the data-flow. To understand this, consider the situation in which the permission to execute a critical task can be granted to employees with less senior roles when the amount of money involved in its execution is less than a certain value. This lack of precision may prevent to verify security properties even for single workflow instances, since their specification requires to precisely characterize the dependency of the possible executions on certain data values.

To overcome these limitations, in this paper, we make two contributions. The **first contribution** is the notion of *parametrized workflow system with access control* (Section 2), which allows us to model a family of workflow instances running concurrently where a (centralized) access control module—based on an extension of the Role-Based Access Control model with delegation [24]—regulates the execution of tasks by users. Each workflow instance is modelled by an extended finite-state automaton whose transitions are guarded by the local state of the instance, the values of the local variables, conditions on the local state and values of local variables of a fixed and known number of other instances, and the state of the access control module. The state of the access control module is changed according to a set of delegation rules. We precisely describe all the possible executions of a parametrized workflow system by defining a transition system on a set of configurations, comprising a finite set of identifiers for the workflow instances, the state of the access control module and all the local states and variables of the automata in the system. Security analysis problems for intra- and inter-instances authorization constraints, such as Separation of Duties, can be stated as infinite-state model checking (reachability) problems for parametrized workflow systems. Without restrictions on the extended automata, it is easy to see that the model checking problem is undecidable even without considering the access control module (see, e.g., [8]).

The **second contribution** of the paper is the definition of a class of parameterized workflow systems with access control whose reachability problem is decidable. We derive this result in the model checking modulo theories approach [13] as follows. First, we define a symbolic representation for the reachability problem of parametrized workflow systems by using simple set-theoretic expressions (Section 3). Second, we describe a symbolic backward reachability procedure that repeatedly computes pre-images and checks whether a fix-point is reached (Section 4). Once a fix-point is obtained, it is checked that no initial state belong to the fix-point in order to certify that the system satisfies the authorization constraint. Otherwise, a violation is reported together with a size of the parametrized system and a finite sequence of transitions causing the violation, that can be used for debugging. Finally, the termination of the backward reachability procedure is stated (Theorem 1) and proved by showing that the the sub-class of parametrized workflow systems satisfy some sufficient conditions that guarantee the representability of fix-points with the chosen symbolic representation.

2   Parametrized Workflow Systems with Access Control

We preliminary recall some notions concerning the Role-Based Access Control model [20] and its extension with delegation [24].

Role-Based Access Control (RBAC) regulates access through roles. Roles in a set R associate permissions in a set P to users in a set U by using the following two relations: $UA \subseteq U \times R$ and $PA \subseteq R \times P$. Roles are structured hierarchically so as to permit permission inheritance. Formally, a role hierarchy is a partial order $\succeq$ on R, where $r_1 \succeq r_2$ means that r_1 is *more senior than* r_2 for $r_1, r_2 \in R$. A user u is an *explicit member* of role r when $(u, r) \in UA$, u is an *implicit member* of r if there exists $r' \in R$ such that $r' \succeq r$ and $(u, r') \in UA$, and u is a *member* of role r if he/she is either an implicit or explicit member of r. Given UA and PA, a user u *has permission* p if there exists a role $r \in R$ such that $(p, r) \in PA$ and u is a member of r. A *RBAC policy* is a tuple $(U, R, P, UA, PA, \succeq)$.

RBAC with Delegation (RBACD). Delegation is used in RBAC policies to provide for flexibility. It allows a user u_2 to acquire a certain permission p from another user u_1. To prevent abuse, delegation usually supports authorization rules, which control who can delegate what privileges to other users. Although our approach can consider more sophisticated models, for the sake of simplicity, we consider here only one-step grant delegation without revocation (see, e.g., [24]). Formally, let $UD \subseteq U \times P$ be the *delegation relation*, a *RBACD policy* is a tuple $(U, R, P, UA, PA, \succeq, UD)$, and a *delegation rule* is a triple of the form $(r_1, r_2, p) \in R \times R \times P$. The semantics of the delegation rules in a finite set δ is given by a transition system whose states are the RBACD policies and a state change is specified by a binary relation $\rightarrow_\delta$ on pairs of RBACD policies as follows: $(U, R, P, UA, PA, \succeq, UD) \rightarrow_\delta (U, R, P, UA, PA, \succeq, UD')$ iff there exists $(r_1, r_2, p) \in \delta$ and users $u_1, u_2 \in U$ such that (a) u_1 is member of role r_1, (b) u_1 has permission p, (c) u_2 is member of role r_2, and (d) $UD' = UD \cup \{(u_2, p)\}$. For simplicity, we assume that conditions (a) and (b) are checked by considering the RBAC policy $(U, R, P, UA, PA, \succeq)$, i.e. a delegatee cannot further delegate the delegated permission to other users. Let $(U, R, P, UA, PA, \succeq, UD)$ be a RBACD policy, a user u *has permission* p if either u has permission p when considering the RBAC policy $(U, R, P, UA, PA, \succeq)$ or $(u, p) \in UD$.

parametrized workflow systems with access control consist of an extended RBACD policy and an arbitrary (but finite) number of identical workflow instances. The RBACD policy is extended by adding a history variable to record which users execute which tasks in a workflow instance. Each workflow instance is modelled by a finite-state automaton which operates on a finite number of local variables ranging over some given sets of data endowed with operations. The parametrized workflow system can change its configuration according to a finite number of state-change rules. Before giving the formal definition, we introduce some technical notions. Let V be a set of state variables and $D = \{D_v\}_{v \in V}$ a family of data sets endowed with some operations. A state σ is a mapping from V to D, such that each $v \in V$ is associated to a value in D_v. A predicate π over V is a function from V to the set $\{true, false\}$ of Boolean values. For a state σ and a predicate π over the state variables in V, we write $\sigma \models \pi$ whenever $\pi(\sigma(V)) = true$, where $\sigma(V) := \{\sigma(v)|v \in V\}$. A *data expression e (associated to a data set D_v in D)* is an expression over the state variables in V and operations inducing a function from V to D_v as follows: given a state σ, $e(\sigma)$ denotes the value of D_v obtained by replacing each $v \in V$ with $\sigma(v)$ in e and then evaluating all operations. A *guarded assignment* is of the form $G \to U$, where G is a predicate over V and U is a finite sequence of assignments of the form $v := e$ for $v \in V$ and e a data expression. A *parametrized workflow system with access control* is a tuple $(U, R, P, UA, PA, \succeq, Q, X, T)$ where $(U, R, P, UA, PA, \succeq, UD)$ is a RBACD policy, Q is a finite set of workflow instance states, X is a finite set of local variables (each one associated to a suitable set of values), and T is a finite set of transition rules of the forms: (I) $t : \langle q_1 \to q_1' \mid G_1 \to U_1 \rangle \cdots \langle q_k \to q_k' \mid G_k \to U_k \rangle$, (II) $\langle G, r_1, r_2, p \rangle$, (III) $\cdot \to q \mid init(X)$, (IV) $q \to \cdot$, where $t \in P$, $q, q_i, q_i' \in Q$, $G_i \to U_i$ is a guarded assignment for $i = 1, ..., k$, $init(X)$ denotes an assignment of values to the variables in X, G is a predicate over X, $r_1, r_2 \in R$, and $p \in P$. The set Q represents the set of states of each of workflow instance, X contains the variables which are local to a workflow instance, and the transition rules describe the transition of the parametrized workflow system.

A *configuration* c of a parametrized workflow system with access control $(U, R, P, UA, PA, \succeq, Q, X, T)$ is a tuple of the form $(Id, UAA, EX, UD, \mathsf{q}, l)$ where Id is a finite index set, $UAA \subseteq U \times R \times Id$ is such that if $(u, r, i) \in UAA$ for some $i \in Id$ then $(u, r) \in UA$, $EX \subseteq U \times P \times Id$, $UD \subseteq U \times P \times Id$, $\mathsf{q} : Id \to Q$, and $l : Id \to (X \to D)$ for $D = \{D_x\}_{x \in X}$. Intuitively, Id is a set of indices, used to uniquely identify workflow instances in the system, that may dynamically change. The state of the access control module is given by (EX, UAA, UD)—where EX is a history variable recording which user has executed which task in which workflow instance, UAA records the role that users has activated to execute the tasks of a certain workflow instance, and UD keeps track of the permission acquired via delegation by a certain user for a certain workflow instance. The states of the workflow instances are given by the mapping q from indices to the states of the workflow instances, and the values of the local variables are given by the mapping l from X to suitable sets of values, once a given workflow instance has been fixed.

We define the transition relation induced by a parametrized workflow with access control on the set of configurations. Let $c = (Id, UAA, EX, UD, \mathsf{q}, l)$ and $c' = (Id, UAA', EX', UD', \mathsf{q}', l')$ be two configurations. We write $c \Rightarrow c'$ to denote that there exists a user $u \in U$ such that

1. for a transition rule of the form (I) and an injection h from the indices $\{1, ..., k\}$ of the transition rule to Id, we have
    (a) $\mathsf{q}(h(i)) = q_i$ and $l(h(i)) \models G_i$ for $i = 1, ..., k$ and u has the permission t in the RBACD policy $(U, R, P, UAA, PA, \succeq, UD)$,
    (b) $\mathsf{q}'(h(i)) = q_i'$ for $i = 1, ..., k$ and $\mathsf{q}'(j) = q_j'$ for each $j \in Id$ not in the range of h,
    (c) $l'(h(i))(x) = l(h(i))(x)$ if $x \in X$ does not occur in U, $l'(h(i))(x) = e(l(h(i)))$ if $x := e$ occurs in U, and $l'(j) = l(j)$ for each $j \in Id$ not in the range of h,
    (d) $UAA' = UAA$, $EX' = EX \cup \{(u, t, h(1)), \ldots, (u, t, h(k))\}$ and $UD' = UD$.
2. for a transition rule of the form (II), an index $i \in Id$, and a user u', we have
    (a) $l(i) \models G$, u has the role r_1 and permission p, and u' has the role r_2 in the RBACD policy $(U, R, P, UAA, PA, \succeq, UD)$,
    (b) $\mathsf{q}'(j) = \mathsf{q}(j)$ and $l'(j) = l(j)$ for each $j \in Id$, and
    (c) $UAA' = UAA$, $EX' = EX$ and $UD' = UD \cup \{(u', p, i)\}$.
3. for a transition rule of the form (III), we have $Id' = Id \cup \{i\}$ for $i \notin Id$, $\mathsf{q}'(j) = \mathsf{q}(j)$ and $l'(j) = l(j)$ for each $j \in Id$, $UAA' = UAA$, $EX' = EX$, $\mathsf{q}'(i) = q$, $l'(i) = init(X)$, and $UD' = \emptyset$.
4. for a transition rule of the form (IV) and $i \in Id$, we have $Id' = Id \setminus \{i\}$, $\mathsf{q}'(j) = \mathsf{q}(j)$ and $l'(j) = l(j)$ for each $j \in Id$ and $j \neq i$, $UAA' = UAA$, $EX' = EX$, and $UD' = UD$.

Condition 1(a) asserts that the transition rule (I) is enabled, i.e. that the workflow instance states $q_1, ..., q_k$ are matched by the corresponding workflow instance states in the configuration c and that the corresponding guarded assignments are enabled. Condition 1(b) means that the states of the workflow instances, matched (via h) with the indices of (I), are changed according to (I) and that the states of the other instances are unchanged. Condition 1(c) asserts that the values of the local variables of the workflow instances, matched (via h) with the indices of (I), are set to the appropriate values specified in the updates or are unchanged those of the unmatched instances. Condition 1(d) asserts that EX is added the facts that user u has executed t in the workflow instances $h(1), ..., h(k)$. Condition 2(a) asserts that the transition rule (II) is enabled, i.e. the values of the local state variables of a certain workflow instance i satisfy the guard G and users u, u' satisfy the RBACD policy $(U, R, P, UAA, PA, \succeq, UD)$. Condition 2(b) asserts that all the states of the workflow instances are unchanged. Condition 2(c) says that the value of EX is unchanged and the permission p is delegated to user u' in the workflow instance i. The index set Id in configurations does not change when executing transition rules (I) and (II). Conditions 3 and 4 say that we can create or delete an instance, respectively, without changing anything else;

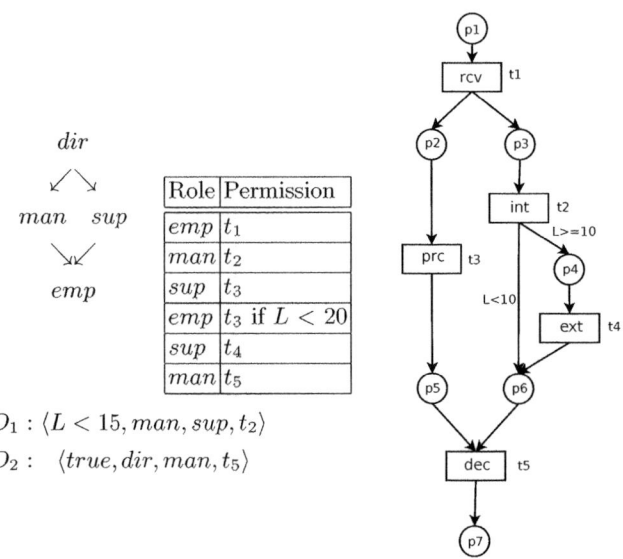

dir

man sup

emp

Role	Permission
emp	t_1
man	t_2
sup	t_3
emp	t_3 if $L < 20$
sup	t_4
man	t_5

$D_1 : \langle L < 15, man, sup, t_2 \rangle$

$D_2 : \quad \langle true, dir, man, t_5 \rangle$

Fig. 1. Informal specification of a Loan Origination Process

in case the instance is created, it is also specified how its local variables should be initialized by the mapping $init(X)$.

An Example. A typical business process is the Loan Origination Process (LOP) shown in Figure 1, adapted from [21]. On the right, the workflow is depicted as an extended Petri net where certain arcs are labelled with conditions and the arc can be traversed only if the condition holds. A workflow instance starts with the input of the customer's data (rcv), consisting of a (unique) identifier C for a customer and the amount L of the loan. Afterwards, a contract for the current customer C is prepared (prc) while the customer's rating evaluation takes place concurrently. If the amount of the loan L is less than 10 KEuros, then an internal rating (int) suffices. Otherwise, the internal rating is followed by an external evaluation (ext) carried out by a third-party financial institution. Finally, the loan request is approved or refused (dec) by the bank. On the left of Figure 1, the role hierarchy (shown as the Hasse diagram associated to the partial order $\succeq$), the role-permission assignments, and the delegation rules of the access control module are given. There are four roles: emp for employee, sup for supervisor, man for manager, dir for director. The permission-assignment relation PA contains permission t_i to execute the task t_i, for $i = 1, ..., 5$. As it is customary in several applications of RBAC, certain tasks can be executed by employees with less senior roles if the loan amount L is lower than a certain value; i.e. $(emp, t_3) \in PA$ if L is less than 20 KEuros. Delegation is specified by the two rules D_1 and D_2 on the left of Figure 1: the former says that a manager can delegate the internal evaluation of a loan to a supervisor if the amount is less than 15 KEuros and the latter formalizes the delegation from the director to a manager for taking the decision about a loan request.

The LOP can be formalized by the following parameterized workflow system with access control: U is a finite but unknown set of users, $R := \{emp, sup, man, dir\}$ and $\succeq$ is the partial order specified in Figure 1, $P := \{t_1, ..., t_5\}$, $UA \subseteq U \times R$, PA is the relation specified in the middle of Figure 1, Q is the finite set of all possible Boolean assignments to the variables $p_1, ..., p_7$, where p_i is associated in the obvious way to a place in the Petri net of Figure 1; $X = \{L, C\}$ and T consists of the following rules: $t_1 : \langle p_1 \to p_2 \wedge p_3 \rangle$(here $\wedge$ is the usual Boolean operator for conjunction), $t_2 : \langle p_3 \to p_4 | L \geq 10 \rangle$, $t_2 : \langle p_3 \to p_6 | L < 10 \rangle$, $t_3 : \langle p_2 \to p_5 \rangle$, $t_4 : \langle p_4 \to p_6 \rangle$, $t_5 : \langle p_5 \wedge p_6 \to p_7 \rangle$, $\cdot \to p_1$ (a workflow instance can be created at any time without initializing any of the local variables), $p_j \to \cdot$ for $j = 1, ..., 6$ (a workflow instance can be killed at any time of its execution except when it is finished), $\langle L < 15, man, sup, t_2 \rangle$, and $\langle true, dir, man, t_5 \rangle$.

So far, we have considered just one instance of the workflow of the LOP. However, in the workflow management system of a bank, it is likely that several instances are concurrently executing and need to synchronize for satisfying some inter-instance authorization constraints, such as "there should not exist more than one instance for which the loan customer is the same," in order to avoid that the customer may escape the *external* rating by asking for two loans whose values is less than 10 KEuros. To formalize this situation, we add to X a Boolean variable F, namely a flag which is set to *true* when two distinct workflow instances have the same loan customer C by means of the following transition rules:

$$t_6^{j,k} : \langle p_j \to p_j \mid C = id \to F := true \rangle \langle p_k \to p_k \mid C = id \to F := true \rangle$$

for $j, k = 1, ..., 7$. When the auxiliary variable F has been set to *true*, the workflow manager should take appropriate corrective measures. For example, it can block the progression of all instances by appending the condition $F = false$ to the guards of the transitions $t_1, ..., t_5$ above.

The Reachability Problem. Given a parameterized workflow system with access control $(U, R, P, UA, PA, \succeq, Q, X, T)$ together with a state $q_0 \in Q$, which we call the *initial workflow state*, and a partial mapping $in(X)$, which we call the *initial value of the local variables*, we define an *initial configuration* c_0 to be the tuple $(Id, UAA_0, \emptyset, q_{in}, l_{in})$ where $UAA_0 \subseteq U \times R$, $q_{in}(j) = q_0$, and $l_{in}(j)$ is any total extension of the partial mapping $in(X)$, for each $j \in Id$. Thus, there is one initial configuration for each index set Id and every total extension of $in(X)$, in which a set of roles has been activated by each user, and no action and no delegation has been performed. A configuration c is *reachable* iff $c_0 \Rightarrow^* c$ for some initial configuration c_0, where $\Rightarrow^*$ denotes the reflexive and transitive closure of $\Rightarrow$. Similarly, a set Γ of configurations is reachable if there exists a reachable configuration $c \in \Gamma$. Let $(U, R, P, UA, PA, \succeq, Q, X, T)$ be a parameterized workflow system with access control, $q_0 \in Q$ be an initial workflow state, $in(X)$ be the initial value of the local variables, Γ be a set of configurations. An instance of the *reachability problem* consists of checking whether Γ is reachable or not. In general, this problem is undecidable. Fortunately, it is possible to identify a decidable sub-class, which is also useful in practice; for example, the LOP described above belongs to this sub-class (this will be discussed in Section 4). We will be interested to verify that a set Γ of "error" configurations, which violate a desired authorization constraint, is unreachable, irrespective of the size of the network. If we include in Γ the error configurations of all possible sizes of the set Id of workflow instance identifiers, and if our analysis finds Γ to be unreachable, then we have verified that the configurations in Γ are unreachable for all possible sizes of the parameterized workflow. To illustrate, consider the LOP. The most important authorization constraint that it should satisfy is *Separation of Duty* (SoD), i.e. two or more critical tasks are executed by different users. So, we can require that "a user cannot perform all the tasks in a workflow instance." By complementing this property, we can define a set Γ of configurations that violate the constraint, which critically depends on the amount L of the loan that cannot be predicted in advance: if $L \geq 10$ then the set of critical tasks comprises all the tasks in the process, otherwise it contains all tasks but *ext*. Formally, this can be expressed by taking Γ to be the union of $\{(Id, UAA, EX, UD, \mathsf{q}, l) \mid (u, t_j, i) \in EX \text{ for } j = 1, 2, 3, 5 \text{ and } l(L) < 10\}$ and $\{(Id, UAA, EX, UD, \mathsf{q}, l) \mid (u, t_j, i) \in EX \text{ for } j = 1, 2, 3, 4, 5\}$.

3   Symbolic Representation of Parameterized Workflow Systems with Access Control

We define a symbolic representation for a class of parameterized workflow systems with access control and its reachability problem.

Formal Framework. We use a very simple fragment of set-theory where sets may only be sub-sets of a finite collection of sets and variables may only range over elements of these sets. Given a set S and a relation $R \subseteq S \times S$, we write $R(x, y)$ or $x \mathrel{R} y$ to denote that $(x, y) \in R$ and $\neg R(x, y)$ or $\neg(x \mathrel{R} y)$ when $(x, y) \notin R$ for $x, y \in S$ (this extends to relations of arity $n > 2$ in the obvious way). We also make use of the usual notations for equality $=$, union $\cup$, intersection $\cap$, set difference $\setminus$, sub-set relation $\subseteq$, enumeration $\{e_1, ..., e_n\}$ and set comprehension $\{\underline{x} \mid exp(\underline{x})\}$ where e_i is an element $(i = 1, ..., n)$, $\underline{x}$ is a tuple of variables, and $exp(\underline{x})$ is a set-theoretic expression containing the variables in $\underline{x}$ as the only free variables. We use the Boolean operators $\neg$ and $\wedge$ for negation and conjunction, respectively, to combine set-theoretic expressions, especially in set comprehensions. We also use the constraints $Reflexive(R)$, $Antisymmetry(R)$, $Transitive(R)$, and $Total(R)$ to characterize the facts that the (binary) relation R is reflexive, antisymmetric, transitive, or total, respectively.

The *set-theoretic specification* of parameterized workflow systems is structured in two parts: one contains *time-independent (TI)* sets and relations which are assumed to satisfy a set of *set-theoretic constraints* and the other is a *set-theoretic transition system* containing the *state variables* and the *set-theoretic guarded assignment rules*. TI sets and relations (with constraints) describe an abstraction of the algebraic structure of the state space of a system. Set-theoretic expressions involving both the state variables and the TI sets and relations are used to describe sets of states. Formally, a *state* is a mapping which associates each state variable with a certain relation, i.e. a subset of the Cartesian product of the TI sets. Let exp be a set-theoretic expression containing state variables from a given set V. With $[exp]$, we denote the set of states identified by exp. We say that a state σ *satisfies* exp iff $\sigma \in [exp]$ and a set Σ of states *satisfies* exp iff σ satisfies exp for every $\sigma \in \Sigma$. A *set-theoretic guarded-assignment rule* is an expression of the form $\ell(\underline{x}) : G \implies U$ where ℓ is the label, G and U are set-theoretic expressions called, respectively, the *guard* and the *update* of the rule. *G is assumed to be a conjunction of (possibly negated) set-membership constraints over the state variables, and the TI sets and relations. U is assumed to be a sequence of assignments of the forms $s := s \cup \{\underline{t}\}$ and $s := s \setminus \{\underline{t}\}$, for $\underline{t}$ a tuple of constants and variables whose length is equal to the arity of s.* Given a set-theoretic guarded-assignment rule $\ell(\underline{x}) : G \implies U$ and a tuple $\underline{e}$ of elements of the same length of $\underline{x}$ (each element belongs to the TI set associated to each variable), we write $\ell(\underline{e}) : G(\underline{e}) \implies U(\underline{e})$ for the instance of the rule obtained by replacing each variable in $\underline{x}$ with the corresponding element of $\underline{e}$ in G and U. The instance $\ell(\underline{e}) : G(\underline{e}) \implies U(\underline{e})$ is *enabled* in state σ iff σ satisfies $[G(\underline{e})]$. The *effect* of executing the enabled instance $\ell(\underline{e}) : G(\underline{e}) \implies U(\underline{e})$ in state σ is the state σ' obtained as follows: if $s := s \cup \{\underline{e}\}$ (resp. $s := s \setminus \{\underline{e}\}$) is in $U(\underline{e})$, then $\sigma'(s) = \sigma(s) \cup \{\underline{e}\}$ (resp. $\sigma'(s) = \sigma(s) \setminus \{\underline{e}\}$); otherwise, i.e. if there is no assignment in U with s as its left-hand-side, $\sigma'(s) = \sigma(s)$. A pair (σ, σ') *satisfies a rule instance* $\ell(\underline{e}) : G(\underline{e}) \implies U(\underline{e})$ iff this is enabled in σ and σ' is the state obtained from σ as the effect of its application. The kind of *reachability problems* we are interested to solve can be stated as follows: given a symbolic transition system $(V, I, \mathcal{R})$ where V is the set of state variables, I is a set-theoretic expression over V, $\mathcal{R}$ is a finite set of guarded-assignment rules, and a set-theoretic expression E encoding the error condition, does there exist a sequence $\sigma_0, ..., \sigma_n$ such that (i) σ_0 satisfies I, (ii) there exists some rule instance τ in $\mathcal{R}$ such that (σ_j, σ_{j+1}) satisfies τ, for each $j = 0, ..., n - 1$, and (iii) σ_n satisfies E?

Symbolic Representation of Parameterized Workflow Systems. Let $\mathcal{S} = (U, R, P, UA, PA, \succeq, Q, X, T)$ be a parameterized workflow system with access control, q_0 be the initial workflow state, and $in(X)$ be the initial value of the local variables. We *assume that no operations are available on the data sets associated to the local variables in X*. Thus, the expression e in an assignment $x := e$ in $\mathcal{S}$ can only be another variable associated to the same data set or a value of the data set. We now define the symbolic representation of $\mathcal{S}$ as a symbolic transition system $(V, I, \mathcal{R})$. Let $c = (Id, UAA, EX, UD, \mathsf{q}, l)$ be a configuration of $\mathcal{S}$. The set V contains id, uaa, ex, and ud corresponding to the elements Id, UAA, EX, and UD in c, respectively and a relation $\tilde{q} \subseteq Id \times \Pi_{v \in L} D_v$ for each $q \in Q$ such that $(j, \underline{x}) \in \tilde{q}$ iff $\mathsf{q}(j) = q$, for each $j \in Id$ and $\underline{x}$ is a sequence of all the variables in X. Below, abusing notation, we write q instead of $\tilde{q}$ and use Q to denote the set $\{\tilde{q} | q \in Q\}$ of relations.

The initial configuration $c_0 = (Id, UAA_0, \emptyset, \mathsf{q}_{in}, l_{in})$ of $\mathcal{S}$ is represented by the following set-theoretic expression $I(id, uaa, ex, ud, Q)$:

$$\{(u,t)|(u,t,i) \in uaa\} \subseteq ua \wedge ex = \emptyset \wedge ud = \emptyset \wedge$$

$$q_0 = \{(j,\underline{x}) \mid j \in id \wedge \bigwedge_{x \in X_{in}} x = l_{in}(x)\} \wedge \bigwedge_{q \in Q \setminus \{q_0\}} q = \emptyset,$$

where $X_{in} \subseteq X$ is the domain of l_{in}. The set id of active workflow instances is left unconstrained so as to consider systems of arbitrary size.

A transition rule of the form (I), namely $t : \langle q_1 \to q_1' \mid G_1 \to U_1 \rangle \cdots \langle q_k \to q_k' \mid G_k \to U_k \rangle$, is represented by the following two symbolic rules:

$$t(i,\underline{x},u,r,r') : \begin{bmatrix} i \in id \wedge \\ \bigwedge_{j=1}^{k}(q_j(i,\underline{x}) \wedge \tilde{G}_j(\underline{x})) \wedge \\ uaa(u,r',i) \wedge \\ r' \succeq r \wedge pa(r,t,i) \end{bmatrix} \implies \begin{bmatrix} q_1 := q_1 \setminus \{(i,\underline{x})\}, \\ q_1' := q_1' \cup \{(i,\tilde{U}_1(\underline{x}))\}, \\ \cdots, \\ q_k := q_1 \setminus \{(i,\underline{x})\}, \\ q_k' := q_1' \cup \{(i,\tilde{U}_k(\underline{x}))\}, \\ ex := ex \cup \{(u,t,i)\}, \end{bmatrix}$$

$$t(i,\underline{x},u) : \begin{bmatrix} i \in id \wedge \\ \bigwedge_{j=1}^{k}(q_j(i,\underline{x}) \wedge \tilde{G}_j(\underline{x})) \wedge \\ uad(u,t,i) \end{bmatrix} \implies \begin{bmatrix} q_1 := q_1 \setminus \{(i,\underline{x})\}, \\ q_1' := q_1' \cup \{(i,\tilde{U}_1(\underline{x}))\}, \\ \cdots, \\ q_k := q_1 \setminus \{(i,\underline{x})\}, \\ q_k' := q_1' \cup \{(i,\tilde{U}_k(\underline{x}))\}, \\ ex := ex \cup \{(u,t,i)\}, \end{bmatrix}$$

where each $\tilde{G}_j$ is a conjunction of set-membership constraints (over V and the TI sets and relations) corresponding to G_j, i.e. G_j satisfies $\tilde{G}_j$, and $\tilde{U}_j$ is a sequence of terms (local variables or data values) corresponding to U_j (if a local variable in $\underline{x}$ does not occur in U_j, then $\tilde{U}_j$ maps such a variable to itself), for $j = 1, ..., k$.

A transition rule of the form (II), namely $\langle G, r_1, r_2, p \rangle$, is represented by the following set of symbolic rules:

$$\begin{bmatrix} i \in id \wedge q(i,\underline{x}) \wedge G(\underline{x}) \wedge \\ uaa(u_1,r_1,i) \wedge r_1 \succeq r \wedge \\ pa(r,t,i) \wedge uaa(u_2,r_2,i) \end{bmatrix} \implies \begin{bmatrix} uad := uad \cup \{(u_2,t,i)\} \end{bmatrix}$$

for each $q \in Q$.

Transition rules of the form (III) and (IV), respectively $\cdot \to q \mid init(X)$ and $q \to \cdot$, are represented by the following symbolic rules:

$$\begin{bmatrix} i \notin id \end{bmatrix} \implies \begin{bmatrix} id := id \cup \{i\}, \\ q_0 := \{(i,\underline{x}) \mid \underline{x} = init(X)\}, \\ \underline{q}^{-q_0} := \emptyset \end{bmatrix} \qquad \begin{bmatrix} i \in id \end{bmatrix} \implies \begin{bmatrix} id := id \setminus \{i\} \end{bmatrix},$$

respectively, where $\underline{x} = init(X)$ denotes the pairwise equality between a variable x in $\underline{x}$ and the corresponding value $init(X)(x)$ and $\underline{q}^{-q_0} := \emptyset$ denotes the sequence of assignments of the form $q := \emptyset$, for each q in $Q \setminus \{q_0\}$.

Symbolic Representation of (negated) Authorization Constraints. We are interested in (*operational*) SoD constraints, which amount to requiring that no employee performs all the "critical" tasks in a given workflow instance (intra-instance) or that a certain employee may not be involved in more than $k > 1$ instances of the workflow at the same time (inter-instance). For simplicity, we only explain how to symbolically represent the configurations violating intra-instance SoD constraints. Inter-instance can be similarly represented albeit with more technicalities. Let $T_c(i, \underline{x}) = \bigcup_{h=1}^{s} T_c^h(i, \underline{x}) \subseteq P$ be the set of critical tasks that should not be executed by the same employee, where $T_c^h(i, \underline{x}) = \{t | t \in P \wedge \pi_h(i, \underline{x})\}$ and π_h is a conjunction of set-membership constraints involving the instance identifier i, the local state variables $\underline{x}$, and the TI sets and relations, for $h = 1, ..., s$. Then, the error condition $E(i, \underline{x})$ is simply the disjunctions of the expressions $q_h(i, \underline{x}) \wedge i \in id \wedge \pi_h(i, \underline{x}) \wedge \bigwedge_{t \in T_c^h}(u, t, i) \in ex$ over $h = 1, ..., s$, for a given instance i and values $\underline{x}$ of the local variables. (Notice that E puts no requirements on workflow instances whose indices are not mentioned in E and thus denotes a possibly infinite set of configurations.) For example, in the case of the LOP, the complement of the SoD intra-instance constraint is the expression obtained by taking the disjunction of $p_7(i, C, L) \wedge i \in id \wedge L < 10 \wedge \bigwedge_{j=1,2,3,5}(u, t_j, i) \in ex$ and $p_7(i, C, L) \wedge i \in id \wedge L \geq 10 \wedge \bigwedge_{j=1,2,3,4,5}(u, t_j, i) \in ex$ for a given workflow instance i, customer C, and loan amount L.

4 Automated Analysis of Parameterized Workflow Systems

We explain how the model checking modulo theories approach [13] can be used to solve the symbolic reachability problems defined in the previous section. The idea is to translate set-theoretic specifications to first-order logic (see, e.g., [11]). We do this by considering the characteristic functions induced by sets or relations and represent them by predicate symbols of first-order logic according to the translation in Figure 2, where A, B, C are sets (the extension to relations is obvious and is therefore omitted), R is a binary relation, and $\widetilde{exp}$ is the first-order translation of the set-theoretic expression exp. Then, we will show that the translation of the set-theoretic expressions are first-order formulae belonging to the *Bernays-Schönfinkel-Ramsey* (BSR) class [19], namely formulae of the form $\exists \underline{x}. \forall \underline{y}. \varphi(\underline{x}, \underline{y})$, where $\underline{x}, \underline{y}$ are (disjoint and possibly empty) tuples of variables and φ is a quantifier-free formula built out of predicate and constant symbols only (i.e. no function symbol occurs in φ). The decidability of the satisfiability problem for BSR formulae is well-known (see again [19]).

BSR Specifications of Reachability Problems. According to Section 3, we assume given some TI sets and relations with a collection $\mathcal{C}$ of set-theoretic constraints, a symbolic transition system $(V, I(V), \mathcal{R}(V, V'))$ representing a parameterized workflow system with access control $(U, R, P, UA, PA, \succeq, Q, X, T)$, and an error condition E, where $V = \{id, uaa, ex, ud\} \cup Q$. Below, we explain how to derive a collection $\tilde{\mathcal{C}}$ of BSR formulae representing the constraints in $\mathcal{C}$, a

Set theory		First-order logic
Membership	$e \in A$	$A(e)$
Empty set	$A = \emptyset$	$\forall x. \neg A(x)$
Enumeration	$A = \{e_1, ..., e_n\}$	$\forall x. A(x) \Leftrightarrow (x = e_1 \vee \cdots \vee x = e_n)$
Set-comprehension	$A = \{x \mid exp(x)\}$	$\forall x. A(x) \Leftrightarrow e\tilde{x}p(x)$
Intersection	$A = B \cap C$	$\forall x. A(x) \Leftrightarrow (B(x) \wedge C(x))$
Union	$A = B \cup C$	$\forall x. A(x) \Leftrightarrow (B(x) \vee C(x))$
Difference	$A = B \setminus C$	$\forall x. A(x) \Leftrightarrow (B(x) \wedge \neg C(x))$
Sub-set	$A \subseteq B$	$\forall x. A(x) \Rightarrow B(x)$
Reflexive(R)		$\forall x. R(x, x)$
Antisymmetry(R)		$\forall x, y. (R(x, y) \wedge R(y, x)) \Rightarrow x = y$
Transitive(R)		$\forall x, y, z. (R(x, y) \wedge R(y, z)) \Rightarrow R(x, z)$
Total(R)		$\forall x, y. R(x, y) \vee R(y, x)$

Fig. 2. Mapping set-theory to first-order logic

symbolic transition system $(\tilde{V}, \tilde{I}(\tilde{V}), \tilde{\mathcal{R}}(\tilde{V}, \tilde{V}'))$ corresponding to $(V, I(V), \mathcal{R}(V, V'))$, and a BSR formula $\tilde{E}$ corresponding to E.

To obtain $\tilde{\mathcal{C}}$ from $\mathcal{C}$, we apply the translation of Figure 2 by mapping symbols for TI sets and relations to predicate symbols with the same identifier and arity. It is easy to see by inspection of the formulae on the right column of the table in Figure 2 that each element in $\tilde{\mathcal{C}}$ is a BSR formula. We also notice that conjunctions of finitely many BSR formulae can easily be transformed to a single BSR formula, so that $\bigwedge_{\psi \in \tilde{\mathcal{C}}} \psi$ (abbreviated below with $\bigwedge \tilde{\mathcal{C}}$) is a BSR formula.

The translation $(\tilde{V}, \tilde{I}(\tilde{V}), \tilde{\mathcal{R}}(\tilde{V}, \tilde{V}'))$ of $(V, I(V), \tilde{\mathcal{R}}(V, V'))$ is obtained as follows. Similarly to the TI sets and relations, we map each state variable in V to a predicate symbol with the same identifier and arity so that $\tilde{V} = V = \{id, uaa, ex, ud\} \cup Q$. The formula $\tilde{I}$ is obtained by using the translation in Figure 2 on I. Recall that (Section 3) I is a conjunction of expressions of the forms $s = \emptyset$, $\{\underline{x} \mid exp(\underline{x})\} \bowtie s$ for $\bowtie \in \{=, \subseteq\}$, s a state variable in V, $\underline{x}$ is a tuple of variables associated to some TI set of appropriate length, and exp is a conjunction of membership constraints. Thus, again by inspection of the corresponding formulae on the right column of the table in Figure 2, it is easy to see that $\tilde{I}$ is a conjunction of BSR formulae, which—as observed above for the constraints in $\mathcal{C}$—can be rewritten as a single BSR formula. Then, consider the collection $\mathcal{R}$ of set-theoretic guarded assignment rules of the form $\ell(\underline{w}) : G \Longrightarrow U$, where $\underline{w}$ is a tuple of variables associated to Id or some TI domain, G is a conjunction of expressions of (possibly negated) membership constraints, and U is a sequence of assignments of the forms $s := s \setminus \{\underline{z}\}$ and $s := s \cup \{\underline{z}\}$ for $\underline{z}$ a sub-tuple of $\underline{w}$ with length equal to the arity of s. Each rule $\ell(\underline{w}) : U \Longrightarrow U$ in $\mathcal{R}$ is mapped to the formula $\exists \underline{w}. \tilde{G} \wedge \tilde{U}$, where $\tilde{G}$ is the conjunction of formulae obtained by translating G according to Figure 2, with the proviso that the variables in $\underline{w}$ are considered as parameters, i.e. as symbolic constants that should not be (universally) quantified as variables, and $\tilde{U}$ is the BSR formula obtained as follows. Let s be a state variable of arity n, s' its primed version (as usual, s denotes the value of the state variable immediately before the execution of the transition and s' its value immediately after), $\underline{t} = t_1, ..., t_n$ a tuple of constants or variables (because of the assumption on updates in Section 3): translate $s' := s \cup \{\underline{t}\}$ as $\forall \underline{z}.(s'(\underline{z}) \Leftrightarrow (s(\underline{z}) \vee \underline{z} = \underline{t}))$ and $s' := s \setminus \{\underline{t}\}$ as $\forall \underline{z}.(s'(\underline{z}) \Leftrightarrow (s(\underline{z}) \wedge \neg(\underline{z} = \underline{t})))$, where $\underline{z} = z_1, ..., z_n$ is a tuple of variables and $\underline{z} = \underline{t}$ abbreviates $z_1 = t_1 \wedge \cdots \wedge t_n = c_n$. Furthermore, for each state variable s not occurring on the left-hand side of an assignment in U, add the formula $\forall \underline{z}.(s'(\underline{z}) \Leftrightarrow s(\underline{z}))$ where $\underline{z}$ is a tuple of variables of length equal to the arity of s. It is not difficult to verify that formulae of form $\exists \underline{w}.G \wedge \tilde{U}$, obtained from the translation of guarded assignment rules of the form $\ell(\underline{w}) : G \Longrightarrow U$, can easily be transformed to BSR formulae.

Finally, the translation $\tilde{E}$ of the error condition $E(i, \underline{x})$ is obtained in two steps. First, derive $\hat{E}(i, \underline{x})$ from $E(i, \underline{x})$ by using the translation in Figure 2, with the proviso that i and $\underline{x}$ are parameters, i.e. they are considered as symbolic constants that should not be (universally) quantified as variables. Then, take $\tilde{E}$ to be the existential closure of $\hat{E}(i, \underline{x})$, namely $\exists i, \underline{x}.\hat{E}(i, \underline{x})$. Since $E(i, \underline{x})$ is, according to Section 3, a conjunction of possibly negated membership constraints, $\tilde{E}$ is a BSR formula by considering the first line of the table in Figure 2.

We are now ready to re-state the reachability problem in terms of the BSR specification derived above, namely $\tilde{C}$, $(V, \tilde{I}(V), \tilde{R}(V, V'))$, and $\tilde{E}$. Verifying that there is no sequence of transitions from a configuration satisfying I to a configuration satisfying the error condition E can be established by checking that there is no $n \geq 0$ such that the formula

$$\bigwedge \tilde{C} \wedge \tilde{I}(V_0) \wedge \bigvee \tilde{R}(V_0, V_1) \wedge \cdots \wedge \bigvee \tilde{R}(V_{n-1}, V_n) \wedge \tilde{E}(V_n) \qquad (1)$$

is unsatisfiable, where V_i is obtained from V by a unique renaming of its elements for $i = 0, ..., n$, and $\bigvee S$ abbreviates $\bigvee_{\psi \in S} \psi$. Notice that, besides checking the satisfiability of (1), we also need to establish an upper bound for the value of n after which we stop enumerating instances.

The Backward Reachability Procedure. We solve this problem by using the following procedure for symbolically computing the set $R(V)$ of (backward) reachable states, iteratively:

$$R_0(V) := \tilde{E}(V) \text{ and } R_{j+1}(V) := R_j(V) \vee \exists V'.(R_j(V') \wedge \bigvee \tilde{R}(V, V')) \text{ for } j \geq 0,$$

where $\exists V'.(R_j(V') \wedge \bigvee \tilde{R}(V, V'))$ is the *pre-image* of R_j with respect to $\bigvee \tilde{R}$. The procedure discovers a fix-point at the n-th iteration iff $\tilde{C} \Rightarrow \forall V.(R_n(V) \Rightarrow R_{n-1}(V))$ is valid or, reasoning by refutation, $\tilde{C} \wedge \exists V.(R_j(V) \wedge \neg R_{j-1}(V))$ is unsatisfiable (*fix-point check*). At this point, $R_n(V)$ is an inductive invariant of the system and if $\tilde{C} \wedge R_n(V) \wedge \tilde{I}(V)$ is unsatisfiable (*safety check*), then the system cannot reach a state satisfying the error condition $\tilde{E}$. In the model checking modulo theories approach [13], the following requirements should be satisfied in order to guarantee the termination of the procedure described above and design an automated analysis procedure for parameterized workflow system with access control: (i) the class of formulae used to represent sets of backward reachable states should be closed under pre-image computation, (ii) the checks for safety and fix-point should be decidable, and (iii) the procedure must terminate. We show that the three requirements are satisfied when considering $\tilde{C}$, $(V, \tilde{I}(V), \tilde{R}(V, V'))$, and $\tilde{E}$ obtained by the translation described above. Preliminary, observe that if $\tilde{R}(V, V') := \bigvee_{i=1}^{n} \tilde{t}_i(V, V')$ then the pre-image of R with respect to $\tilde{R}$ is $\bigvee_{i=1}^{n} \exists V'.(R(V') \wedge \tilde{t}_i(V, V'))$, i.e. pre-images distribute over disjunction. Thus, without loss of generality, we focus on a single disjunct $\tilde{t}_i$ of the transition formula $\bigvee \tilde{R}$.

Fact 1 (Closure under pre-image computation) *Let R be a formula of the form $\exists \underline{x}.\varphi(V)$, where $\underline{x}$ is a tuple of variables and $t(V, V')$ be a formula of the form $\exists \underline{y}.(\tilde{G}(V) \wedge \tilde{U}(V, V'))$ obtained by the translation described above. Then, the pre-image of R with respect to $\tilde{t}$ (in symbols, $\exists V'.(R(V') \wedge \tilde{t}(V, V'))$) can be rewritten to a formula of the form $\exists \underline{x}, \underline{y}.\psi(V)$, where φ and ψ are quantifier-free.*

Thus, formulae in the sequence $R_0, R_1, \dots$ generated by the backward reachability procedure are all of the form $\exists \underline{x}.\varphi(V)$ and it is easy to see that the formulae $\tilde{C} \wedge \tilde{I} \wedge R_j$ and $\tilde{C} \wedge R_j \wedge \neg R_{j-1}$ for safety and fix-point, respectively, are all equivalent to BSR formulae for $j \geq 1$.

Fact 2 (Decidability of safety and fix-point checks) *The safety and fix-point checks of the backward reachability procedure on a BSR specification $\tilde{C}$, $(V, \tilde{I}(V), \tilde{R}(V, V'))$, and $\tilde{E}$ obtained as described above are decidable.*

The proof consists of transforming the formulae for safety and fix-point into BSR formulae whose decidability is well-known [19].

Fact 3 (Termination of backward reachability) *The backward reachability procedure on a BSR specification $\tilde{C}$, $(V, \tilde{I}(V), \tilde{R}(V, V'))$, and $\tilde{E}$ obtained as described above always terminates.*

This fact can be derived from a more general result in [13] and guarantees that any fix-point can be expressed as BSR formula.[1] We can now state the main result of this paper (which is an immediate consequence of the three facts above).

Theorem 1 (Decidability). *The reachability problem for parameterized workflow systems with access control, symbolically represented by a set C of set-theoretic constraints and a set-theoretic transition system $(V, I(V), R)$, and the complement of a SoD constraint, specified by a (finite) conjunction of (possibly negated) set-membership constraints, is decidable.*

The scope of applicability of our decidability result is the sub-class of parameterized workflow systems with access control manipulating data with "simple" algebraic structures and whose updates assign (local) variables given values or

---

[1] The proof of this fact and those of the previous two can be found in the extended version of this paper, available at http://st.fbk.eu/SilvioRanise

(the content of) other variables. The formal characterization of "simple" algebraic structure is given by the set $\tilde{\mathcal{C}}$ of set-theoretic constraints in the table of Figure 2 (in the restricted fragment of set-theory introduced at the beginning of Section 3). The restriction on the updates of the local variables— (introduced in the paragraph **Symbolic representation of parameterized workflow systems** of Section 3 and stated as "no operations on the data sets in which the variable take their values are available")—implies that the updates of the set-theoretic guarded assignment rules in $\mathcal{R}$ obtained by the translation described above can be described as additions or deletions of a tuple $\underline{t}$ to each state variable s, i.e. $s' = s \cup \{\underline{t}\}$ or $s' = s \setminus \{\underline{t}\}$, respectively. As an example, the LOP discussed in Section 2 falls in the sub-class of parameterized workflow systems covered by Theorem 1. (Recall that the LOP requires to specify total orders in order to describe the interplay between the data- and the control-flow as well as the access control policies.)

5   Related Work and Discussion

The formal specification and automatic analysis of workflows under authorization constraints has received and is receiving a lot of attention; e.g., [14,6,9,15,23] to name a few. In [14], the safety problem for protection systems in the access matrix model is introduced. A protection system is safe with respect to a certain right r if r cannot be "leaked," i.e. the execution of an operation cannot cause r to be entered into a cell in the access matrix where it does not already exist. The main result in [14] is that the safety analysis problem is undecidable in general but becomes decidable for a certain sub-class of protection systems. This seminal paper has stimulated a series of works which can be roughly classified in two categories. The former (e.g., [6,9,15]) is to augment the access control model with authorization constraints so that the safety of configurations can be ensured at run-time. According to [16], the main problem of this approach is the difficulty of expressing authorization constraints, which usually requires a language based on first-order logic thereby making it difficult to determine if the desired safety properties are correctly specified. However, much of the research in the run-time enforcement of authorization constraints has focused on different problems with respect to safety, namely satisfiability—i.e. establishing whether a set of users can complete a workflow under a set of authorization constraints [6,9]—and resiliency—i.e. a workflow can be completed even if a number of users may be absent [15,23].

Our approach is more related to the second category of works derived from [14], which consists of restricting the access control model so that the safety problem can be shown decidable [17,22].[2] It is interesting to notice that the expressivity

---

[2] Technically, we adopt the same notion of safety proposed in [17] which is argued to be more natural than that of [14] in [22]. Our notion of unsafety amounts to establishing whether there is some sequence of commands in which a right is entered in some place in the matrix where it did not exist in the initial state; instead, unsafety in [14] is referred to the state that immediately precedes a command introducing a leak.

of the sub-class of BSR formulae which we use to specify (the complement of) authorization constraints (such as SoD or BoD) is greatly reduced with respect to full first-order logic. This makes it usually easy to determine if the desired safety properties are correctly specified. In this line of works, less attention has been paid to the automated analysis of authorization constraints when considering multiple workflow instances that may need to synchronize as we do in this paper. For example, only [15]—among the papers listed above—considers inter-instance authorization constraints and proposes simple static analysis checks to detect conflicting constraints; more complex anomalies are handled only at run-time. In contrast, our work proposes a specification language for describing multiple workflow instances and shows the decidability of automatically analysing SoD constraints for an interesting sub-class. More recently, it has been proposed to leverage state-of-the-art model checkers for developing more expressive static analysis techniques. Contrary to the approach presented here, these works are not concerned with the question of decidability of the verification problems but are rather oriented to the practical applications of state-of-the-art tools. For example, in [21] it is shown that business processes with RBAC policies and delegation can be formally specified in the NuSMV specification language and that SoD properties can be formally expressed as LTL formulae. The paper [10] presents a similar approach with the SPIN model checker. The work in [7] describes a reduction to the specification language of the SAL model checker. An alternative approach is pursued in [4], where it is possible to separate the specification of the workflow from that of the access control policy, security properties are given by LTL formulae, and model-checking is used for the analysis of the composed specification. All these works provide a variety of important contributions but they all assume that the workflow given as input is finite state, e.g. the number of workflow instances is finite and known in advance (and it is usually one). For this reason, these techniques can be profitably used for debugging only while our approach allows us to certify that for any number of workflow instances in the system, the SoD constraint will not be violated. Another important difference is that we are able to specify more precisely the data-flow of the system and its interplay with the control flow with respect to the works in [21,10,7,4] where data is bounded to make the search space finite and thus amenable to available model checkers. This limitation is shared with the techniques for analysing business processes developed in the field of Petri nets where data is abstracted away and only the control flow is taken into account. Another limitation of Petri net based techniques is that only a single instance of the workflow is considered. Thus, besides lacking precision in describing the interplay between the data- and the control-flow, it is not possible to specify and verify inter-instance authorization constraints. A recent paper [18] has proposed extensions of Petri net with fragments of first-order logic to augment the precision of existing verification techniques; even in this case, only one workflow instance is considered.

To summarize, the approach proposed in this paper improves on available techniques in two respects. First, it is capable of specifying parameterized workflow system with a finite but unknown number of instances which run concurrently, synchronize, and are marshalled by a centralized module for access control. Second, the automated analysis technique can explore infinite states in order to verify that a parameterized workflow system does not exhibit undesired behaviours. Thus, it is also an improvement on our previous work [5,3,2] where only administrative access control policies were considered and the workflow was completely abstracted away.

We have three main lines of future work. First, we intend to implement the technique described here in our tool ASASP [2]. Second, we want to investigate how the organisational structure underlying business processes (such as LDAP) and the activity of role provisioning can be incorporated in our model. Third, we want to study if and how transitions in which a finite but unknown number of workflow instances change states, can be included in our model while maintaining decidability.

Acknowledgements. This work was partially supported by the "Automated Security Analysis of Identity and Access Management Systems (SIAM)" project funded by Provincia Autonoma di Trento in the context of the "team 2009 - Incoming" COFUND action of the European Commission (FP7).

References

1. Abdulla, P.A., Delzanno, G., Ben Henda, N., Rezine, A.: Regular Model Checking Without Transducers (On Efficient Verification of Parameterized Systems). In: Grumberg, O., Huth, M. (eds.) TACAS 2007. LNCS, vol. 4424, pp. 721–736. Springer, Heidelberg (2007)

2. Alberti, F., Armando, A., Ranise, S.: ASASP: Automated Symbolic Analysis of Security Policies. In: Bjørner, N., Sofronie-Stokkermans, V. (eds.) CADE 2011. LNCS, vol. 6803, pp. 26–33. Springer, Heidelberg (2011)

3. Alberti, F., Armando, A., Ranise, S.: Efficient Symbolic Automated Analysis of Administrative Role Based Access Control Policies. In: 6th ACM Symp. on Information, Computer, and Communications Security, ASIACCS (2011)

4. Armando, A., Ponta, S.E.: Model Checking of Security-sensitive Business Processes. In: Degano, P., Guttman, J.D. (eds.) FAST 2009. LNCS, vol. 5983, pp. 66–80. Springer, Heidelberg (2010)

5. Armando, A., Ranise, S.: Automated Symbolic Analysis of ARBAC Policies. In: Cuellar, J., Lopez, J., Barthe, G., Pretschner, A. (eds.) STM 2010. LNCS, vol. 6710, pp. 17–34. Springer, Heidelberg (2011)

6. Bertino, E., Ferrari, E., Atluri, V.: The specification and enforcement of authorization constraints in workflow management systems. ACM Trans. Inf. Syst. Secur. 2, 65–104 (1999)

7. Cerone, A., Xiangpeng, Z., Krishnan, P.: Modelling and resource allocation planning of BPEL workflows under security constraints. Technical Report 336, UNU-IIST (2006)

8. Comon, H., Jurski, Y.: Multiple counters automata, safety analysis and presburger arithmetic. Technical Report LSV-98-1, LSV ENS Cachan (1998)

9. Crampton, J.: A reference monitor for workflow systems with constrained task execution. In: 10th ACM SACMAT, pp. 38–47. ACM (2005)

10. Dury, A., Boroday, S., Petrenko, A., Lotz, V.: Formal verification of business work-flows and role based access control systems. In: SECURWARE, pp. 201–2010 (2007)
11. Enderton, H.B.: A Mathematical Introduction to Logic. Academic Press, New York (1972)
12. Fu, X., Bultan, T., Su, J.: Formal Verification of E-Services and Workflows. In: Bussler, C.J., McIlraith, S.A., Orlowska, M.E., Pernici, B., Yang, J. (eds.) CAiSE 2002 and WES 2002. LNCS, vol. 2512, pp. 188–202. Springer, Heidelberg (2002)
13. Ghilardi, S., Ranise, S.: Backward reachability of array-based systems by smt solving: Termination and invariant synthesis. In: LMCS, vol. 6(4) (2010)
14. Harrison, M.A., Ruzzo, W.L., Ullman, J.D.: Protection in operating systems. Communications of the ACM 19(8), 461–471 (1976)
15. Warner, J., Atluri, V.: Inter-Instance Authorization Constraints for Secure Workflow Managment. In: SACMAT, pp. 190–199. ACM (2006)
16. Jaeger, T., Tidswell, J.: Practical safety in flexible access control models. ACM Transaction on Information and System Security 4(2), 158–190 (2001)
17. Li, N., Tripunitara, M.V.: Security analysis in role-based access control. ACM Transactions on Information and System Security (TISSEC) 9(4), 391–420 (2006)
18. Monakova, G., Kopp, O., Leymann, F.: Improving Control Flow Verification in a Business Process using an Extended Petri Net. In: 1st Central-European Workshop on Services and their Composition, ZEUS (2009)
19. Ramsey, F.P.: On a Problem of Formal Logic. Proceedings of the London Mathematical Society s2-30(1), 264–286 (1930)
20. Sandhu, R., Coyne, E., Feinstein, H., Youmann, C.: Role-Based Access Control Models. IEEE Computer 2(29), 38–47 (1996)
21. Schaad, A., Lotz, V., Sohr, K.: A model-checking approach to analysing organisational controls in a loan origination process. In: SACMAT, pp. 139–149. ACM (2006)
22. Tripunitara, M.V., Li, N.: The Foundational work of Harrison-Ruzzo-Ullman Revisited. Technical Report CERIAS TR 2006-33, CERIAS and Department of Computer Science. Purdue University (2006)
23. Wang, Q., Li, N.: Satisfiability and resiliency in workflow authorization systems. ACM Trans. Inf. Syst. Secur. 13, 40:1–40:35 (2010)
24. Wang, Q., Li, N., Chen, H.: On the Security of Delegation in Access Control Systems. In: Jajodia, S., Lopez, J. (eds.) ESORICS 2008. LNCS, vol. 5283, pp. 317–332. Springer, Heidelberg (2008)

The Role of Data Integrity in EU Digital Signature Legislation — Achieving Statutory Trust for Sanitizable Signature Schemes*

Henrich C. Pöhls and Focke Höhne

Institute of IT Security and Security Law,
University of Passau, Germany
hp@sec.uni-passau.de,
focke.hoehne@uni-passau.de

Abstract. We analyse the legal requirements that digital signature schemes have to fulfil to achieve the *Statutory Trust* granted by the EU electronic signature laws ("legally equivalent to hand-written signatures"). Legally, we found that the possibility to detect subsequent changes is important for the Statutory Trust. However, detectability was neither adequately nor precisely enough defined in the technical and legal definitions of the term "Data Integrity". The existing definition on integrity lack a precise notion of which changes should not invalidate a corresponding digital signature and also lack notions to distinguish levels of detection. We give a new definition for Data Integrity including two notions: Authorized changes, these are changes which do not compromise the data's integrity; and their level of detection. Especially, the technical term "Transparency" introduced as a security property for sanitizable signature schemes has an opposite meaning in the legal context. Technically, cryptography can allow authorized changes and keep them unrecognisably hidden. Legally, keeping them invisible removes the Statutory Trust. This work shows how to gain the Statutory Trust for a chameleon hash based sanitizable signature scheme.

1 Introduction

Legislative bodies, like the European Union (EU), recognized that system complexity, technical failure, human mistake, accidents or attacks may all have negative consequences for the physical infrastructures that deliver important services to citizens [13]. In the EU, the national regulatory authorities should therefore ensure that the integrity and security of public communications networks are maintained[1]. As such, the topic of reliable and secure communication of information over electronic communications networks is increasingly discussed by law and policy-makers. Laws and regulations, like the EU Signature Regulations [16] of 1999, have been introduced to build a foundation for trusted electronic communication by defining how an electronic document can gain Statutory Trust.

---

* Research funded by BMBF [FKZ:13N10966] and ANR as part of ReSCUeIT project.
[1] Recital 44 of Directive 2009/140/EC of 25 November 2009 [13].

C. Meadows and C. Fernández-Gago (Eds.): STM 2011, LNCS 7170, pp. 175–192, 2012.
© Springer-Verlag Berlin Heidelberg 2012

To earn this trust we expect information technology (IT) to comply with the law and to behave as society would expect. Integrity is one of the classical security goals in computer science (CS). Technically, digital signatures are used to link the signatory to the signed document by ensuring technical properties such as: Data Integrity. As a central term, Data Integrity shall be clearly defined. Nevertheless, we found ambiguity within and between legal and technical definitions.

Legal codes and regulations are drafted to be technology neutral and to hold, even in case of technological advances. Especially, IT law is in need of definitions that are also technically sound and precise. Deviations in terms must not lead to wrong technical decisions when lawyers demand for legal compliance with respect to Data Integrity.

This paper is based on the research question we asked ourselves: Can Statutory Trust be given to a document signed with a Sanitizable Signature Scheme (SanSig)? We first found that the integrity definitions, neither within computer science nor within IT law, are well enough aligned to clearly answer or argue about this. Hence, in this paper we present a new aligned definition of Data Integrity. Being able to distinguish between several levels of detectability for subsequent changes we can finally answer the question: A document signed with a detectable sanitizable signature is given Statutory Trust, if and only if no authorized subsequent changes are detected.

1.1   Introduction to Sanitizable Signatures Schemes (SanSig)

RSA-based signatures are well understood, both technically and legally. Using SHA-256 for hashing and padded securely they build the technical basis for todays realization of advanced electronic signatures that induce Statutory Trust. However, neither in general nor for other, more specialized, signatures schemes the role of integrity for Statutory has been looked at. This paper first determines the general impact of integrity for Statutory Trust and focuses on SanSig like [3, 24] as one example of a specialized signature scheme. There are many more signature schemes that have not yet been analyzed with respect to their Statutory Trust.

In a nutshell, a SanSig allows to retain a verifiable valid digital signature on a document even if it has undergone changes. The changes are done by a third party called the sanitizer, not the signer, nor the verifier. The sanitizer and the position of changes that do not harm the validity are chosen by the signer by choice of parameters or the scheme itself. One possible action of a sanitizer is "redaction". Redaction removes the original data and leaves a blinded version of the data behind. An occurred sanitization can be kept unrecognisably hidden from the verifier, thus for verifiers sanitization can stay invisible. Note, sanitization does not involve the original signer.

Applications for SanSig can be found in the original works, i.e. [3][24]. We want to restate just two examples: A personal data set is given to a chain of processors, they do forward, store and process the data subject's data set in order to carry out a process. To preserve the data subject's privacy each processor only hands over the parts of data that are necessary. A forward sanitizable signatures would allow to still verify the integrity of the remaining partial personal data. Additionally, the signature key can be used as a form of indirect later authorization of the data subject at all sites that hold his personal data [20]. Another example allows the privacy preserving release of signed documents [3] due to transparency regulations. These documents would often contain confidential information, that is not covered by the otherwise reasonable release request. The latter is one application of sanitizable signatures, also mentioned in nearly all the schemes' motivation.

1.2   Contribution

We focus on the property of Data Integrity and, whenever possible or needed, further specialize to the application domain of digital, respectively electronic, signatures. This focus is well aligned with the legislative bodies; the protection goal of integrity got recognized by the law as being essential for trust in IT. We first provide an adequate understanding of regulations and technical terms. Then, we present the differences between the law's definitions of integrity with respect to IT systems and the computer security's definitions.

Our analysis of laws and regulations lead us to two technical questions: (1) What constitutes an allowed and thus authorized change after the digital signature has been applied? (2) To what degree can that change be detected or is it unrecognisably hidden? Hence, we give a new harmonized definition of Data Integrity that differentiates along two axes: Authorized changes and detectability. Finally, we show how Statutory Trust for SanSig can be achieved.

2   State of the Art

We are not aware of any other work discussing in detail the role of detection with respect to Data Integrity and their consequences for the Statutory Trust of digital signatures in the EU. This problem is different from the longstanding problem of representation, such that the act of signing binds the signer to what he actually sees when he carries out the act of signing. Dynamically changing content has been discussed in [2] and also how to build trusted viewers in [28]. From the legal point of view, the work of Zanero [31] showed in 2005 that the Italian Legal Digital Signature Framework's had problems with faulty software implementations, as well as legal, and methodological issues. Zanero's work from 2005 predates the current EU legislation and has a broader scope, our work is focussed on integrity and analyzes current EU legislation. The impact of the detection level on Statutory Trust has not yet been discussed.

Several different SanSig exists [30], [3] or [24]. Ateniese et al. described the property of "Transparency" in their work in [3] in 2005. Note, in CS something "transparent" is unrecognisably hidden or invisible. So technically the *Transparency* allows a statement about the complete absence of detectability of authorized changes in SanSig: Ateniese et al.'s definition of Transparency has been partially formalized by Brzuska et al. in [6]. Recently, Pöhls et al. refine this definition further and show that the property of Transparency is independent on the level of a complete sanitizable signed message in [27]. Transparency is technically and legally an important concept. It is important to note that technical Transparency is different from the legal transparency. Hence, the quite opposite definitions are discussed in detail in Sect. 4. The impact of the Property of Transparency of a `SanSig` for the Statutory Trust and has not yet been discussed.

3   Discussion/Analysis of Existing Terms and Definitions

Technology is following legal obligations or legal codes follow technological advances. Hence, we first examine definitions by the European Union for the terms "integrity" and "Data Integrity" in its laws and regulations in the Sections 3.1 to 3.3. We go from general legal definitions of integrity with respect to IT (Sect. 3.1), over the term "Data Integrity" given in EU and the US HIPAA act (Sect. 3.2), down to the area of Digital Signatures as a special case (Sect. 3.3). We quote the according legal code passages in full, to provide the reader with useful insight into the legal framework and its definitions. For a better legal understanding we highlight the most important parts in **bold-face**. We will comment on each legal definition from the CS and IT security perspective.

We analyse technical definitions of integrity from IT security: The term "integrity" in general (Sect. 3.4), with respect to digital signatures (Sect. 3.5), and we state technical definitions Data Integrity in digital signatures

3.1   EU Regulation: Integrity in Information Technology

To establish a more general understanding of the EU legislation, we will first look at EU wide legislation that can be used to define the term "integrity" in the general context of IT. Then we provide the reader with the legal definitions of "Data Integrity" given in EU regulation and in the HIPAA act of the United States of America (US).

In the end of 2009 the European legal texts [13] made, for the first time, a distinction between network-integrity and network-security[2]:

> The national regulatory authorities shall promote the interests of the citizens of the European Union by inter alia: a) ... f) ensuring that the **integrity** and security of public communications networks are maintained. [13]

Article 13a of the same EU regulation[2] further differentiates this:

> (2) Member States shall ensure that undertakings providing public communications networks take all appropriate steps to **guarantee the integrity of their networks, and thus ensure the continuity**.
> (3) Member States shall ensure that undertakings providing public communications networks or publicly available electronic communications services notify the competent national regulatory authority of **a breach of security or loss of integrity** that has had a significant impact on the operation of networks or services. [13]

[2] Art. 4 lit. f and Chapter IIIa "Security and Integrity of Networks and Services", Articles 13a, 13b, and Recital 28 of Directive 2009/140/EC from Nov. 2009 [13]

Comments. EU legislators see "integrity" as means to ensure continuity (13a(2)) and another time they list "loss of integrity" and "breach of security" as distinct problems (13a(3)). Both usages of "integrity" are not in line with the CS's one. However, let us interpret "security" as "secrecy" or "confidentiality", and take the technically better known term of "availability" instead of "continuity": Now, Article 13a(2,3) requires that Member States shall ensure confidentiality, integrity and availability. These are the three classical IT security goals, often referred to as CIA. Also Article 13a(3) would read: "a breach of **secrecy** or loss of integrity". Note, the link between "integrity" and "continuity", as given in Article 13a(2), is technically correct. Loss or unavailability of data are also defined as integrity breaches in CS definitions.

The German constitutional court identified a new fundamental right in 2008:

> The constitutional right in the **confidentiality and integrity** of information technology systems. [7]

This right protects the personal and private life of rights holders from the state accessing any IT devices. In particular, it protects citizens against state access to the IT system as a whole, rather than offering only protection against state access to individual communications or certain stored data. The German constitutional court wanted to make sure that integrity is not harmed by the state and that users of IT have legitimate expectations not being spied at by the state (confidentiality protection).

To sum up, following the technically redefined Article 13, the EU also contrasts integrity and confidentiality as the German constitutional court did. Thus, EU legislation has put "integrity" in line with other known IT security goals.

3.2   EU / US Regulation: Data Integrity

What constitutes "Data Integrity" also varies in legal texts, even though the EU heard experts during the drafting process. According to the Regulation establishing the European Network and Information Security Agency (ENISA):

> "**Data Integrity**" means the confirmation that data which has been sent, received, or stored are **complete and unchanged** [14][3].

Integrity is an essential part of ENISA's "network and information security":

> "network and information security" means the ability of a network or an information system to **resist**, at a given level of confidence, accidental events or **unlawful or malicious actions that compromise the** availability, authenticity, **integrity** and confidentiality of stored or transmitted data and the related services offered by or accessible via these networks and systems [14][4].

---

[3] Article 4 lit. f of the REGULATION (EC) No 460/2004 [14].
[4] Article 4 lit. c of the REGULATION (EC) No 460/2004 [14].

The US Health Insurance Portability And Accountability (HIPAA) act defines:

Integrity. Implement policies and procedures to protect electronic protected health information from **improper alteration** or destruction. [8][5]

Comments. ENISA's definition misses that "integrity" is technically a status and needs a trusted process of verification to gain confirmation of this status. Thus, it mixes processes and states, which makes it technically complex if not infeasible to follow. Our second critic of ENISA's definition is its notion of completeness. Technically, "complete" means nothing has been removed or dropped, CS calls this "availability". For brevity, we do not discuss if Data Integrity implicitly or explicitly implies availability, thus HIPAA's "destruction" is not discussed.

ENISA's definition for Data Integrity, "complete and unchanged" [14][3], is very strict. It does not mention "improper alteration" [8], and it forbids any form of subsequent change. On the other hand, the same ENISA regulation wants integrity for network and information systems to resist "[...]unlawful or malicious actions that comprise [...] integrity [...]" [14][4]. Hence, ENISA's definition for network and information security allows speculation if lawful or benign actions exists that would not harm the integrity.

3.3   EU Regulation: Data Integrity in Electronic Signatures

From the broader legal scope of integrity and Data Integrity we will now turn to the specific application domain of electronic or digital signatures. Foremost, computer scientists are confused by the term "electronic", and would prefer the term "digital". Indeed, the early German legislation from 1997, as well as the Italian and the US legislation, who all predated the EU Signature Regulations [16] of 1999, were talking about "digital" signatures. We have found no other reasons for the now widespread term of "electronic" in many places of EU legislation than the explanation of Dumortier in [11]. Durmortier reasons that the EU needed to introduce a EU wide legislation prohibiting each member state from regulating the legal status of signatures differently, and wanted to be "technology neutral". As a consequence, we find legal terms like "electronic document" and "electronic signature" in many EU regulations instead of technical terms "digital documents" and "digital signatures". Member state legislation adopted these, thus in Germany the "electronic document" covers more than only the digitized version of a paper document. So technically, digital signatures can be used to create advanced electronic signatures. The European Directive 1999/93/EC on electronic signatures [16] has the clear intention to build trust in technical systems. The Directive's goal is given in Article 5 [16], where it describes the legal effects it has for electronic signatures:

1. Member States shall ensure that advanced electronic signatures which are based on a qualified certificate and which are created by a secure-signature-creation device:

---

[5] HIPAA Technical Safeguard Standard, Paragraph 164.312(c)(1) [8].

(a) satisfy the legal requirements of a signature in relation to data in electronic form in the same manner as a handwritten signature satisfies those requirements in relation to paper-based data; and
(b) are admissible as evidence in legal proceedings. [16]

The legislative body produced very precise technical and organizational requirements which electronic signatures system have to meet to become trusted to the above extend. Requirements for the signature creation devices are given in Annex II and for a secure signature verification process in Annex IV of [16]. One goal of the Directive is to allow signatory identification. So, a lot of clauses deal with certification and linkage of persons or entities with the signature-creation-data or the signature-verification-data.

However, the Directive lacks a clear definition of the term Data Integrity and never defines it explicitly. Instead, Article 2 of [16] offers the definition of the term "advanced electronic signature", stating a requirement that resembles known definitions of Data Integrity:

1. "electronic signature" means data in electronic form which are attached to or logically associated with other electronic data and which serve as a method of authentication;
2. "advanced electronic signature" means an electronic signature which meets the following requirements:
(a) it is uniquely linked to the signatory;
(b) it is capable of identifying the signatory;
(c) it is created using means that the signatory can maintain under his sole control; and
(d) **it is linked to the data to which it relates in such a manner that any subsequent change of the data is detectable;** [16]

As cited above, Directive 1999/93/EC Article 2 (d) [16] clearly states that the advanced signature allows to detect any change the signed data was subjected to after it was signed. Further, in Annex III of [16] the recommendations for a secure signature-creation device ensure that after signature creation, it cannot be forged. And that the data to be signed by the device should not be manipulated during the signing process. Annex III lists the following:

1. Secure signature-creation devices must, by appropriate technical and procedural means, ensure at the least that:
(a) the signature-creation-data[6] used for signature generation can practically occur only once, and that their secrecy is reasonably assured;
(b) the signature-creation-data used for signature generation cannot, with reasonable assurance, be derived and **the signature is protected against forgery using currently available technology**;
(c) the signature-creation-data used for signature generation can be reliably protected by the legitimate signatory against the use of others.

---

[6] Signature-creation-data: Technical example: Private key in asymmetric crypto.

2. Secure signature-creation devices **must not alter the data to be signed** or prevent such data from being presented to the signatory **prior to the signature process**. [16]

Comments. The EU legislation on electronic signatures itself defines the protection goals of electronic signatures without using the term integrity. This is positive, as we have seen the term integrity understood differently in different EU regulations. Section (1b) of the requirements states that a signature cannot be forged once created. Further the definition requires that the signature has to offer protection against undetected "subsequent changes". To sum up, the EU legislation on electronic signatures simply postulates that changes of signed data must be detectable. Technically, it does not state when an electronic signature is invalid. However, legally: Statutory Trust is removed once a subsequent change, authorized or not, has been detected by the digital signature verification process.

Further, the requirements define properties of the technical processes and systems involved: Section 2 postulates that data to be signed is not subject to changes within a secure signature-creation device. The technical process standardized in the XML Digital Signature Syntax and Processing standard [12] does not adhere to this: The standard process involves that the data to be signed is transformed into a canonical form, hence changed, which we discuss in Sect. 5.1.

3.4   Technical: Data Integrity

Finding the term "integrity" defined differently or different definitions having a different scope is not a legal problem. We start with two definitions from sources we consider classical for the terms of "Data Integrity" in CS: Clark and Wilson, and Trusted Computer System Evaluation Criteria (TCSEC).

In 1987 Clark and Wilson saw that in the commercial world data must be manipulated. So, they introduced "well-formed transactions" [9] instead:

Data Integrity: No user of the system, even if authorized, may be permitted to modify data items in such a way that assets or accounting records of the company are lost or damaged.
[...]
The concept of the well-formed transaction is that a user should not manipulate data arbitrarily, but only in constrained ways that preserve or ensure the **integrity** of the data. [9]

While Clark and Wilson modeled a system, where it would be possible to control data manipulations such that the economic value of the data was not harmed, the US Department Of Defense set out to define more technical properties that must be present in a trusted computer system. The Trusted Computer System Evaluation Criteria (TCSEC) [23] from 1985, defines Data Integrity as follows:

Data Integrity – The state that exists when computerized data is the same as that in the source documents and has not been exposed to accidental or malicious alteration or destruction. [23]

Clark and Wilson see "modifications" that "damage the asset" as the security threat, the TCSEC speaks of "malicious alteration". However, they allow benign or non-damaging modifications. Hence, both definitions allow authorized changes that do not violate the integrity. Note, both definitions see complete loss or destruction of data as a violation of integrity.

Turning to more recent literature we find that Stallings defines Data Integrity with respect to a message stream or single message or parts thereof in two forms: connection-oriented and connectionless integrity services [29].

> [...] Thus, the **connection-oriented integrity service** addresses both message stream **modification** and denial of service.
>
> [...] a **connectionless integrity service**, one that deals with individual messages only without regard to any larger context, generally provides protection against message **modification** only. [29]

Stallings mentions that integrity services are concerned "with detection rather than prevention" [29].

Gollmann defines Data Integrity along with data origin authentication in [19]:

> [...]**Data Integrity:** integrity check functions provide the means to detect whether a document has been changed; data origin authentication: [...] provide the means to verify the source and integrity of a message. [19]

Hence, Gollmann includes Data Integrity in origin authentication, as "you cannot claim to have verified the source of a message that has been changed in transit" [19]. However, Gollmann also makes clear that "a separate notion of Data Integrity makes sense in other applications, e.g. file protection" [19].

Bishop definition given in [4] in 2002 allows to change data, which is integrity protected, as long as the change is authorized. Hence, Bishop's definition is in line with Clark and Wilsons's view on well formed transactions, when it defines:

> [...]modification or alteration, an **unauthorized change** to information[...] [4]

Comments. The technical definitions for Data Integrity either explicitly state or forbid authorized changes. All are concerned with detecting changes.

3.5   Cryptographic: Data Integrity in Digital Signatures

Cryptographic problems have been mathematically defined, including an attacker model, the security goals, and the attacks. The strongest security notion is to withstand the most sophisticated attacker that only needs to mount an attack with the lowest severity. For digital signatures the strongest security notion is: Existential forgery under an adaptive chosen message attacks (EF-CMA), as defined by Goldwasser, Micali, and Rivest in 1988 in [18]. For an EF-CMA an attacker has no algorithm to produce a valid signature over a new message that allows him a notable gain over guessing, even after the attacker was able to analyse valid signatures for messages of his choice.

Existential Forgery: Forge a signature for at least one message. The enemy has no control over the message whose signature he obtains, so it may be random or nonsensical. [18]

Adaptive Chosen Message Attack: [...] the enemy is also allowed to use A^7 as an "oracle"; not only may he request from A signatures of messages which depend on As public key but he may also request signatures of messages which depend additionally on previously obtained signatures. [18]

Comments. A technically clear definition: Digital signatures detect forgeries of the signed message done by an enemy. In an EF-CMA secure digital signature scheme nobody other than the signer can produce a valid signature for a changed message. Note, sanitizers produce "forgeries", they are said to be semi-trusted. Thus, this model cannot be directly applied to SanSig.

3.6 Sanitizable Signatures: Data Integrity Protection

As stated in the introduction, a sanitizable signature allows a third party to remove or change, in other words modify, specific parts of an already signed message and keep the signature valid. A document protected by the sanitizable signature is changed during such authorized sanitization. These authorized changes no longer result in a failed signature verification, however integrity is protected according to Agrawal et al.:

The verifier confirms the **integrity of disclosed parts** of the sanitized document from the signature and sanitized document. [1]

Comments. Only sanitizers that hold the secret can do changes which do not invalidate a signer's signature. So in general, a SanSig codifies authorized changes by giving cryptographic tokens to sanitizers. To judge the scope of integrity protection requires knowledge of (1) the possibility of sanitization as well as (2) knowledge about occurred sanitization. This focus on detection of integrity violations was already found in Stallings in Sect. 3.4.

4   Transparency: Legally the Opposite of Technical

We already stated that technical Transparency describes very much the opposite of what transparency legally means. We will shortly provide you with the term's legal concept and then with the technical security property.

4.1   Legal Transparency

Transparency is an important legal principle. Transparency means openness of procedures. Such openness enables citizens to participate more closely in the

---

[7] The user whose signature method is being attacked.

decision-making process and guarantees that the system enjoys greater legitimacy and is more effective and more accountable to the citizen in a democratic system. [[25], para 54]. Therefore the Treaty on European Union highlights transparency e.g. in Art. 1 Sec. 2 and Art. 11 Sec. 2 [17]. In data protection law transparency accordingly denotes that the affected person must be informed, which data is being collected about him, for which purpose, for how long and which rights he can exercise. With respect to IT systems transparency is designed to make (IT-) procedures understandable and controllable. This implies the free and easy access to readily available government information, the enactment of swift control and participation procedures, the creation of specialised and independent bodies to control and check [21]. The balance between the right to privacy with respect to the processing of personal data and the principle of transparency when restricting the free flow of personal data was addressed in the Regulation No. 45/2001 [15] and concretized by the European Court of Justice in Case C-28/08 P of 29th June 2010 [25].

4.2   Technical Transparency of Sanitizable Signature Schemes

Amongst others the following security properties are present in meaningful SanSig schemes: Unforgeability, Immutability, Privacy, Transparency, and Accountability [6]. Technically, the sanitizable signature still verifies if subsequent changes are the result of authorized sanitizations. So an authorized subsequent change will no longer be detected by signature verification. Thus, detection, if a sanitization has taken place, becomes an important property, not known to classical signature schemes. Ateniese et al. described the absence of such a detection as the property of "Transparency" in [3] in 2005:

> Given a signed message with a valid signature, no party — except the censor and the signer — should be able to correctly guess whether the message has been sanitized. [3]

Transparency can be controlled on the document level. Pöhls et al. have given technical solutions and hence adjusted the scope of the above definition in [27]:

> Transparency makes a statement about a sanitized document as a whole. [27]

Comments. Generally, a transparent SanSig renders the occurred authorized changes unrecognisably hidden for the verifier. This emphasizes the importance of detection as already found in Stallings in Sect. 3.4.

5   Role of Integrity for Statutory Trust in Signatures

Legally, all EU definitions are stringent and they strictly forbid undetectable subsequent changes of signed data. The EU signature regulation lacks an explicit definition of the term Data Integrity, still any subsequent change of signed data must be detectable. More technically, ENISA's definition also implies that integrity protected data has to remain "unchanged" [14]. However, ENISA's definition defines the security goals (amongst it integrity) with respect to "accidental events or unlawful or malicious actions" [14]. Thus, ENISA leaves open whether lawful or benign actions negatively affect the integrity status or not.

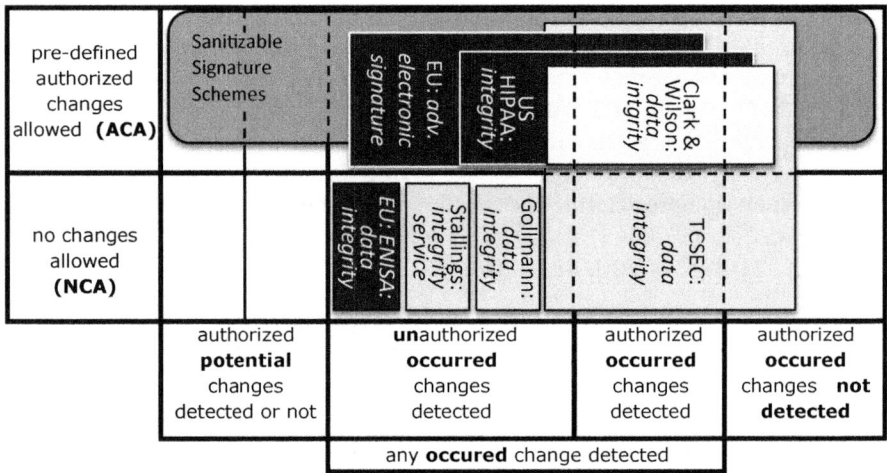

Note: Touching an area means: "having the property of the touched area".

Fig. 1. Comparison of analyzed integrity definitions and position of "Sanitizable Signatures". Vertically: Authorized or not?; Horizontally: Detected or not?.

The technical definitions differ whether Data Integrity protection shall tolerate authorized or well-defined changes, or not. A graphical overview in Fig. 1 compares the definitions along two axes: *Allowed Changes* and *Detected Changes*.

5.1 1st Axis: Allowed Changes

Whether the application would like to tolerate subsequent changes to signed and thus integrity protected data and which subsequent changes are detectable, influences the choice of the technical digital signature method and process.

Classical Signature Schemes. For example, the signature process for RSA first computes a digest of a padded bit-representation of the data using a cryptographically secure hash function (i.e. SHA-256). Second, it applies a asymmetric encryption algorithm (i.e. RSA) to compute the signature for this digest. As a result of the secure hash function, a change of one bit in the signed bit-representation results in a different hash value and invalidates the signature. Thus, classical digital signatures protect the bit-representation against any modification. Hence, all changes are unauthorized and detected.

Sanitizable Signatures. A sanitizable signature allows certain parties to do certain changes to the signed data without affecting the signature verification result. We cannot give a full classification of existing research here, but `SanSigs` allow the signer, among other properties, to specify:

1. which parts of a signed document are mutable;
2. which changes are allowed (blinding, substitution of values, or arbitrary);
3. who is allowed to perform such changes;
4. if the potential for changes can be detected;
5. if an actual change can be detected.

However, there is always a form of control. This can legally be seen as some form of delegation. Thus, Fig. 1 shows sanitizable signature schemes horizontally covering all detection levels for allowed pre-defined authorized changes.

XML Signatures. Another technical compliance problem can be found in XML Signatures. The standardized XML-Signature process [12] applies, so called, transformations as part of the signature process to generate a bit-representation from the XML document. Nearly in all applications the same standardized canonicalization (C14n) method [5] is performed on the XML document **before** it is hashed, so prior to signing or verification. XML's high degree of freedom would even allow any transformation to take place during signature generation. Brad Hill points out that XSLT [10], also allowed as a transform, is "Turing-complete" [22]. Transforms need to be understood by both signer and verifier. If not they can introduce errors by changing the input document in ways that lead to unexpected loss of coverage of the digital signature's scope of protection [26]. Hence, Annex III of [16] states that "Secure signature-creation devices **must not alter the data to be signed** or prevent such data from being presented to the signatory **prior to the signature process**" [16]. We recommend that XML input data must be canonicalized beforehand using exactly the same C14n algorithm as the signing process, i.e. `xml-exc-c14n#`. Only then, the XML signature generation process with its C14n transform is in line with the EU Directive, because the second C14n transformation during signing does not alter the already C14n transformed input data.

5.2 2nd Axis: Detection of Changes

Fig. 1 shows five different degrees of detection, for brevity we combined the *potentially authorized change detection* and did not list the sixth: *no detection*. Legally, ENISA's Data Integrity definition does not really differ from the EU legislation for advanced electronic signatures. While the latter generally covers all subsequent changes (allowed or not) as long as they are detected, ENISA generally forbids subsequent changes. Thus, following ENISA all changes are not allowed and all occurred changes are detected as unauthorized. This is inline with the technical definitions of Stallings and Gollmann. Technically different in their detection are Clark and Wilson, TCSEC, and US HIPAA; they all allow authorized changes to take place, but lack a clear definition if these allowed changes can be performed undetected or must be detected.

Sanitizable Signatures. Technically, sanitizable signatures can allow subsequent changes to signed data to go undetected, this is a clear contrast to the legal definition of an advanced electronic signature. Pöhls et al. show in [27] combinations that make detection of an authorized change possible. For example, while a signer could allow arbitrary changes to certain data even by everyone. With sanitizable signatures we can allow a verifier to detect that the signer, and only the signer, has removed change detection for this certain data.

In general, sanitizable signatures are not advanced electronic signatures following the strict definition of the EU Directive 1999/93/EC on electronic signatures [16]. The same holds when we judge its technical integrity protection following TCSEC or US HIPAA. Only if the changes, even if authorized, remain detectable a sanitizable signature could be considered as an advanced electronic signature. This property of detectability is known as "transparency". As stated before and in [27], an occurred sanitization can be detected on the message level if the scheme does not have the property of "transparency" on the message level. Previous definitions have missed this [3, 6].

6   New Definition: Data Integrity

Due to the role integrity plays for the definition of Statutory Trust and the lack of precise terminology to capture existing definitions we introduce levels for "detected changes" and levels for "allowed changes". We then define integrity protection as set of tuples. Each tuple contains a level of allowed change and its level of detection. We differentiate three mutually exclusive levels that describe the *allowed changes* to protected data:

- **No Changes Allowed (NCA):** A subsequent change to protected data results in a negative integrity status.
- **Authorized Changes Allowed (ACA):** The integrity status remains unchanged if the applied change to protected data was authorized.
- **Unauthorized Changes Allowed (UCA):** The integrity status remains unchanged regardless of the change.

NCA covers the typical hash and sign paradigm of a digital signature with a cryptographic hash function. For ACA we first have to define what is "authorized". This can be achieved either by coding it into the signature creation and verification process itself or by introducing an extra policy verification step outside signature verification. We consider sanitizable signature schemes as a promising way to include the policy into the signature creation and verification process. While transformations within XML Digital Signature would allow to externally encode such policies, the high flexibility of transforms introduces new security problems due to complexity. For brevity we will not further discuss the technical issues of implementing policies for authorized changes here. ACA, as strange as it might sound, can be used to authorize any change by anyone. Hence, ACA allows to describe the delegation of a signed form with empty fields, i.e. a blank cheque. Entry of signed data is delegated to the delegatee, while the delegator still signed the data. For the sake of completeness, UCA covers if no form of authorization is needed.

As integrity protection is about the detection of changes, we offer six degrees of detection. We differentiate between the detection of *occurred* and materialized allowed changes or future *potential* changes to protected data.

- **no detection of occurred changes (ND):** Any occurred change to protected data is unrecognisably hidden to a verifier.
- **one or more occurred changes detected (1CD):** The verifier detects that at least one change to protected data has occurred. The exact number of occurred changes or where they happend remain invisible to the verifier.
- **all occurred changes detected in detail (CD):** All occurred changes to protected data are detectable by a verifier offering a certain grade of detail (i.e. regarding their locations or types of changes).
- **no detection of potential future changes (NFD):** The verifier cannot detect the potential of future change to protected data.
- **one or more potential future changes detected (1FD):** The verifier detects that at least one potential change to protected data could happen in the future. The exact number of potential changes or where they might happen remain invisible to a verifier.
- **all potential future changes detected in detail (FD):** All potential changes that could happen to the protected data in the future are detectable by a verifier offering a certain grade of detail (i.e. regarding their locations or types of changes).

Hence, the classical digital signature with a cryptographic hash offers **NCA-1CD integrity** protection, because any change is detected and results in a failed verification outcome. Ateniese et al. originally further defined the property of "strong transparency": "the verifier [...] does not know which parts of a signed message could potentially be sanitizable" [3]. A sanitizable signature scheme that has strong transparency offers **ACA-ND/ACA-NFD/UCA-1CD integrity**, as authorized changes by sanitizers are not detected, not even their potential. Pöhls et al. refine an independent transparency property on the message's scope; their extended construction allows **ACA-1CD/ACA-NFD/UCA-1CD integrity** protection: Detect that at least one authorized change has occurred, detect unauthorized changes, hide what changed, and hide potential for further changes [27]. Detection of just the potential for change was defined by Ateniese et al. as "weak transparency" [3] and formalized by Brzuska et al. [6]. Following our new definition a scheme with weak transparency results in protection of **ACA-FD/UCA-1CD integrity**, as authorized changes by authorized sanitizers go undetected, just their potential is detected.

7   Conclusion: Detectable Sanitizable Signature (ACA-1CD)

Laws and regulations certainly more and more influence the technical decisions made, as IT systems have to comply with rules and regulations. More than ten years after the EU Directive on electronic signatures, we have analysed the role of Data Integrity for the Statutory Trust. However, detection of changes plays a central role when deciding the Statutory Trust given to electronic signatures. The term Integrity has recently been explicitly defined in EU legislation when grounding the ENISA. ENISA's strict definition of "complete and unchanged" is very strict and no changes are allowed (=NCA). The detectability of changes is also the main concern in legal as well as in all technical integrity protection definitions: EU's Electronic Signature Legislation requires "that any subsequent change of the data is detectable" [16]. Compliance, requires NCA-1CD integrity protection (=no changes are allowed and one or more occurred changes are detected). This general legal rule excludes business cases for sanitizable signatures.

In 1987 Clark and Wilson already allowed commercial data to be manipulated by authorized "well-formed transactions" without destroying its integrity [9]. If authorized changes are allowed (=ACA) and Statutory Trust can be gained the applicability of signatures can be extended to more use cases. We postulate technically allowing authorized subsequent changes to signed data which not automatically removes Statutory Trust. Sanitizable signatures schemes (SanSig) in general are not advanced electronic signatures following the strict definition of the EU Directive 1999/93/EC on electronic signatures [16]. For example, a transparent SanSig opposes the EU Directive's requirement to detected "any subsequent change" [16]. A transparent SanSig, or even any digital signature scheme which unrecognisably hides occurred authorized changes (ACA-ND), will not gain Statutory Trust. This conclusion is harsh, but must be seen in the light that Directive 1999/93/EC was drafted more than ten years ago, when technical solutions like sanitizable signatures were not well established.

Following our definition, Statutory Trust would require 1CD or CD detection. If we remove a SanSig's Transparency an authorized change becomes detectable, hence legally transparent, and Statutory Trust in the unchanged sanitizable signed document is granted. So in order to gain Statutory Trust and be usable in e-commerce scenarios sanitizable signature schemes must be enhanced with a detection of occurred authorized changes (ACA-1CD). These enhancements could build a *seal* or *"break glass"-like* which is needed to achieve Statutory Trust for sanitizable signatures. As future work we plan to give concrete technical constructions that do not harm the other useful properties of SanSigs.

During our comparison between legal requirements we found that the EU demands that "Secure signature-creation devices must not alter the data to be signed or prevent such data from being presented to the signatory prior to the signature process". To comply an XML signature creation device must either not carry out transformations or can be used only on already transformed input data. Strictly, only then the XML signature can be given Statutory Trust.

It still remains unclear if the legal exclusion of sanitizable signatures was indeed intended by legislative bodies. Sanitizable signatures could solve legal compliance issues technically. Our work showed the differences. We hope to start a discussion in both fields, legislation and IT, to see more precise and aligned technical definitions, like our definition of Data Integrity, in the future.

References

[1] Agrawal, S., Kumar, S., Shareef, A., Rangan, C.P.: Sanitizable Signatures with Strong Transparency in the Standard Model. In: Bao, F., Yung, M., Lin, D., Jing, J. (eds.) Inscrypt 2009. LNCS, vol. 6151, pp. 93–107. Springer, Heidelberg (2010)

[2] Alsaid, A., Mitchell, C.J.: Dynamic content attacks on digital signatures. Information Management & Computer Security 13 (2005)

[3] Ateniese, G., Chou, D.H., de Medeiros, B., Tsudik, G.: Sanitizable Signatures. In: di Vimercati, S.D.C., Syverson, P.F., Gollmann, D. (eds.) ESORICS 2005. LNCS, vol. 3679, pp. 159–177. Springer, Heidelberg (2005)

[4] Bishop, M.: Computer Security: Art and Science. Addison-Wesley Professional (2002) ISBN: 0201440997

[5] Boyer, J.: Canonical XML V 1.0 (March 2001)

[6] Brzuska, C., Fischlin, M., Freudenreich, T., Lehmann, A., Page, M., Schelbert, J., Schröder, D., Volk, F.: Security of Sanitizable Signatures Revisited. In: Jarecki, S., Tsudik, G. (eds.) PKC 2009. LNCS, vol. 5443, pp. 317–336. Springer, Heidelberg (2009)

[7] Bundesverfasssungsgericht (BVerfG). Urteil vom.1 BvR 370/07, 1 BvR 595/07 - NJW, 822 (February 27, 2008)

[8] Caplan, R.M.: HIPAA. health insurance portability and accountability act of 1996. Dent Assist. 72(2), 6–8 (1997)

[9] Clark, D.D., Wilson, D.R.: A comparison of commercial and military computer security policies. In: IEEE Symposium on Security and Privacy, p. 184 (1987) ISSN: 1540-7993

[10] Clark, J.: XSL Transformations (XSLT) version 1.0, www.w3.org/TR/xslt

[11] Dumortier, J.: Legal status of qualified electronic signatures in europe. In: ISSE 2004 - Securing Electronic Business Processes. Vieweg (2004)

[12] Eastlake, Reagle, Solo.: XML-signature syntax and processing. W3C recommendation (February 2002), www.w3.org/TR/xmldsig-core/

[13] EU. Directive 2009/140/EC of 25 November 2009 amending Directives 2002/21/EC on a common regulatory framework for electronic communications networks and services, 2002/19/EC on access to, and interconnection of, electronic communications networks and associated facilities, and 2002/20/EC on the authorization of electronic communications networks and services. Official Journal L 337/8 (December 2009)

[14] EU. Regulation 460/2004/EC of the European Parliament and of the Council of 10 March 2004 establishing the European Network and Information Security Agency. Official Journal L 77/1 (March 2004)

[15] EU. Regulation 45/2001 of the European Parliament and of the Council of 18 December 2000 on the protection of individuals with regard to the processing of personal data by the Community institutions and bodies and on the free movement of such data. Official Journal, L 8/1 (January 2001)

[16] EU. Directive 1999/93/EC of the European Parliament and of the Council of 13 December 1999 on a Community framework for electronic signatures. Official Journal L 12, 12–20 (2000)

[17] EU. Consolidated version of the treaty on european union. Official Journal of the European Union (March 2010)

[18] Goldwasser, S., Micali, S., Rivest, R.L.: A digital signature scheme secure against adaptive chosen-message attacks. SIAM Journal on Computing 17 (1988)

[19] Gollmann, D.: Computer Security 2e. John Wiley & Sons (2005)

[20] Herkenhöner, R., Jensen, M., Pöhls, H.C., de Meer, H.: Towards automated processing of the right of access in inter-organizational web service compositions. In: IEEE Int. Workshop on WebService and Business Process Security (WSBPS). IEEE (2010)

[21] De Hert, P., Gutwirth, S.: Privacy, data protection and law enforcement. Opacity of the individual and transparency of power. In: Privacy and the Criminal Law, pp. 61–104. Intersentia nv (2006)

[22] Hill, B.: Attacking xml security. Black Hat Briefings USA (2007)

[23] Latham, D.C.: Department of defense trusted computer system evaluation criteria (1985)

[24] Miyazaki, K., Iwamura, M., et al.: Digitally signed document sanitizing scheme with disclosure condition control. IEICE Transactions (2005)

[25] EU Court of Justice. Judgment of the court Case C28/08P (June 29, 2010)

[26] Pöhls, H.C., Tran, D., Petersen, F., Pscheid, F.: MS Office 2007: Target of hyperlinks not covered by digital signatures (December 2007), www.securityfocus.com/archive/1/485031/30/0/

[27] Pöhls, H.C., Samelin, K., Posegga, J.: Sanitizable Signatures in XML Signature — Performance, Mixing Properties, and Revisiting the Property of Transparency. In: Lopez, J., Tsudik, G. (eds.) ACNS 2011. LNCS, vol. 6715, pp. 166–182. Springer, Heidelberg (2011)

[28] Posegga, J., Vogt, H., Kehr, R.: Eine Vorrichtung zur Erhöhung der Sicherheit bei Digitalen Signaturen. German Patent (Akz 199 23 807.3); European Patent (EP 1 054364 A2), Patentblatt 2000/47 (1999)

[29] Stallings, W.: Network Security Essentials: Applications and Standards, 3rd edn. Prentice-Hall (2006) ISBN: 0132380331

[30] Steinfeld, R., Bull, L., Zheng, Y.: Content Extraction Signatures. In: Kim, K. (ed.) ICISC 2001. LNCS, vol. 2288, pp. 285–304. Springer, Heidelberg (2002)

[31] Zanero, S.: Security and Trust in the Italian Legal Digital Signature Framework. In: Herrmann, P., Issarny, V., Shiu, S.C.K. (eds.) iTrust 2005. LNCS, vol. 3477, pp. 34–44. Springer, Heidelberg (2005)

Mutual Remote Attestation: Enabling System Cloning for TPM Based Platforms

Ulrich Greveler, Benjamin Justus, and Dennis Loehr

Computer Security Lab
Münster University of Applied Sciences
D-48565 Steinfurt, Germany
{greveler,benjamin.justus,loehr}@fh-muenster.de

Abstract. We describe a concept of mutual remote attestation for two identically configured trusted (TPM based) systems. We provide a cryptographic protocol to achieve the goal of deriving a common session key for two systems that have verified each other to be a clone of themselves.

The mutual attestation can be applied to backup procedures without providing data access to administrators, i. e. one trusted systems exports its database to another identical trusted system via a secure channel after mutual attestation is completed.

Another application is dynamically parallelizing trusted systems in order to increase the performance of a trusted server platform.

We present details of our proposed architecture and show results from extensive hardware tests. These tests show that there are some unresolved issues with TPM-BIOS settings currently distributed by PC hardware manufacturers since the specification regarding measurement of extended platform BIOS configuration is either not met or the usage of undocumented options is required.

Keywords: Mutual Attestation, Trusted Computing, Data Cloning, Key Exchange Protocol.

1 Introduction

Recent developments related to the legal and social aspects of privacy issues call for technical measures enforcing strict restrictions and requirements on the collection, use and disclosure of personal data. Trusted systems can be used for secure storage of sensitive data.

Once a system state is defined as a trusted state and the system is set up to this state, its security characteristics can be transferred to a system clone that is composed of identical software (boot chain components, operating system, and applications) and matching hardware. A system clone can be generated via methods such as copying the contents of one system hard disk image to another disk, or automatic installation using an install-script. The execution of these procedures will result into a run-capable system clone (depending on operating system characteristics). Mutual attestation is the key functionality to *verify* the secure cloning of trusted platforms.

C. Meadows and C. Fernández-Gago (Eds.): STM 2011, LNCS 7170, pp. 193–206, 2012.

Applications using cloned trusted platforms include

- Database synchronization: database management systems that offer a restricted access to its databases. Further, the database can be synchronized and backed up without the need of low-level table access for administrators.
- Parallel computing: clustering synchronous trusted servers increase the output performance and reduce the response time compared to stand-alone servers.
- Enforcing restrictions expressed through rights expression language (RELs) across systems: a REL description might require the system to restrict access and maintain a state (i. e. a maximum of n queries are permitted on a database in order to avoid illegitimate database duplication). This state needs to be distributed across physical systems in a way that one logical system stays consistent (i. e. set up 2 physical systems that allow $n/2$ requests each until the next synchronization takes place).

The implementation of any of the above projects requires an efficient and reliable remote attestation scheme. The ideal architecture should possess the following components: **1** systematic integrity measurement and automated integrity measurement verification procedures; **2** a secure key exchange protocol that allows both systems to possess a common session key. Existing Trusted Computing Standards provide extensive architectures and opensource components for the purpose of carrying out trust based applications. To our dismay, we have not found any off-the-shelf protocol or software which may provide a ready implementation of our trust-cloning project. A search of web shows that there are (section 2.2) some available opensource software tools that are designed to carry out functionalities of attestation for TPM based systems. These tools are mostly experimental, and do not take into account the implementation architecture of mutual attestation as an whole. A tailor-designed and ready-to-implement mutual attestation architecture is desired.

Contributions: Our contributions in this paper are as follows

1. We propose a mutual remote attestation protocol for two identically configured TPM hardware and provide implementation details.
2. We describe in details the hardware test results and discuss to what extent *system cloning* is possible for TPM based hardware.

Our mutual remote attestation scheme has particular merit in a corporate setting where database synchronization and backup are constantly required between available servers. The protocol is easy to implement and requires no intervention of a third party, such as a trusted certification authority once the attestation procedure has started. Our mutual attestation scheme can be viewed as a small step in the development of much needed peer-to-peer (P2P) attestation techniques.

The plan of the paper is as follows. Section 2 presents the related work on remote attestation, its applications and the available tools to perform the attestation. Our *Mutual Attestation Scheme* is explained in section 3. Section 4 provides a discussion and conclusion on the scheme. The appendices A and B give a detailed design of our proposed protocol and some test values respectively.

2 Background and Related Work

2.1 Remote Attestation

Specifying the notion of trust in computing platforms has been a goal of computer science research for decades. The use of secure operating system environments were proposed in the 1970s [23]. The premise of a *secure system* is built upon the philosophy that any system is only as secure as the foundation upon which it is built.

The Trusted Computing Group (TCG) is an industry standards body formed to develop and promote specifications for trusted computing and security technologies. The TCG proposed a trust model where each device is equipped with a hardware root-of-trust associated with the platform that can measure integrity metrics and may confirm these metrics to other parties. Regarding PCs this hardware is a chip called the Trusted Platform Module (TPM) and the process of reporting the integrity of a platform is known as *remote attestation*. When the TPM reports the values of the integrity metrics that it has stored, the TPM signs those values using a TPM identity.

To achieve the goals of *remote attestation*, TCG has introduced in version 1.1 specifications the concept of privacy certification authority (Privacy CA) [14]. It works briefly as follows. Each TPM is equipped with a RSA key pair called an Endorsement Key (EK). The Privacy CA is assumed to know the Endorsement Keys of all valid TPMs. Now, when TPM needs to authenticate itself to a verifier, it generates a second pair of RSA key called an Attestation Identity Key (AIK), it sends the AIK public key to the Privacy CA, and authenticates this public key w.r.t the EK. The Privacy CA will check whether it finds the EK in its list and, if so, issues a certificate to the TPM's AIK key. The TPM can then forward this certificate to the verifier and authenticate itself w.r.t. this AIK.

As discussed by Brickell, Camenisch and Chen [4], version 1.2 of the TCG specifications incorporate the Direct Anonymous Attestation (DAA) protocol. This protocol is designed to address anonymity issues of remote attestation. The DAA scheme is rather sophisticated [4,5] whose implementation requires novel techniques and methods [7,9,10]. Many applications related to privacy preserving and privacy enhancing are built upon the concept of DAA [2,6,18,20].

There have been several proposal in the literature to combine DAA with key exchange protocols. Balfe et al. [3] proposed anonymous authentication protocol in peer-to-peer networks by embedding DAA with TLS and IPSec. Cesena et al. [8] proposed an anonymous authentication protocol based on TLS and DAA including a reference implementation. Recently, Li and Walker [26] incorporated DAA scheme into a key exchange protocol. Further, they introduced a security model for key exchange with anonymous authentication, and provided rigorous security proof under the proposed model.

2.2 Available Remote Attestation Opensource Tools

The implementation of our trusted system cloning applications as described in the introduction requires the initiation of a mutual attestation protocol. Even though anonymity of the systems is not required during the attestation, we do require that the session keys to be authenticated with respect to some certification authorities. The successful authentication of critical keys assures a system that a remote platform who is trying to access the database is truly operating on trusted hardware modules.

As stated in the previous section, the certification of AIK keys ideally calls for the interaction with a Privacy CA. Theoretically, a Privacy CA should hold a list of all valid EK certificates delivered from TPM manufacturers. However, this kind of trust chain infrastructure at present is still lacking. To the authors' knowledge, currently only Infineon [27] is providing TPMs with Endorsement certificates.

Despite the lack of certification authorities, there exists several opensource tools that allow users to carry out experimentally the steps of mutual attestation. The *TPM Quote Tools* [25] contain a collection of programs that provides functionalities such as AIK key generation, TPM quote operations, and TPM quote verification operations.

Another ongoing project is *Trusted Computing for the Java Platform* [13]. The project is developed and maintained at the Institute for Applied Information Processing and Communication, Graz University of Technology. The package at present stage includes a basic implementation of a Privacy CA Server.

In the next section, we shall describe a mutual attestation protocol for two identically configured TPM based systems. During the protocol, AIK keys are generated, and we do make the assumption that all genuinely generated AIK keys are certifiable by some means. This assumption should be reasonable as Trusted Computing technologies and its related infrastructure are ever growing at present.

3   Mutual Attestation Scheme

3.1   High-Level Description

Our scheme allows mutual remote attestation between two identically configured TPM based systems, and provides a common session key for both systems at the end of the protocol. The scheme is an integrity based attestation. The reader can find the details of the protocol in appendix A. Figure 1 gives a pictorial representation of the protocol. We shall in this section explain the underlying ideas and discuss some of the implementation issues.

Though anonymity is not required during the attestation, we do require on-site systematic integrity measurement and automated measurement verification procedure. In fact, our mutual attestation scheme is very much driven by the the Cloning-Applications at hand, whereas schemes proposed in [26,17] are much more theoretical and are not implementable at present. The security proof of our protocol can be derived along the line as described in [26]. The protocol is of the challenge-and-response type. Both TPM based systems during attestation issue a sequence of challenges. The systems then mutually attest towards each other by demonstrating that they satisfy the specified attestation criterion.

The attestation criteria are: system integrity (PCR values) and integrity of the AIK keys.

Initially, *system I* generates an AIK key AIK_I and obtains a certificate $Cert_I$ from a certification authority (e.g. Privacy CA). The purpose of the certificate is to verify the integrity of AIK_I. Similarly, *system II* generates an AIK key AIK_{II} and obtains a certificate $Cert_{II}$. Both systems now exchange and then verify each others' certificates.

Assuming the certificates are valid, both systems start a Diffie-Hellman key exchange protocol. This is achieved as follows. From a list of agreed-upon primes, *system I* selects a prime with required security parameter and a primitive root $g \mod p$. Next, *system I* selects an secret integer a and computes its public Diffie-Hellman parameter $(A = g^a)$. Similarly, *system II* generates its public Diffie-Hellman parameter $(B = g^b)$ where b is *system II*'s secret parameter.

Next, *system I* and *system II* exchange their public Diffie-Hellman parameters. This allows each system to compute the shared Diffie-Hellman key. For example, *system I* computes its key as **skey$_I$** $= B^a$ where B is *system II*'s public DH parameter. And *system II* computes its key as **skey$_{II}$** $= A^b$ where A is *system I*'s public DH parameter. Notice, we have not assumed **skey$_I$** $=$ **skey$_{II}$** at this point of the protocol. The keys **skey$_I$** and **skey$_{II}$** are to be compared at the next step of integrity check. This assumption is needed to prevent man-in-the-middle type of attacks.

System integrity check is the next step. To prove system integrity, *system I* uses the TPM Quote utilities to sign a set of PCR values using its AIK key. If the AIK key is genuine and controlled by the TPM, it will only sign true and correct PCR values, which may therefore be taken to accurately represent the state of the signing system. Also to keep the quote fresh, the quote also includes a hashed **skey$_I$**. *System I* sends $sign(\mathbf{PCR} \,\|\, \mathbf{hash(skey_I)})$ to *system II*. After verifying the signature, *system II* checks the integrity of *system I* by comparing *system I*'s PCR values with its own. *System II* also checks that **skey$_I$** is correctly formed. This is achieved by comparing **hash(skey$_I$)** with his own key **hash(skey$_{II}$)**. The hashed exchange of **skey** is pivotal here as eavesdroppers will not have access to **skey** (one-wayness of the cryptographic hash function) and the fresh key is linked to the trusted system state.

This completes the steps of mutual attestation. And since **hash(skey$_I$)** $=$ **hash(skey$_{II}$)**, both systems at this point possess the common session key **skey$_I$** $=$ **skey$_{II}$** $=:$ **skey**.

3.2   Diffie-Hellman Key Exchange

The key **skey** is computed by both systems following the Diffie-Hellman key exchange protocol [11]. Since the finite field Diffie-Hellman algorithms has roughly the same key strength as RSA for the same key size, we have chosen the DH parameter to be of the size 2048 bits. The key length is reckoned sufficient until the end of 2016 [12].

We fix a group generator g, and find a safe 2048-bit prime whose group generator is g. This can be easily implemented using for example the open source software OpenSSL. The private key for *system I* (w.r.p. *system II*) is then a randomly generated integer a in the interval $[2, p-1]$. *System I*'s public Diffie-Hellman parameter is then computed as

$$A = g^a \bmod p.$$

And *system II*'s public DH parameter is computed as

$$B = g^b \bmod p$$

where b is *system II*'s private key.

In practice, a list of such safe primes is pre-generated and stored on both systems. At the beginning of each session of mutual attestation, a agreed-upon prime p will be selected from the list.

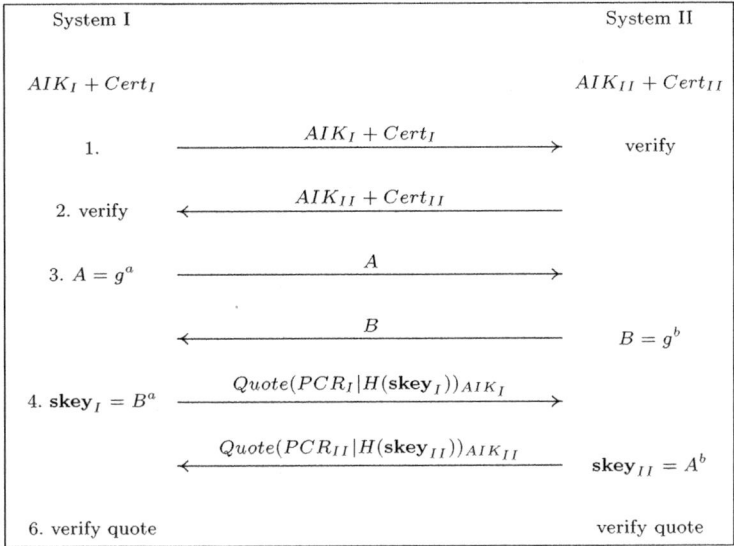

Fig. 1. Mutual Attestation Scheme for Identically Configured TPM Systems

3.3   TPM Quote and Verify

The most important part of the attestation is the system integrity check. TPM has a set of special volatile registers called *platform configuration registers* (PCRs). These 160-bit long registers are used to keeping track of the integrity information during a bootstrap process. The TCPA specification defines a set of functions for reporting PCR values [14,15]. The TPM Quote operation is able to sign a specified set of PCRs. The input of the Quote function also includes a 160 bit challenge file. By including this value in the Quote signature, the verifier knows that the Quote is fresh and is not an old replay of an old quote. In our protocol, the challenge file is a SHA-1 hash on **skey**. Each system can verify the integrity of the other system by comparing received PCR quote with its own PCR values.

3.4   Hardware Test Results

Table 1. Test Environment

System name	Machine Model	BIOS Version	TPM Manufacturer & Chip Version
Lenovo T510 System 1	4384-GEG	1.35 (6MET75WW)	STM 1.2.8.16
Lenovo T510 System 2	4384-GEG	1.35 (6MET75WW)	STM 1.2.8.16
Lenovo T60	1951-WWA	2.20 (79ETE0WW)	ATML 1.2.11.5
Lenovo T61	8889-ABG	2.26 (7LETC6WW)	ATML 1.2.13.9
Lenovo M58p	9965-A5G	(5CKT61AUS)	WEC 1.2.2.16

Table 2. Hardware Test cases for a Single System

No	System(s)	Description	Result
1	T510 System 1	reboot system	same PCR 0–15 values
2	T510 System 2	**1.** Boot order changed, **2.** dynamic selection of different bootmedia	PCRs 1,4 are changed for **1.** as well as **2.**
3	T510 System 1	booting two different OSs	PCRs 4,5 differ as well as OS specific PCRs 8–15
4	T510 System 1	without extended reporting switch on/off Ultrabay switch on/off Firewire	same PCR 0–15 values in all 4 subcases
5	T510 System 1	activated *CMOS Reporting* switching Ultrabay on/off	PCR 1 differs → on/off is detected
6	T510 System 1	BIOS default settings plus SMBIOS extended reporting switch on/off Ultrabay	same PCR 0–15 values → on/off is undetected
7	T510 System 1	BIOS default settings plus NVRAM extended reporting switch on/off Ultrabay	PCR 1 differs → on/off is detected
8	T510 System 1	BIOS default settings plus ESCD extended reporting switch on/off Ultrabay	PCR 1 differs → on/off is detected

The root of trust in the mutual attestation protocol lies at the fact that two identically configured TPM based hardware have the same boot-up values in certain platform configuration registers. This is a claim laid out in the relevant TCG specifications [16] which we have rigorously tested in the lab. Together with the BIOS CRTM, the TPM forms a root of Trust: the TPM allows a secure storage and the reporting of relevant security metrics into PCRs. These metrics can be used to detect changes to previous configurations from which it can easily be deduced whether a system clone is comparable in its security metrics or not. In our tests, we compared extensively the boot-up PCR values among different TPM hardware.

Table 3. Hardware Test cases Multiple Systems

No	System(s)	Description	Result
1	T510 System 1, T61,M58p	measure different hardware configurations with same boot chain without extended reporting[a]	differences in PCRs 0,1,2,4,6 (please note next test case!)
2	T510 System 1, T60	measure different hardware configurations with same boot chain without extended reporting	PCR 1 is equal on both systems
3	T510 System 1, T510 System 2	BIOS default settings plus maximum extended reporting (BIOS ROM String and ESCD[b] and CMOS and NVRAM and SMBIOS)	PCR 1 differs between (identical hardware) systems
4	T510 System 1, T510 System 2	BIOS default settings plus CMOS extended reporting	PCR 1 differs between (identical hardware) systems
5	T510 System 1, T510 System 2	BIOS default settings plus NVRAM extended reporting	PCR 1 differs between (identical hardware) systems
6	T510 System 1, T510 System 2	BIOS default settings plus ESCD extended reporting	PCR 1 is equal on both (identical hardware) systems

[a] *without extended reporting* does refer to the BIOS menu *Security Reporting Options* settings: BIOS ROM String and ESCD and CMOS and NVRAM and SMBIOS are in the state *Disabled*.

[b] ESCD (Extended System Configuration Data) is a subset of the nonvolatile BIOS memory (still named CMOS in the BIOS settings.)

Despite the fact that there exists a *TCG Generic Server Specification* we could not supply our test bed environment with ready-to-use server hardware since TPM-based servers are still a shortage with respect to the IT hardware market. Thus, for our test results we limited ourselves to the testing of TPM equipped notebook and desktop hardware. Table 1 shows the hardware test environment. The tested hardware include : IBM Lenovo T510, IBM Lenovo T61, IBM Lenovo T60, and IBM Lenovo M58p (Desktop computer). All the platforms have a TPM 1.2 chip on main-board[1].

There are similar hardware test results in the literature. Sadeghi et al. [1,22] tested a core set of TPM functionalities on TPM chips from different vendors. The compliance test results show that there exist discrepancies in the behaviors among different TPM chips. Several TPMs show non-compliant behavior with respect to the TCG specification and errors occur sometimes in the runtime library [24].

For single system testings (Table 2), we fix a TPM platform and record the boot-up PCR values for the various system settings. For instance, we have booted up two different Linux OS systems (No. 3 in Table 2). The boot-up PCR values

---

[1] TPM hardware details: Atmel TPM 97SC3203 (on T60, T61), Chipset integrated TPM (on T510), 9965-A5G TPM 1.2 Winbond (on the M58p Desktop).

are recorded in Figure 4.4. We have found resulted differences in PCRs 4, 5 and 8 - 15. Changing boot order or dynamically selecting a different bootmedia (No. 2 in Table 2) results differences in PCRs 1 and 4 (Figure 3.3). We have also tested the effects of on/off DMA activation on PCRs. Our test results show that the vendor default configuration does not include Extended Security Reporting Options (in BIOS submenu) in the PCRs measurement. And the activation of BIOS DMA features (No. 4 in Table 2) results in no differences in PCRs. The activation of BIOS DMA features is detected only after we switch on the CMOS, NVRAM and ESCD reporting in the Extended Security Reporting Options.

The significance of the DMA tests is the following: DMA allows devices to transfer data without supervision by the CPU. An attacker with physical access to the trusted system may activate DMA options in the BIOS and subsequently connect a hardware to the system to access its memory [21,19]. To prevent such a security flaw, DMA can be disabled in the BIOS settings and any change of this setting should be reflected in the configuration register values. A system with a changed DMA setting will then not be able to qualify as a clone of a trusted system .

Among different hardware platforms (Table 3), there exists expected PCRs discrepancies (No. 1 in Table 3). We also extensively tested among the Extended Security Report Options (No. 3 - 6 in Table 3) between two similar hardware. While the activation of most of the Extended Reporting features resulted differences in PCRs 1, the only exception is being the BIOS ESCD extended reporting feature whose activation has produced the same PCRs 1 on both platforms. This system behavior is not documented in the system documentation. Our testing on the T510s show that the ESCD reporting option is the only feature fulfilling the double requirements:

1. same PCR 1 value return after identical system hardware (here T510 vs. T510) measurement
2. a change of DMA related BIOS options (stored in the non-volatile BIOS memory) is detected and results in a changed PCR 1 value (see test cases 8 in Table 2 and 6 in Table 3)

The other available reporting option (CMOS, NVRAM, SMBIOS) do not meet the specified TCG requirement [16]: *platform configuration information being either unique (e.g. serial numbers) or automatically updated (e.g. clock registers) must not be measured into PCR 1.* The activation of any one of the three extended security reporting options above on two identical systems results in different PCRs 1 (see test cases 3–5 in Table 3).

4 Discussion and Conclusion

Our contribution in this paper is the proposal of a mutual attestation protocol for identical TPM based platforms. We also provide source code and bootable prototypes on our project website[2].

---

[2] http://www.daprim.de/

Trusted Platform Modules are deployed in many PC clients (especially laptop computers) since 2006 and they can be therefore viewed as commodity goods. However, software applications using the TPM attestation functions are still rare and to our knowledge limited to project prototypes.

While the ability of attesting a remote platform is supposed to be one of the main functionalities of the Trusted Platform Module, TPM based remote attestation is still no ready-to-use technology. Real-world attestation applications require not only that the system architecture to have a ready-to-implement TCG Software Stack, but it must also have compatible hardware to support the relevant TPM operations.

The hardware issues we have identified in section 3.4 require us to use two identical hardware for the purpose of cloning TPM based systems, taking into account the fact that the BIOS machine code needs to be part of the trusted boot chain. Though hardware equivalence is rather a strong requirement for the cloning procedures, it is still insufficient in the following sense: We were unable to add security relevant BIOS settings to the verifiable state of the system in an appropriate way. The activation of the extended reporting options results into different PCR values for identical systems. Only by rigorously testing the undocumented options in the BIOS setup submenu, we were able to derive a BIOS configuration from which our mutual attestation scheme can be carried out: i.e. the cloned system has the same PCR values and a change of security relevant BIOS variables (e.g. DMA activation) is detected.

Our results show that the specified requirement [16] that "platform configuration information being unique or automatically updated must not be measured" is apparently violated. The full activation of extended security reporting options results in different values on identical systems.

Note that the situation for *TPM-Sealing* is quite different from attestation since there are ready-to-use software libraries and only one TPM platform is involved per sealing or de-sealing procedure. An application architecture making use of this TPM-based function would run on any compatible hardware since sealed files are not to be migrated to different platforms in any case.

The purpose of Trusted Computing is to enable each endpoint to make a trusted decision about the other endpoint, regardless of hardware background and software configurations. Indeed in reality, it is hard to expect a homogeneous enterprise with identical hardware, and completely synchronized BIOS settings, and globally verified Service Packs installed. Future research in trusted computing should focus on more robust and flexible mechanism for trust establishment and infrastructure. In the meantime, we will require from the system vendors a well documented TPM platform together with a full disclosure of BIOS internal integrity checks regarding the extended security reporting options. The present situation that the platform owner is required to test undocumented options, and to find out which of these options being in line with the TCG specifications is not acceptable.

Acknowledgements. Many thanks go to the anonymous reviewers who provided detailed and insightful commentary on this paper.

References

1. Sirrix, A.G.: TPM Compliance Test Results (2006),
   http://www.sirrix.com/content/pages/test_results_en.htm
2. Armknecht, F., Chen, L., Sadeghi, A.-R., Wachsmann, C.: Anonymous Authentication for RFID Systems. In: Ors Yalcin, S.B. (ed.) RFIDSec 2010. LNCS, vol. 6370, pp. 158–175. Springer, Heidelberg (2010)
3. Balfe, S., Lakhani, A.D., Paterson, K.G.: Trusted Computing: Providing Security for Peer-to-Peer Networks. In: Peer-to-Peer Computing, pp. 117–124 (2005)
4. Brickell, E.F., Camenisch, J., Chen, L.: Direct Anonymous Attestation. In: ACM Conference on Computer and Communications Security, pp. 132–145 (2004)
5. Brickell, E., Chen, L., Li, J.: A New Direct Anonymous Attestation Scheme from Bilinear Maps. In: TRUST, pp. 166–178 (2008)
6. Brickell, E., Li, J.: Enhanced privacy id: A Direct Anonymous Attestation Scheme with Enhanced Revocation Capabilities. In: WPES, pp. 21–30 (2007)
7. Brickell, E., Li, J.: A Pairing-Based DAA Scheme Further Reducing TPM Resources. In: Acquisti, A., Smith, S.W., Sadeghi, A.-R. (eds.) TRUST 2010. LNCS, vol. 6101, pp. 181–195. Springer, Heidelberg (2010)
8. Cesena, E., Löhr, H., Ramunno, G., Sadeghi, A.-R., Vernizzi, D.: Anonymous Authentication with TLS and DAA. In: Acquisti, A., Smith, S.W., Sadeghi, A.-R. (eds.) TRUST 2010. LNCS, vol. 6101, pp. 47–62. Springer, Heidelberg (2010)
9. Chen, L.: A DAA Scheme Using Batch Proof and Verification. In: Acquisti, A., Smith, S.W., Sadeghi, A.-R. (eds.) TRUST 2010. LNCS, vol. 6101, pp. 166–180. Springer, Heidelberg (2010)
10. Chen, L., Page, D., Smart, N.P.: On the Design and Implementation of an Efficient DAA Scheme. In: Gollmann, D., Lanet, J.-L., Iguchi-Cartigny, J. (eds.) CARDIS 2010. LNCS, vol. 6035, pp. 223–237. Springer, Heidelberg (2010)
11. Diffie, W., Hellman, M.E.: New Directions in Cryptography. IEEE Transactions on Information Theory IT-22, 644–654 (1976)
12. Federal Office for Information Security. Algorithms for qualified electronic signatures. Technical Report (February 19, 2010)
13. Trusted Computing for the Java(tm) Platform,
    http://trustedjava.sourceforge.net/
14. Trusted Computing Group. Trusted computing platform alliance (TCPA) main specification, version 1.1b (2001), www.trustedcomputing.org
15. Trusted Computing Group. Trusted computing platform alliance (TCPA) main specification, version 1.2 (2003), www.trustedcomputing.org
16. Trusted Computing Group. TCG EFI Platform Specification V1.20 (2006), www.trustedcomputing.org
17. Leung, A., Mitchell, C.J.: Ninja: Non Identity Based, Privacy Preserving Authentication for Ubiquitous Environments. In: Krumm, J., Abowd, G.D., Seneviratne, A., Strang, T. (eds.) UbiComp 2007. LNCS, vol. 4717, pp. 73–90. Springer, Heidelberg (2007)
18. Li, J., Rajan, A.: An Anonymous Attestation Scheme with Optional Traceability. In: Acquisti, A., Smith, S.W., Sadeghi, A.-R. (eds.) TRUST 2010. LNCS, vol. 6101, pp. 196–210. Springer, Heidelberg (2010)

19. Marchesini, J., Smith, S., Wild, O., MacDonald, R.: Experimenting with TC-PA/TCG hardware, or: How I learned to stop worrying and love the bear. TR2003-476, Dartmouth College (2003)
20. Nauman, M., Khan, S., Zhang, X., Seifert, J.-P.: Beyond Kernel-Level Integrity Measurement: Enabling Remote Attestation for the Android Platform. In: Acquisti, A., Smith, S.W., Sadeghi, A.-R. (eds.) TRUST 2010. LNCS, vol. 6101, pp. 1–15. Springer, Heidelberg (2010)
21. Piegdon, D.R., Pimenidis, L.: Hacking in Physically Addressable Memory. In: Hämmerli, B.M., Sommer, R. (eds.) DIMVA 2007. LNCS, vol. 4579, pp. 1–19. Springer, Heidelberg (2007)
22. Sadeghi, A.R., Selhorst, M., Stueble, C., Wachsmann, C., Winandy, M.: TCG Inside? A Note on TPM Specification Compliance. In: Proceedings of the First ACM Workshop on Scalable Trusted Computing, pp. 47–56. ACM (2006)
23. Schroeder, M.: Engineering a security kernel for multics. In: Fifth Symposium on Operating Systems Principles, pp. 125–132 (November 1975)
24. Shubina, A., Bratus, S., Ingersoll, W., Smith, S.W.: The Diversity of TPMs and its Effects on Development. In: ACM STC 2010 (2010)
25. TPM Quote Tools, http://sourceforge.net/
26. Walker, J., Li, J.: Key Exchange with Anonymous Authentication using DAA-SIGMA Protocol. In: IACR eprint archive (2010)
27. Infineon Technologies Website, http://www.infineon.com/cms/en/product/channel.html?channel=ff80808112ab681d0112ab692060011a

A   Mutual Attestation Protocol

0. *System I* generates a AIK key AIK_I and obtains a certificate $Cert_I$. *System II* generates a AIK key AIK_{II} and obtains a certificate $Cert_{II}$.

1. *System I* and *system II* exchange their certificates and public AIK keys:

$$I \xrightarrow{\left(AIK_I^{pub}, Cert_I\right)} II, \quad II \xrightarrow{\left(AIK_{II}^{pub}, Cert_{II}\right)} I$$

2. *System I* verifies *system II*'s certificate. *System II* verifies *system I*'s certificate. The protocol continues upon successful verifications of both certificates.

3. Let p be the agreed-upon prime of required security parameter and a group generator g that will be used to generate the Diffie-Hellman parameters. *System I* randomly selects an integer a in the interval $[2, p-1]$. *System II* randomly selects an integer b in the interval $[2, p-1]$. *System I* computes value A and *system II* computes value B:

$$A = g^a \bmod p, \quad B = g^b \bmod p.$$

4. System I sends A to system II. System II sends B to system I:

$$I \xrightarrow{A} II, \quad II \xrightarrow{B} I$$

5. *System I* computes the key $\mathbf{skey}_I$. *System II* computes the key $\mathbf{skey}_{II}$:

$$\mathbf{skey}_I = B^a, \quad \mathbf{skey}_{II} = A^b$$

6. The systems process mutual system integrity check. The steps are:

a *System I* signs the PCR values and hashed $\mathbf{skey}_I$ and forwards it to *system II*. *System II* signs the PCR values and hashed $\mathbf{skey}_{II}$ and forwards it to *system I*.

$$I \xrightarrow{Quote(PCR_I \,||\, H(\mathbf{skey}_I))} II, \quad II \xrightarrow{Quote(PCR_{II} \,||\, H(\mathbf{skey}_{II}))} I$$

b *System I* verifies the signature. *System I* compares the received PCR_{II} values with its own PCR values, then it compares the received $H(\mathbf{skey}_{II})$ with its own hashed key $H(\mathbf{skey}_I)$. If all the values agree, *system I* grants database access to system II. The session key is the common keys $H(\mathbf{skey}_{II}) = H(\mathbf{skey}_I)$.

c *System II* verifies the signature. *System II* compares the received PCR_I values with its own PCR values, then it compares the received $H(\mathbf{skey}_I)$ with its own hashed key $H(\mathbf{skey}_{II})$. If all the values agree, *system II* grants database access to *system I*. The session key is the common keys $H(\mathbf{skey}_{II}) = H(\mathbf{skey}_I)$.

B   Example PCR Values

```
multiple systems – test case 2
Lenovo T510 System 1                   IBM T60
PCR–00: 42 A2 AF 18 81 7C  ...         PCR–00: A2 7B 2C EF 5B 0B  ...
PCR–01: 48 DF F4 FB F3 A3  ... <===>   PCR–01: 48 DF F4 FB F3 A3  ...
PCR–02: 24 5B 5C E4 FF F1  ...         PCR–02: 53 DE 58 4D CE F0  ...
PCR–03: 3A 3F 78 0F 11 A4  ...         PCR–03: 3A 3F 78 0F 11 A4  ...
PCR–04: 1E F2 2E 55 6D 02  ...         PCR–04: C0 D0 F2 DF 3D F9  ...
PCR–05: 3F C8 89 02 05 59  ...         PCR–05: 13 E3 62 E8 6D 4B  ...
PCR–06: 58 5E 57 9E 48 99  ...         PCR–06: 58 5E 57 9E 48 99  ...
PCR–07: 3A 3F 78 0F 11 A4  ...         PCR–07: 3A 3F 78 0F 11 A4  ...
PCR–08: 03 B3 B2 AE 7E 2B  ...         PCR–08: 03 B3 B2 AE 7E 2B  ...
PCR–09: F6 E5 F7 35 B0 2F  ...         PCR–09: F6 E5 F7 35 B0 2F  ...
PCR–10: 00 00 00 00 00 00  ...         PCR–10: 00 00 00 00 00 00  ...
PCR–11: 00 00 00 00 00 00  ...         PCR–11: 00 00 00 00 00 00  ...
PCR–12: F0 22 54 28 39 D1  ...         PCR–12: F0 22 54 28 39 D1  ...
PCR–13: 34 42 7B 49 32 23  ...         PCR–13: 34 42 7B 49 32 23  ...
PCR–14: A8 28 2F BD A7 BC  ...         PCR–14: A8 28 2F BD A7 BC  ...
```

Fig. 2. Boot-up PCR Values of IBM T510 and IBM T60 Without Extended Reporting: different hardware configurations with the same bootchain, but without extended reporting results the same PCR 1

```
single system – test case 2
Lenovo T510 System 2                    Lenovo T510 System 2
PCR–00: 42 A2 AF 18 81 7C  ...          PCR–00: 42 A2 AF 18 81 7C  ...
PCR–01: 56 6E BA FB 53 FE  ... <***>    PCR–01: CB B7 0F E9 7A D0  ...
PCR–02: 24 5B 5C E4 FF F1  ...          PCR–02: 24 5B 5C E4 FF F1  ...
PCR–03: 3A 3F 78 0F 11 A4  ...          PCR–03: 3A 3F 78 0F 11 A4  ...
PCR–04: 78 6E AD 00 83 A0  ... <***>    PCR–04: 1E F2 2E 55 6D 02  ...
PCR–05: 3F C8 89 02 05 59  ...          PCR–05: 3F C8 89 02 05 59  ...
PCR–06: 58 5E 57 9E 48 99  ...          PCR–06: 58 5E 57 9E 48 99  ...
PCR–07: 3A 3F 78 0F 11 A4  ...          PCR–07: 3A 3F 78 0F 11 A4  ...
PCR–08: 03 B3 B2 AE 7E 2B  ...          PCR–08: 03 B3 B2 AE 7E 2B  ...
PCR–09: F6 E5 F7 35 B0 2F  ...          PCR–09: F6 E5 F7 35 B0 2F  ...
PCR–10: 00 00 00 00 00 00  ...          PCR–10: 00 00 00 00 00 00  ...
PCR–11: 00 00 00 00 00 00  ...          PCR–11: 00 00 00 00 00 00  ...
PCR–12: F0 22 54 28 39 D1  ...          PCR–12: F0 22 54 28 39 D1  ...
PCR–13: 34 42 7B 49 32 23  ...          PCR–13: 34 42 7B 49 32 23  ...
PCR–14: A8 28 2F BD A7 BC  ...          PCR–14: A8 28 2F BD A7 BC  ...
```

Fig. 3. Boot-up PCR values of IBM T510 Before and After Boot Order is Changed: changing bootorder or dynamically selecting a different bootmedia results differences in PCR 1 and 4

```
single system – test case 3
Lenovo T510 System 1                    Lenovo T510 System 1
PCR–00: 42 A2 AF 18 81 7C  ...          PCR–00: 42 A2 AF 18 81 7C  ...
PCR–01: 48 DF F4 FB F3 A3  ...          PCR–01: 48 DF F4 FB F3 A3  ...
PCR–02: 24 5B 5C E4 FF F1  ...          PCR–02: 24 5B 5C E4 FF F1  ...
PCR–03: 3A 3F 78 0F 11 A4  ...          PCR–03: 3A 3F 78 0F 11 A4  ...
PCR–04: 1E F2 2E 55 6D 02  ... <***>    PCR–04: A3 CE B1 EF AC 90  ...
PCR–05: 3F C8 89 02 05 59  ... <***>    PCR–05: 99 21 E8 EA 42 08  ...
PCR–06: 58 5E 57 9E 48 99  ...          PCR–06: 58 5E 57 9E 48 99  ...
PCR–07: 3A 3F 78 0F 11 A4  ...          PCR–07: 3A 3F 78 0F 11 A4  ...
PCR–08: 03 B3 B2 AE 7E 2B  ... <***>    PCR–08: 00 00 00 00 00 00  ...
PCR–09: F6 E5 F7 35 B0 2F  ... <***>    PCR–09: 00 00 00 00 00 00  ...
PCR–10: 00 00 00 00 00 00  ...          PCR–10: 00 00 00 00 00 00  ...
PCR–11: 00 00 00 00 00 00  ...          PCR–11: 00 00 00 00 00 00  ...
PCR–12: F0 22 54 28 39 D1  ... <***>    PCR–12: 00 00 00 00 00 00  ...
PCR–13: 34 42 7B 49 32 23  ... <***>    PCR–13: 00 00 00 00 00 00  ...
PCR–14: A8 28 2F BD A7 BC  ... <***>    PCR–14: 00 00 00 00 00 00  ...
```

Fig. 4. Boot-up PCR values of IBM T510 based on two different Operating Systems: identical hardware runninig on different Linux Operating Systems results differences in PCR 4,5 and 8 - 15

Secure Architecure for the Integration of RFID and Sensors in Personal Networks*

Pablo Najera, Rodrigo Roman, and Javier Lopez

University of Malaga, Campus de Teatinos s/n 29071, Spain
{najera,roman,jlm}@lcc.uma.es
http://nics.uma.es

Abstract. The secure integration of RFID technology into the personal network paradigm, as a context-aware technology which complements body sensor networks, would provide notable benefits to applications and potential services of the personal network (PN). RFID security as an independent technology is reaching an adequate maturity level thanks to research in recent years; however, its integration into the PN model, interaction with other network resources, remote users and service providers requires a specific security analysis and an architecture prepared to support these resource-constrained pervasive technologies. This paper provides such PN architecture and analysis. Aspects such as the management of personal tags as members of the PN, the authentication and secure communication of PN nodes and remote users with the context-aware technologies, and the enforcement of security and privacy policies are discussed in the architecture.

Keywords: RFID security, BSN, personal network, secure architecture.

1 Introduction

The emerging personal network paradigm enables the communication of all the user's devices and services in a flexible, secure, self-organizing and user friendly manner. This network paradigm should provide a base for personal and context-aware service provision as well as enable the communication with wide area networks (e.g. Internet of Things) in order to connect to remote devices or networks and offer complex and comprehensive services.

A key technology in the realization of this network paradigm are wireless body sensor networks (BSNs), formed by tiny wearable sensor nodes which, depending on the desire applications, consistently monitor user's physiological parameters (e.g. blood pressure, electrocardiogram or glucose level), recognize

---

* This work has been partially supported by the European Community through the NESSoS (FP7-256890) project and the Spanish Ministry of Science and Innovation through the ARES (CSD2007-00004) and SPRINT (TIN2009-09237)projects. The latter is cofinanced by FEDER (European Regional Development Fund). The first author has been funded by the Spanish Ministry of Education through the National F.P.U. Program.

C. Meadows and C. Fernández-Gago (Eds.): STM 2011, LNCS 7170, pp. 207–222, 2012.

the user's current activity in, either, personal (e.g. walking, reading, sleeping) or professional (e.g. repairing an airplane or controlling a fire) arenas, or monitor parameters such as temperature, humidity or radiation levels of the surrounding environment. These features are driving the adoption of BSNs in several areas ranging from elderly care and patient monitoring to novel applications in military and consumer electronics.

Although commonly overlooked as a member of the emerging personal network paradigm, another key and crucial technology in the realization of the pervasive computing vision, and the technology that is really enabling the integration of computation and communication capabilities to common and low-cost everyday objects is RFID (Radio Frequency IDentification). RFID enables the unique identification of an object as well as provide additional data about the item (e.g. characteristics or history log) by attaching or embedding an RFID tag. ITU describes RFID technology as one of the pivots that will enable the upcoming Internet of Things, turning regular objects into smart ones[1], while the European Commission expects that the use of this technology will multiple by five during the next decade. The widespread adoption of this technology combined with the novel applications enabled collides with the potential privacy and security threats that its penetration on the user's personal belongings and documentation may arise. Due to this, the research community has devoted notable efforts in minimizing potential security risks by proposing a huge range of mutual authentication protocols[2], privacy protection schemes[3] and lightweight cryptographic algorithms[4] for this promising technology, in order to avoid unauthorized access to personal RFID tags, user's tracking and profiling.

As presented later in this paper, the secure integration of RFID technology into the PN paradigm as a context-aware technology which complements BSNs provides notable benefits to the knowledge and potential services of the PN. Security of RFID as an independent technology is reaching an adequate maturity level thanks to research advances in recent years; however, its integration into the PN model, interaction with other network resources, remote users and service providers requires a specific security analysis and a secure PN architecture prepared to support these heterogeneous pervasive technologies. Although an increasing amount of research is focusing on the personal network paradigms with the proposal of some network architectures[5,6,7], and the benefits of the integration of wireless sensor networks and RFID technology have already driven the proposal of several architectures for the collaboration of these technologies in different scenarios[8,9,10], to the best of our knowledge, no architecture has introduced the secure integration of RFID and wireless sensor networks technologies in personal networks. This paper exposes the benefits of the collaboration of RFID and sensor technologies in PN networks, analyzes how this integration could be achieved and defines a secure PN architecture which provides the foundations in order to securely register and maintain the personal tags as members of the PN, authenticate and authorize PN nodes and remote devices in their requests to access these context-aware technologies, provide a secure tunnel to communicate with this non IP-enabled entities and enforce the fulfilment of security and privacy policies in these communications.

The paper is organized as follows. Section 2 reviews the advantages and limitations of the integration of RFID and BSNs in personal networks. Section 3 presents our concept of the personal network, types of nodes and alternatives in the integration of RFID and sensors. Section 4 introduces the modules of our secure PN architecture proposal. Section 5 analyzes the secure management of PN nodes and communication with context-aware technologies in the architecture. Finally, section 6 concludes the paper.

2   Convenience of the Integration of RFID and PNs

Even if BSNs provide context awareness to the PN gathering information on the physiological parameters of the owner, his activities and environment, the snapshot of the surrounding reality is far from complete and the knowledge handled by the information system to monitorize and support the user is open to further contributions. RFID technology greatly complements BSNs in order to provide a more comprehensive vision of the user's current state and context. In particular, RFID enhances the features of the network in the following aspects:

- *Reach further*: thanks to the extreme miniaturization of RFID tags, ability to harvest the energy required for operation during the reading process and low cost, RFID allows spreading computation and communication capabilities to a much wider range of consumer products, furniture, building components and personal belongings than wireless sensor nodes, substantially enhancing the number of nodes, quality and quantity of data handled by the personal network. However, at the same time, these novel RFID-enabled personal items only feature highly resource-constrained capabilities and lightweight cryptography rising potential security and privacy risks into the PN.
- *Detect presence*: RFID technology allows the network to recognize the presence and absence of individual objects which are carried by the user or in his context in a specific period of time. The fact that a particular item is present denotes information about the tools the user has available and range of potential actions, in order to support and help the user, enable services of the network triggered by the current activity or achieve special privileges in the surrounding environment thanks to the possession of distinguished items. Therefore, such presence information should be accessible to authorized local or remote entities in the provision of their services, but blocked from potential attackers and rogue users.
- *Characteristics of personal items*: tags can provide further information on the characteristics of each objects. The description and metadata about the items must be provided in a standardized format in such a way that the personal network can seamlessly obtain this information, increase its knowledge on the situation where the user is immerse and features of available items, and use it to improve its services.

- *On-item history log*: tags can maintain a log about previous interactions of the personal item, places, ownerships or relevant facts. This type of historical item data defined for each type of personal object would further enhance the quality of the information handled by the PN, as well as the forensic data gathered to detect rogue actors, intrusions and attacks.
- *Secure and transparent management of personal data*: a significant portion of personal data (including certificate of personal life events, academic qualifications, medical and monetary documents, personal writings and reports) are currently handled in paper-based documentation. The integration of RFID technology into personal documentation will provide a seamless link with the digital world for agile and automated processing of its contents, as well as enable the use of advanced security mechanisms extensively addressed in electronic documents and piooner hybrid personal documents (e.g. the comprehensive ePassport security mechanisms) without sacrificing the reliability and convenience provided by the physical support.
- *User authentication*: the integration of this technology in identification cards and documentation enables the secure identification and authentication of the user in his PN, surrounding context or even access remote networks and services with minimal user interaction, but advanced security properties.

Therefore, a secure integration of RFID technology into the PN can greatly enhance the context aware services of the network. In fact, RFID technology can be considered as an additional sensing source, where, instead of sensing parameters such as temperature or humidity, the network senses which items are present and relevant metadata. From this perspective, the RFID reader acts as an additional sensor node, which senses this particular type of data about the context based on the support of passive nodes (i.e. the RFID tags). Although the integration of RFID and sensor technologies brings multiple benefits to the personal network, most RFID tags only implement lightweight cryptography and feature highly constrained memory and computation capabilities rising potential security risks in the PN. Moreover, the heterogeneous resources between RFID, sensors and other personal devices highlight the need of an adequate secure communication model with personal tags in the PN architecture.

3   Network Architecture of the PN

Our vision of the personal network paradigm focuses on the definition of a secure network architecture for the integration of RFID technology in the core PAN, the immediate sphere of nodes surrounding the user, and the communication of this enhanced core network with remote nodes (e.g. clusters of personal devices at remote locations, other personal networks or central monitoring servers). As related literature [6,7], we consider a centralized network architecture where the master device supports PN communications and network management, while special emphasis is focused on the integration of the two foundation technologies for context awareness: wireless sensor networks and RFID technology. In particular, we assume the following types of nodes (see Figure 1):

- *Master device*: a device with no serious computational and memory constraints. This node incorporates reasonable battery life; the user interacts with it frequently and guarantees its functional state or incorporates energy harvesting features so that its continuous operation can be assumed. The node integrates communication interfaces to interact with external and wide area networks (e.g. 3G/UMTS, LTE or Wimax) and is usually carried by the user. Although specific devices could emerge in the upcoming future to fulfil this role, the widespread smartphones already satisfy this profile.
- *Wireless sensor nodes*: provide a significant amount of information about physiological parameters of the user and his activity. A wide range of sensor features, sensing variables and locations on the user are possible, and they should be adapted to the purpose and potential applications of the personal network. The PN could include a base station which manages the sensor nodes and aggregates their data or this function could be integrated in other nodes such as the master device.
- *RFID tags*: identify and keep data related to the personal tagged items. Different types of RFID technology would coexist for different purposes. For example, passive UHF tags such as EPC Gen2 tags are more adequate for personal objects (e.g. clothes, glasses or professional tools) as they fulfil the identification and reduced data management requirements of these items while featuring low cost per tag and long reading distance, however they present more constrained resources. On the other side, personal documentation would benefit from advanced cryptographic security mechanisms such as the ones available in passive HF RFID tags based on ISO/IEC 14443. Along the same lines as wireless sensor nodes, active RFID technology provide sensing and less constrained computational capabilities in case a more advance item monitorization is necessary.
- *RFID reader(s)*: in charge of identifying and recovering the data stored in the personal tagged items. Multi-standard or more than one reader is required to communicate with the different types of RFID technology. Portable and handheld UHF passive readers are able to seamlessly access tagged personal items in the sphere surrounding the user while HF passive readers (such as those integrated in some smartphone models[12]) do require close proximity to hybrid personal documentation during the communication process. In case the personal tag requires a short reading distance, notification (through input/output devices) and explicit user interaction could be required to complete de communication.
- *Input/output devices*: in addition to all-in-one smartphones, additional technologies are expected to emerge in order to provide convenient and unobtrusive methods for explicit interaction of the user including data input (e.g. tactile panels in clothes, sensor equipped bracelets) and output (e.g. head-mounted displays, augmented reality glasses).
- *Advanced gadgets*: appliances and devices owned by the user and useful for particular jobs (e.g. GPS device, music players, digital cameras and gaming devices). These devices participate in a non-continuous basis in the network enabling additional features and services, and present less resource

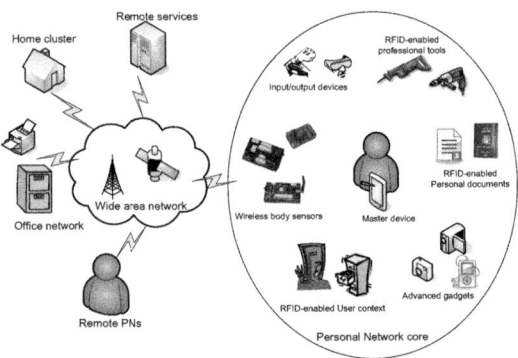

Fig. 1. Outline of communications in the personal network

constrained characteristics than the core context-aware technologies of the PN (i.e. sensor and RFID nodes).

4   Software Components in the PN Architecture

Our proposal is not the first contribution of a software architecture for personal networks. Existing literature[5,6,7] has already worked in this arena providing a general architecture for this novel network paradigm which already addresses a wide spectrum of network management issues for generic personal devices. While these previous works provide a good foundation for the development of PNs, a generic approach do not take into account how to achieve the secure integration of RFID technology in the PN.

Remote entities which require communicating with the tags are not able to address them directly (e.g. RFID tags do not have their own IP address and remote entities should not burden with their current location inside the PN or RFID readers in range). Furthermore, due to the potential leakage of personal data and potential threats to owner's privacy, user's privacy policies should be enforced in any communication with personal items. Due to this, the PN should manage the secure addressing and access to personal tags, ensuring the fulfilment of security requirements in these communications.

In the realization of our vision, the PN should provide support to the secure collaboration of the heterogeneous nodes which coexist in the network, as well as their interaction with external entities. To achieve this purpose, personal devices need to be recognized as members of the PN, providing secure mechanisms to initialize new nodes or transfer ownership from other parties. The members of the PN and authorized external entities require maintaining updated keys and credentials in the network, as well as being able to establish secure communications with other network nodes (including nodes based on incompatible network technologies). During the communications, entities must be authenticated and the fulfilment of security and privacy policies must be enforced. In order to meet these requirements, we propose a PN architecture based on the following modules and behaviour (see Figure 2):

- *PN Members Database*: in charge of maintaining a database of the nodes that are recognized as nodes of the personal network. The database should maintain metadata related to each unique node during their membership in the network such as addressing data (e.g. IP, MAC, PN address), cryptographic materials (e.g. digital certificates, keys), roles, reputation levels and privileges in the network.
- *Member Discovery and Maintenance Module*: PN is a dynamic network paradigm where new personal devices are required to be incorporated on-demand, while previous PN members can change ownership, be compromised or disposed. This module handles the secure lifecycle of the devices associated with the PN, whether with a permanent or temporal relationship, including secure device incorporation to PN (i.e. imprinting process, key and cryptographic material exchange), refresh of shared keys and cryptographic resources during devices lifetime, as well as node disassociation protocols.
- *Naming Resolution and Communication Management*: receives requests from PN members or remote devices which are willing to communicate with a PN network node identified by a recognizable naming convention. The module handle the request by checking the applicant node and its privileges in the network (supported by the Authentication and Authorization module), and later forwarding the connection to the appropriate network module (i.e. PN Routing or Secure Context Management).
- *Authentication and Authorization Module*: in order to (re-)connect to the PN and establish queries or secure connection to PN devices, both PN members and remote nodes require to authenticate in the personal network. This module handles the secure process and, based on the node privileges, provides authorization to the node for further interactions with the PN members during its communication.
- *PN Routing*: determines the most adequate route to interconnect the applicant (local or remote) node with the requested PN network entity. The route takes into account the mobility of PN nodes in the network, as well as the heterogeneity in communication technologies and computational capabilities in order to locate the current position of the final node and include the required gateway nodes in the path.
- *Secure tunnel Manager*: secure communications are required between PN members and to/from remote devices and servers. However, due to the limited communication capabilities and strongly resource-constrained characteristics presented by some personal devices, secure connections cannot be directly established between any pair of devices. This submodule is in charge of enabling the secure communication between end-to-end nodes, including the use of intermediate proxy and gateway nodes in the PN which may act as a bridge between different networking technologies, adapting the security mechanisms used at each hop-to-hop connection in order to maximize the security level according to the capabilities of each pair of nodes.

- *Privacy policies and profile DB*: manages the information regarding the user profile and personal information, as well as the privacy policies which define how its personal information, as well as the data stored or generated by the PN should be managed. The process to define the most adequate privacy policies could be based on different alternatives and it is open to innovative proposals. In a basic approach, the user could initially select between a range of predefined privacy levels associate to a set of privacy policies which can be later updated and fine-tuned based on the user input during the PN lifetime.
- *Secure Context Management*: in charge of managing the information generated by context-aware technologies (i.e. RFID and sensor networks). This data must be properly processed according to the security and privacy restrictions desired by the user. Based on this input, context-aware data is properly filtered, anonymized and aggregated depending on the requesting entity and related privileges.

In our centralized PN model, the master device has a distinguished position featuring a global vision of the underlying network of personal devices, providing external interfaces to wide area networks and expected continuous presence in the network. As a result, the complete PN architecture could be deployed in the master device which would be in charge of all the management and communication functions in the network. However, part of the modules of the architecture and related functions could also be outsourced to other PN devices with adequate computation and communication capabilities, as well as reliable power supply and availability in the network. For example, a wireless base station could be in charge of the Secure Context Management module or an advanced gadget could store the PN Members Database or Privacy Policies and User Profile repository. This distributed network architecture may be statically defined, although novel proposals could provide secure mechanisms for dynamic delegation of PN functions in the network.

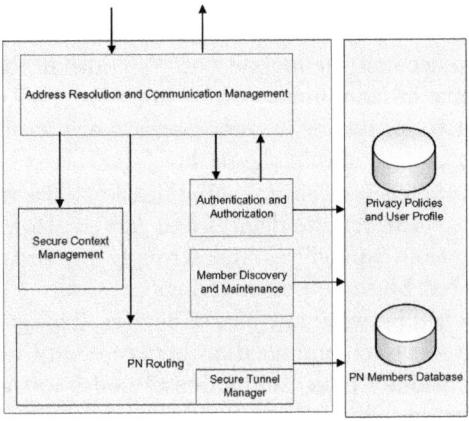

Fig. 2. Software components of the PN architecture

5 Secure Management of RFID Nodes and Sensors in the Architecture

The integration of RFID technology in the personal network requires specific considerations on the functions carried out by the modules of the architecture. Following, we will discuss how this integration can be achieved, and the aspects to be required in the architecture. In particular we will analyze the discovery and management of personal tagged objects, the secure communication with context-aware technologies and the enforcement of security and privacy policies.

5.1 Discovery and Management of RFID-Enabled Items in the Architecture

As members of the PN, the personal RFID tags should also be included in the PN Members Database in order to know which tags from the user context do belong to the network and how to authenticate and access the tag. In order to properly manage the tags, the database should store adequate identification data, such as the unique identification code (UID) of each tag, along with other naming conventions which could be used in the PN to provide uniform and more convenient naming of PN nodes (e.g. using a prefix to recognize the PN, a type-of-node code and a sufix unique code in the category), a mobile IPv6 address as proposed in[18] or pseudonyms for privacy protecting purposes. Moreover, the database should maintain the adequate cryptographic material and keys so that authorized remote or PN nodes can successfully accomplish mutual authentication protocols, access and update specific memory sectors or even kill the tags.

From an ideal perspective, the deployment from scratch of a PN would allow the selection of a (set of) common security mechanism(s) and authentication protocol(s) to be used by all the RFID tags embedded in personal items. As characteristics of RFID tags differ widely from basic tags which behave as state machines with extremely limited memory to advanced tags capable of performing high level cryptographic operations (including public key cryptography), the PN network should adopt not only one, but a range of authentication and privacy protection mechanisms, in order to maximize the security level achieved with the resources available for each type of personal tag. This ideal solution would allow standardizing the secure communication protocols and unifying the management of the cryptographic materials involved in the secure storage and key refreshment processes. However, in real-world conditions, the tags adopted in the PN will be embedded in the personal items by different sources, so that a wide range of heterogeneous tags, based on different RFID technology branches and/or different authentication protocols, will coexist in the PN. Therefore, a common set of authentication protocols (depending on the type of tag, purpose and computational resources) could be defined for the RFID tags directly deployed for the applications of the PN, while the PN architecture (including the PN Members Database, Secure tunnel manager or Authentication and Authorization modules) should be prepared to manage the cryptographic data and authentication protocols required by adopted RFID tags in the PN.

As new RFID-enabled objects are owned by the user or tags are explicitly embedded in personal belongings, these tags should be securely recognized and included into the personal sphere. The process of incorporating an RFID tag into the PN is managed by the Member Discovery and Maintenance Module. In the case of virgin RFID tags, deployed specifically for PN applications, an imprinting protocol should be used to initialize the tag, exchange the appropriate cryptographic materials (e.g. keys, pseudonyms and/or certificates) and register the tag in the PN Members Database. The specific mechanism to securely identify the tag and imprint the adequate cryptographic materials to prepare the tag is out of the scope of this paper and will depend on the RFID authentication protocol(s) selected for later accesses from the wide range available in the literature. The incorporation process could require some explicit interaction of the PN owner with the master device (or some other PN device with input/output capabilities) in order to confirm which tagged objects should be accepted as members of the network (e.g. by selection in a display or physically bringing the reader in close proximity of a tag) and participate in the generation or establishment of keys with a high level of entropy (e.g. by shaking a device enabled with an accelerometer or providing input through a keypad).

If the tag has not been initially deployed in this network, a tag ownership transfer protocol is required to obtain the rights to securely access the tag, dissociate it from the previous owner and refresh its cryptographic materials. Several RFID ownership transfer schemes are available in the literature[14,15] and could be adopted (and adapted) in the PN context. However, novel protocol proposals could take into account the services and resources available in the personal network and the integration of the PN into wide area networks, as well as potential explicit user interaction in order to achieve secure remote tag ownership transfer between distant parties. In scenarios where the tag is still required in the original application where it was deployed (e.g. products under warranty which take advantage of RFID, or private/public identification documents), the goal of the incorporation process could change to securely share tag ownership[16] between the PN and a external entity or the original owner could maintain its role but enable the PN to securely access the tag by the execution of a key management protocol or granting the required privileges to query a key management server.

5.2 Secure Access and Communication with RFID Nodes and Sensors

In order to gather information from the pervasive computing technologies present in the PN, obtain awareness about the user context, sense the physical parameters and conditions or recognize and authenticate the personal items in close proximity, the PN nodes, as well as remote parties from wide area networks, require an appropriate scheme to reach and communicate with RFID nodes and sensors in the PN. The Naming and connection management module has a particular importance in accessing the RFID tags as it provides flexibility to remote devices which may use a pseudonym scheme or PN naming scheme instead of the physical and technology specific code recognized by the tag. Moreover, the PN routing module releases the requesting node from knowing the path to the smart node or RFID reader where the tag can be found in reading range.

In our vision, a PN member or a remote device could be interested in the information provided by an RFID tag in two possible ways:

- *Direct access*: the device wants to establish a direct communication with the tag in order to identify the item, authenticate it, update its memory or retrieve specific data.
- *Aggregated knowledge*: the device requires context-awareness about the current (or past) state where the user is immersed. For its convenience, this knowledge can be better represented by the aggregated data provided by RFID-enabled personal items and sensors, rather than directly accessing each node and composing the picture on its own.

Our architecture handles both kind of interaction requirements. In case of direct access request, the applicant first requires to authenticate itself in the PN. Once it has been authenticated and authorized, the naming and routing modules are responsible to resolve the identity of the requested tag as well as its current location in the PN and provide an adequate path to reach it. In case secure communication is required, the Secure tunnel Manager submodule supports the establishment of a tunnel from the point-of-access of the PN to the smart node or RFID reader close to the requested tag, or if the intermediate nodes do not allow such a tunnel, hop-by-hop secure links inside the PN in order to maximize the security of the end-to-end channel according to the communication and computational resources of each node in the path.

On the other side, if aggregated knowledge is required, the Secure Context Management module is used after the initial authentication to provide the required context data on sensing parameters and personal items nearby. The context aware data is gathered and processed by the module as background procedures which make use of the secure naming and routing services provided by the PN to access the RFID tags and sensor nodes in the network. These behind-the-scenes communications between Secure Context Management and the pervasive computing resources available in the PN could be triggered directly by a request to the module or take place periodically to update context awareness, decoupling the remote or internal network queries from the actual secure communications with the RFID or sensor nodes.

The direct access mechanism allows the applicant to control the communication with the final tag at low level, in order to read or update specific information in the tag. This approach is very convenient for example in the remote interaction with personal documentation, as the secure communication with the advanced RFID-enabled documents may be used to authenticate the owner of the PN and even obtain non-repudiable proofs of interaction with the PN.

However, due to the low level communication with the final tag, controlling the fulfilment of security requirements and privacy policies becomes a binay decision with low granularity control. That is, queries and commands to the tag could be blocked or forwarded, but, without filtering and processing the raw data, granularity of disclosed personal information can not be properly adjusted. Therefore, authorization mechanisms could be reinforced increasing the requirements to grant direct access privileges to remote devices as once the direct access is performed the low level data transferred could potentially contain sensitive private data. Section 5.3 provides further discussion of direct access alternatives.

On the other side, the aggregated knowledge approach allows the network to further protect the security requirements and user privacy by filtering the data obtained by the context-aware technologies, anonymize the specific nodes where the data was generated and enforce the privacy policies established by the user before the data is presented to the applicant. Therefore, this mechanism to access personal data would allow to reduce the requirements on the applicant node (e.g. trust/reputation levels or explicit privileges grant by user) in order to authorize the node to interact with the Secure Context Management module, as this module would be responsible of ensuring the privacy of the final personal data accessed, at the cost of reducing the flexibility of the applicant node in its interaction with the final tag, as well as burdening the PN with additional processing tasks. Additional discussion on the use of privacy policies in the PN architecture is provided in Section 5.4.

5.3   Alternatives in Secure Direct Access to RFID Nodes

In the direct access approach, a remote or local entity request to establish a communication with a specific node of the PN. While the routing module could provide a direct path to PN nodes which feature IP connectivity (including sensor nodes[17]), one or more proxy nodes will be required in case of devices based on incompatible communication technologies or extremely constrained cryptographic and computational resources. In particular, in the case of personal RFID tags which lack from a TCP/IP stack and feature highly constrained communication, computation and memory resources, the direct access mode (for non-local RFID readers) requires proxy nodes to establish a bridge between communication technologies and enforce the fulfilment of the security and privacy policies during the communication.

In the secure routing of direct access communications to personal RFID tags, the following alternatives could be adopted (see Figure 3):

- *Proxy node as a command forwarder*: the remote node is first required to contact an external interface of the PN (e.g. the PN master device) and authenticate itself in the network. Once the applicant has been successfully authenticated, it requests accessing a node of PN (in this study case, an RFID tag) through any addressing scheme recognized by the naming module and a secure tunnel is established from the remote node to an RFID reader or smart node in reading range of the requested RFID tag.

Once or more proxy nodes could participate in the path in order to reach the final tag, however, the secure communication links between this entities are only used to forward the communication between both final entities. In this case, the remote node is required to understand the particular RFID technology which the tag is based on and send commands which are compatible with this final entity. The RFID reader or smart node close to the tag extract the commands received through the secure tunnel and send them to the personal tag. On reply, the response from the RFID tag is encapsulated and sent back to the remote device through the tunnel.

In this scheme, apart from being able to assert compatible RFID commands, the applicant is responsible to successfully complete the (mutual) authentication protocol against the final tag. Therefore, the applicant should know or be able to gather the necessary cryptographic materials (e.g. keys or digital certificates) required in the process. In case tag ownership is shared with an external service or the tag adopted in the PN belongs to an application external to the PN (e.g. RFID tags in private or governmental personal documentation), the applicant could obtain the cryptographic materials from third parties (e.g. a key management server[18]) before accessing the PN. Otherwise, the PN could directly provide them to the applicant once he has been authenticated in the PN. In the latter case, the PN would be responsible of refreshing the involved keys by means of the Member Discovery and Maintenance Module (e.g. once the communication has finished or in a periodic schedule) in order to prevent future unauthorized communications. As direct commands are sent to the final tag, the PN has a low control on the personal and private data recovered or modified by the applicant; however, a proxy node in the path (e.g. the master device or RFID reader) could further analyze the traffic flow and block those messages which do not fulfil the security policies, warning the applicant node.

– *Proxy node as a command gateway*: the initial authentication of the remote node in the PN and resolution of the final tag to be addressed and authorization is identical to the previous scenario. However, a gateway node in the secure route between the applicant and the tag would be required to intermediate and translate any communication between both final entities.

In this case, the applicant does not need to know the RFID standard the tag is based on, compatible commands or required cryptographic materials to complete the (mutual) authentication with the personal tag. The applicant could send his commands based on a set of normalized operations for generic RFID tags, while the gateway node would be responsible of translating the generic requests into specific commands to be executed on the RFID tag, as well as interpreting and translating the tag replies.

In this solution, the applicant only requires to maintain the adequate credentials to authenticate itself in the PN. Once authenticated and authorized, the gateway node gathers the necessary cryptographic materials through the mechanisms provided by the PN and performs the (mutual) authentication with the personal tag, therefore unburdening the applicant from the dual authentication process and the management of credentials with the individual nodes of the PN. The secure management and maintenance of personal tags also benefits from the gateway approach as the required cryptographic materials in internal secure communications are not disclosed to external entities. Furthermore, a deeper control is reached during the 'direct' low level communication with the tag, enabling a more convenient supervision of the operations and data transferred (e.g. commands issued, memory zones accessed) in order to check sensitivity of data and applicant privileges and enforce the fulfilment of the security policies. Although the security and privacy in the PN is enhanced in this solution, this approach could not fulfil purposes where a fine control of the communication with personal tag is required by the applicant (e.g. during the authentication and validation of RFID-enabled personal documents).

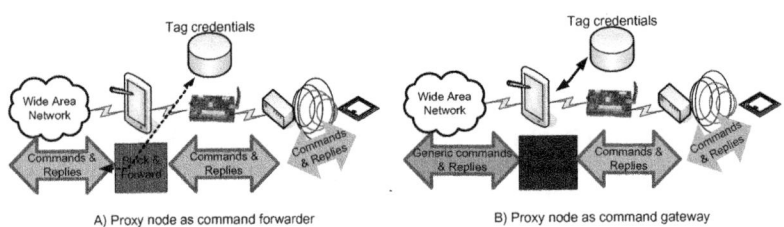

Fig. 3. Alternatives in secure direct access to RFID nodes

5.4   User Privacy in the Access to Context-Aware Technologies

The privacy policies will have an important role in the integration of RFID technology in the PN. These policies should be flexible enough to manage the ecosystem of personal RFID-enabled items, as they will belong to a wide range of categories and type of objects, as well as the potential diversity of personal and professional remote devices and service providers who may request access to the personal tags and their associated data. In this context, the privacy policies should provide a mechanism to represent which categories or individual tags maintain private data, which ones do not represent a privacy threat, when public or restricted access to selected actors can be provided, and even which personal data should be filtered and desassociated from the individual objects where it was generated before being shared with external actors.

In the case of direct access to individual tags from external actors, access control mechanisms (e.g. ACL or RBAC) can be used to define which actors are allowed to execute which commands on which tags. Additional parameters related to the context of the user (e.g. location, current activity or other PNs around) could also be used in the access policies. In the case of aggregated knowledge from multiple sensors and/or tags, the solution could also be based on these techniques, but, in this case, the targets to be accessed would be the types of knowledge that the PN is able to generate after processing and filtering the sensed data, instead of the individual sensors and RFID tags.

In the literature, a relevant solution in this direction is the RFID Guardian device which maintains a centralized security policy defining which RFID readers are authorized to access which tags in which situations. The device achieves its purpose by eavesdropping the communication process and applying tag emulation tactics to block unauthorized readers. However, this device considers RFID as an isolated technology without taking into account data generated by other technologies to evaluate the context of the user. Moreover, it focuses on the local access to RFID tags, and does not consider the communication of personal devices with remote service providers and PNs. Our vision of RFID technology integrated in the PN takes into account both aspects and provides the appropriate architecture to securely access the context-aware technologies also from WANs, while leaving the door open to specific privacy policies for this context.

6   Conclusions

As presented, the emerging personal network paradigm could benefit from the integration of RFID-enabled personal items and BSNs, however, the special characteristics of tagged items (e.g. passiveness, non-IP enabled, constrained computation capabilities) and potential security and privacy risks require a PN architecture prepared to support these context-aware technologies.

In this paper, we have defined the foundations of an adequate secure PN architecture for this purpose. In our model, personal tags should be recognized as nodes of the PN handling related crypto materials, naming information and metadata on sensitive information to enable secure communications with other members and external entities. The deployment of RFID-tagged items from scratch would allow the selection and definition of a set of common authentication protocols to standardize personal tags management, however, the PN should support the adoption of heterogeneous tags and incorporate mechanisms for secure ownership transfer and sharing.

Authentication and authorization of entities are also controlled by the architecture before granting privileges in the network and enabling communications. In our approach, requests on resource-constrained pervasive technologies would be provided in two alternatives: direct access to final nodes and aggregated context-aware knowledge. As previously discussed, each one presents their own benefits and handicaps and should be managed independently, through secure context management and direct access schemes.

On direct access, the PN would be able to resolve and establish a secure route to reach the final node, in particular non-IP-enabled tags. As discussed, the role of proxy nodes as message forwarders or gateway nodes does also have an impact on the requirements of the applicant and enforcement of security requirements. Last, but not least, the privacy policies have a crucial role in the PN and must be able to represent which members of the PN and external parties should be able to access which context-aware nodes or types of knowledge in which situations.

Previous research in aspects such as the integration of RFID and sensor technologies, RFID security, secure tag ownership, access control schemes and RFID privacy management devices could be adopted and adapted to this purpose providing the foundations to the realization of such architecture. However, the global vision of RFID and sensor network technologies as components of the heterogeneous and user-centric PN paradigm integrated in wide area networks leaves the door open to novel proposals specifically designed for the requirements and resources of this emerging paradigm.

References

1. International Telecommunication Union, ITU Internet Reports: The Internet of Things (November 2005)
2. Yum, D.H., et al.: Distance Bounding Protocol for Mutual Authentication. IEEE Transactions on Wireless Communications, 592–601 (2011)
3. Alomair, B., Poovendran, R.: Privacy versus Scalability in Radio Frequency Identification Systems. Computer Communication (2010)
4. Peris-Lopez, P., et al.: Cryptographic Puzzles and Distance-bounding Protocols: Practical Tools for RFID Security. In: IEEE International Conference on RFID 2010, Orlando, USA, pp. 45–52 (2010)
5. Anggraeni, P.N., Prasad, N.R., Prasad, R.: Secure personal network. In: IEEE 19th International Symposium on Personal, Indoor and Mobile Radio Communications, pp. 1–5 (2008)
6. Ibrohimovna, M., et al.: Secure and Dynamic Cooperation of Personal Networks in a Fednet. In: 6th IEEE CCNC 2009, pp. 8–14 (2009)
7. Project IST-FP6-IP-027396, Magnet Beyond, http://magnet.aau.dk (last accessed March 2011)
8. Anggorjati, B., et al.: RFID Added Value Sensing Capabilities: European Advances in Integrated RFID-WSN Middleware. In: IEEE SECON 2010, pp. 1–3 (2010)
9. Xiaoguang, Z., Wei, L.: The research of network architecture in warehouse management system based on RFID and WSN integration. In: IEEE International Conference on ICAL 2008, pp. 2556–2560 (2008)
10. Tolentino, R.S., Lee, K., Kim, Y.-T., Park, G.-C.: Next Generation RFID-Based Medical Service Management System Architecture in Wireless Sensor Network. In: Kim, T.-H., Chang, A.C.-C., Li, M., Rong, C., Patrikakis, C.Z., Ślęzak, D. (eds.) FGCN 2010. CCIS, vol. 119, pp. 147–154. Springer, Heidelberg (2010)
11. Memsic WSN product family, http://www.memsic.com/products/wireless-sensor-networks.html (last accessed March 2011)
12. Google Nexus S, http://www.google.es/nexus/tech-specs (accessed on March 2011)
13. Dominikus, S., Schmidt, J.-M.: Connecting Passive RFID Tags to the Internet of Things. In: Interconnecting Smart Objects with the Internet Workshop, Prague (2011)
14. Yu Ng, C., et al.: Practical RFID Ownership Transfer Scheme. Journal of Computer Security - Special Issue on RFID System Security (2010)
15. Song, B., Mitchell, C.J.: Scalable RFID Security Protocols supporting Tag Ownership Transfer, Computer Communication. Elsevier (2010)
16. Kapoor, G., et al.: Single RFID Tag Ownership Transfer Protocols. IEEE Transactions on Systems, Man, and Cybernetics, 1–10 (2011)
17. Mulligan, G.: The 6LoWPAN architecture. In: 4th Workshop on Embedded Networked Sensors, pp. 78–82. ACM, New York (2007)
18. Najera, P., Moyano, F., Lopez, J.: Security Mechanisms and Access Control Infrastructure for e-Passports and General Purpose e-Documents. Journal of Universal Computer Science 15, 970–991 (2009)

Accepting Information with a Pinch of Salt: Handling Untrusted Information Sources

Syed Sadiqur Rahman, Sadie Creese, and Michael Goldsmith

e-Security Group, WMG Digital Laboratory, University of Warwick,
Coventry CV4 7AL, UK
{S.S.Rahman,S.Creese,M.H.Goldsmith}@warwick.ac.uk
http://digital.warwick.ac.uk

Abstract. This paper describes on-going research developing a system to allow incident controllers and similar decision makers to augment official information input streams with information contributed by the wider public (either explicitly submitted to them or harvested from social networks such as Facebook and Twitter), and to be able to handle inconsistencies and uncertainty arising from the unreliability of such sources in a flexible way.

Keywords. Crowd-Sourcing, Incident Management, Mash-up, Situational Awareness, Trust, Uncertainty.

1 Introduction

Situation awareness is a key requirement in managing civil contingencies, since major incidents, accidents and natural disasters are by their very nature highly confused and confusing situations. It is important that those responsible for dealing with them have the best available information. The mash-up approach brings together information from multiple public and specialist sources to form a synoptic view, but the controller is still faced with multiple, partial and possibly conflicting reports. The aim of our research is to investigate how the varying provenance of the data can be tracked and exploited to prioritise the information presented to a busy incident controller and to synthesise a model or models of the situation that the evidence pertains to. Our approach is to develop a system which takes in situational data in a structured format, such as the Tactical Situation Object (TSO) proposed by the OASIS project[1]. The TSO is an object containing language-independent situation information encoded in XML. The system then creates a set of possible world views, each internally consistent, which are ranked based upon an initial provenance metric (configured by the user) which is used to score the individual data items. The result is a prioritized set of world views according to the metric. Additional intelligence and intuitions

---

[1] Open Advanced System for dISaster & emergency management, a European Framework 6 Project addressing the strategic objective, "Improving Risk Management"; www.oasis-fp6.org/

C. Meadows and C. Fernández-Gago (Eds.): STM 2011, LNCS 7170, pp. 223–238, 2012.

can then be used to re-measure the world views over time. The user is then presented with an ability to access open-source information with an increased awareness of likely provenance according to the metrics set. We present here our approach, including the factors which might be considered by judging provenance of a data item, how we propose to exploit TSO and proposed extensions, the types of policy our system will use in order to measure data items, how we propose to create the world views and consider uncertainty and our system architecture. First we elucidate the challenges faced when attempting to crowd-source from social network forums in order to gain intelligence.

2   Uncertainty in the Crowds

Social networks (e.g. Twitter) and Photo/Video hosting services (e.g. Flickr) received a large amount of postings during the November 2008 Mumbai attacks. Twitter started to receive messages from eye witnesses both from inside and outside the affected locations [6] after a series of coordinated attacks took place in different locations of Mumbai which started shortly before 10:00 pm on 26 November 2008 [29,2]. During the attacks eyewitnesses sent an estimated 80 SMS to Twitter every 5 seconds i.e. about 1000 SMS messages per minute [6].

Twitter and Facebook were also flooded with updates soon after the January 2010 Haiti earthquake of magnitude 7.0. People used these social networks to collect and share information about the disaster and its victims. Twitter posts appeared within seconds of the earthquake [21] and Facebook claims that they were receiving about 1,500 Haiti related messages per minute [21,7]. The earthquake was very powerful and its destruction was so widespread that it affected the majority of the people in the country. Although a handful of people were twitting from inside Haiti, a significant portion of the status updates on Twitter appeared to come from people outside Haiti who were showing concern or sympathy. This could be explained by the fact that only 10 percent of the Haiti population had access to the internet [12] before the disaster took place. As a result, the status updates on Twitter mostly contained information like *Earthquake 7 Richter in Haiti, help Haiti, please donate, looking for ...., no phones*, etc.

Many such social network postings might be useful to agencies charged with responding to such situations (whether natural disasters or terrorist bombings). In order for such data to have utility it must be of appropriate quality, which may, in part, be a question of provenance particularly in the face of uncertainty due to apparently conflicting reports.

2.1   Uncertainty in Mumbai

We have collected 948 twitter statuses from six twitter accounts in order to assess the degree to which conflicting reports exist, and the resulting window of uncertainty. We found that Twitter users don't always give information based on first-hand experience; in many cases they just relay the messages that they received from different sources (which may or may not be reliable) including the main stream media. Here are some example tweets that relay messages from other sources. The second and third tweets refer to CNN News and CNN-IBN and are in contradiction with each other as they differ on the number of deaths of terrorists and they are coming from the same (Twitter) account.

1. At 23:11:53 on 26/11/2008 **mumbaiattack**, a twitter user, relayed this message from an unspecified source: "#mumbai 78 reported dead >200 injured".
2. At 03:03:42 on 27/11/2008 **MumbaiAttacks**, a twitter user, relayed this message from CNN News: "87 are reported dead. 9 of the terrorists are reported dead by a CNN News report. #mumbai"
3. At 03:10:03 on 27/11/2008 **MumbaiAttacks**, a twitter user, relayed this message from CNN-IBN: "5 terrorists now reported to be shot dead, while 9 are detained. #mumbai CNN-IBN"

Table 1 below shows some contradictions found in the tweets.

According to the official statement of the Indian Government, the total number of people injured was 308 [17]. Not only do the Twitter users sometimes give contradictory information but at times, they go beyond that and spread rumour or hoax (although possibly without malicious intent). A hoax, apparently created by a Twitter user **mumbaiupdates**[2], was used in an effort to stop people from reporting live about the military operations against the terrorists [8]. Table 2 contains some of the tweets of **mumbaiupdates** that came before and after he created (or at least propagated) the hoax.

This hoax was so convincing that even BBC was fooled to report *Indian government asks for live Twitter updates from Mumbai to cease immediately* with a reference to the tweet made by **mumbaiupdates** on 27/11/2008 at 04:10:35 [14,8]. However, another twitter user, **dina**, challenged the authenticity of the message and asked for a proof. When **dina** asked another Twitter user **cool_technocrat** about the source of the information and told him to stop spreading the rumour, **cool_technocrat** responded with the following message with a reference to the BBC website:

@dina read from bbc website http://tinyurl.com/5al54e [TweetID: 1026242175, created_at: 27/11/2008 11:53:27]

dina again tried to convince them, saying:

@Kimota please read it carefully - BBC says they got it from a tweet. These rumours have been tweeted all day. BBC is NOT god!!! #mumbai [TweetID: 1026241807, created_at: 27/11/2008 11:53:04]

Yet some twitter users were still not convinced, as one of them, **Mumbai Attacks**, tweeted:

---

[2] Note however that **mumbaiupdates** has contributed to the discussion on [8], denying that he was the ultimate source of the rumour.

Table 1. Contradictions Found in Tweets about Mumbai Incident

Time	Tweet	Screen_name
26/11/2008 19:58:54	#mumbai - ndtv says 60 dead 200 injured. so far.	dina
26/11/2008 20:08:11	#mumbai 55 dead 190 injured. hostages uk and americans taken	mumbaiattack
26/11/2008 21:15:01	#mumbai 78 dead 200 injured	mumbaiattack
26/11/2008 21:37:48	#mumbai 15 policemen killed so far in intense fighting	mumbaiattack
26/11/2008 23:11:53	#mumbai 78 reported dead > 200 injured	mumbaiattack
26/11/2008 23:12:21	#mumbai 11 members of Police force perish	mumbaiattack
26/11/2008 23:38:04	#mumbai ndtv fm mantralaya. 76 dead 116 injured. 2 terrorists dead. 9 arrested. 2 topcops dead. Chief Minister evasive on who's responsible.	dina
27/11/2008 00:05:56	#mumbai 87 reported dead 200 injured.	mumbaiattack
27/11/2008 01:45:22	87 are reported dead with 185 wounded. #mumbai CNN.com	MumbaiAttacks
27/11/2008 02:08:44	Injured reports rise from 185 to 187 now. #mumbai CNN.com	MumbaiAttacks
27/11/2008 02:59:54	Reports say Mumbai Government has control of situation. 84 dead, 200 wounded, 2 terrorists dead, 9 in custody. #mumbai CNN.com	MumbaiAttacks
27/11/2008 03:03:42	87 are reported dead. 9 of the terrorists are reported dead by a CNN News report. #mumbai CNN News	MumbaiAttacks
27/11/2008 03:10:03	5 terrorists now reported to be shot dead, while 9 are detained. #mumbai CNN-IBN	MumbaiAttacks
27/11/2008 06:31:08	5 terrorists dead, 1 terrorist arrested, and at least 6 still present in the two luxury hotels; Taj and Oberoi. #mumbai CNN-IBN	MumbaiAttacks
27/11/2008 16:01:09	125 reported dead, 327 wounded in the Mumbai attacks. #mumbai CNN.com	MumbaiAttacks
27/11/2008 19:09:02	RT @BreakingNewsOn The death toll from the Mumbai terrorist attacks has risen to at least 131 with 330+ reported injured	mumbaiupdates
27/11/2008 20:19:36	8 terrorists in total have been killed in shootouts so far. #mumbai CNN-IBN on CNN.com Live	MumbaiAttacks
29/11/2008 00:50:48	#mumbai Casualty total: 155 killed 327 injured	mumbaiattack

Table 2. mumbaiupdates' Tweets Before and After the Creation of the Hoax

Time	Tweet	Screen_name
27/11/2008 03:52:00	Due to military action happening very soon, @mumbaiupdates may have little information to report to protect the rescue operations	mumbaiupdates
27/11/2008 03:54:27	I am not updating on any details about #mumbai operations until further notice to protect the operation	mumbaiupdates
27/11/2008 04:02:59	Indian government is asking that the twitter search page #mumbai be shut down	mumbaiupdates
27/11/2008 04:07:51	or possible clarification: to just stop live updating about the situation pertaining to #mumbai	mumbaiupdates
27/11/2008 04:10:35	ALL LIVE UPDATERS - PLEASE STOP TWEETING about #Mumbai police and military operations.	mumbaiupdates

CNN-IBN is, unfortunately, yet again reporting specifics as to tactics. They must stop to protect final operations on this assault. #mumbai [TweetID: 1026241807, created_at: 27/11/2008 11:53:04]

This particular case of rumour highlights an inconsistent behavior of a trusted and reliable source (BBC) and shows how misleading it can be.

2.2 Uncertainty in Haiti

We conducted a similar analysis for the Haiti disaster collecting 306 Twitter status updates from twelve users that were created in the first three days (from 12-15 January 2010) after the quake. It appears from the tweets that at least ten out of these twelve users twitted from inside Haiti and one of these users reported the earthquake within three minutes of the incident. We only considered those Tweets written in English, resulting in about 5% of tweets being excluded (they were written in local languages such as French and Haitian Creole). Some of the tweets appeared to contain valuable information relating to people being stuck under rubble, or children caught in collapsing buildings. Some of the tweets appeared to spread a lot of rumour and hoax which could make it difficult to believe the messages or make decisions based on them, such as the presence and degree of local flooding.

2.3 Windows of Uncertainty

For both case studies we analysed the content of the tweets and constructed the timelines for those creating uncertainty around a specific topic. It is possible to observe the facts of the situation as over a period of time the content of the tweets did converge, and we refer to said period of time as being the window of uncertainty. Figure 1 shows the window of uncertainty relating to the flooding in the Haiti disaster.

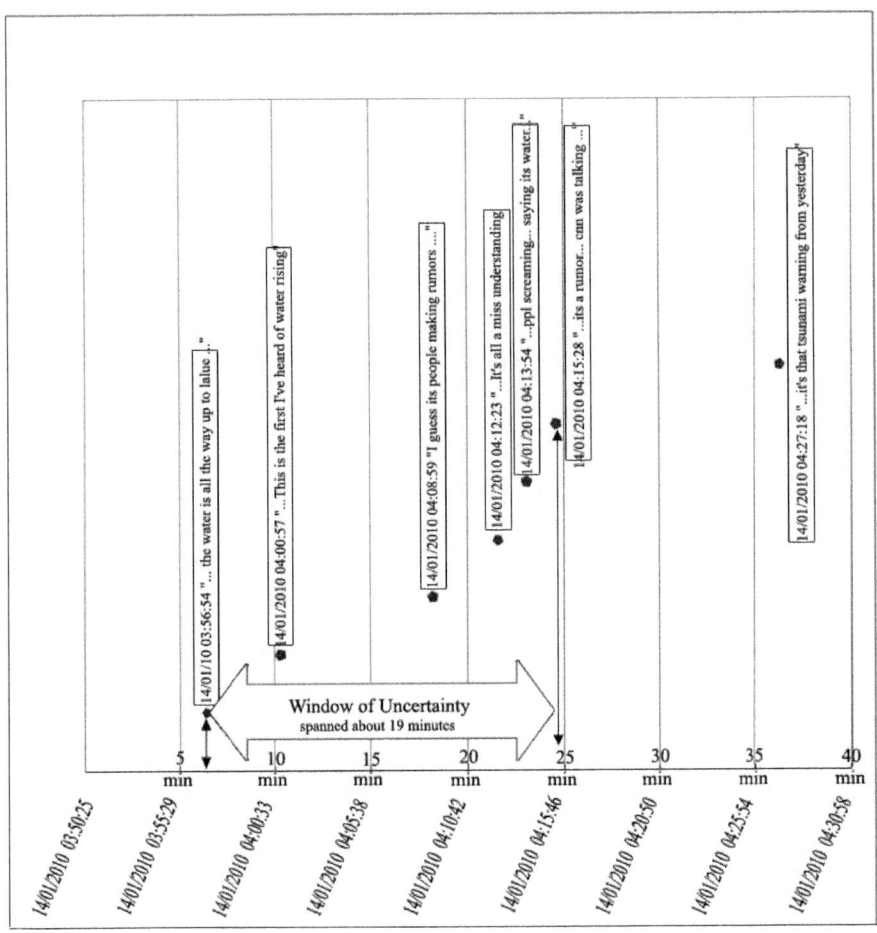

Fig. 1. Rumour created Uncertainty about Flood for about 19 minutes

3   Provenance Factors Affecting Trust in Information

Provenance of information refers to the source of information such as who gave (or produced) the information, the derivation history of information, what data was used to generate it, and also finding the trail of how the information has passed from one source to the other and how it has been changed. A recent study shows that one of the main factors that influence the trust of users in web content is provenance [11]. Provenance of information also helps to assess the quality of information (correctness, authenticity, etc.) and thus, helps to determine the level of trust that can be attributed to it [15,28]. We propose to use measures of provenance in order to score open source data and provide a method for filtering through the various world views resulting from uncertainty; we can give more priority to the information from the more trusted source. (However, security of provenance information is a critical issue since there is a potential risk of having the provenance information tampered by malicious agents that will ruin the purpose of keeping provenance information.) There are many factors proposed for judging provenance, sometimes explicitly and sometimes implicitly, designed to provide evidence or measures of trustworthiness. The selection of factors may depend upon context, since their reliability as a provenance indicator may vary according to their vulnerability to compromise and the likelihood of a compromise (malicious or accidental) taking place. We outline below the results of a survey into factors commonly in use and we indicate the potential points of vulnerability.

3.1   Identity of Informer

Identity provides a base for trustworthiness, risk assessment, and provenance [30,9]. If we know the identity of the informer and other demographic information related to him/her then it may help us to understand their motive. Generally, when we trust a person we believe the information s/he provides. So establishing identity can be essential to underpinning trust. Various pieces of information contribute to an identity, and could include name or pseudonym (user name) which remains consistent over time and can be linked to an individual, phone number, email/IP address, age, education, profession and membership of social groups. It has been argued that adult people are more trustworthy than children and adolescents [27]. We may believe an old lady more than a 13 year old boy unless there is a doubt that someone might have masqueraded as an old lady by changing his/her voice. There may be more reasons to act upon a tip-off received from an off-duty police officer than from a member of the public. Similarly, information from someone with a track record in providing quality information may be more believable than information provided by a previously unknown entity. It is clear that identity itself doesn't signify anything in relation to the person's trustworthiness unless we know more attributes (which we might refer to as competence in part). For example, we have received messages from two email addresses e.g. abc@defence-administration.uk and xyz@defence-administration.uk. Since we do not have any more information about the sources (except their identities), so we do not know whether they are the two most senior intelligence officers or two blue-collar workers. Hence, we cannot treat their information as very dependable despite the fact that we have the identities of the informers (their email addresses are their identity). Having said that, we may treat the messages coming from the server of "National Defence Administration" as more reliable than the messages coming from a Hotmail account even though the messages were sent by blue-collar workers of "National Defence Administration". This is because of two reasons:

Firstly, someone sending messages from "defence-administration.uk" is more traceable and therefore, they are less likely to be malicious.

Secondly, the sever that belongs to the "National Defence Administration" is expected to be more secure against attacks and Identity Theft. Forged identity and credentials are widely used by scams to steal money from people's bank accounts through Phishing [24]. Use of forged identity is also causing troubles in social networks. For example, it was found that some of the twitters on US president Barak Obamas Twitter account were not made by him [3], someone else who hacked his account made those twitters.

3.2   Location of Informer

The location from which an informer reports an incident may also have a bearing on the believability of information; we might always give more importance to the information received from an eyewitness as we believe it to be more accurate. We can use location as a method for determining whether claims to eyewitness accounts are credible; we can rule out informers who are not within a given radius of the incident. However, collecting location and other private information pertaining to information providers may be extremely difficult because of legal and privacy issues (unless they give consent to providing it), and there is a potential risk of having location information faked. A researcher at the University of Illinois at Chicago has demonstrated such attack using only 9 Perl statements [19]. There is also software for faking location of mobile phones which is easily accessible in the market at a very low price e.g. Fake-A-Location[3] Although IP addresses could be used to find an approximate but true location of an informer, yet IP address can also be faked with readily available software e.g. Hide My IP 5.2[4]., Hide My IP Address[5].

3.3   Freshness of Information

Freshness or timeliness is another factor that determines the quality or believability of information [4,16]. We need to know when the information was published or message was sent in order to judge how fresh it is, and assign a probability of correctness or trustworthiness accordingly. When we have conflicting information then freshness may play a part in deciding which information to base a decision on (although the decision is likely to be based on more than just a freshness factor). In some cases, there may be a significant time-gap between sending information and receiving it at the other end. As a result, old information will appear as fresh and correct information. If we can ensure that each message published in the mash-up comes with a time-stamp then it will be possible for us to know whether the information is old or fresh. For example, mobile phone network operators inform the recipients of the time when a text message was sent to them by adding a time-stamp to each message when they receive it from the sender [26].

---

[3] www.excelltechmobile.com/, Accessed on 19/12/2010.

[4] www.hide-my-ip.com/, accessed on 18/12/2010.

[5] www.hide-my-ip-address.com/hideip/, accessed on 18/12/2010.

3.4 Reputation

We can predict someone's behaviour with a known history (reputation) to a certain extent, while it is almost impossible to predict their behaviour with a little or no history about them. So, we may trust an informer with a good reputation more than another with a bad reputation (or no reputation at all). However, there is risk associated with using reputation for evaluating trustworthiness because there is no guarantee that an informer with a very good reputation will not give wrong information [11]. A trusted source may suddenly (willingly or inadvertently) issue a patently false statement, or a typically distrusted source may post information that is trustworthy [1]. Therefore, this factor will not be reliable in situations when a source has purposefully built up a positive reputation specifically to act as cover for the time at which they wish to act maliciously (equivalent to an insider threat whose reputation had been built up over time and who suddenly steals some data). Misinformation from previous apparently-reliable source may be subtle and hard to detect immediately (as in the case of Advanced Persistent Threat). Hence, we need to be cautious while using reputation as a measure of trust.

3.5 Popularity

When a message appears on a social network (e.g. Twitter, Facebook, etc..) informing about an incident, many other people repeat that message and many people start following that first informer for more updates. Thus, a number of popular users are found on social networks that frequently provide a lot of timely information about incidents. Of course, it is questionable the degree to which popularity should be considered a measure of trustworthiness, as it is entirely possible that many are following someone who is incorrect in their assertions. However, some believe that popularity must mean that either the source is providing accurate information or is infamous for something related to the incident, as there appears no other rationale explanation for their popularity (they are not celebrities). Who is being mentioned how many times can be worked out from Twitter messages and a corresponding score can be assigned (positive or negative) to each popular user according to their popularity. It is also possible to capture the average number of times someone's message gets repeated by others. The two combined could give a rough estimate of popularity, should such a factor be considered important to provenance in a given situation.

3.6 Context/Situation, Interest and Ethics

People's trustworthiness varies depending on the situation or context [5,25,4]. It is easy for someone to be unbiased and trustworthy in a situation when his/her own interest is not concerned. We may doubt a trader's word when s/he says that s/he is not making any profit by selling a particular product. However, we will have no reason to doubt the same person when s/he reports an accident. However, intention itself is sometimes context dependant and driven by ethics.

For example, a journalist who is also a share holder of a company may write a true report about the company because of his/her ethics, despite the fact that the report will cause the share price to fall.

However, in reality, we cannot judge someone's trustworthiness based on their intention or ethics as there is no practical way of reading someone's mind and knowing their intention. We have to use their history/reputation to know about their ethics. So this factor will be vulnerable in the same way as reputation (discussed above).

3.7   Social Relation

A person, X, is likely to trust another person, Y, to a certain degree if Y is trusted by many other people who are trusted by X even though X doesn't know Y [18,20]. This transitive nature of trust is also seen in social networking websites (virtual society) e.g. Facebook, LinkedIn, etc.. However, the degree of transitivity of trust depends on other factors. For example, a cousin A of X's mother, and a friend C of X's friend B are unlikely be trusted by X to the same degree. This is because the trust is rooted in two different ways (cousin of mother and friend of a friend respectively). Social relations can be easily manipulated with a little use of social engineering and masquerading. For example, Alice and Bob are very good friends and their houses are on the same street. On an evening a scam, Mallory, knocks on Alice's door and identifies him as Bob's brother. Mallory asks Alice that whether he could sit in her sitting room while he is waiting for Bob and it is very cold outside. There may be a good chance that Mallory will get access to Alice's house and run away with her mobile phone. This manipulation is even easier in social networks as there is a lot of private information publicly available on the net which will facilitate social engineering.

3.8   Corroboration

When the same information comes from many different and unrelated sources we tend to believe the information, even though the sources aren't very trusted or they have no previous reputation [1,9]. But, if it is found that the sources are related to each other then it may cast doubt on the information. ENISA's survey shows that most web users trust the content of a website because it is found on many other websites [22]. However, the potential risk in establishing trust based on corroboration is that it may not be possible to unearth the fact that some websites are related to each other, although they are maintained by the same crime syndicate. For example, it was found that false rumours have been spread using web 2.0 applications in order to manipulate stock prices [23].

3.9   Competence

Trustworthiness of information also partly depends on the competence of the information provider. If someone does not have adequate level of knowledge and expertise (competence) to securely generate/collect some information in a specific context then, the information provided by him/her may not be trustworthy and reliable [13]. Hence, if someone reports an incident and says that some of the casualties are suffering a brain haemorrhage then we will think of either of two possibilities: 1. Some casualties are suffering a brain haemorrhage and the informer is a doctor/nurse/paramedic. 2. There are some casualties but possibly nobody is suffering a brain haemorrhage if the informer doesn't have the necessary knowledge, expertise or skills to diagnose the problem. Likewise, if a fireman recognises and reports a shooting incident as an organised terrorist attack then we cannot be certain about it. However, this factor may be vulnerable if a competent person is biased, since his/her judgement may be biased or prejudiced.

3.10   Conviction/Certainty

When someone receives a piece of information, they can believe or disbelieve it to a certain degree. Likewise, a person may not completely believe a message even though s/he passes it on. People, despite being a sender of a piece of information, believe/disbelieve the information to a varying degree. Therefore, it is important to ask information providers as to how certain they are about the veracity of the information they are providing, especially when they have received that information from others. If the source itself is doubtful about the veracity of a piece of information, then we should automatically give less priority to that information provided that we believe the source is honest. Since, source certainty i.e. the conviction of a source about the veracity of information solely depends on the source's honesty and personal view, it will be quite risky for us to make a decision based on this factor alone; as this is an extremely vulnerable factor [10]. A source that expresses a higher certainty about the veracity of a piece of information which turns out to be untrue may be penalised with a diminished reputation or trustworthiness.

4   System Architecture

Our approach is to design a system which enables the user (decision maker) to measure data inputs and resulting combinations of data inputs based on the provenance factors discussed above. Here we present the system architecture, see Fig. 2, and how each of the components works.

4.1   Information Source Filter

Whilst the system will collect open-source information from any source (limited only by the ability to construct TSO messages) we expect that user organisations may wish to filter out sources in order to reduce noise. The Information Source Filter will simply provide a mechanism for either subscribing to a set of known information sources, or conversely blocking inputs from a set of known information sources. This forms one component of the *Organisational Policy*.

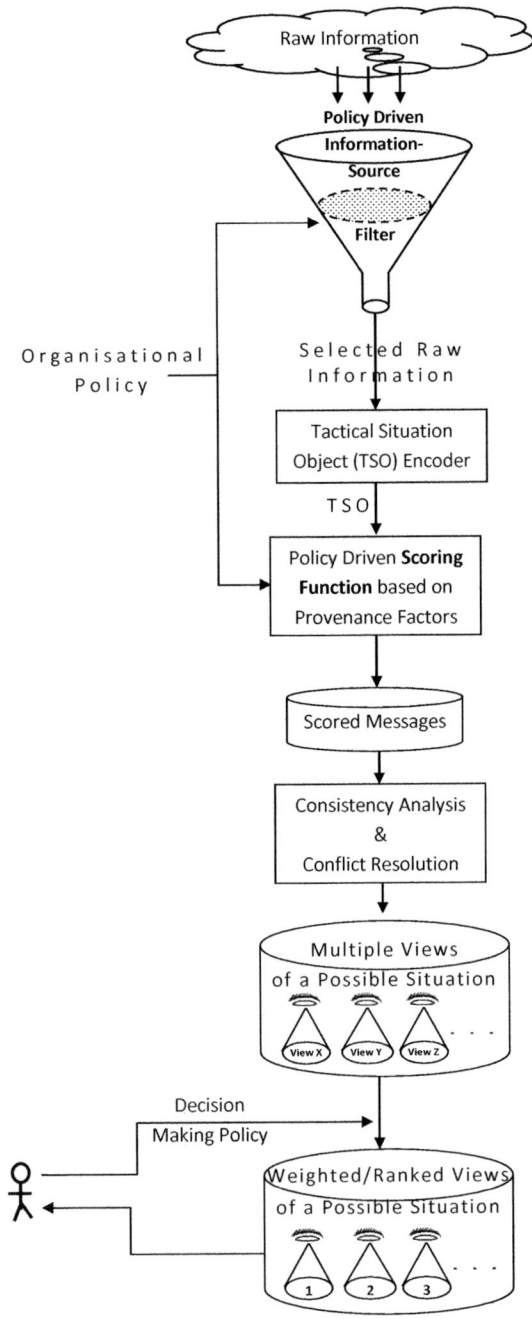

Fig. 2. Data Flow in the System Architecture

4.2   Tactical Situation Object (TSO) Encoder

We use the TSO format to ensure that data is encoded in a single format, which enables us to easily determine where the information contained in messages is in conflict with that in other messages (the limited vocabulary makes consistency analysis tractable). We currently show the encoding into TSO as internal to our system architecture, where the TSO may be created manually by trained staff or an automated system. We currently provide a tool for manually creating TSO, see later discussion for the challenges we faced in doing this. Of course, should information sources provide inputs already in the TSO format this stage would be avoided (although validity checks would need to be made). Whether we can automatically generate TSO using natural language processing is a topic for future research.

4.3   Scoring Function

The scoring function constitutes the second half of the *Organisational Policy*. This essentially captures the provenance factors of interest (for a given context or incident) and how to assign scores to messages for each factor. The selection of factors will depend upon context, since their reliability as a provenance indicator may vary according to their vulnerability to compromise and the likelihood of a compromise (malicious or accidental) taking place, as well as their perceived inherent value (such as location in a disaster situation). The scoring function will assign a vector of (normalised) scores to each piece of information, one score for each of the provenance factors in use. In other words, the overall score given to a piece of information is a vector constituted of multiple scores; each score assigned against each of its provenance factors. The policy will contain the provenance factors that will be used to evaluate the veracity of a message and will specify how large a score should be assigned to each factor in a particular situation. For example, in an incident where eye-witness accounts are of paramount interest then a policy would be constructed which penalised heavily locations not in the immediate area of interest. Where identity is of paramount interest, it would be possible to define a sets of information sources which are given higher scores than those not inside the sets. The scored messages will be stored in a database for consistency analysis and conflict resolution.

4.4   Consistency Analysis and Conflict Resolution

The scored messages will be analysed to cluster the consistent messages together. Inconsistent or conflicting messages will be kept in different clusters. Thus, multiple clusters will be created with all messages in a cluster consistent and coherent. Hence, each cluster represents a different view of the possible situation that we call a *World View*, where some or all messages may be included in multiple world views. Intuitively, each cluster consists of a maximal consistent subset of messages, although in practice some fuzziness will be desirable in order to prevent a proliferation of highly-similar world views.

4.5   Decision Making Policy

The actual tool user, the decision maker, will then be able to influence the ranking of world views according to their own policy, which we refer to as the *Decision Making Policy*. This policy will allow the decision maker to amplify or attenuate one or more provenance factors that may appear to be more or less important in a particular situation, in their opinion, by increasing or decreasing the weight given to the corresponding score across all messages in all world views. We envisage this being implemented in part via a tool akin to a graphic equaliser, where the user can effectively turn up or turn down the relative importance of a factor against others. This will change the ranking of the world views of a possible situation. (Note that this does not change the value of any single provenance factor for any individual message, just overall score applied to the collection of messages.) The policy maker may also set some threshold values for different factors when s/he doesn't want to consider messages with a score above/below the threshold value for the specified provenance factors. For example, if the decision maker wants to receive messages only from the affected area, then s/he may set a threshold value of 6 (say) for the provenance factor Location. Hence, any message that receives a score less than 6 for location will be ignored.

The overall score may be calculated for each cluster of information by averaging (or applying some other suitable mathematical operation to) the score vectors of individual messages within that cluster. There will also be the potential to set a corroboration threshold to be applied across a world view, whereby worlds can be penalised for not having enough messages which corroborate each other (or conversely enabling the decision maker to focus on worlds which are outliers and conveying information which is not being widely published). The user will then be able to easily see how changes in their policy affect the rankings of the worlds, and to switch between them.

5   Generating TSO Inputs

We have developed an application tool that combines the OASIS schema and data dictionary in order to build a complete schema to facilitate the creation of Tactical Situation Objects with the data from Twitter and other similar sources. At present each message needs to be coded manually with the aid of our tool. Our future work may include investigating the practicality of natural language processing for this purpose.

While combining the OASIS XML schema for Tactical Situation Objects with their supplied Data Dictionary in order to provide guided data-entry, we discovered a couple of difficulties with the detail of the implementation, arising from (a) the use of non XML-friendly codewords for values which would naturally map into enumeration values of the extended schema, and (b) codes duplicated in distinct contexts (**HUM** standing for both humid weather conditions and human resources, for instance). We have also had to make a few minor changes to the original TSO schema, including enabling empty content in some contexts and making some introduced elements optional.

6   Conclusions and Future Work

The majority of the system components described in this paper have been prototyped and we are currently working on integrating them. Our future work includes the application of the technique to a range of case studies, in order to understand the utility of provenance factors for various contexts. If appropriate we will also explore the use of template policies in order to support rapid configuration of the tool. Theoretically our focus will be on how best to resolve uncertainty and provide a tractable set of possible worlds, and we expect this to mean introducing a notion of fuzziness.

References

1. Artz, D., Gil, Y.: A survey of trust in computer science and the semantic web. Journal of Web Semantics: Science, Services and Agents on the World Wide Web 5(2), 58–71 (2007)
2. BBC News: As it happened: Mumbai attacks (November 27, 2008), http://news.bbc.co.uk/1/hi/world/south_asia/7752003.stm
3. Bellantoni, C., Dinan, S.: Obama's twitter site hacked. The Washington Times (January 2009), http://www.washingtontimes.com/news/2009/jan/05/obamas-twitter-site-hacked/
4. Bizer, C.: Quality-Driven Information Filtering in the Context of Web-Based Information Systems. VDM Verlag (2007)
5. Blomqvist, K.: The many faces of trust. Scandinavian Journal of Management 13(3), 271–286 (1997)
6. CNN International (2008), http://edition.cnn.com/2008/WORLD/asiapcf/11/27/mumbai.twitter/index.html
7. (2010), http://www.computerworld.com/s/article/9145259/Facebook_creates_site_dedicated_to_providing_earthquake_info
8. Tracking a rumor: Indian government, twitter, and common sense (2008), http://www.contentious.com/2008/11/27/tracking-a-rumor-indian-government-twitter-and-common-sens/[sic]
9. Dai, C., Lin, D., Bertino, E., Kantarcioglu, M.: An Approach to Evaluate Data Trustworthiness Based on Data Provenance. In: Jonker, W., Petković, M. (eds.) SDM 2008. LNCS, vol. 5159, pp. 82–98. Springer, Heidelberg (2008)
10. Fullam, K.K., Barber, K.S.: Using policies for information valuation to justify beliefs. In: Third International Joint Conference on Autonomous Agents and Multi Agent Systems (AAMAS 2004) (July 2004)
11. Gil, Y., Artz, D.: Towards content trust of web resources. Journal of Web Semantics: Science, Services and Agents on the World Wide Web 5(4), 227–239 (2007)
12. Google Public Data Explorer: Internet users as percentage of population, Haiti, http://www.google.com/publicdata?ds=wb-wdi&met=it_net_user_p2&idim=country:HTI&dl=en&hl=en&q=internet+user+in+haiti#met=it_net_user_p2&idim=country:HTI
13. Grandison, T., Sloman, M.: A survey of trust in internet applications. IEEE Communications Surveys and Tutorials, 2–16 (Fourth Quarter 2000)
14. Bbc admits it made mistakes using Mumbai Twitter coverage (November 2008), http://www.guardian.co.uk/media/pda/2008/dec/05/bbc-twitter

15. Hartig, O.: Provenance information in the web of data. In: Linked Data on The Web (LDOW 2009) (April 2009),
    http://ceur-ws.org/Vol-538/ldow2009_paper18.pdf
16. Hartig, O., Zhao, J.: Using web data provenance for quality assessment. In: First International Workshop on the Role of Semantic Web in Provenance Management (SWPM 2009) (2009)
17. P.I.B.G. of India, HM announces measures to enhance security (December 2008) (press release), http://pib.nic.in/release/release.asp?relid=45446
18. Kelton, K., Fleischmann, K.R., Wallace, W.A.: Trust in digital information. Journal of the American Society for Information Science and Technology 59(3), 363–374 (2008)
19. Lahiri, M.: Gaming foursquare with 9 lines of perl (August 2010),
    http://compbio.cs.uic.edu/~mayank/4sq.html
20. Lewis, J.D., Weigert, A.: Trust as a social reality. Social Forces 63(4), 967–985 (1985)
21. (2010), http://nationnewmedia.com/2010/01/17/opinion/opinion_30120439.php
22. Network, T.E.: (ENISA), I.S.A.: Web 2.0 survey, http://www.enisa.europa.eu/act/it/oar/web-2.0-security-and-privacy/enisa_survey_web2.pdf/view
23. Network, T.E.: (ENISA), I.S.A.: Web 2.0 security and privacy (December 2008), http://www.enisa.europa.eu/act/it/oar/web2sec/report
24. Rahman, S.S.: Phishing Attack. Master's thesis, University of East London (2006)
25. Sheppard, B.H., Sherman, D.M.: The grammars of trust: A model and general implications. Academy of Management Review 23(3), 422–437 (1998)
26. SMS packet format, http://www.gsmfavorites.com/documents/sms/packet format/
27. Suttera, M., Kocher, M.G.: Trust and trustworthiness across different age groups. Games and Economic Behavior 59(2), 364–382 (2007)
28. Tan, W.C.: Provenance in databases: Past, current, and future. IEEE Data Engineering Bulletin 30(4), 3–12 (2007)
29. http://simple.wikipedia.org/wiki/November_2008_Mumbai_attacks
30. Xu, S., Sandhu, R., Bertino, E.: TIUPAM: A Framework for Trustworthiness-Centric Information Sharing. In: Ferrari, E., Li, N., Bertino, E., Karabulut, Y. (eds.) IFIPTM 2009. IFIP AICT, vol. 300, pp. 164–175. Springer, Heidelberg (2009)

Author Index